Classical and Neoclassical Theories of General Equilibrium

Classical and Neoclassical Theories of General Equilibrium

Historical Origins and Mathematical Structure

VIVIAN WALSH   HARVEY GRAM

New York   Oxford
OXFORD UNIVERSITY PRESS
1980

Copyright © 1980 by Oxford University Press, Inc.

Printed in the United States of America

Library of Congress Cataloging in Publication Data

Walsh, Vivian Charles.
  Classical and neoclassical theories of general equilibrium.

  Includes index.
  1. Equilibrium (Economics)   2.   Economics—Mathe-
matical models.   3.   Economics—History.   I.   Gram,
Harvey Nelson, 1946–   joint author.   II.   Title.
HB145.W34   330'.01'8   78-31129
ISBN 0-19-502674-8

For
Winifred Anne Macaulay Walsh and
Eileen Louise Collins

Acknowledgments

Joan Robinson and William Baumol read and commented in detail on several versions of this book. William Jaffé also read much of the final version and our interpretation and occasional translations of Walras have been influenced by his many comments. Oskar Morgenstern read early versions of our work and helped us to see the pivotal role of John von Neumann in the development of modern classical theory. Edward Nell used a manuscript version of the book in his graduate seminar at the New School and provided us with comments.

We also owe a general debt of gratitude to our students who are invariably fascinated to learn of the contrasting structures of classical and neoclassical theories of general equilibrium. Their probing questions have done much to sharpen our treatment of the essential distinctions between these two traditions. In turn, one of the authors owes his introduction to the classical revival to Donald Harris who was lecturing in this field at the University of Wisconsin during the late 1960's.

Finally, we are grateful to Richard Roud for editorial assistance.

V.W.
Graduate Faculty,
New School for Social Research,
New York, New York

H.G.
Queens College and The Graduate School,
City University of New York,
New York, New York

May, 1979

Contents

Introduction

The use of mathematical formulations in economic theory was introduced in the last quarter of the nineteenth century with high hopes that thereby the subject could be made truly scientific. It was developed mainly in connection with consumers' demand and market equilibrium. In the second half of the present century it has grown and proliferated. Though the analysis of markets is still at the center, it now covers all branches of the subject and is beginning to invade sociology and history as well.

Contrary to the hopes of its practitioners, the apparent precision of mathematics has generated vagueness. Mathematical operations are performed upon entities that cannot be defined; calculations are made in terms of units that cannot be measured; accounting identities are mistaken for functional relationships; correlations are confused with causal laws; differences are identified with changes; and one-way movements in time are treated like movements to and fro in space. The complexity of models is elaborated merely for display, far and away beyond the possibility of application to reality.

As a prophylactic against these aberrations, this book makes use of extremely simple models with the absolute minimum of elements, each defined in physical terms, subject only to linear relationships. A student who has learned to pass the arguments with which he is presented through this fine sieve will understand their true meaning and will have learned a great deal about the relationship between theoretical statements and the reality that they purport to describe. The dry and formal reasoning is deployed in the setting of a history of ideas, enlivened by entertaining sketches of the characters involved.

Two topics are chosen for treatment in this way—the classical concept of surplus as the source of accumulation, and the neoclassical concept of the allocation of existing resources between alternative uses which, developed in neo-neoclassical mathematical form, is dominant in orthodox teaching. There is no discussion of effective demand; finance or international trade and the evolution of industry is touched upon only incidentally. The chosen topics, however, cover the main span of basic economic theory as it exists today.

The art of constructing models that contribute to understanding is to make the most drastic simplifications that are possible without eliminating any element essential to the problem in hand. In this art, Ricardo was preeminent, but all the great classics, from Sir William Petty to Karl Marx, practiced it in some degree. The method came to them by instinct; now it has to be practiced systematically, in mathematical terms.

The concept of an economic surplus is of a flow of production in excess of *necessary* consumption. To compensate for the ingredients of necessary consumption, so as to permit the flow of output to be maintained, means to replace both the depletion of the stock of pre-existing means of production and the fund of subsistence of the labor force. To present this in cut-and-dried physical terms, two drastic simplifications are necessary. First, the technique of production must be assumed constant, so that means of production used up are replaced in identical form; when changes in technique and in the composition of output are taking place, as they normally are in an industrial economy, the replacement of capital goods used up is made in a physically different form so that it is impossible to make an absolutely precise distinction between net and gross output. Second, the flow of necessary consumption of the labor force must be treated as a specified quantity of specified commodities.

The Physiocrats, who set out the first systematic model of a self-sustaining economy, represented the producers, peasants and artisans, as managing their own activities and controlling a revolving fund of working capital adequate to keep means of production intact and to support their families. The peasants harvested an annual surplus of output in excess of the replacement of stock, which they handed over as rent to landlords, by whom it was devoted to improductive consumption, both private and public. The Physiocrats treated the level of consumption of producers as being a technical datum and attributed the surplus to the productivity of land.

In reality, as Adam Smith pointed out, the share of surplus in net product is not determined only by technology; it depends also upon the balance of power between the classes of the community. As we see in South Asia today, there is no bottom limit to subsistence below which landlords cannot squeeze down the livelihood of cultivators.

Our authors are well aware of this problem but they make the two simplifications mentioned above and so are able to deploy and manipulate models in which surplus is defined in physical terms.

Adam Smith was living amidst the transition from artisan production to wage labor; both systems are reflected in his observations. When he speaks of appealing to the self-interest of the baker, the butcher, and the brewer to get us a dinner, he is evidently thinking of a gentleman of independent means spending money on the products of self-employed tradesmen, but for the most part he discusses industry, in which masters employ workers and surplus accrues in the form of net profits. It is to be observed that the famous "invisible hand" guides capitalists to invest in the most profitable ventures rather than competitive sellers to meet consumers' preferences.*

For the Physiocrats, the prices of manufactures were such as to cover the replacement of stock and the subsistence of the artisans who produced them. Adam Smith was not quite clear about the distinction between gross and net output. Otherwise his theory of the relative prices of commodities is in accordance with common sense—the selling value of a flow of output of any particular commodity must cover the cost of wages, rents, and profits that go into it, each at the rate prevailing at that time in the place where production is carried out. What he lacked was a theory of the determination of the level of profits and rents (except for the power of masters and landlords to grab a share of the product of labor) and of their relations to each other and to the level of wages.

Ricardo, who is the hero of our author's tale, took the level of real wages as given and worked out a consistent theory of the formation of rents and of the rate of profit on capital. He was interested in finding the laws which determined the distribution of the produce of the earth among the classes of the community, but he got deflected into the search for an invariable standard of value which tormented him till his dying day.

Rescued by Piero Sraffa, Ricardo's theory of the rate of profit in fact solves the problem of the analysis of relative prices. The value of a unit of each commodity depends upon the quantity of labor time directly and indirectly required to produce it and upon profit, at the ruling rate, on the investment required to "bring it to market."

---

*Wealth of Nations, Book IV, Chapter 2, part II.

The simple model used in this book makes it possible to explain Sraffa's measure of value, the standard commodity, even more thoroughly than he did himself. Here it is important to emphasize the assumption of unchanging technique. Each system of equations, describing a particular technique, has its own standard commodity, and only in very restricted cases can one be compared with another. Ricardo, hankering after an "invariable standard" like weight or length was pursuing a Will O' the Wisp.

The authors are rather shy of tackling the Marxian "transformation problem." The labor theory of *value* carries a strong charge of ideology that makes it precious to its supporters and abhorrent to its opponents, but, at the level of formal analysis, it is sufficient to postulate a technology in which the ratio of labor embodied in means of production to labor currently employed is the same in all industries. Then prices proportional to *values* are compatible with a uniform rate of profit. This will not serve where relative prices are the center of interest, but it is adequate for many large problems in which they are not particularly important.

A case in point is the discussion of expanded reproduction in *Capital* Volume II, which, somewhat neglected by professed Marxists, has provided the basis for the analysis of savings and investment, of accumulation, and of development in socialist economies and in the Third World.

Turning to the so-called problem of allocation, the authors put all the theorems of general equilibrium through the sieve of their simple linear model. There are two factors of production called labor and land and two commodities, called rice and wheat. In these terms, an analysis is provided of the relation of prices to output and to inputs, of supply to demand, and of returns to factors, of the attainment of positions on a production possibility surface, and of the meaning of "scarcity" of commodities and of factors of production.

In this sphere, unfortunately, the simplification of the assumptions has not stopped short of eliminating the problem to be discussed, for both historical time and social structure are ruled out by these assumptions. General equilibrium, as it has been developed in neo-neoclassical theory, elaborates the analysis of exchange in a competitive market without giving a plausible account of the manner in which exchangeable commodities are produced or of the setting in which exchange takes place.

How is the "factor" labor combined with land? If the workers are independent peasants, the distinction between rent and wages does not arise. If they

are share-cropping tenants, their livelihood depends upon their ability to reconstitute their working capital from harvest to harvest so as to keep out of the
clutches of money-lenders. If they are hired by landlords at wages, working
capital is provided by employers, whose returns therefore include an element
of profit along with rent. (To introduce man-made means of production into
the model would make the problem all the worse.)

However, the above inquiry is not in the spirit of the general equilibrium
model. There, society consists only of indistinguishable "transactors," some
of whom happen to have an "endowment" of labor power and some of property; output emerges instantaneously from exchanges between them. (Many
efforts have been made in recent times to patch up the model but none has
overcome its basic self-contradictions.)

A teacher who maintains that general equilibrium is the central topic in economic theory will be grateful for the drill provided in this book, but it will not
help him to persuade his pupils that it ought to be taken seriously.

Every economic doctrine has a purpose. Economics is an ill-developed branch
of the biology of the human species; an economist is (presumably) a human
being and cannot regard his fellowmen with the same detachment as his col-
league in the laboratory regards a collection of fruit flies. Thus there is always
an element of ideology in any discussion of social problems.

The main preoccupation of the classical economists was the growth of the
wealth of nations—that is, each of his own nation; they were favorable to the
system of private enterprise because it was seen to promote accumulation.
Even Marx, to whom capitalism appeared cruel and oppressive, was in favor
of growth, for he believed that the system would destroy itself by its own success.

A theory which is unable to account for the pace and direction of technological change cannot find an answer for the problems that perplex us today,
but the classics at least laid a foundation on which it ought to be possible to
build.

The preoccupation of the neoclassics was primarily with the freedom of the
individual, in particular the right of anyone who has some money to spend, to
spend it as he chooses. Their own analysis, however, does not really support
their favorite doctrine of consumers' sovereignty. Given the stocks of means
of production in existence, created by past investment, and the present state of
technology, the decision as to what commodities to offer rests with the producers. The main influence upon the pattern of demand is the distribution of

wealth and income amongst households. This is tucked away in the model under the heading of "endowments" and factor prices, while all the emphasis is on "tastes."

The slogan that all economic action is governed by "choice under restraint" is not of much use unless we know who, in particular, can choose between what range of alternatives.

There is, however, an important area where neo-neoclassical theory comes into its own. The concept of a production possibility surface and of the distribution of scarce means between alternative uses are the very foundation of economic planning. While the theory of allocation is withering in the free-market world, it is blossoming afresh in socialist economies.

JOAN ROBINSON

Classical and Neoclassical
Theories of General Equilibrium

1

Prologue

A Classical Revival

A sharp distinction can be drawn in the theory of general equilibrium between the classical theme of the accumulation and allocation of surplus output, and the neoclassical theme of the allocation of given resources among alternative uses. Without this distinction neither the history of economic analysis nor the structure of modern mathematical models of general equilibrium can be clearly understood.

Our point of view concerning the intellectual history of our subject is consistent with Schumpeter's distinction between a history of economic *analysis* and a history of economic *thought*. Schumpeter defined economic thought as, "the sum total of all the opinions and desires concerning economic subjects, especially concerning public policy bearing upon these subjects, that, at any given time and place, float in the public mind."[1] He held that the historian could reasonably claim to be able to demonstrate that progress had taken place in economic analysis, but not in economic thought. A study of intellectual history supports the contention that sustained, though not uninterrupted, progress took place in the analytical development of the classical theme of surplus and the accumulation of capital. This theme is clearly stated by Sir William Petty in 1662 and is developed systematically, together with the classical theory of the allocation of surplus output, by Richard Cantillon in 1732. The themes of classical theory developed steadily up to the death of Ricardo in 1823 after which there was a significant decline ending as we can see today with the mature work of Marx, in, for example, his 1857 *Grundrisse*. Since Marx's work was long unpublished and longer unread in England, this historical influence came too late to revive classicism in that country. Then, in the

3

early 1870's, the special neoclassical form of allocation theory—the alloca-tion of given resources—displaced classical theory and came to dominate the-oretical economics. Since Léon Walras is usually considered the most impor-tant of the great nineteenth century founders of neoclassicism, this version of general equilibrium theory will be referred to as post-Walrasian.

Interest in classical theory was never completely extinguished. Early in the twentieth century the mathematical methods of analysis which had come to characterize neoclassical theory were applied in the construction of models of a recognizably classical type. Piero Sraffa was working on such models at Cambridge from the mid-twenties, and Adolphe Lowe and others were doing so at Kiel at the same time. John von Neumann presented a seminal paper containing a model of this type in Princeton in 1932, and in Vienna in 1936, and published it in 1937.[2] An important generalization of Neumann's model of an expanding economy appeared in a paper by John G. Kemeny, Oskar Morgenstern, and Gerald L. Thompson in 1956.[3] Meanwhile, Joan Robinson had made fundamental contributions to the revival and development of classical theory in her *Accumulation of Capital*.[4] Then, in 1960, Sraffa published his *Production of Commodities by Means of Commodities*.[5] The work of Robinson and Sraffa was developed extensively in the journals by Pierangelo Garegnani, Luigi Pasinetti, and others.[6]

Recently, several books have appeared which further elaborate the classical theme of surplus and the accumulation of capital. Michio Morishima uses modern mathematical methods to formalize part of the work of Marx, the last great nineteenth century classical economist.[7] Oskar Morgenstern and Gerald Thompson have generalized the work of Neumann in their *Mathematical Theory of Expanding and Contracting Economies;*[8] Luigi Pasinetti has pub-lished his *Lectures on the Theory of Production;*[9] and Adolphe Lowe has de-veloped modern classical theories of growth in *The Path of Economic Growth*.[10] Finally, a number of economists celebrated for their work in the neoclassical tradition, including Kenneth Arrow, Sir John Hicks, and Paul Samuelson, have made contributions to the literature in which the properties of modern classical models are compared with those of conventional neoclas-sical models.[11]

Such a revival of classical themes is as rare in science as it is common in art, music, and literature where one often sees a "classical" period of sub-stantial duration overthrown by a new theory or movement only to reappear in another form some generations later. A study of the historical roots and for-mal structure of classical and neoclassical theories of general equilibrium brings out this fascinating renaissance of classical ideas. The revival of classical theory also sheds light on a much debated question concerning the history of neoclassical analysis: was there a marginal revolution and, if so, in what did it consist?[12]

In short, there was a major change of theme in economic analysis in the later nineteenth century, one which showed itself vividly in the work of Jevons, Menger, and Walras. Their view has been summarized thus:

> As far as pure theory is concerned, the essential idea on which they concurred was in recognizing scarcity of given means in relation to alternative ends as *the* economic problem.[13]

This, in contrast to the classical theme of the production, extraction, and accumulation of surplus was what distinguished the new ideas. Vexed questions about the genealogy and implications of the concept of "utility" are therefore relatively unimportant in deciding how and when neoclassical theory emerged. The early development of the theory of "utility" (in the hands of Ferdinando Galiani, Mountiford Longfield, Hermann Heinrich Gossen, and others) can therefore be passed over since the ancient philosophical idea of utility was not a crucial component of the truly new neoclassical concept of allocation. As has been well said, what was important about marginal utility was the adjective rather than the noun.*

History and Analysis

It is a well-known characteristic of general equilibrium models of the neoclassical, post-Walrasian kind that the economic problem is seen as consisting in the (essentially timeless) allocation of given resources among alternative uses. Here the inputs of the model are the services of given factors which are treated as parameters of its structure.† It is equally characteristic of general equilibrium models of the classical type that inputs are produced commodities which are treated as variables, and *not* as parameters. Commodities are produced by means of commodities so that time enters essentially into the economic problem: will the corn produced this year be enough to provide the necessary inputs (seed plus subsistence) for next year's production? Here the fundamental concepts are viability and surplus, and the problem of allocating the surplus between the accumulation of capital and luxury consumption (over and above subsistence) come to the fore.

Many of the newest works on general equilibrium theory are largely con-

---

*See chapter 5, pp. 130–31.
†On parameters and variables in economic models see chapter 7.

fined to models of the neoclassical type. In this work, however, modern classical models are developed alongside the usual neoclassical model of the allocation of given resources, thus making clear the relations and differences between the two traditions. Initially, we investigate their origins in the history of analysis, offering evidence that one class of simple models can be regarded as "classical," and another as "neoclassical." An elementary mathematical analysis of the two types of models is then presented with a view to highlighting their contrasting features, and to showing why we hold them to be legitimate simplifications of their less formal historical antecedents. In this, the chronological order of the theories is reversed; a neoclassical allocation model is offered first since it will be familiar and so provide a basis for comparison with the structure of a modern classical model.

Throughout the formal analysis, points fundamental to the distinction between classical and neoclassical theory are made in terms of simple two-sector linear models. This raises the question of the proper use of mathematics in formalizing the "models" of classical writers, and (to a much lesser extent) of neoclassical writers (whose original works were often expressed mathematically). There are different levels at which this enterprise can be undertaken. At the most pretentious, one may write out a system formalized in modern mathematics and announce that it is Quesnay's *model*, or Smith's, or Ricardo's. When this is done serious questions of historical interpretation arise. A reading of primary sources clearly shows that the classical authors, from Petty to Marx, allow themselves a richness of texture and a subtlety and complexity of construction which eludes representation in a convenient mathematical form.

Take the case of constant returns to scale. Eighteenth and nineteenth century English political economists, since they did not construct what are now regarded as formal models, did not feel compelled to restrict themselves to constant-returns models, although they might have believed constant returns to be likely in certain circumstances. Smith's view on the increasing returns resulting from progressive division of labor is the most obvious case of a belief in *non*-constant returns. Still, it is tempting to offer "models" of Smith's system, or of the other classics, based on linearity assumptions, while granting that, as in the ready-made copies of Paris originals, something is evidently lost when such "copies" are made.

Just as an artist can capture in a few lines a recognizable sketch of a person's face, a mathematical model can be used to give only the simplest sketch of the salient characteristics of an original thinker's work or of a school of thought. And this is our intention: to show by a careful use of the primary sources of the history of economic analysis that classical writers may best be distinguished from neoclassical writers by the use of very simple models—outlines of the most important aspects of their theories. Our use of mathematics therefore makes no claim to have captured all the components of a classical or neoclassical theory, or to render superfluous a recourse to primary sources. But mathematics does have precedence in the following sense. Suppose it can be shown that a model constructed in modern terms validly expresses certain aspects of a classical theory. If the model proves to be inconsistent, or overdetermined, this must cast doubt on the coherence of the original theory. Conversely, mathematical model building may demonstrate that a constituent of a theory can be so interpreted that it is valid and important where previous informal historical criticism had pronounced it false. An example of this is the way in which Sraffa's analysis of value undermined the validity of neoclassical criticisms of Ricardo's theory of value;[14] another concerns the Pasinetti Theorem as a basis for reinterpreting classical views on saving.[15] History and analysis thus complement each other. As has been said of another area which requires the successful mixture of two very disparate components, we must remember that:

> . . . not only in the history of opera but in any individual opera the balance between 'drama' and 'music' is continually shifting, that the scales are only rarely exactly even, and that one side or the other almost always bears the heavier weight.[16]

Our reliance on history extends back more than two centuries before the writings of Léon Walras, William Stanley Jevons, and Carl Menger in the 1870's, a decade often used to mark the beginnings of general equilibrium and microeconomics. This is because the present day general equilibrium model which we have labelled modern classical is in many ways the descendant of models implicit in the work of Sir William Petty, Richard Cantillon, François Quesnay, Adam Smith, David Ricardo, and Karl Marx. The present-day neoclassical model can then be seen as typical of a much later tradition. The revival of classical ideas in modern form therefore carries with it the thesis that a major theme of classical political economy did not appear in the type of model used during the neoclassical period. And it implies a thesis about the needs of current theory: that models of the classical type must be reintegrated into the structure of economic theory.

Notes

1. Joseph Schumpeter, *A History of Economic Analysis,* Oxford University Press, New York, 1954, p. 38.

2. John von Neumann, "Uber ein Oekonomisches Gleichungs-System und eine Verallgemeinerung des Browerschen Fixpunktsatzes," in Karl Menger, ed., *Ergebnisse eines Mathematischen Kolloquiums,* No. 8, 1935–36, published 1937; trans. "A Model of General Economic Equilibrium," *Review of Economic Studies,* Vol. 13 (1945–46), pp. 1–9.
3. J. G. Kemeny, O. Morgenstern, and G. L. Thompson, "A Generalization of the von Neumann Model of an Expanding Economy," *Econometrica,* Vol. 24 (1956), pp. 115–35.
4. Joan Robinson, *The Accumulation of Capital,* Macmillan, London, 1956.
5. Piero Sraffa, *Production of Commodities by Means of Commodities, Prelude to a Critique of Economic Theory,* Cambridge University Press, 1960.
6. Pierangelo Garegnani, "Heterogeneous Capital, the Production Function, and the Theory of Distribution," *Review of Economic Studies,* Vol. 37 (1970), pp. 407–36; Luigi Pasinetti, "Changes in the Rate of Profit and Switches of Techniques," and other papers in "Paradoxes in Capital Theory: A Symposium," *Quarterly Journal of Economics,* Vol. 80 (1966), pp. 503–83. See also, D. J. Harris, "Capital, Distribution, and the Aggregate Production Function," *American Economic Review,* Vol. 63 (1973), pp. 100–13.
7. Michio Morishima, *Marx's Economics, A Dual Theory of Value and Growth,* Cambridge University Press, 1973.
8. Oskar Morgenstern and Gerald L. Thompson, *Mathematical Theory of Expanding and Contracting Economies,* D. C. Heath, Lexington, Mass., 1976.
9. Luigi Pasinetti, *Lectures on the Theory of Production,* Columbia University Press, 1977.
10. Adolphe Lowe, *The Path of Economic Growth,* Cambridge University Press, 1976.
11. Kenneth J. Arrow and David Starrett, "Cost and Demand-Theoretic Approaches to the Theory of Price Determination," in Sir John Hicks and W. Weber, eds., *Carl Menger and the Austrian School of Economics,* Oxford University Press, London, 1973, pp. 128–48; Sir John Hicks, *Capital and Growth,* Oxford at the Clarendon Press, 1965, and *Capital and Time, A Neo-Austrian Theory,* Oxford at the Clarendon Press, 1973; Paul A. Samuelson, "Understanding the Marxian Notion of Exploitation: A Summary of the So-Called Transformation Problem Between Marxian Values and Competitive Prices," *Journal of Economic Literature,* Vol IX (1971), pp. 399–431.
12. Mark Blaug, "Was There a Marginal Revolution?" in R. D. Collison Black, A. W. Coats, and Craufurd D. W. Goodwin, eds., *The Marginal Revolution in Economics, Interpretation and Evaluation,* Duke University Press, 1973, pp. 3–14. See also the other contributions.
13. Donald Winch, "Marginalism and the Boundaries of Economic Science," in *The Marginal Revolution,* p. 62. Winch's italics.
14. Sraffa, *Production of Commodities,* pp. 18–33, 94.
15. Pasinetti, *Growth and Income Distribution, Essays in Economic Theory,* Cambridge University Press, 1975, pp. 86–146.
16. Alfred Einstein, *Mozart, His Character, His Work,* Oxford University Press, New York, 1945, p. 386.

2

The Roots of Classical Theory

Petty [had] a not inconsiderable share in carrying into practise the principles which Bacon had formulated half a century earlier. . . .

THE MARQUIS OF LANSDOWNE[1]

The working of the price system is portrayed by Cantillon with such clarity that scientific economics, it is sometimes claimed with considerable justification, makes its appearance with his demonstration of the essential interdependencies of the system of production and exchange.

SAMUEL HOLLANDER[2]

And this is the great merit of Physiocracy. The Physiocrats put themselves the question: how is surplus-value . . . produced and reproduced?

KARL MARX[3]

Theories of Accumulation and Theories of the Allocation of Given Resources

Of the two great themes of economic analysis with which we shall be concerned, the first to be heard dealt with the capacity of an economy to reproduce itself and to grow. Its focus was on the manner in which capitalist production generates a social surplus, on the way in which the given social relations of this production govern the extraction and accumulation of the surplus by the capitalist class, and on the effects upon the growth of the economy of the division of the surplus between capital accumulation and luxury consumption. The emergence and development of this theme is coextensive with the rise of classical political economy, and with the efforts of the classical economists to explain the rise of the capitalist mode of production. Indeed, the classical economists, in whose works we first find a clear statement of this theme, may be adequately characterized for the moment by the fact that, being in a position to observe the great economic transformation from feudal into capitalist production, they regarded the explanation of this historical phenomenon as their primary task.

Our other major theme appeared as a reaction to the classical, and so it emerged much later in history, not becoming dominant until late in the nineteenth century. It developed into an interpretation of capitalism, in terms of the phenomena of market exchange, as a system which allocates given resources among alternative uses by means of competitive prices. Indeed, the theory of resource allocation (linked with the theory of the ''rational consumer'' in the modern fashion) is often regarded as the core of what has been called neoclassical economics.* Certainly, this theme of the allocation of given resources bulks very large in standard neoclassical treatments of general equilibrium.

A tradition seems to have grown up of confining ''classical economics'' to the English successors of Adam Smith. In this book we follow the older usage, that of Marx, who appears to have first used the term ''classical Political Economy.'' Marx wrote that ''by classical Political Economy, I understand that economy which, since the time of W. Petty, has investigated the real relations of production in bourgeois society. . . .''[4] To the classical economists, thus defined, it early became evident that all economic development depended on the existence of a disposable surplus—that is to say, upon the capacity of an economy to produce (say, in a year) more commodities than those which had to be used up in the annual process of production. They seem to have sensed from the beginning that it was of the essence of capitalist production to generate an *accumulating* surplus, and that the manner of this accumulation was crucially related to the character of the newly emerging social relations of bourgeois society.

This theory of the accumulation of surplus has been regarded, with some justice, as the core of classical economics:

Both Quesnay and Smith, then, and the schools which they represent, were primarily concerned with the scientific analysis of capitalist *production*. . . . In their theoretical analysis they both tended to concentrate much of their attention on the question of the origin and disposition of the social surplus, which they regarded as the only possible source of new capital. In this common interest and emphasis they are so sharply distinguished . . . from the Marginalist [neoclassical] writers who followed them, that it seems proper . . . to stress their community by treating them as working within a broadly similar framework of aims and concepts. The most convenient name for this framework is probably 'classicism.'[5]

Of course, it is true that what have been called ''revenue economies''— economies ''in which a surplus is extracted from cultivators''[6]—are of truly ancient origin. In fact, they precede the development of the market as an eco-

---

* In chapters 5 and 6, we show that the ''neoclassical school,'' beginning with William Stanley Jevons, Carl Menger, and Léon Walras, in the 1870's, can be seen as united because of the special stress on the theme of allocation of given resources, despite many differences of emphasis in other areas.

nomic institution. What were new, however, about the emerging industrial capitalist economies were the uses to which the surplus was being put. A lord who had once had no option but to use the surplus produce he extracted to feed bands of retainers, including craftsmen, and thus maintain political power, could now spend the surplus on manufactured luxuries. He could seek to maximize the surplus available to him by letting his lands to capitalist farmers, and these, in turn, would use their profit for the accumulation of capital. And, as the market spread and peasant was replaced by agricultural laborer and artisan by wage-earner, the *manner* in which surplus or "revenue" was now being extracted had altered. It was no longer a matter of custom backed by force, as in earlier history. The extraction of surplus now depended on production relations, the newly emerging capitalist relations, which were themselves intertwined with market phenomena.

The extraction of a customary surplus, year by year, and its use to feed retainers, had not called for explanation by economic theory. The extraction, distribution, and, above all, accumulation of surplus through capitalist production and market relations *did* seem to the classical economists to call for this kind of analysis.

The Rise of Capitalist Production and Classical Political Economy

Feudal society or, if that term be objected to, the lord and peasant system,[7] had been characterized by tradition, status, and production for use. Exchange took place at the great fairs, and exotic products were brought at great hazard all the way from the Far East, but exchange in a marketplace was not the central economic experience it became under capitalism. Most industrial production was in the hands of artisans, who sold the product of their labor under rigidly organized conditions, in guilds, and owned the means of production and the lore of their crafts. Thus, they were not compelled to sell their labor-power for a wage. Agriculture was traditionally organized in a manner that bound both landlord and peasant to the land, and dictated how the land should be cultivated and the produce distributed. The landlord certainly collected the surplus produce—what was left after the necessary outlay for seed and the peasant's subsistence had been accounted for. But he could not treat the land as capitalist "private property." He could not transform the method of cultivation, substituting an efficient technology using a small number of wage-laborers doing specialized tasks, for the tradition bound peasant cultivation which had been handed down. He could not forthwith rent the land to large capitalist farmers, who would use wage labor, and throw the peasantry, who had feudal rights just as the lord had, off the estate.

As a matter of history, the capitalist mode of production first penetrated society on a large scale in agriculture. As feudal bonds loosened, the open fields of the manorial system were enclosed; the peasants lost their land and their rights to common land and became wage-laborers. There began to appear a class of capitalist farmers, employing wage labor. Such a farmer would not think in terms of traditional roles, but in terms of maximizing the surplus which he extracted from production—the profit on his capital investment. He was in effect a capitalist.

Classical political economy developed in England and France, but this transformation of agriculture took place much earlier in England. The early English classical economists were aware of it and the French, who could not observe it in their own society, picked it up from the English writers. Thus, we shall shortly see the vitally important influence of Sir William Petty on Richard Cantillon, and of Cantillon on François Quesnay and the Marquis de Mirabeau. "Just when the English peasantry disappeared, and English farming came to be dominated by the triple division into landlords, tenant-farmers and hired laborers, has been a matter of argument for a long time. The most common opinion today is that this structure had come into existence in broad outline by the middle of the 18th century at the latest, i.e., before the start of the Industrial Revolution."[8]

Side by side with the transformation of the relations of production in agriculture, went the development of a *market* in which agricultural produce could be sold in return for the products of the growing towns. The capitalist farmer wanted an agricultural surplus *for sale in a market,* not just to maintain a great household of dependents, as the feudal lord had done. The emergence of a widespread market, to which ever more products are brought for exchange, was crucial to the development of capitalism. Products were no longer produced for use; they were commodities, made to be exchanged.

The Simplest Formulation of the Concept of Surplus

The simplest way to give formal expression to the idea of surplus is in the context of a one-sector model. Consider a highly simplified economy where the only thing produced is corn. Suppose further that land of a given fertility is freely available; and also that the only input into production is corn, which is needed as seed and as food over the growing season. In this way, we ignore, for the moment, all inputs other than corn. (Later in the book we take up the whole question of representing technology in more realistic situations where there are a number of inputs that go into defining a method of production, a "process," and also a set of these processes from which to choose.) Now, suppose that the amount of corn needed to produce a unit of corn is constant for all levels of output—if it takes a half bushel of corn to produce one bushel, then it takes five bushels to produce ten. This is a further simplification; namely, the assumption that returns to *scale* are constant. It is then possible to represent the technology for producing corn by a single "coefficient": the fraction of a unit of corn needed to produce a unit of corn a_{cc}. This standard notation is used throughout the book to represent technology. In general, a_{ij} will measure the quantity of input i per unit of output j, always assumed to be *independent* of the actual number of units of output j that are produced.

Defining Y_C as gross output of corn, it follows that the product $a_{cc} Y_C$ measures the input of corn needed to produce Y_C units of corn. We are now in a position to state the condition that is necessary in order for the corn economy to be *viable:*

$$Y_C - a_{cc} Y_C \geq 0 \qquad \text{or} \qquad 1 - a_{cc} \geq 0 \qquad\qquad (1)$$

The first inequality states that, for *any* output Y_C, the input of corn needed does not exceed the output produced; the second inequality states the same condition with reference to a *unit* level of production (where $Y_C = 1$), to show more clearly that *viability* is simply a restriction on technology, i.e., a restriction on the size of the per-unit input coefficient a_{cc}. Finally, in terms of the concept of *surplus,* a strict inequality in (1) means that a surplus *exists;* a strict equality means that surplus is zero and the economy is, therefore, *just* viable.

In the corn model, the notion of surplus is very concrete. It is simply a quantity of corn: $Y_C(1 - a_{cc}) \geq 0$. In defining surplus, however, it is necessary to suppose that the quantity of corn used as seed is fixed (by the technology), and that the quantity of corn which has to be provided to the workers for sustenance during the period of production is also given. For the classical economists, this *real wage* was usually thought of as fixed at subsistence, though not necessarily subsistence in a strict biological sense. "Subsistence" might be determined by some historical or social standard. In any event, subsistence had to cover the upkeep of the worker and his wife and enough of his children to keep the work force at least constant from one generation to another.

The existence of a surplus in this strictly physical sense of a net output is clearly a necessary prerequisite for the extraction of surplus in the sense of capitalist "profit." The latter demands, in addition, the development of appropriate technical and social relationships for the extraction of the surplus by a social class which owns the means of production and purchases labor-power in return for subsistence. At the same time, the existence of surplus, as such, does not necessarily imply a positive rate of accumulation. It only makes accumulation possible. The surplus may, in fact, be *consumed*—though not necessarily by the social class engaged in producing it.

Simple, this model certainly is—the cultivators must plant and harvest the corn with their hands (or with pieces of wood picked up at random) since we have no sector producing tools of any kind! Nevertheless, and despite the unreality of its assumptions, it will be found that the structure of the corn model illuminates a number of fundamentally important notions, and we shall return to it again in chapters 11 and 12. In more complicated models it is often convenient to let "corn" stand for whatever is produced by that sector of an economy which extracts products directly from nature, whether agricultural produce (including animals or raw materials) timber, or mineral ores. The contrast intended will be with the industrial, or manufacturing, sector. This use of a "corn" sector is, it will become evident, in the tradition of classical political economy. Needless to say, such a sector is adopted solely to simplify exposition; mathematically there is no problem about disaggregating a "sector" into its components, conceived as finely as may be desired.

It is convenient, at this point, to use our simple one-sector corn model to introduce an alternative way of measuring surplus which is of historical importance. Suppose that the year's output of our economy is 1000 units of corn, and that 100 units must be set aside to replace the stock of seed. Let the yearly subsistence of the labor force be 500 units of corn. Then the surplus is 400 units. Suppose that the work force, over the year, has put in 100,000 hours. We may now say that the labor *embodied* in the stock of seed is 10,000 hours; in the subsistence of the work force, 50,000 hours; and in the surplus, 40,000 hours. We shall find that, from the beginnings of classical political economy, surplus was described sometimes as a quantity of produce (our "corn") and sometimes in terms of the quantity of labor embodied in its production. This may be seen immediately from the writings of Sir William Petty, to which we now turn.

Sir William Petty and the Beginnings of the Classical Theory of Surplus

The mass of writings on economic subjects during the latter half of the seventeenth century—and, indeed, during the first half of the eighteenth century

—have certain characteristics which justify their being labelled "mercantilist." They stressed the analysis of *trade,* above all foreign trade, and its regulation by the powerful new bureaucracies of the emergent nation states in the interest of national power and aggrandisement. One looks in vain for any deep analysis of the nature and structure of *production,* in either agriculture or industry. However, this characteristic does not imply that these writings are without merit. For one thing, they are mainly directed toward policy, and, in this respect, they belong in the history of economic *thought* (in Schumpeter's sense) rather than economic analysis. Mercantilist policies, it is now recognized, were far from being as absurd as the nineteenth century liberals had believed. And then, insofar as they contained pieces of *analysis* (which, it is now recognized, they are by no means devoid of in some cases), that analysis was directed toward the explanation of foreign trade. Enormous fortunes were being made in foreign trade during this period, providing the capital for expansion in industry. Mercantilist analysis addressed itself to trade, international monetary mechanisms, and shifts in employment in the short run. It was *not* directed toward the explanation of long-term capital accumulation through the generation of surplus within *production.*

To understand the reasons for this emphasis, an important point about the mercantilist age must be borne in mind. It is true that by the late seventeenth century the preparation of the world for industrial capitalism was well under way. But the transformation of *industry* (destined to owe so much to the scientific revolution in the seventeenth century), that was to make the nature of capitalist production so pressing a problem for the mature classical economists, was more than a hundred years away. Men of active intellect in the seventeenth century were absorbed in two phenomena which were, indeed, ultimately to be crucial for the development of the capitalist relations of production: the emerging science, and the emerging *nation state.* Thus, economic thinking was wholly devoted to the service of "reasons of state"—the control of foreign trade in the interest of the state—and in this sense it was "mercantilist."

Sir William Petty (1623–1687) was in many ways a typical man of his age. As we shall see, he was fascinated by the new science, and he faithfully served the new absolutist state power—in this case, that of Oliver Cromwell. Characteristically for the time, Petty's highly original analysis of surplus is embedded in work written for the instruction of the bureaucratic power of the new state, and gives advice on the raising of taxes and contributions. In *this* sense, Petty belongs in the mercantilist tradition. But certain chance events put him in a unique position to see beyond the mercantilist economic ideas of his age to the analysis of the anatomy of capitalist surplus.

Regarded by Marx as the founder of classical political economy in England, Sir William Petty has been consistently praised, as Joseph Schumpeter remarks, by "economists whom no other topic could unite. . . ."[9] What is more to the point, Petty had, in his own lifetime, exactly the background, and precisely the successes and failures, most suitable for a man who was to be the father of classical economics in the conditions of the seventeenth century. His poverty-stricken youth offered him no comfortable berth in England's feudal past. His intensely inquiring mind led him to a thorough knowledge of existing technology by the age of twelve, and kept him (often to his cost) an inventor all his life. His burning ambition, combined with his poverty, brought out in him a striking business ability which was to make his fortune and mar his reputation. His mathematical talent stood him in good stead when he produced, in an amazingly short time and to his great financial profit, the first scientific survey of the land of 22 counties of Ireland. But this talent was also to give him the entrée to the brightest intellectual circles of his time, and lead to his being one of the original charter members of the Council of the Royal Society. Doubtless it was no handicap for the founder of scientific economics to be the kind of man who, in the last few months of his life, was able to read Newton's *Principia* and appraise it accurately.

Petty's study of medicine, and in particular anatomy, took him to the Low Countries, whose economy was then the most advanced in existence. What is more, this study led to his appointment as Professor of Anatomy at Oxford and Fellow of Brasenose, thus forging for Petty an important link with the best minds of his day. It also caused some little celebrity when Petty, attending a hanging in search of bodies for dissection, revived the servant girl, Ann Green, who had just been hanged, supposedly until dead.

But the specific experience which made Petty the first delineator of the concept of surplus as the rent of agricultural land, came when he abandoned his recently begun Oxford career and followed Cromwell's armies to Ireland. He went initially as physician to the army, but his real work was in masterminding the Down Survey. Even the most scrupulously fair account of Cromwell's proceedings in Ireland[10] cannot describe them as anything but an "effusion of blood."[11] He and his Ironsides had conquered and devastated the country, and it lay bleeding and ready to be carved up in the light of Petty's survey: "The Irish rebels had been driven into exile or killed by the sword and the rope, and the main business to be completed was the division of the spoils."[12] Petty produced his survey of Ireland with a view to the extraction of the last ounce of surplus from the lands of that country for the hungry soldiery who, having laid it low, were ready to carve it up, and for the circling adventurers who waited to settle upon its remains. What an anatomy lesson in the cutting up of a country the Down Survey must have been! And what instruction in the extracting of surplus for a man who, arriving with a few hundred pounds, found himself, after the completion of the survey, heavy with estates and laden with rents!

It is quite evident from Petty's numerous writings how well he understood the concept of an agricultural surplus. For example, as early as the *Treatise of Taxes and Contributions,* which was published in 1662 and was the first of his economic works, he writes:

Suppose a man could with his own hands plant a certain scope of Land with Corn, that is, could Digg, Plough, Harrow, Weed, Reap, Carry home, Thresh, and Winnow so much as the Husbandry of this Land requires; and had withal Seed wherewith to serve the same. I say, that when this man had subducted his seed out of the proceed of his Harvest, and also, what himself hath both eaten and given to others in exchange for Clothes, and other Natural necessities; that the remainder of Corn is the natural and true Rent of the Land for that year; and the *medium* of seven years, or rather of so many years as make up the Cycle, within which Dearths and Plenties make their revolution, doth give the ordinary Rent of the Land in Corn.[13]

This is a remarkably clear description of surplus as a quantity of corn, extracted by the landlord as rent. We shall find it to be characteristic of early classical political economy, both in England and in France, that surplus is first clearly seen in the context of the rent yielded by agricultural land. The mature classical concept of industrial profit as a reflection of surplus comes later. Profit, among the early classical economists, is not distinguished clearly from wages, since most trades were in the hands of artisans.

To return to Petty, it may be observed that he often measures surplus as a quantity of labor time: "If a man can bring to *London* an ounce of Silver out of the Earth in *Peru,* in the same time that he can produce a bushel of Corn, then one is the natural price of the other. . . ."[14] Of this kind of argument in Petty, Meek comments that he is "virtually resolving the value-difference between output and input into surplus labor, much in the manner of the later Classical economists."[15] As Marx had remarked, "In fact for Petty, therefore, since the value of Corn is determined by the labour-time contained in it, and the rent is equal to the total product minus wages and seed, rent is equal to the surplus-produce in which the surplus labour is materialized. Rent here includes profit; the latter is not yet separated from rent."[16] Petty, who sought for a "par" between land and labor, sometimes expressed the surplus as a quantity of the produce of the land (corn) and sometimes as a quantity of labor time.

Richard Cantillon, the Founder
of Classical Allocation Theory

Richard Cantillon, who reproduced and extended Petty's analysis of surplus, and who first systematically developed the theory of the allocation of surplus output, is in some ways a rather mysterious figure. Not that there was anything obscure about his origins: he came of an old Anglo-Irish family with connections and descendents in several branches of the British nobility. Nor did he hide himself away. He lived much in Paris where he was a highly successful banker, but he and his wife were well known in English as well as French society. Lady Mary Wortley Montague, the celebrated eighteenth century letter writer, notes in a letter from Paris that "Madame Cantillon . . . eclipses most of our London beauties." [17] And the Cantillons' only surviving child, Henrietta, was a noted heiress. Horace Walpole writes that, "Lord Stafford is come over [to Paris] to marry Miss Cantillon, a vast fortune. . . ." [18]

Yet there is a sense in which Cantillon *is* a mysterious figure. Despite his British connections, he was destined to influence the development of classical political economy mainly in France. In that country, as we shall shortly see, his influence was profound. Several occurrences help to explain Cantillon's lack of influence on the English classical economists. His only surviving work, the *Essay on the Nature of Trade in General,* [19] is believed to have been written between 1730 and his death in 1734. But it was only published in a French translation, and that not until 1755. No complete English version appeared until the French text was translated by Henry Higgs in 1931.

Cantillon is thought to have been born between 1680 and 1690. He died on May 14, 1734, in circumstances which account for the loss of all his other manuscripts. They perished in the flames of his London town house in Albermarle Street: a raging fire which nevertheless failed to conceal the evidences of a murderer's knife. Cantillon's French cook, one Joseph Denier, who had been dismissed ten days before, fled to Holland and evaded capture. We have it on the authority of the Marquis de Mirabeau, who will appear shortly as one of the best-known members of the French school of early classical economists, the Physiocrats, and who was deeply influenced by Cantillon, that, "A mass of precious manuscripts perished with him by a remarkable and deplorable catastrophe." [20] Probably much more of Cantillon's work than we possess today was known to Mirabeau, whose writings show an intimate knowledge of Cantillon's habits and character. We learn, for example, that, "Cosmopolitan, or rather equally a citizen everywhere, he had houses in seven of the principle cities of Europe, and the least knowledge to acquire or calculation to verify made him cross the continent from one end to another.''[21]

Mirabeau makes the amazing statement that the manuscript from which the *Essay* was printed in 1755 was in his hands for sixteen years, after which he had to return it to its rightful owner. Mirabeau had proposed to publish the manuscript himself, but it needed revision, and lacked a statistical supplement. The supplement apparently perished in the fire. Ironically, given Cantillon's destined influence, mainly on French economics, Mirabeau tells us that Cantillon ''never intended that the work should appear in French and only translated it for a friend whose solidity of mind was known to him, so he paid little attention to its phrasing.''[22] But, as we shall shortly see, François Quesnay, the founder of Physiocracy, read the first edition of Cantillon's *Essay*. He noted the concept of surplus in Cantillon, and based his whole system on this idea. And Quesnay's first convert to physiocracy and for many years his co-worker, was Mirabeau. Schumpeter, with much justification, has claimed that ''few sequences in the history of economic analysis are so important for us to see, to understand, and to fix in our minds as is the sequence: Petty–Cantillon–Quesnay.''[23]

For Richard Cantillon, as for Petty, the notion of social class is basic to his theory. In the *Essay,* however, it is systematically worked out for the first time as a fundamental concept of a whole system of theory. He insists right at the beginning that ''all the classes and inhabitants of a state live at the expense of the Proprietors of Land.''[24] Each proprietor will either manage his land himself, or rent it to one or more farmers. The subsistence of the farmers* and laborers must then be deducted, and the surplus goes to the proprietor.[25] Merchants, artisans, and professional people of all sorts, live off part of the surplus, which the proprietors pay them in return for their services.[26] This notion that only land generates a true surplus was destined to be adopted by Quesnay, and to form a fundamental assumption of physiocracy. Recall that the capitalist mode of production (and of thought) appeared first in the context of agriculture. In Petty's England, and to a lesser extent, in Cantillon's and Quesnay's France, capitalist social and technical relations were penetrating agriculture, but most industry, especially in France, was in the hands of artisans who sold the product of their labor, assisted by an appropriate stock of means of production (tools, material, etc.) which they owned, and from whom a surplus was not extracted in the course of production by another class.

---

* And, apparently, their profit. See below, pp. 20, 26 (note 48), 39–40 (notes 77 and 78).

Cantillon devotes a whole chapter to discussing critically the concept of a par or relation between the value of land and labor, while acknowledging the priority of "Monsieur le Chevalier Petty."[27] Cantillon calculates how much land will be needed under various conditions of agriculture to enable the laborer to subsist and to bring up a replacement for the next generation. This amount of land for, say, one year has the same value as the labor* of one laborer for the same period. It is quite clear from the argument of the *Essay* that he is well aware of the social relativity of the concept of subsistence. He refers to some figures which he had caused to be drawn up in the supplement (which, it will be recalled, has been lost) "to determine the amount of land of which one man can consume the produce under each head of Food, Clothing, and other necessities of life, according to the mode of living in Europe where the Peasants of diverse countries are often nourished and maintained very differently."[28] In a most important passage Cantillon tells us that:

The Farmers have generally two thirds of the Produce of the Land, one for their costs and the support of their assistants, the other for the Profit of their Undertaking: on these two thirds the Farmer provides generally directly or indirectly subsistence for all those who live in the Country, and also several Mechanics or Undertakers in the City in respect of the Merchandise of the City consumed in the Country.

The Proprietor has usually one third of the produce of his Land and on this third he maintains all the Mechanics and others whom he employs in the City as well, frequently, as the Carriers who bring the produce of the Country to the City.[29]

It can hardly be doubted in the light of this and many other passages that Cantillon regarded the farmer as a capitalist entrepreneur, who made a profit from production, over and above his subsistence. He offers the suggestion that for the majority, "their Labour or Superintendence may be valued at about thrice the produce of the land which serves for their maintenance."[30] Even when he is stressing the great wealth of the few large landowners, the reasonable prosperity of the farmer in comparison to a *small* landowner comes through: "If a Proprietor had only the amount of Land which he lets out to one Farmer, the Farmer would get a better living out of it than himself; but the Nobler and Larger Landowners in the Cities have sometimes several hundreds of Farmers. . . ."[31] As we shall see later, one of the paradoxes of Physiocracy lies in the refusal by Quesnay and his followers to recognize that part of the agricultural surplus extracted by the farmers remains with them as their profit, and is not passed on to the landlords. The paradox is heightened by the fact that both Quesnay and Mirabeau had studied Cantillon's *Essay*.

* More correctly, the labor-power, but Cantillon did not use this distinction.

What Quesnay, Mirabeau, and the other physiocrats *did* clearly derive from Cantillon, however, is the idea, repeatedly stressed throughout the *Essay,* that *all* nonagricultural classes live off the surplus produce of the land. In one sense, this was a sound insight: if there is no agricultural surplus, no workers can be maintained while they engage in industrial development and thus no industrial sector can be set up. Both Cantillon and the physiocrats, however, slip into the inference, which does not follow, that an industrial sector, when it exists, is barely viable—that industrial production yields no surplus.*

Having explained how the agricultural surplus is extracted by the farmers and part of it passed on to the landlords, Cantillon now proceeds to analyze how the demands of landlords (and to some extent the demands of the farmers and prosperous merchants) determine the allocation of the surplus between different areas of production—that is to say, how these demands determine the composition of surplus output. In particular, he shows how, in a free market, prices will serve to allocate the surplus so as to satisfy the demands of the landlords, farmers, and well-to-do merchants, just as well as if they had owned slaves and directly ordered their overseers what to produce. The title of Chapter XIV of the *Essay,* where the allocation theory is set out with condensed brilliance, is itself highly suggestive: "The Fancies, the Fashions and the Modes of Living of the Prince, and especially of the Landowners, determine the use to which Land is put in a State and cause the variations in the market-prices of all things." [32] What a modern description of the determinants of demand for luxury goods†—"Les Humeurs, les modes et les façons de vivre. . . ." [33] And Cantillon would satisfy any modern economist in his clear understanding of how demand acts, through variations in market prices, to alter the composition of output. Thus, the theory of the allocation of surplus output, an essential part of classical analysis, begins with the *Essay.*

To set out his theory of allocation, Cantillon constructs a highly articulated model of an economy. We are to analyze the decision making of the landlord of a large estate, "which I wish to consider here as if there were no other in the world." [34] Cantillon takes up two cases. First, we are to suppose that the landlord has the estate cultivated himself, and makes all the decisions as to how everything is to be allocated. Nevertheless, he is bound by the technology in use to lay aside certain outputs to be used as inputs in order to keep production going: "He will necessarily use part of it for corn to feed the

---

*On surplus in an industrial sector, see below, pp. 35–44; also, chapter 3, pp. 51–77.
†Note that demand affects only the composition of surplus output (luxury goods). Workers' wages are treated in the same way as is fodder for draft animals: as a set of subsistence requirements.

Labourers, Mechanics, and Overseers who work for him, another part to feed the Cattle, Sheep and other Animals necessary. . . ." [35] Thus, the subsistence requirements of the animals, laborers, mechanics, and overseers are treated simply as technological data. They may be summarized as the amount of corn needed to produce a unit of corn, and regarded as a parameter of the model. The total amount of corn produced can be varied, and so the corn available as an input in the next period of production is a variable open to the landlord's decision. The total amount of land is a given primary resource, but it need not all be used in production. Labor is not treated as given: as we have seen it is available, in any amount considered optimal by the landlord, at a fixed per unit cost, namely, the amount of corn needed to provide a laborer and his family with subsistence for a unit of time. Surplus output can be allocated as the landlord desires: "He will turn part of the land into Parks, Gardens, Fruit trees or Vines as he feels inclined and into meadows for the Horses he will use for his pleasure, etc." [36]

Having described how allocation might be carried out by the landlord himself, Cantillon then considers the case where the allocation process is turned over to the operations of a free market. "Let us now suppose that to avoid so much care and trouble he makes a bargain with the Overseers of the Labourers, gives them Farms or pieces of Land and leaves to them the responsibility for maintaining in the usual manner all the Labourers they supervise. . . ." [37] The landlord now "fixes a common measure, like silver, to settle the price at which the Farmers will supply [the Master-Craftsmen] with wool and they will supply him with cloth, and that the prices are such as to give to the Master-Craftsmen the same advantages and enjoyments as they had when Overseers, and the Journeymen Mechanics also the same as before. . . . The merchandise . . . will be sold to the Landowner, the Farmers, the Labourers, and the other Mechanics reciprocally at a price which leaves to all of them the same advantages as before. . . ." [38] Cantillon shows that a pricing system can achieve the same allocation as a complete economic plan. Thus a set of prices will be an *equilibrium* price system if it satisfies the demands of the landlord exactly as these demands would have been satisfied in the case when the economy was planned. "The Owner, who has at his disposal the third of the Produce of the Land, is the principal agent in the changes which may occur in demand." [39] The landlord's demands then determine the composition of output (slightly reinforced by the demands of a few farmers or master craftsmen; but Cantillon feels that these people will follow the mode set by the landlord). This clear picture of the generation of surplus, and of the allocation of surplus output, was passed on by Richard Cantillon to the French physiocrats.

Physiocracy: The Final Development of the Theory of Surplus in Agriculture Alone

The theory of the generation, extraction, and allocation of an agricultural surplus began in the British Isles. With Cantillon, however, its influence moved to France. We should hardly be surprised that it prospered and achieved its final flowering on French soil. The enormous development of foreign trade and the profits made by merchant capitalists in Britain distracted the minds of British economic thinkers from the sphere of production. The fact of agricultural surplus alone was not enough to make them concentrate upon the analysis of what happened in actual production. When they did return to the analysis of production, led by Adam Smith, the interest lay in demonstrating the existence of a surplus *throughout industry* and not just in agriculture. To the France of the mid-eighteenth century, on the other hand, foreign trade was of relatively less importance, and manufacturing was underdeveloped.[40] There was thus less to distract the mind of an economic theorist from the prospect of developing, in the rich lands of France, a progressive capitalist agriculture like that of Britain. French cultivation, except in a few northern provinces, lay in a state of feudal stagnation that must have been an open challenge. At the same time, France could harldly have offered a fertile environment for Adam Smith's theory of a surplus throughout industry: the turbulent Glasgow of the 1770's, with the transformation to industrial capitalism going on before his eyes, was just what Smith needed for his ideas to develop. But France did offer exactly the soil in which the concepts of Petty and Cantillon could reach their final and most developed form.

Victor de Riquetti, Marquis de Mirabeau (1715–1789), had been sitting on the manuscript of Cantillon's *Essay*. Finally he had to return it, and it appeared in print. This persuaded Mirabeau to publish, as a book of his own, some material he had planned to bring out together with Cantillon's *Essay*. He published the *Friend of Mankind* in 1757, and this brought him to the attention of François Quesnay (1694–1774), and led to their meeting twice in Quesnay's room in the palace of Versailles one summer day in 1757. The first interview went badly. Curiously, although they were discussing Cantillon, they were not debating his theory of agricultural surplus, which was to become the foundation of physiocracy. They were bogged down over Cantillon's views on population—Mirabeau had maintained in the *Friend of Mankind* that the way to increase prosperity was to encourage population. Fortunately, this side issue did not provoke a quarrel, and Mirabeau returned to Dr. Quesnay in the evening, to become a devoted disciple and the doctor's lifelong friend, and, eventually, equal collaborator. From that moment, as Jacqueline Hecht remarks, the proud aristocrat gave himself up completely to the doctor's influence.[41]

The group of thinkers influenced by Quesnay and Mirabeau, known originally as *les économistes,* but later as the physiocrats,[42] liked to date their beginnings from that fateful summer evening of 1757. The life of the circle was intense and brilliant, but surprisingly short. Its immediate vogue was over by the time of the political fall of Turgot* in 1776. which led to the undoing of the physiocratic reforms which Turgot, though holding himself aloof from the school, had carried out as a minister of the crown. The publication in 1776 of Smith's *Wealth of Nations* then overshadowed them, and, as Ronald Meek observes, "It is only in our own time, with a revival of interest in certain of the basic theoretical and practical questions upon which the Physiocrats concentrated, that their full stature as economists is gradually being revealed."[43]

At the time of their meeting, Mirabeau was 42 and only beginning to understand physiocratic theory, and Quesnay, who was 63, had so far published only one minor paper on economics. Yet they founded a school of economic analysis which would show a faithfulness to its master's teaching for which, as Schumpeter remarks, there are "but two analogues in the whole history of economics: the fidelity of the orthodox Marxists to the message of Marx and the fidelity of the orthodox Keynesians to the message of Keynes."[44],† But then, Quesnay and Mirabeau enjoyed valuable advantages for founding such a school. Mirabeau was a figure of the first degree of fashion, and a highly popular writer. Everything he wrote would be read and discussed at court and throughout intellectual France, and he began at once to write extensively in support of his master's doctrines, submitting every last word to Quesnay and receiving each manuscript back with careful annotations. Quesnay, on the other hand, had come to court through the protection of the Marquise de Pompadour as her personal doctor, and was besides her intimate friend, confidante, and adviser. For all his modest origins, he was, in effect, as well connected at court as Mirabeau. Certain little incidents show this vividly. For example, when Quesnay wanted to run off copies of his *Tableau Économique,*

---

*On Turgot, see below, pp. 40–44.
† No doubt, this is more true of the Marxists than of the Keynesians!

he persuaded Madame de Pompadour that manual work was therapeutic relaxation, and Louis XV installed a beautifully made printing press at Versailles, and helped to set up and proofread the *Tableau Économique*. And when Mirabeau was sent to prison at Vincennes at the instigation of the tax farmers, for publishing in 1760 his *Theory of Taxation,* Quesnay and the Marquise de Mirabeau worked with the Pompadour to mollify the king and defeat the reactionary interests who farmed the taxes. Mirabeau had been sent to Vincennes on December 19. He was released on December 24 and was simply banished to his estates for two months.

The physiocrats, believing that all surplus came from agriculture and ended in the hands of the landlord, naturally argued that the landlords should be taxed. Again, wishing for a prosperous agriculture, they opposed the taxation of the cultivators, arguing that this would deprive the latter of the means to maintain the land. Clearly, this was not going to make them popular with vested interests in a country where most great landlords were noblemen or prelates, and exempt from taxation, and where the right to collect the taxes on peasant cultivators and others had been sold by the Crown to the so-called "tax farmers," who had thus a strong interest in the status quo. Under the circumstances, what is perhaps surprising is that Mirabeau got off so lightly. Meanwhile the marquis had been attended by crowds on his journey home, and his popularity had never been higher.

Rumor had it that Quesnay himself was actually author of the book which resulted in Mirabeau's problems. As a matter of fact the marquis seems to have collaborated with several people besides Quesnay. But in any case, Quesnay could be said to be joint author of everything Mirabeau wrote for the rest of the doctor's life. And, if Quesnay caused Mirabeau problems, he would also defend him to the death. One of the doctor's great qualifications as founder of physiocracy was that he had already defended the rights and claims of a school in a hard campaign. He had risen to fame as a writer through his brilliant and widely discussed defenses of the surgeons in their fight for status and recognition against the Faculty of Medicine of Paris. Many an eminent doctor could have certified that Quesnay was a valuable ally and a devastating opponent.

And then, most pertinent to the founding of physiocracy, was Quesnay's lifelong love for the soil of France. Despite his many years as a courtier at Versailles, despite his distinguished practice of medicine as first doctor-in-ordinary to Louis XV and doctor to Madame de Pompadour, and his equally notable medical writings, there were things in the background of François Quesnay that made it natural for him to be the great developer of the theory of *agricultural* surplus. A story exists that Quesnay's father Nicolas was an attorney; but, in fact, Nicolas had been a farmer and Quesnay was born on a farm, and grew up close to the soil.[45] All his life he retained an interest in farming and crops, not immediately to be expected of a man who had moved continually in the glittering society of the court of Versailles from 1749 until the year of his death, 1774.

Quesnay's first work on economics, the article on "Farmers" in the *Encyclopedia,*[46] reveals clearly his interest in agriculture. But it is with the second *Encyclopedia* article, "Corn,"[47] in 1757, that the great theme of surplus first appears in his work. Here Quesnay explicitly acknowledges the influence of Cantillon.[48]

It has been suggested that the general influence of Cantillon on Quesnay was perhaps first recognized by Marx.[49] What confronts one in reading Quesnay is that the concept of surplus, already the major theme in Cantillon, is now developed throughout all its variations in a whole system of political economy, and presented in an elaborate and sophisticated economic model. The key to Quesnay's work, as Marx saw quite clearly, is that it is a study of the accumulation of *capital*. It is a study of how the replacement of small farms, cultivated by peasants, by capitalist agriculture, leads to an enormous growth in the corn surplus making possible general economic growth.

It should not seem strange by now to the reader that the first systematic study of capitalist accumulation (by Quesnay and the physiocrats) was an analysis of how to make agriculture an efficient capitalist industry. Of course, all industrial development requires an agricultural surplus as a precondition: if everyone must work full-time on the land for there to be subsistence, no industrialization can take place. But, aside from the prior need for an agricultural surplus, there were, as we have seen, factors which prevented the physiocrats from seeing the generation of a surplus in industry. For one thing, French industry was largely at the artisan stage, so that the craftsman owned the tools of his trade and sold the product of his labor. He was not forced to sell his labor-power in return for subsistence to another class who had acquired ownership of the means of production. Thus the technical and social conditions for the sale of labor-power by one class and the extraction of surplus by another did not yet exist on a large scale in French industry. There were some factories, and a strictly wage-earning class was emerging in France throughout the latter half of the eighteenth century. But, as late as the beginning of the French Revolution, the case was such that its great scholar, Georges Lefebvre, could write:

Yet when all is said only a small minority of wage workers were yet assembled in factories, residentially concentrated or brought together in labor organizations. The famous revolutionary areas of the city, Saint-Antoine with its wood workers, Saint-Marceau with its tanners, had an abundance of small shops in which master craftsmen and their journeymen employees fraternized on the great insurrectionary "days." On the whole the wage workers had no clear consciousness of class. If they had had, it is very doubtful whether the Revolution of 1789 would have been possible.[50]

Subsequent historians have confirmed the view of Lefebvre. George Rudé has recently written:

There was as yet no factory system or industrial "belt," though enterprising textile manufacturers had set up establishments that, on occasion, employed up to 400 or 500, or even 800 workpeople under one roof. Apart from the multifarious petty trades plied in the markets, on the riverside, in the Place de Grève or on the Pont Neuf, the prevailing mode of production was still that of the traditional workshop in which the journeyman, though his prospects of promotion were becoming more and more remote, still shared the work and gossip, and often the board and lodging, of his master.[51]

François Quesnay had already formed his views of the respective characters of agriculture and industry in 1757. It is reasonable to suppose that he would have based his analysis on the France he had experienced: that of the first half of the eighteenth century. So, we are entitled to conclude that what was still true on the eve of the Revolution would have been even more so in the earlier period of which Quesnay wrote. And, one must also remember that where large fortunes *were* made in commerce and industry, it was easy for the physiocrats to point to the notorious monopoly privileges which existed and deny that these fortunes represented the creation of any new surplus.

Previous writers, with the exception of Petty and Cantillon, had searched for the source of surplus only within the sphere of circulation, exchange, and trade. Sixteenth and seventeenth century publicists had thought that one country could gain a "surplus" from trade, but only as the cost of the other country's loss. For these mercantilist writers, surplus "was explained purely from *exchange,* the sale of the commodity above its value."[52] The physiocrats, however, following the suggestions in Petty and Cantillon, transferred the enquiry as to the origin of surplus "from the sphere of circulation into the sphere of direct production and thereby laid the foundation for the analysis of capitalist production."[53] Since their specific contribution was to show how to derive surplus within production, "they necessarily begin . . . with that branch of production which can be thought of in complete separation from and independently of circulation, of exchange; and which presupposes exchange not between man and man, but only between man and nature."[54]

What the physiocrats saw clearly (even if only for the case of agriculture) was that a surplus, a "net product," can be derived from *production:* it need not result from beggar-my-neighbor trade, either foreign or domestic, but from production itself. If one is to analyze surplus within production in physical product terms (say, as so much corn), then the easiest place to see this principle in operation is in agriculture. "The sum total of the means of subsistence which the laborer consumes from one year to another . . . is smaller than the sum total of the means of subsistence which he produces. In manufacture, the workman is not generally seen directly producing either his means of subsistence or the surplus in excess of his means of subsistence."[55] The analysis of the extraction of this agricultural surplus was carried to new heights of refinement and precision by Quesnay in the *Tableau Économique.*

The Tableau Économique

We are at a great turning point in the development of classical analysis. Cantillon had given a brilliant verbal sketch of a general equilibrium in the allocation of surplus output, and Quesnay, as we know, had learned from this. His notion of an agricultural surplus is Cantillon's (and, beyond Cantillon, Petty's), and his fundamental division of society into three classes: a class of proprietors (classe des propriétaires), a productive class (classe productive), and a sterile class (classe stérile), is precisely Cantillon's. But, in the *Tableau Économique,*[56] he presents for the first time a fully developed, quantitative model of general equilibrium in the production of commodities by means of commodities. This model was destined, as we shall see,* to have a profound influence on the development by Marx of his schemes of simple and expanded reproduction, and in the twentieth century, upon the development of general equilibrium models of the classical type, such as those of Neumann and Sraffa.

The general characteristics of the *Tableau* are what we would expect after studying Cantillon, and knowing something of agriculture and industry in mid-eighteenth century France. The productive class is shown cultivating the soil, and producing a net product, or revenue, over and above its necessary expenses, i.e., subsistence, seed, repairs to farm equipment, etc. The class of landlords, Quesnay assumes, receives the entire surplus which results from

* See chapter 4, pp. 108–15.

the cultivation of the soil. Finally, the "sterile" class produces luxury goods which it sells to the landlords; and farm implements, etc., which it sells to the productive class. Those who sell services, high or low—lawyer, harlot, soldier, and government minister alike—are also treated as members of the sterile class.

In becoming a formal model, however, the *Tableau* has developed certain unique features which are vital to its understanding and appraisal. The first of these arises over the issue of economic growth. The physiocrats were deeply concerned that French agriculture should awaken out of its feudal slumbers and be reorganized into large farms (as in England) on a capitalist basis. The *Tableau* in its original form, however, does not show growth of output. It shows a state of affairs in which the physiocrats were acutely interested—the end-result of a process of agricultural reform which they were advocating. In the best-known versions of the *Tableau,* Quesnay presented a model of the French economy, using figures which he believed represented its possibilities in his time, if and only if French agriculture were relieved of tax burdens, and optimally organized into large farms.[57] Thus, to anticipate a little, this model is one of what Marx was to call *simple* reproduction rather than of reproduction on an extended scale. In both Quesnay's model and Marx's, the economy depicted is more than barely viable—a surplus is being generated. But that surplus is wholly devoted to luxury consumption (in Quesnay, by the proprietors; in Marx, by the capitalists), and no further growth is going on.

This does not mean that Quesnay could not adapt his *Tableau* to show the effects of wise or foolish policies in causing the economy's output to expand or contract. He made much of this (remember the strong policy orientation of the physiocrats) and used a modified *Tableau* for this sort of analysis. In the *Explanation* which accompanies the "third edition" of the *Tableau Économique,*[58] he describes how an economy can grow or contract, and this kind of analysis is typical of the later works of both Quesnay and Mirabeau, where *Tableaux* are used to illustrate such growth or contraction. This can be seen, for example, in chapter 7 of the *Rural Philosophy*[59] of Mirabeau, a chapter which is usually attributed to Quesnay, as well as in works by the latter such as the *First Economic Problem*[60] and the *Second Economic Problem.*[61]

Since many versions of the *Tableau Économique* were published, and since we do not have space to discuss variants here, we must, of necessity, pick a particular specimen for our purposes. Such a choice, obviously, must be to some degree arbitrary, although certain criteria do exist. We may begin by noting that many physiocrats never knew the *Tableau* in its original form, but only in later works by Quesnay and Mirabeau, and today we have only had a

TABLE 2-1. Formula of the *Tableau Économique*
Total Reproduction: Five Milliards

	Annual advances of the productive class	*Revenue for the proprietors*	*Advances of the sterile class*
	2 milliards	2 milliards	

Sums which serve to pay the revenue and the interest on the original advances	G B 1 milliard
	  F 1 milliard
	  D 1 milliard
		A	E 1 milliard
			
			C 1 milliard
			
			H 1 milliard

Expenditure of the annual advances	2 milliards		
TOTAL	5 milliards		2 milliards
			of which one-half is held back by this class for next year's advances

definitive text of the "third edition" of the *Tableau Économique* since the recent work of Marguerite Kuczynski and Ronald Meek.[62]

In the late 1750's, Quesnay privately printed three versions of a short manuscript, containing the *Tableau Économique,* together with an explanation and some other material. These have become known as the three "editions" of the *Tableau,* but they were simply run off on the King's press for private circulation among a few friends of Quesnay's, and were never, properly speaking, published. Of these "editions," the second and third agree as to the contents of the zig-zag. (The earlier versions of the *Tableau,* which had zig-zag lines to illustrate the flow of money and goods throughout the system, were referred to affectionately as the "zic-zac.") We know from an undated letter by Quesnay to Mirabeau that Quesnay regarded his second "edition" as an improvement on the first since he writes that, "I shall be sending you a second edition, enlarged and amended in the usual way."[63] And, since we now possess an excellent text of the third "edition," we can see that Quesnay retained his "amended" version there. Progressive change in the *Tableau,* however, did not stop here. In the *Rural Philosophy,* the geometrical progression which had given its name to the zig-zag is dropped as an unnecessary complication. Finally, in his *Analysis of the Tableau Économique,*[64] which first appeared in the *Journal de l'Agriculture, du Commerce et des Finances* in June, 1766, the *Tableau* takes on its final form. We shall concentrate on this last version.[65]

Quesnay begins by assuming a large kingdom whose territory, cultivated by the most modern methods, yields every year a reproduction worth five milliards. Initially, the productive class has two milliards of produce. These are its "annual advances" ("avances annuelles")—in effect, the inputs necessary to produce the annual output. The class of proprietors has a revenue of two milliards in money—the rents resulting from the last annual production. The artisan, or sterile class, has one milliard—its annual advances, or, to use modern terminology, the necessary inputs for the period of production. The productive class, as a result of its annual production, changes its two milliard annual advances into five milliards. Two of these five are net product or revenue. The sterile class produces one milliard luxuries and one milliard new equipment for the productive class. Exchange then takes place in a manner illustrated by the *Tableau,* of which we present a slightly modified version in Table 2-1.

The proprietors now spend one milliard on food from the productive class (AB), and one milliard on manufactured goods from the sterile class (AC). The sterile class buys one milliard of raw materials from the productive class

(EF) together with one milliard of food (CD). "Thus the *sterile class* receives *two milliards,* which it employs in making purchases from the *productive class* for the subsistence of its agents and for the raw materials for its goods."[66] It should be noted that the annual advances of the sterile class do not include an allowance for food, which, as we have just seen, it obtains from the productive class. The productive class's annual advances, on the contrary, *do* include one milliard worth of food, which, in their case, is generated within their own sector. This explains the somewhat confusing character of the top line of the *Tableau,* where the sterile class is shown as having only one milliard worth of annual advances, whereas its output is two milliards.[67] On the face of it, it thus looks as if the sterile class produces a surplus. In fact, however, the sterile class has to obtain food from the productive class, so it uses up one milliard of annual advances *plus one milliard of food*[68] in producing two milliards of output and therefore, consistent with physiocratic theory, yields no net product or surplus.

The productive class, on the other hand, uses up two milliards of annual advances (which in its case *include* its food) in producing five millards of output. The five milliards are disposed of in the following way. One milliard represents the interest on what Quesnay called "original advances" ("avances primitives") at ten percent. This original advance is the fixed capital used in farming, and Quesnay is assuming that it has to be replaced at the rate of ten percent each year out of what is produced that year by the productive class (i.e., animals that die, repair of fencing or drainage, farm buildings, etc.). This original advance is abstracted from in early versions of the *Tableau.* Two milliards serve to pay the revenue to the proprietors, and two milliards serve to replace the annual advances. One will be consumed by the productive class in the next period and the other will pay for the manufactured necessities of the next period (GH). Thus, Quesnay assumes that the agricultural sector produces annually a net product of two milliards equal to its necessary inputs, but excluding interest on the "avances primitives."[69]

Ever since the various versions of the *Tableau* appeared, scholars have seen massive problems lurking like sharks beneath its smooth, formal surface. We shall resist the temptation to hunt them here; the bare sketch we have just given of the final *Tableau* of the *Analysis* is sufficient for our needs.

The First Formal Model of a Viable Economy

Certain broad characteristics of the *Tableau Économique* remain true of every classical model constructed subsequently, down to the most recent contemporary work. Most fundamental, perhaps, is the concept of viability: the model is shown to be capable of reproducing itself, together with its constant annual surplus of two milliards, without change (although, as we have already noted, change in the size of the surplus was studied in some of the later *Tableaux*).

Nearly as fundamental is the notion of analysis by sector. Quesnay showed that certain crucially important properties of an economy could be captured by dividing it into a few broad sectors. This insight was to be fundamental to Marx's reproduction schemes, and is equally so for today's model building. It is important to see, however, that Quesnay's sectors do not partition the economy in precisely the way in which a general equilibrium model would be partitioned today. The *Tableau* divides the total flow of *expenditure* into productive expenditure—expenditure of the revenue, i.e., of surplus—and sterile expenditure. This division by types of expenditure corresponds exactly to the division of the economy into *classes* which Quesnay took over from Cantillon: a class of agricultural producers, a class of proprietors, and an artisan (sterile) class.

Modern sectoral analysis, however, is in terms of industries or significant aggregates of industries. Part of the *Tableau* does have this feature: the segregation of all forms of agriculture into a sector corresponds to modern practice. We shall do this, and call the sector thus defined the corn sector. Likewise the segregation of all manufacturing (leaving aside for the moment the sterility assumption) into one sector is similar to modern practice, and we shall be introducing such a sector, which we shall call the industrial, or "iron," sector shortly. So far the strengths and weaknesses of the *Tableau* are exactly those of modern general equilibrium models. But Quesnay also has a sector devoted to expenditure of the revenue, and this does not, unlike his other sectors, represent an industry or an aggregation of industries. It represents the extraction, by the feudal nobility, of the surplus output of the land, and the consumption of this, partly as agricultural luxury products, and partly as luxuries manufactured by the sterile class.

In modern times, neoclassical historians of economic analysis have responded to the situation by a drastic expedient: that of inventing an industry for the class of proprietors to engage in, so that they may be regarded as producing landlord services and so that the revenue they receive is composed of payments for these services.[70] This move is perfectly consistent with the assumptions of neoclassical theory, which we leave for a later discussion, but, as the basis for an interpretation of physiocracy, it has serious problems. Thus, on this analysis the surplus disappears—indeed, one cannot even introduce the concept—and there are three industries, each producing a product for which the return just covers its opportunity cost.* But the primary sources of physiocracy reveal an intense, consistent, and long-continuing concern with revenue, net product, or surplus: how to maximize it, and how to allocate it. Equally consistent and omnipresent is the insistence that there is a fundamental distinction between agricultural production by capitalist farmers and industrial production by artisans; namely, that the former is *productive* (yields the revenue or net product) while the latter is *sterile* (yields no revenue or net product). All this shows clearly on the face of the *Tableau* throughout its many versions.

To preserve the historical integrity of the *Tableau,* therefore, and to show its role in the development of *classical* theory, it is necessary to recognize that one of its sectors (the class of proprietors) cannot appear as a sector in the modern sense in any attempt to present a formalization of the *Tableau* in modern notation. Thus, from a modern classical point of view, the *Tableau* visibly disaggregates the economy into *two* sectors: agriculture and artisan production; and shows the receipt of income by *three* classes: agricultural producers, artisans, and the proprietors who receive the agricultural surplus. Once one looks at the *Tableau* in this way, one is struck by a curious fact. The *Tableau* is obviously much concerned with viability, showing the generation of a surplus in one sector and exhibiting the flow of commodities. Yet, the whole thing runs in *money* terms: the figures stand for quantities of commodities *valued at current prices,* not for so many physical units of output. We wish to suggest that this feature of the analysis has caused many of the problems which, from its first appearance down to our own day has perplexed its students. Thus, Quesnay wrote to Mirabeau in an undated letter whose manuscript survives today:

Madame the Marquise de Pailli tells me that you are still bogged down in the zig zag. It is true that it relates to so many things that it is difficult to grasp the way they fit together, or rather to understand it self-evidently.[71]

It will be our contention that part of the reason why the marquis and subsequent readers were bogged down has to do with the fact that the zig-zag presents at one and the same time two aspects of a general equilibrium theory which nowadays are always separated.

An economy is viable if it can produce at least enough of all commodities used up in a period of production to replace the necessary inputs for the next

---

* For the significance of this characteristic of neoclassical models, see chapters 8 and 9, especially the latter where opportunity cost and relative factor scarcity are linked.

period. It is purely a matter of technology; of the capacity to reproduce commodities in a certain set of balanced amounts. This aspect of an economy can be studied quite apart from its price system, and is independent of the question of whether a price system even *exists*. As Cantillon brilliantly demonstrated, the economy may be centrally planned and achieve in principle exactly the same results as under a system of equilibrium prices. This particular insight of Cantillon's—of the logical separation between physical viability and the system of prices—was not embodied in the *Tableau Économique*. In this regard, we speak in modern terms of the "quantity relations" of a model as being concerned with viability, that is to say, with strictly physical questions; and of the "price relations," which focus on the characteristics of a pricing system that transforms surplus into profit. As two sets of equations (or inequalities) the quantity and price relations are intimately connected, but they are not identical.* Thus, it is through the fusion, in the *Tableau,* of two related, but distinct, aspects of an economic model that a number of confusions have arisen.

Matters may best be clarified by considering, in terms of the modern distinction between quantity and price relations in a model, what has been perhaps the most discussed issue throughout physiocratic scholarship: the insistence of Quesnay, Mirabeau, and their followers that a true original surplus—a net product, or revenue—arises only in agriculture.[72] To achieve this, we add to our little corn model, which is already familiar, an industrial or manufacturing sector, which we shall for brevity call the "iron" sector. The technology of production is now a little more complicated since we drop the assumption that nothing but corn is used in corn production. In particular, a unit of corn output requires an input of manufactured implements (say, plows) which we write a_{IC}, the input of iron per unit of corn, following our earlier notation. (For reasons of simplicity, we assume that iron implements wear out and must be renewed each year.) We likewise assume that, besides the amount of iron goods needed per unit of output in the industrial sector, denoted a_{II} (which, like a_{CC}, must be some fraction not greater than unity), there is also an input of corn in the industrial sector (to feed iron workers). Again, the corn required *per unit* of industrial output is written as a coefficient a_{CI}. As for outputs we have the symbol Y_C for corn production, and now introduce Y_I for industrial output.

Given arbitrary levels of production Y_C and Y_I, the total input of corn can be expressed as the sum of two products: $a_{CC} Y_C$, the corn needed to produce

---

*Quantity and price relations in models of general equilibrium are linked via the concept of duality. See chapters 11 and 12 for the classical theory.

Y_C units of corn, plus $a_{CI}Y_I$, the corn needed to produce Y_I units of iron. In the same manner, the total input of iron that is needed is the sum of $a_{IC}Y_C$, the iron needed in the corn sector, plus $a_{II}Y_I$, the iron needed in the iron sector. The two-sector economy is then viable if and only if:*

$$a_{CC}Y_C + a_{CI}Y_I \le Y_C \qquad (2)$$
$$a_{IC}Y_C + a_{II}Y_I \le Y_I \qquad (3)$$

Earlier in this chapter we set out formally the viability condition for the simplest possible economy: a one-sector corn economy. Here we are generalizing the viability condition to an economy with two sectors. Observe, however, that the two-sector model is essentially more complex that the one-sector model because *both* (2) and (3) must be satisfied before the economy is viable. Thus, a surplus in one sector, indicated by a strict inequality in either (2) or (3), combined with a deficit (where total input requirements *exceed* gross output) in the other sector would not be viable and, of course, a deficit in both sectors would also indicate nonviability.† We may therefore express the later classical idea of a surplus in every branch of production by supposing that Y_C and Y_I are such that, given the technical coefficients:

$$a_{CC}Y_C + a_{CI}Y_I < Y_C \qquad (2)'$$
$$a_{IC}Y_C + a_{II}Y_I < Y_I \qquad (3)'$$

We are now in a position to develop our point about quantity relations, physiocracy, and the claim that surplus arises only in agriculture. Consider how the physiocrats might have reacted to inequalities (2)′ and (3)′. They might have closed this model by specifying that the surplus in the corn sector is partly consumed directly by the proprietory class and partly consumed by that part of the sterile class engaged in producing luxury goods, e.g., carriages. In the iron sector, part of the gross output is for replacement of implements used up, measured by the sum on the left-hand side of inequality (3)′, while the remainder, which cannot be consumed directly, is entirely devoted to the production of luxuries.

Formally, we define that part of corn output directly consumed by the proprietory class as a proportion of Y_C, namely, $\lambda_C Y_C$, where λ_C is a fraction less

---

* Inequalities (2) and (3) will again be discussed in chapter 11, devoted entirely to the quantity relations of a modern classical model. At that point it will be helpful to reread this chapter in order to link the history of classical analysis with its more recent formulations.
† When we return to consider the viability of a two-sector corn and iron economy in chapter 11, it will be found that the *viability condition* can be stated, as in the one-sector corn economy, simply in terms of input–output coefficients.

than unity. This is subtracted from the right-hand side of (2)'. Then we add to the left-hand side of each inequality the required input from the agricultural and industrial sectors, respectively, into the production of luxuries. Let a_{CX} and a_{IX} be the corn and iron required per unit of output of carriages. Then $a_{CX} Y_X$ and $a_{IX} Y_X$ measure the allocations of corn and iron to the production of Y_X carriages, i.e., to the production of luxuries. Inequalities (2)' and (3)' become:

$$a_{CC} Y_C + a_{CI} Y_I + a_{CX} Y_X = (1 - \lambda_C) Y_C \qquad (2)''$$

$$a_{IC} Y_C + a_{II} Y_I + a_{IX} Y_X = Y_I \qquad (3)''$$

This pair of equations defines all possible values for λ_C and Y_X, where λ_C corresponds to direct consumption of surplus corn (corn as a luxury commodity fed to family and friends, retainers, harlots, priests, etc.) while Y_X implies indirect luxury consumption of corn and iron in the form of carriages.

Quesnay makes it quite explicit in his *Explanation* of the *Tableau Économique* that, out of the total revenue:

one half is spent by the proprietor in purchasing bread, wine, meat, etc., from the productive expenditure class, and the other half in purchasing clothing, furnishings, utensils, etc., from the sterile expenditure class.

This expenditure may go more or less to one side or the other, according as the man who engages in it goes in more or less for luxury in the way of subsistence or for luxury in the way of ornamentation. We assume here a medium situation. . . .[73]

Quesnay's "luxury in the way of subsistence" is what we are calling the direct luxury consumption of corn, our $\lambda_C Y_C$. His "luxury in the way of ornamentation" is what we are calling carriages. Our formalization is thus consistent with the fact that in the *Tableau* the *whole* surplus is shown as devoted to luxury consumption. Desired growth is assumed to have already taken place. The assumption that half of the luxury consumption is on products of the agricultural sector, and half on the products of the artisan sector is a standard one in Quesnay, and is to be found in his earliest as well as his later expositions of the *Tableau*. He only abandons it when he wants to show distortions.

It is of note that in the formal structure we have just outlined, there is an output of iron (for carriages) *over and above* what is needed to keep the economy viable, i.e., to replace its stocks. There is an obvious sense in which this is a physical surplus being generated in the iron sector. Once one sets out the formal relations of the model, it is inescapably there. In the actual model described in the *Tableau,* the sterile class unquestionably manufactures luxury goods in addition to supplying necessary implements to the productive class. If so, the technology must be as described above. It is difficult to make the technology implicit in the *Tableau* consistent with the oft-repeated physiocratic claim that only agriculture yields a surplus.*

The inequalities and equations that make up our little two-sector representation of certain aspects of the *Tableau* are defined wholly in terms of physical quantities: the iron needed to produce corn, etc. The concepts of viability and surplus are physical output concepts. Not a single price appears anywhere in these expressions, as is appropriate, since what we have written down are simply the *quantity* relations of a modern model. But, look again at the *Tableau* reproduced earlier in this chapter, bearing in mind Quesnay's explanation of it. Is it reasonable to conclude that what the *Tableau* was intended to give expression to was an analysis of viability and surplus? Yet, right at the top, what the proprietors receive is not the physical net product, a quantity of corn, but the *revenue:* its monetary value at current prices. Stress thus shifts from the question: "What must a sector physically produce for the economy to be viable?" to the question: "What revenue can be extracted from a sector by a proprietory class?" The question of physical surplus therefore becomes confused with the problem of determining "revenue" as money rent and profit extracted, a problem which, as we shall see in chapter 12, pertains to the price relations of the model.

We are assured by modern French scholarship on the economic and social history of the *ancien régime* that French industry was overwhelmingly in the hands of artisans even well *after* the physiocrats had written, and on the eve of the Revolution. So we need not be surprised that when thinking of money revenue they did not show rent or profit being extracted from the sterile class. Treating surplus simply as revenue received by the land-owning class gave the *Tableau* a superficial simplicity that glossed over deep problems. Progressively, later physiocratic writings show these suppressed issues emerging in a number of different guises until, at the hands of Turgot, the way is opened up for the next great stage of classical theory. This came with the explicit recognition, in the work of Adam Smith, that surplus is generated throughout industry, and with the final development, in his mature writings, of the concept of a uniform rate of profit on stock.

Meanwhile, as physiocracy declined, problems inherent in its treatment of profit became more and more acute. We have seen that the physiocrats denied that profit, in the sense of a true original revenue, was extracted in industry;

---

* This is not to be confused with the perfectly valid claim that only in the case of land was the money value of the surplus extracted by one class from another, i.e., by the landlords, as rent.

and that they often made the further claim that industrial production, unlike agriculture, produced no physical net product. The former claim is understandable, given the artisan character of French industry during their period; the latter claim we have had to regard as a mistake.

Even if the capitalist entrepreneur was not yet a figure characteristic of French industry, he *was* becoming characteristic of at least some French agriculture. And the physiocrats had done all they could to promote the trend to adopt capitalist farming on the English model. So the question as to what role to give the capitalist, and his profit, arose *within* agriculture, where the physiocrats themselves held that a disposable surplus was being extracted. Quesnay is at pains to insist that the final state of reformed French agriculture, whose great possibilities are illustrated by the kind of figures he habitually chose for the *Tableau Économique,* depends on the assumption "that the land employed in the cultivation of corn is brought together, as far as possible, into large farms worked by rich husbandmen." [74] In the original, the phrase is "riches Laboureurs," and it is instructive to hear Georges Lefebvre on what class of men this phrase would stand for. Commenting on the structure of rural society, he writes:

The most well to do were the large farmers, who often owned no land themselves. Next came the substantial class, called *laboureurs,* who worked considerable tracts which they owned wholly or in part. They were followed, in downward order, by the small farmer, the sharecropper, the peasant having the use of some land. . . .[75]

That such men were not retaining part of the surplus as capitalist profit would be utterly implausible to anyone not committed to physiocratic dogma, especially to someone acquainted with Britain's already long history of capitalism in farming, as the physiocrats themselves were, and as Adam Smith was later to be. Yet Quesnay explicitly denies that the farmer keeps any of the surplus. The class of landlords "subsists on the revenue or *net product* of cultivation, which is paid to it annually by the productive class, after the latter has first deducted, out of the reproduction which it causes to be annually regenerated, the wealth necessary for the reimbursement of its annual advances and for the maintenance of the wealth it employs in cultivation." [76]

In their mature work, the physiocrats habitually insist that the farmers have no "disposable" revenue, or net product. Quesnay did not take this view quite from the beginning of his writings, however. An important early deviation from the mature physiocratic view has been pointed out by Ronald Meek. In *Corn,* Quesnay follows Richard Cantillon in attributing a share of the net product as profit to the farmer.[77] Meek regards this early view of Quesnay, differing as it does from nearly all his later statements,[78] as strong evidence of Cantillon's influence on the foundations of physiocracy.

Why did the physiocrats want to deny that farmers (however large!) got any share of the surplus? Cantillon, who saw the generation of surplus only in agriculture, nevertheless divided the net product between farmers and landlords.* A possible explanation (it is no more) is that the physiocrats were eager to have the taxing of agricultural entrepreneurs stopped, so that the latter would have ample funds to invest in maintaining and improving their lands. But, of course, any net investment in developing land is the use of surplus for capital accumulation.[79] It is hard to resist the idea that the physiocrats, in their desire to promote the accumulation of surplus, were discreetly turning a blind eye to the fact that some of the surplus was absorbed by the agricultural capitalists, instead of all of it going to the landlords.

Finally, in the last days of physiocracy, Turgot introduced the notion of capitalist production into all branches of industry, thus taking a vital step toward Adam Smith. Much ink has been spilled on the question of whether Turgot was a physiocrat. He himself denied that he was. He was certainly a member of a French society imbued with physiocracy; and he mixed with, and learned from, the great figures of physiocracy. This, however, did not prevent him from introducing into the model presented in his *Reflections,* an analysis of social class which distinguished between capitalist and worker both in agriculture and in *industry.* As we shall see, he is an enigmatic figure in the emergence of mature classical political economy, linking the work of Cantillon to that of his contemporary, Adam Smith, whom he knew personally and by whose early ideas he could easily have been influenced.

Turgot and Capitalism throughout Industry—
The Link with Smith

Anne Robert Jacques Turgot, Baron de l'Aulne (1727–1781) was a dazzling figure, even against the shimmering backdrop of the Versailles and Paris of Louis XV. In some ways he was a man of the feudal past. Of an old Norman family, he was, as third son, destined for the church and cut quite a figure as an abbé at the Sorbonne. But then he abandoned the life of religion for that of administration, and, as Schumpeter puts it, "nobody would think of writing a volume on Great Ministers of Finance without including Turgot."[80]

Despite his duties, Turgot planned, and to a large extent carried out, nu-

* See above, p. 20.

merous works on amazingly diverse subjects. In these writings his originality, and the sense in which he belonged to the future, show vividly. For example, in his work on universal history, stages in the mode of production are distinguished, and it is suggested that the arts and sciences arise out of men's economic and psychological needs, and change as these change.[81] "Turgot's intellectual development was very similar to that of Smith and Marx: all three thinkers began by working out the elements of a universal 'sociological' system, embodying a theory of history which laid emphasis on economic causes, and then developed *from* these 'sociological' systems the great systems of economic theory by which we mainly know them today."[82] Turgot's way of looking at history echoes the work of the Scottish Historical School, an outstanding member of which was, of course, Adam Smith.[83]

In his brilliant *Reflections on the Formation and the Distribution of Wealth,*[84] Turgot introduced a model with capitalist production in all branches of industry. The book contains certain polite bows toward physiocratic doctrines, but its basic structure is an economy with capitalist organization of production not simply in agriculture, but in all sectors of industry. To see the striking implications of this, one must realize that Adam Smith, who was soon to carry the analysis of industrial capitalism even further, grew up in one of the most advanced centers in the most advanced industrial country in the world, while Turgot was living in the France of the physiocrats. We know that Turgot was close to Smith while the latter lived and moved in Parisian intellectual society, between Christmas of 1765 and October of 1766. It has been customary to speak of the influence of Turgot on Smith, but we shall offer reasons in the next chapter for the view that the major influence may have been the other way. Turgot did not begin to publish his *Reflections* until the end of 1769, long after Smith had left France, and, as we shall see shortly, Smith had shown plenty of evidence, in work written before he met Turgot, of understanding the concept of capitalist production throughout industry.

Whatever these two men may have learned from each other, however, no one can deny the dazzling intellectual quality of the *Reflections,* or its originality in the France of 1770. Ronald Meek wrote that the system in the *Reflections* "is basically 'capitalist' and that the particular form of 'capitalism' which it envisages and analyses is by no means a primitive one. This can be brought home if one contrasts Turgot's system with Cantillon's, which was certainly the most advanced prior to Turgot's and from which Turgot may well have learned a great deal."[85]

The physiocrats, for all their rich development of the theory of surplus in agriculture, had been inhibited by their belief in the sole productivity of agriculture from learning from and developing those aspects of Cantillon's *Essay* which would prove inconsistent with their fundamental viewpoint. Thus, a case can be made for the claim that Cantillon came nearer than the physiocrats to recognizing the existence and significance of industrial profits.[86] There are many instances of this phenomenon in intellectual history. A seminal mind produces a rich work; certain of its leading ideas are seized upon and developed, while other important concepts present in the texture of the original work are ignored, misunderstood, or eliminated as inconsistent. Later, these ignored aspects of the original work are rediscovered by thinkers to whose theoretical viewpoint they are congenial.

Of course, the physiocrats never denied that artisans, tradesmen, manufacturers, and such like could make a *living,* or that this living could include a return for wages of management and also, presumably, to cover risks. And, given the riskiness of enterprise, the few really lucky entrepreneurs might even get rich while their rivals were ruined. Monopoly privileges made a killing of this sort all the easier. If one chooses to call these incomes, "profits," then even the purest physiocrat could afford to recognize the existence of "profits." The point at issue, however, is that for Adam Smith and the mature English classical political economy, "profits" originated from a true original *surplus* yielded by capitalist manufacturing industry precisely as a surplus was yielded by capitalist farming industry. The classics were concerned with the *ultimate* source of surplus output and therefore of capital accumulation and economic growth—not with its redistribution as a result of trade.

Now, as we know, the physiocrats always denied that industrial profits represented any genuine *creation* of surplus. Profits, rather, were seen as a *redistribution,* and this view indeed appears to have originated in Cantillon's *Essay.* But there are some passages in the *Essay* where Cantillon seems to regard the entrepreneur's profit as representing a true surplus. He makes a sharp distinction between "entrepreneurs" and "hired people." The entrepreneurs are those who work for uncertain returns, as distinct from a wage. However, as Samuel Hollander notes, "the 'net' return to the master manufacturer or farmer to which Cantillon refers is not *formally* related to their functions as capitalist employers; for all recipients of uncertain incomes were profit earning entrepreneurs. . . ."[87] And, indeed, Cantillon had included under his category of "entrepreneurs" what he called "undertakers of their own Labour who need no Capital to establish themselves, like Journeymen artisans,

Copper-Smiths, Needle-Women, Chimney Sweeps, Water-Carriers. . . ."[88]
This is a far cry from the mature classical theory of capitalist profits.

There are, however, certain passages where Cantillon appears to come
nearer to the concept of net profit as the reflection of surplus:

Again a Master Hatter who has capital to carry on his manufacture of Hats, either to
rent a house, buy beaver, wool, dye, etc., or to pay for the subsistence of his workmen
every week, ought not only to find his upkeep in this enterprise, but *also* a profit *like
that of the Farmer* who has a third part for himself. This upkeep and the profit should
come from the sale of the Hats whose price ought to cover not only the materials but
also the upkeep of the Hatter and his Workmen *and also the profit in question.*[89]

The key phrase is "like that of the Farmer." The farmer in Cantillon's view
shared *part of the original surplus* produced by agriculture. Did Cantillon
sense that the capitalist manufacturer also enjoyed a surplus? On the other
hand, as Hollander observes, for Cantillon, "profits and wages were said to
have a common source in, or to be dependent upon, the property of landowners."[90] And, indeed, Cantillon never tires of insisting on this. In a typical
passage he tells us that, "As all these Artisans and Undertakers serve each
other as well as the Nobility it is overlooked that the upkeep of them all falls
ultimately on the Nobles and Landowners."[91]

Now, to set Turgot, who said he was not a physiocrat, in his proper context, one must see how he had improved, not on Quesnay, but on Cantillon;
and, on the other hand, how he fell short of Adam Smith. Unlike Cantillon,
Turgot makes a clear distinction between the *different social classes* entailed
by the emergence of capitalist industry, telling us that "the Class of Cultivators, like that of Manufacturers, is divided into two orders of men, that of the
Entrepreneurs or Capitalists who make all the advances, and that of the ordinary Workmen on wages."[92] Clearly, he took a major step toward that analysis of industrial capital which was to characterize classical political economy
from Smith onward. What is then of the greatest interest is to compare
Turgot's analysis of capitalist production with that of Adam Smith.

The great virtue of the early classics was that they understood and insisted
on the paramount importance of an agricultural surplus. The mercantilists had
seen England's treasre in foreign *trade;* the early classics saw that it lay in a
transformed capitalist agriculture. Without an agricultural surplus, no economic development is possible. Their limitiation, on the other hand, arose
precisely out of their virtue: they saw surplus *only* in agriculture. Turgot (and
perhaps Cantillon) had given hints of profit in industry, but the clear under-

standing of industrial capitalism, and thus the coming of age of classical theory, had to await Adam Smith.

Notes

1. The Marquis of Landsdowne, *The Petty Southwell Correspondence, 1676–1687 Edited from the Bowood Papers,* Augustus M. Kelly, New York, New York, 1967, p. xii.
2. Samuel Hollander, *The Economics of Adam Smith,* University of Toronto Press, 1973, pp. 38–9.
3. Karl Marx, *Theorien über den Mehrwert,* Teil 1, Dietz Verlag, Berlin, 1956; trans. *Theories of Surplus Value,* Progress Publishers, Moscow, 1963, Part I, p. 383.
4. Marx, *Das Kapital,* Vol. 1, Otto Meissner, Hamburg, 1867; trans. *Capital,* Vol. I, Progress Publishers, Moscow, n.d., p. 85, note.
5. Ronald L. Meek, *The Economics of Physiocracy,* Harvard University Press, Cambridge, Mass., 1963, p. 347. Meek's italics.
6. Sir John Hicks, *A Theory of Economic History,* Oxford University Press, 1969, pp. 23–4.
7. *Ibid.,* pp. 101–21.
8. E. J. Hobsbaum and George Rudé, *Captain Swing,* Lawrence and Wishart, London, 1970, p. 27.
9. Joseph A. Schumpeter, *History of Economic Analysis,* Oxford University Press, New York, 1954, p. 210.
10. See Lady Antonia Fraser, *Cromwell Our Chief of Men,* Weidenfeld and Nicolson, London, 1973, Panther Books, London, 1975 especially chapter 13, "Ireland, Effusion of Blood," pp. 326–57.
11. Oliver Cromwell, Letter to Parliament after the storming of Droheda; cited in Fraser, *Cromwell,* pp. 326, 338.
12. E. Strauss, *Sir William Petty, Portrait of a Genius,* Bodley Head, London, 1954, p. 55. In this section we have made extensive use of the Strauss biography.
13. Sir William Petty, *A Treatise of Taxes and Contributions,* printed for N. Brooke, at the Angel in Cornhill, London, 1662. All our citations will be from C. H. Hull, ed., *The Economic Writings of Sir William Petty,* A. M. Kelly, New York, 1963. The present citation is from *Economic Writings,* Vol. 1, p. 43. Petty's italics.
14. Petty, *Economic Writings,* pp. 50–1. Petty's italics.
15. Meek, *Studies in the Labour Theory of Value,* 2nd ed., Lawrence and Wishart, London, 1973, p. 36.
16. Marx, *Theories of Surplus Value,* part I, p. 357.
17. Henry Higgs, ed., *Essai sur la Nature du Commerce en Général,* by Richard Cantillion, edited with an English Translation and other material, A. M. Kelly, New York, 1931, p. 379.
18. *Ibid.,* p. 380.
19. *Essai sur la Nature du Commerce en Général,* Traduit de L'Anglois à Londres,

Chey Fletcher Gyles dans Holborn, 1755. All our citations come from the Higgs translation, citing either Higgs or Cantillon where appropriate.

20. Higgs, *Essai,* p. 382.
21. *Ibid.*
22. *Ibid.*
23. Schumpeter, *History of Economic Analysis,* p. 218.
24. Cantillon, *Essai,* p. 15.
25. *Ibid.,* p. 6.
26. *Ibid.,* pp. 15–7.
27. *Ibid.,* p. 42.
28. *Ibid.,* pp. 37–9.
29. *Ibid.,* pp. 43–5.
30. *Ibid.,* p. 41.
31. *Ibid.,* p. 45.
32. *Ibid.,* p. 59.
33. *Ibid.*
34. *Ibid.,* p. 59.
35. *Ibid.*
36. *Ibid.*
37. *Ibid.*
38. *Ibid.,* pp. 59–61.
39. *Ibid.* p. 63.
40. We do not intend to deny the existence of an important trade with the French colonies. On the state of manufacturing, Lefebvre, writing about the eve of the French Revolution—a period some thirty years later than the founding of physiocracy—remarks that, "Industry remained socially and economically subordinate." Georges Lefebvre, *Quatre-Vingt-neuf,* Institute for the History of the French Revolution, University of Paris, 1939; trans. R. R. Palmer, *The Coming of the French Revolution,* Princeton University Press, 1947; paperback edition, 1967, p. 43.
41. Jacqueline Hecht, "La Vie de François Quesnay," in *François Quesnay et la Physiocratie,* Institut National d'Études Démographiques, Paris, 1958, Vol. I, p. 256; hereafter cited as *I.N.E.D.*
42. The term "physiocracy" appears to have been used for the first time by the Abbé Baudeau, a follower of Quesnay, who gave it the following definition: "L'ordre Naturel et social, fondé sur la nécessité physique et sur la force irrésistible de l'évidence," *Éphémérides,* April, 1757. Cited in *I.N.E.D,* Vol, I, p. 2. The term did not become popular, however, until Du Pont de Nemours published a collection of Quesnay's writings under the name *Physiocratie,* probably in 1767. On the disputed date of *Physiocratie,* see Luigi Einuadi, *I.N.E.D,* Vol. I, pp. 1–9.
43. Meek, *Physiocracy,* p. 34.
44. Schumpeter, *History of Economic Analysis,* p. 223.
45. Hecht, "La Vie de François Quesnay," p. 212.
46. François Quesnay, "Fermiers," *Encyclopédie,* ed. D. Diderot, Vol. VI, 1756; *I.N.E.D.,* Vol. II, p. 427.
47. Quesnay, "Grains," *Encyclopédie,* Vol. VII, 1757; *I.N.E.D.,* Vol. II, p. 459.

48. In "Grains," Quesnay writes, "Les terres ne doivent pas nourir seulement ceux qui les cultivent, elle doivent fournir à l'État la plus grande partie des subsides, produire des dimes au clergé, des revenus aus propriétaires, des profits aux fermiers, des gains à ceux qu'il emploient à la culture. . . . Un auteur [Cantillon, Essai sur le commerce, chap. V, VI.] a reconnu ces verités fondamentales. . . ." *I.N.E.D.*, Vol. II, p. 482. The reference in brackets is Quesnay's footnote.

49. Meek, *Physiocracy,* p. 266. Given the importance of Cantillon in the development of the concept of surplus, the provoking thing is how *little* Marx refers to Cantillon's work. In the three volumes of *Capital,* plus the three parts of *Theories of Surplus Value,* there are a total of four references, mostly trivial footnote references.

50. Lefebvre, *The Coming of the French Revolution,* p. 99.

51. George Rudé, "14 July 1789. The Fall of the Bastille," *History Today,* Vol. IV, No. 7; reprinted in *Paris and London in the 18th Century,* Fontana/Collins, London, 1974, p. 84.

52. Marx, *Theories of Surplus Value,* Part I, p. 44. Marx's italics.

53. *Ibid.,* p. 45.

54. *Ibid.,* p. 49.

55. *Ibid.,* p. 46.

56. The first "edition" of Quesnay's *Tableau Économique* is given in I.N.E.D. as 1758. There has been some doubt since all three "editions" were simply printed on a press in the palace of Versailles, and privately circulated. For the definitive text of all three "editions," see Marguerite Kuczynski and Ronald L. Meek, eds., *Quesnay's Tableau Économique,* A. M. Kelly, New York, 1972.

57. *Quesnay's Tableau Économique,* pp. 20–1.

58. *Ibid.,* p. ij.

59. Victor de Riquetti, Marquis de Mirabeau, *Philosophie Rurale, ou Économie Générale et Politique de l'Agriculture,* Paris, November 1763, Amsterdam, 1764, Les Libraries Associés; reprinted by photocopy, Scientia Verlag, Aalen, Germany, 1972, chapter VII, pp. 330–420.

60. Quesnay, "Problème Économique," *Journal de l'Agriculture, du Commerce et des Finances,* August 1766; enlarged and corrected edition published in *Physiocratie,* ed. Du Pont de Nemours, Merlin, Paris, 1767–8; reproduced in *I.N.E.D.,* Vol. II, pp. 859–77; trans. Meek, *Physiocracy,* pp. 168–85.

61. Quesnay, "Problème Économique," *Physiocratie;* reproduced in *I.N.E.D.,* Vol. II, pp. 977–92; trans. Meek, *Physiocracy,* pp. 186–202.

62. See note 56.

63. Quesnay to Mirabeau, no date, first published by Stephen Bauer in *Economic Journal.* Vol. V, March 1895, pp. 20–1; trans. Meek, *Physiocracy,* p. 117.

64. Quesnay, "Analyse du Tableau Économique," *Journal de l'Agriculture, du Commerce et des Finances,* June 1766; published in an enlarged version in *Physiocratie;* reproduced in Auguste Oncken, ed., *François Quesnay, Oeuvres,* Frankfurt, 1888; reprinted by Scientia Verlag, Aalen, Germany, 1965, pp. 304–28; also in *I.N.E.D.,* Vol. II, pp. 793–812; partially trans. Meek, *Physiocracy,* pp. 150–67.

65. *I.N.E.D.*, Vol. II, p. 801; Meek, *Physiocracy,* p. 158, also pp. 281–2.
66. *I.N.E.D.*, Vol. II, pp. 799–800; Meek, *Physiocracy,* p. 156.
67. This characteristic is by no means confined to later versions of the *Tableau*. See, for example, *Quesnay's Tableau Économique* for the first three "editions" of the *Tableau*.
68. *Ibid.*, p. iij. Quesnay clearly states, with regard to the *Tableau* of the third "edition," that the sterile class needs a sum for wages equal to the sum represented by its annual advances.
69. *Ibid., passim.* This is characteristic of the various versions of the *Tableau*.
70. See, for instance, A. Phillips, "The Tableau Économique as a Simple Leontief Model,"*Quarterly Journal of Economics,* Vol. LXIX, February 1955, pp. 137–44.
71. Meek, *Physiocracy,* p. 115.
72. See the exhaustive treatment in Meek, *Physiocracy,* pp. 265–96.
73. *Quesnay's Tableau Économique,* p. i.
74. *Ibid.,* p. 15.
75. Lefebvre, *The Coming of the French Revolution,* p. 133. Lefebvre's italics.
76. Quesnay, "Analyse du Tableau," in Meek, *Physiocracy,* p. 150. Quesnay's italics.
77. Meek, *Physiocracy,* p. 268. See note 48, where we reference Quesnay following Cantillon in allowing the farmer some of the surplus.
78. *Ibid.,* pp. 298–301, for a discussion of the few minor exceptions.
79. On these questions, see the interesting discussion in Meek, *Physiocracy,* pp. 297–312; also Meek, *Turgot on Progress, Sociology, and Economics,* Cambridge University Press, 1975, pp. 24–6.
80. Schumpeter, *History of Economic Analysis,* p. 246.
81. Meek, *Turgot,* pp. 12, 27, 91–3, 102–4, 116–7.
82. *Ibid.,* p. 27.
83. *Ibid.,* pp. 10–11, and references cited there. See further, Meek, *Studies in the Labour Theory of Value,* p. 52, and the reference cited there.
84. Turgot's *Réflections sur la Formation et la Distribution des Richesses* first appeared in three issues of *Éphémérides* for 1769, nos. 11 and 12, and 1770, no. 1, ed. Du Pont de Nemours. Our citations are from Meek's translation (basically of the later edition of 1788) in Meek, *Turgot.* On the problems at issue, see pp. 36–40.
85. Meek, *Turgot,* p. 30.
86. See, for example, Hollander, *Economics of Smith,* p. 40.
87. *Ibid.* Hollander's italics.
88. Cantillon, *Essai,* p. 53.
89. *Ibid.,* p. 203. Our italics.
90. Hollander, *Economics of Smith,* p. 40. n. 48.
91. Cantillon, *Essai,* p. 15.
92. Turgot, *Réflections;* trans. Meek, *Turgot,* p. 155.

3

Adam Smith: The Beginning of Mature Classicism

> I shall always remain with the impression of having lost a friend whom I loved and respected, not only for his great talents, but for every private virtue.
>
> THE DUKE OF BUCCLEUCH TO DUGALD STEWART [1]

> The writer, in combating received opinions, has found it necessary to advert more particularly to those passages in the writings of Adam Smith from which he sees reason to differ; but he hopes it will not, on that account, be suspected that he does not, in common with all those who acknowledge the importance of the science of Political Economy, participate in the admiration which the profound work of this celebrated author so justly excites.
>
> DAVID RICARDO [2]

> The main credit for putting economic development on the map as a subject for general analysis belongs undoubtedly to Adam Smith.
>
> LORD ROBBINS OF CLAREMARKET [3]

The early classical economists from Petty to Turgot clarified the concepts of viability, surplus, and the distinction between luxury consumption and the accumulation of capital. But, in effect, they did so only for the case of capitalist agriculture. Adam Smith (1723–1790) changed all this. In his early works he made quite clear the concept of surplus arising *throughout* industry, capitalist agriculture being only one special case of a capitalist industrial undertaking. Then, in his great mature work, the *Wealth of Nations,* he set out in detail what would nowadays be called the fundamental duality of surplus (in the quantity relations) and profit (in the price relations) obtained at a uniform rate throughout industry. The structure of classical theory had now been laid bare—mature classicism had begun.

Adam Smith and the Scottish Enlightenment

The scene to which we now turn seems at first sight utterly different from the France of Quesnay and Mirabeau. Yet appearances prove deceptive, for Scottish society in the late eighteenth century was in an intellectual ferment, and her universities (unlike the Oxford and Cambridge of the period) were coming to brilliant life. The Scottish Enlightenment does not sparkle with diamonds and champagne, but it does with wit and ideas. It was run on oatmeal porridge and high aspirations.

Adam Smith was, on his father's side, "descended from a family of Aberdeenshire lairds at one time identified with Rothiebirsben and later with Inveramsay." [4] His mother was a Douglas of Strathenry, a great-great-granddaughter of Sir William Douglas of Lochleven, later Earl of Morton, the sinister laird who held Mary Queen of Scots prisoner in his castle on an island in Loch Leven.[5] But there were gallant Douglasses too: the laird's brother, dashing young George ("pretty Geordie") Douglas, and a little orphan cousin, young Willie Douglas ("the little Douglas") together engineered the Queen's escape, and served her faithfully until her death.[6] For all Adam Smith's vision of the historically liberating forces of industry under his new system of natural liberty, one can hear a hint of the tones and assumptions of an eighteenth century country gentleman throughout his many comments on the qualities of capitalists.

It has recently been remarked that "Adam Smith for the most part was a perfunctory, dilatory correspondent." [7] It is not simply that Smith was averse to writing letters, although this was notoriously the case. The matter goes deeper than that. Smith's whole social and intellectual circle was one in which self-revelation was neither indulged in nor thought to be good form. In the case of two great founders of neoclassical theory, Jevons and Walras, we shall later have reason to be grateful for the intimate revelations about the development of their thought to be derived from private journals and letters. They breathed the heavily scented air of the later years of the Romantic Rebellion, and it shows in their writings.

Such exotic flowers did not flourish in the cool crisp northern climate of the Scottish Englightenment. Those sober Augustans admired the eighteenth century English poets, and Smith appears to have agreed with the view that Shakespeare had written good scenes but no good play, and to have "thought Racine's Phaedrus [sic] the finest tragedy extant in any language in the world." [8] Not a view which would cut Smith off, it may be noted, from the French Enlightenment which he was later to know intimately. In any case, as Jacob Viner remarked of Smith:

In the circle in which he lived, a high value was set both on the privacy of one's own affairs and on the protection of the privacy of those with whom one had had intimate personal relations. It was then quite common, therefore, for men in their old age to carry out, or to leave instructions for carrying out after their death, a massive destruction of their private papers. Adam Smith did this. . . .[9]

Nevertheless, certain biographical questions simply cannot be avoided if one is to give the barest sketch of Smith's role in the development of mature classical political economy. One of the most celebrated of these questions concerns his relations with the French economists, and therefore makes it important to know how early in his work he was acquainted with French economic writings, and, on the other hand, how early he developed certain characteristic ideas.

Adam Smith as Student

The question as to how much Adam Smith owed the French economists of his period has long been in dispute among historians of economic analysis. Indeed the issue had already been raised by Smith's close friend and first biographer, Dugald Stewart, only five years after Smith died. After spending the years from 1737 to 1740 as a student at the University of Glasgow, Smith had been sent as an exhibitioner to Balliol College, Oxford. Of the seven years he spent there, Dugald Stewart wrote, "I have heard him say, that he employed himself frequently in the practise of translation, (particularly from the French), with a view to the improvement of his own style. . . ."[10] So we know that Smith was reading French literature more than fifteen years before Quesnay began to publish on economic subjects. Dugald Stewart goes on to remark:

It was probably also at this period of his life, that he cultivated with the greatest care the study of languages. The knowledge he possessed of these, both ancient and modern, was uncommonly extensive and accurate. . . . How intimately he had once been conversant with the more ornamental branches of learning; in particular, with the works of the Roman, Greek, French, and Italian poets, appeared sufficiently from the hold which they kept on his memory. . . .[11]

The modern reader can see the justice of Stewart's opinion if he samples the elegant prose of Smith's posthumously published essays on the "History of the Ancient Logic and Metaphysics," on the "Imitative Arts," on "Music, Dancing and Poetry," and on "English and Italian Verses."[12] It should be recalled that an intensely scholarly youth like Smith, coming from Glasgow when the University there was in the ferment of the Scottish Enlightenment, would, in the decadent Oxford of the eighteenth century, be thrown back largely on his inner intellectual resources. The Scottish Enlightenment, it must again be remembered, had influenced, and been influenced by, the French. The Scottish philosopher, historian, economist, and *belle lettrist,* David Hume, for example, was revered in French intellectual society. And Hume was to become a lifelong friend and admirer of Smith. It has been recognized that Smith shared with other members of the Scottish Historical School a certain conception of the importance of economic forces in history which has striking similarities to that of Turgot.*

After coming down from Oxford in 1746, Smith spent two years of quiet study at his birthplace, Kirkaldy, with his mother, to whom he remained devoted throughout his life. In 1748 he moved to Edinburgh, and in these years entered a crucial phase of his development. From this period date the first of his speculations on economic theory of which we have any report.

The Edinburgh Lectures

It has been remarked that a certain mystery surrounds both the circumstances and the subject matter of the lectures which Adam Smith gave at Edinburgh during the three years, 1748 to 1751.[13] Public lectures, not sponsored by or given at the university, were fashionable in Edinburgh just then. And Smith could offer lectures on a newly modish topic: English Literature. It has been suggested that there were probably two courses on Literature and Literary Criticism, and then a final course on Jurisprudence.[14] Fragments of the lectures on jurisprudence, discovered in the present century, suggest that here "Adam Smith had already laid the foundation of a great part of his economic work."[15]

Dugald Stewart published in 1795 an extract from a paper drawn up by Smith in 1755 (now lost) in which Smith describes his early economic views:

Man is generally considered by statesmen and projectors as the materials of a sort of political mechanics. Projectors disturb nature in the course of her operations in human affairs; and it requires no more than to let her alone, and give her fair play in the pursuit of her ends, that she may establish her own designs.[16]

And, in another passage:

Little else is requisite to carry a state to the highest degree of opulence from the lowest barbarism, but peace, easy taxes, and a tolerable administration of justice; all the rest being brought about by the natural course of things. . . .[17]

---

*For a summary of the case for and against French influence on Smith before he went to France, see the section below, "Smith in France."

The significance of these passages, and of other less direct evidence concerning Smith's early work, is brought out in a hypothesis which was advanced by William Robert Scott:

One conclusion that can be stated with a fair degree of certainty is that Book III of the *Wealth of Nations* entitled "The different progress of Opulence in different nations" is traceable back through the early draft . . . ,* and the *Glasgow Lectures* to this final course at Edinburgh. It . . . is confirmed by the quotation Adam Smith himself gave in 1755, which in effect contrasts the slow progress of opulence with what would happen if the natural course of things were allowed free play.[18]

We shall take the position in this book that the fundamental concern of Smith's economic thought is with the allocation of surplus output so as to attain the greatest possible growth of the economy. It seems plain to us that early in his economic writings Smith shows a clear understanding of the notions of viability and surplus, and of the bearing on growth of the allocation of surplus as between luxury consumption and accumulation; and that his concern with natural liberty derives from his observation of the way in which feudal survivals and mercantilist restrictions diverted capital stock from the uses in which it would lead to maximal growth. If, as Scott suggested, "The different progress of Opulence in different nations" is one of the oldest parts of Smith's corpus of work on economics, we believe it also to be one of the most central. A consideration of the development of this core into a whole system and the influences to which it was or was not subject, and a glance at the leading analytical features of the developed system, will show us Smith's place as the founder of mature classical political economy.

The Two Reports of Smith's Lectures on Jurisprudence

In 1751 Smith was elected professor of logic in the University of Glasgow, and then, in 1752, he became professor of moral philosophy and remained so with the greatest distinction—on the testimony of his contemporaries—for thirteen years. During these years the acquaintance between Smith and the Scottish philosopher, David Hume, had grown into friendship, as is amply testified by about fifteen friendly letters from Hume. Smith's replies are (predictably) few and far between, but no less warm in tone: "Tho you have resisted all my Sollicitations, I hope you will not resist this. I hope, I need not tell you that it will give me the greatest pleasure to see you."[19]

Meanwhile, Smith had published his brilliant essay on the foundations of

* An "Early Draft" of the Wealth of Nations was discovered by W. R. Scott. See below, pp. 57–58.

moral judgment, *The Theory of Moral Sentiments* (1759),[20] to Hume's enthusiastic admiration. So Smith now had a direct link with the French Enlightenment: he was author of a book admired by French intellectual society, and the close friend of its darling, David Hume.

Then, during the academic years of 1762–63 and (probably) 1763–64, Smith gave at Glasgow the lectures on Jurisprudence of which two reports, one for each (academic) year, have come down to us. As is well known, the first of these, written by a student, was discovered by Edwin Cannan and published in 1896 under the title *Lectures on Justice, Police, Revenue and Arms*.[21] This report was dated 1766, but is thought to be of lectures given during 1763–64. We shall follow the notation of the Glasgow Edition's editors and refer to it for brevity as LJ(B). The earlier report, that for the session 1762–63, which is referred to in the Glasgow Edition as LJ(A), was discovered by the late John M. Lothian in 1958, and is published for the first time in The Glasgow Edition of the Works and Correspondence of Adam Smith.

Ever since a report, LJ(B), of Smith's lectures at Glasgow upon Jurisprudence first became available in Cannan's edition, the tendency of critical opinion has been to stress the gap between these lectures and Smith's mature work in the *Wealth of Nations* (1776).[22] This was already to be seen in the position taken by Cannan in the introduction to his edition of the *Lectures* published in 1896. Of course, Cannan was quick to point out that the discovery of the lectures disposed of the crude myth, which had surfaced here and there throughout the nineteenth century, to the effect that Smith had borrowed everything that seemed original in the *Wealth of Nations* from the French economists. And the *Lectures* indeed contain many of the doctrines traditionally thought of as Smithian: the analysis of the advantages of the division of labor, the advocacy of the removal of mercantilist restrictions, the establishment of a regime of economic liberty, the attack on monopolies, the theory of natural and market prices, and so on. Cannan (and subsequent scholars), however, have been more concerned with those respects in which the *Lectures* fall short of Smith's later work. Writing of the development of Smith's thought on economics, Cannan remarked that the manuscript of the *Lectures* "enables us to follow the gradual construction of the work almost from its very foundation, and to distinguish positively between what the original genius of its author created out of British materials on the one hand and French materials on the other."[23]

Cannan found the main ideas of the mature work, which are missing in the lectures, to be the scheme of distribution of the total product of a year's industry into wages, profits, and rent; and the theory of capital:

There is no trace whatever in the lectures of the scheme of distribution which the *Wealth of Nations* sets forth. The main body of Book II, "Of the Nature, Accumulation and Employment of Stock," is also entirely unaccounted for. There is nothing at all about capital in the lectures, and stock is not given an important place.[24]

Yet, despite Cannan's view, there are a number of places in the version of the lectures which he had before him, where Smith shows a clear awareness of the role of the accumulation of capital stock in the emergence of capitalist production. He is well aware of the consequences of administrative measures which prevent prices from reaching their natural (long run) level:

If the price of one commodity is sunk below its natural price, while another is above it, there is a smaller quantity of the stored stock left to support the whole. On account of the natural connection of all trades in the stock, by allowing bounties to one you take away the stock from the rest. This has been the real consequence of the corn bounty.[25]

Smith's whole argument implies an understanding of the way in which a government policy (such as a bounty on the export of corn) diverts capital stock from what would otherwise be the most productive uses, thus making the growth of the economy less than what it could have been. Similarly, Smith believed that the necessity to tie up a proportion of the country's stock in precious metals so as to have money for circulation forces one to have so much dead stock so that "the poverty of any country increases as the money increases, money being a dead stock in itself, supplying no convenience of life. . . ."[26]

Viability is tersely stated: "an industrious people will always produce more than they consume."[27] And he argues quite clearly that luxury at home can destroy a country's accumulation of capital—to the contrary of mercantilist prejudices.[28] Similarly, luxury consumption by the country's rentier creditors (payments on the national debt to idle people) means that "industry is taxed to support idleness,"[29] and the accumulation of capital impeded. Likewise, his discussion of lending at interest is much concerned with the relations between interest and stock.[30] But perhaps the most telling passages of all come where Smith is discussing the slow progress of opulence. The division of labor, Smith's famous principle, is seen entirely in terms of its tendency to promote accumulation. Given its effects, why has every nation remained poor for so long? It all turns on the accumulation of capital:

Before labour can be divided some accumulation of stock is necessary. A poor man with no stock can never begin a manufacture. Before a man can commence farmer, he must at least have laid in a years provision, because he does not receive the fruits of his labour till the end of the season.[31]

The other cause of the slow progress of growth is the weakness of government: when people expect to be robbed they have no motive to be industrious, and therefore there can be little accumulation of stock. When the power of government grows, wars endanger growth, and it becomes next to impossible that any accumulation of stock can be made. Finally, governmental policies oppress agriculture which Smith regards as being of all arts the most beneficient to society, and early stages of land tenure, such as the feudal, are highly inefficient in maximizing accumulation. The whole study of the impediments to the growth of agricultural surplus is dazzling.[32]

Having summed up the causes which hinder the growth of surplus in agriculture, which he describes as the most important branch of industry, Smith proceeds to show that the slow growth of manufacturing has similar causes. Slave labor postponed the development of machinery, and contempt for trade prevented the investment of talent and capital in manufactures. Thus, merchants ''could never amass that degree of stock which is necessary for making the division of labour, and improving manufactures.''[33]

Finally, when he turns to the discussion of revenue, Smith is concerned to show that the use of land to raise revenue is a cause of the slow progress of opulence. Were the British government supported by the rent of land, the land in its hands would be much worse cultivated: ''By this therefore the stock of the country would be greatly diminished and fewer people maintained.''[34] One of his principal concerns about taxes is that they increase the stock needed to carry on a business. It is typical of this whole discussion that his primary objection to taxes on imports is that they divert stock from its optimal allocation for growth: ''The more stock there is employed in one way, there is the less to be employed in another. . . .''[35]

Thus we have shown that a reading of the report of Smith's *Lectures,* LJ(B), which was available to Cannan demonstrates that between 1751 and 1764 Smith had in fact powerfully developed one great theme of all of his work: the allocation of surplus throughout industry so to ensure its maximal growth. If we may be excused for putting our point in modern terminology, the *quantity* relations of a viable economy, and of an economy using surplus generated throughout industry so as to promote overall growth, are surely to be found clearly expressed in Cannan's version of the *Lectures.* On the other hand, if the role of surplus was clear in that version, the nature and role of its dual, profit, was not. The concept of profit as a return earned on stock by its owner simply in proportion to the amount of stock invested in a given enterprise, which, as we shall see, is treated in detail in the *Wealth of Nations,* is not made explicit in the only report of Smith's *Lectures,* LJ(B), which was available until recently. Now, it happens that the newly published version of the *Lectures,* LJ(A), offers possible light on these matters, and to this we therefore turn.

Profit in ~~the Newly Discovered Lectures~~

The editors of The Glasgow Edition suggest that:

A number of scholars, basing themselves on LJ(B) have argued that in Smith's Glasgow lectures capital and the accumulation of capital did not yet play anything like the central role which they were later to do in [the *Wealth of Nations*]; that the concept of profit on capital as a basic category of class income was still missing; and that the concept of a normal *rate* of profit on capital was also missing. Now . . . it is possible that these judgements may require *some*—although perhaps not very much—modification.[36]

As far as the accumulation of capital is concerned, we have already shown that it indeed played a major role, even in the Cannan version—on this our case rests. With regard to profit and the normal rate of profit, however, there are significant differences between the two reports of Smith's *Lectures.* On this question, three passages singled out for comment by Meek, Raphael, and Stein will bear examination. In the first of these, Smith describes how:

. . . each branch of trade will afford enough both to support the opulence and give considerable profit of the great men, and sufficiently reward the industry of the labourer. Every trade can afford something* for those who do not work, and give enough to the industrious. Thus . . . if we should suppose that the pin makers can furnish 1000 pins in the day, that these (including the price of the metall which is about 20^d per pound, out of which many thousand pins can be made) can be sold at the rate of 3 half-pence per 100. The whole thousand will then be worth 15^d, of which the artizan can afford 3 to his master and have 12 as the price of his labour, or may give him 200 and retain 800 to himself, *for it is the same thing whether we suppose each † one to have the commodity he works in or the value of his share.*[37]

It would be hard to find a more precise statement of the relation between physical surplus and profit, short of the use of matrix algebra. We leave the detailed discussion of the duality of profit to surplus for our treatment of the *Wealth of Nations* below, where Smith repeatedly invokes it. But it must surely be granted that the idea was clear to him when he lectured in Glasgow.

Now, as regards the concept of a tendency toward a uniform *rate* of profit throughout industry in the long run, the editors of The Glasgow Edition note a passage where Smith states that the price of a good must be enough to repay

---

* Replaces "sufficient." Glasgow Editors' reference.
† Replaces an illegible word. Glasgow Editors' reference.

the costs of education and the apprentice fee "not only in principall but with the interest and profit which I might have made of it."[38] Admittedly, apprentices become master craftsmen, not capitalists, but the point is that Smith is arguing that one would not lay out the capital for an apprentice fee if one expected less yield in the long run than the same capital would have yielded as profit if used as stock anywhere in industry.

Finally, there is a passage where Smith describes, as the Glasgow Editors note, what may be expected to take place in a competitive market in the long run when a trade is overprofitable:

For if any trade is overprofitable all throng into it till they bring it to the naturall price, that is, the maintenance of the person and the recompence of the risque he runs; that is, what is sufficient to maintain the person according to his rank and station.[39]

If Smith had stopped after the phrase "naturall price," one might be willing to grant his having his complete theory of profit by this time. The remainder of the passage, however, shows an obvious uncertainty of touch, if compared with the perfectly clear understanding of the nature of capitalist profit as a return paid exactly in proportion to the value of the stock invested (not to the investor's "station"!) which we shall see in due course in the *Wealth of Nations*. For all that, a reading of the newly published report must surely convince one that Smith's theory of profit was already well advanced (and vastly ahead of its time) by his lectures of the academic year, 1762–63.

The "Early Draft"

One further manuscript of Smith's work before he went to France has been known for some time through the efforts of W. R. Scott and the help of the then Duke of Buccleuch. The manuscript was found among papers at Dalkeith House, a seat of the Dukes of Buccleuch. As Scott remarks, "There is a certain appropriateness in its home, since Dalkeith at one time belonged to the head of the branch of the Douglas family from which Adam Smith's mother descended till it was sold in 1642 by William, eighth Earl of Morton, to Francis Scott, second Earl of Buccleuch."[40]

Cannan had claimed that, "It is plain that Adam Smith acquired the idea of the necessity of a scheme of distribution from the Physiocrats, and that he tacked his own scheme (very different from theirs) on to his already existing theory of prices."[41] We have seen that the discovery of the new report of Smith's *Lectures* shows that he had quite developed ideas about the distribution of the product between wages and profit by the academic year 1762–63. About rent, he was always to remain somewhat unclear. Scott's publication of the "Early Draft" in 1937, however, in itself was quite an effective answer to Cannan's hypothesis.

The manuscript at issue begins with "Chapter 2" which is entitled "Of the nature and causes of public opulence." [42] In this, Smith addresses the question of the accumulation of stock specifically in relation to the question of how the total product is distributed. For instance, he asks how it comes about that in a civilized society the poor are better provided than in a savage state where each retains the whole product of his own labor:

> In a civilized society the poor provide both for themselves and for the enormous luxury of their superiors. The rent, which goes to support the vanity of the slothful landlord, is all earned* by the industry of the peasant. The monied man indulges himself in every sort of ignoble and sordid sensuality, at the expense. of the merchant and the trades man to whom he lends out his stock at interest. All the indolent and frivolous retainers upon a court are, in the same manner, fed, cloathed, and lodged by the labour of those who pay the taxes which support them. Among savages, on the contrary, every individual enjoys the whole produce of his own industry. . . . We might naturally expect, therefore, if experience did not demonstrate the contrary, that every individual among them should have a much greater affluence of the necessaries and conveniencies of life, than can be possessed by the inferior ranks of people in a civilized society. [43]

Smith's answer, of course, is that the division of labor "can alone account for that superior opulence which takes place in civilized societies, and which, notwithstanding the inequality of property, extends itself to the lowest member of the community." [44] And again: "So great a quantity of every thing is produced, that there is enough both to gratify the slothful and oppressive profusion of the great, and at the same time abundantly to supply the wants of the artizan and the peasant." [45]

One comes away from the "Early Draft" with the feeling that Adam Smith had now fully filled out his picture in quantity terms of the role played by the extraction of surplus, and the allocation of surplus output to growth or luxury consumption. What was missing from this manuscript, however, was an explicit treatment of the dual of surplus—profit. The full-dress development of the theory of the uniform rate of profit in the price relations of a mature classical model would be found only in the *Wealth of Nations*.

Smith in France

Smith was now about to leave for France, and we may conveniently ask how much, up to this point, he could have owed to physiocratic influence. We

---

* Replaces "earned," possibly mis-spelt. Glasgow Editors' reference.

have seen that, at least from his Oxford years, he was well read in French literature. The issue as to how much specific physiocratic work Smith could
have read has long been debated, and each new piece of information about the
contents of Smith's library has rekindled the fire. We must content ourselves
here with a few general points. First of all, as will be recalled, Quesnay's
Tableau Économique, in its three "editions" during the 1750's, was shown to
only a few of Quesnay's friends at Versailles. The *Tableau* was not made
available to the reading public until it appeared in Mirabeau's *Rural
Philosophy.* As we know, Quesnay's early article, "Corn," had appeared in the *Encyclopedia* in 1757, and Mirabeau's work (to which Quesnay
certainly contributed), the *Theory of Taxation,* came out in 1760, while Mirabeau's *Rural Philosophy* was first printed in 1763. Scott argues that the "balance of probability"[46] is that Smith acquired these books, which *were* in his
library, while in France, and not while still in Glasgow. In any case, most of
this work was published too late to have deeply influenced Smith's early
thought. And, above all, as we have been at pains to show, Smith was already
concerned in his early writings with the surplus which is yielded by the
employment of capital stock *throughout* industry, not just in agriculture, and
with the profit that results from this. These ideas, however, he could not have
learned from *any* physiocratic literature. More suggestive is the fact that Cantillon's *Essay* was in Smith's library. From Cantillon, as we have seen, one
could develop a picture of surplus not being confined to the agricultural sector, and possibly even some notion of profit. Perhaps Smith and Quesnay
were both inspired by that brilliant and mysterious figure, each taking from
Cantillon what he, in the circumstances of his country and experience, could
use.

It was late in the year 1763 that Smith made the momentous decision to accept the offer to travel on the continent with the young Duke of Buccleuch.
Remarking that the system of political economy, of which the princples had
already been delivered in the *Glasgow Lectures,* was now the leading object
of Smith's studies, Dugald Stewart wrote:

The coincidence between some of these principles and the distinguishing tenets of the
French economists, who were at that very time in the height of their reputation, and
the intimacy in which he lived with some of the leaders of that sect, could not fail to
assist him in methodizing [*sic*] and digesting his speculations. . . .[47]

In this passage Dugald Stewart launched the tradition of looking for a French
influence on Smith. Now, it is indeed true that Smith moved in a French society imbued with physiocratic ideas and was intimately acquainted with the
leading physiocrats. This began slowly. The first visit to Paris of Smith and

the young duke lasted only ten days, after which they stayed eighteen months at Toulouse; and then traveled extensively in the south of France, after which they spent two months in Geneva. They returned to Paris around Christmas of 1765, where they remained till the next October. Of their life there, Stewart wrote:

The society in which Mr. Smith spent these ten months, may be conceived from the advantages he enjoyed, in consequence of the recommendations of Mr. Hume. Turgot, Quesnai, [sic] Necker, d'Alembert, Helvétius, Marmontel, Madame Riccoboni, were among his acquaintances; and some of them he continued ever afterwards to reckon as friends.[48]

These people were all to be seen about town in the salons which, as the financier and statesman Jacque Necker put it, formed "the invisible power which, without finances, without troops, without an army, imposes its laws upon the town, on the Court, and even on the King himself."[49] Jean le Rond d'Alembert, for instance, a close friend of David Hume and one of the greatest of the contributors to the *Encyclopedia,* held a salon with Julie de Lespinasse which was frequented by Turgot and Smith. Most of them wrote for the *Encyclopedia;* Claude-Adrien Helvétius was a noted philosopher. Marie-Jeanne Laboras de Mézières, Mme. Riccoboni, the novelist, was a friend of Hume's and a great admirer of Smith. Smith, evidently, was in the thick of it: he was meeting all intellectual Paris.

Nor did they forget him when he left France—he was no nine-days wonder. Writing on March 3, 1778, Louis-Alexandre, Duc de la Rochefoucauld,[50] sent Smith a copy of a new edition of his grandfather's *Maxims,* and informed Smith that he had nearly finished a translation of *The Theory of Moral Sentiments* when he found that another translation had been published. La Rochefoucauld, who was a close friend of Turgot and a disciple of Quesnay,[51] continued to be a friend of Smith all his life. La Rochefoucauld's enthusiasm for Smith's work was quite unimpaired by the fact that Smith had been unkind to the author of the *Maxims* (François VI, Duc de La Rochefoucauld, grandfather of Smith's friend) in early editions of his *Theory of Moral Sentiments.*[52] Smith, for his part, sent word to the duke in 1789 that future editions of the *Moral Sentiments* would no longer contain the unfavorable reference to the *Maxims,* and this change was indeed made in the sixth edition, which appeared in 1790. Thus the Scotsman was no less generous in his gestures than the French. Stewart tells us that, "If he had not been prevented by Quesnai's [sic] death, Mr. Smith had once an intention (as he told me himself) to have inscribed to him his 'Wealth of Nations'."[53]

So it is hardly surprising that the issue of Adam Smith's relation to the Physiocrats was already being raised by Stewart in 1795, five years after Smith's death. For us, however, one great theme of all Smith's work, the analysis of the allocation of surplus generated throughout industry, had been developed long before Smith went to France—by its very nature, it could not have been derived from physiocratic writings. And the treatment of the dual problem, the uniform rate of profit, which plays a minor role in Smith's early work and which is for us the outstanding originality of the *Wealth of Nations,* is utterly at variance with physiocratic thinking. Turgot alone could have been sympathetic to it, and, as we know, he had the benefit of Smith's close friendship *before* he wrote his *Reflections.*

The Wealth of Nations

On July 5, 1764, at Toulouse, when Smith and the duke had not yet begun to go much into society, Smith had written to his friend, Hume, "I have begun to write a book in order to pass away the time. You may believe I have very little to do."[54] In October of 1766, Smith and his pupil returned to London, and we are told by Dugald Stewart that during the next ten years Smith "remained with his mother at Kirkaldy, occupied habitually in intense study. . . ."[55] Finally, in 1776, there appeared the masterpiece to which we now turn. Classical political economy had come of age.

When one reads the *Wealth of Nations,* it is to find the great theme of the allocation of surplus output to the maximum possible accumulation of capital, developed continually through endless variations, as Smith ranges over the whole of economic life as he knew it. Indeed, some of the most vivid expressions of the theme come in contexts where one would least expect to find them. Yet, strangely enough, in discussions of the *Wealth of Nations,* "allocation" has been assumed to mean "allocation of *given* resources," and it has been seriously debated whether Smith's basic concern was with "growth" or with "allocation" (of given resources).

Commenting on this issue, Samuel Hollander has recently contrasted two views of the *Wealth of Nations:* Smith's basic concern, according to one view, "is with the increasing of material wealth rather than the efficient allocation of scarce resources among alternative uses. . . . But we must refer at this point to an alternative well known view according to which the very essence of Smithian economics lies precisely in the statement of the role of relative product and factor prices in making an optimum allocation of scarce resources."[56] He cites Lord Robbins, who has written that "from the point of view of theoretical economics, the central achievement of [Smith's] book was his demonstration of the mode in which the division of labour tended to be kept in equilibrium by the mechanics of relative prices—a demonstration which . . . is in harmony, with the most refined apparatus of the modern School of Lausanne."[57,*]

However, we must note with Hollander that "a more recent statement by Lord Robbins of the main purpose of the *Wealth of Nations* suggests a change of emphasis."[58] He goes on to cite Robbins as saying recently that, "The main credit for putting economic development on the map as a subject for general analysis belongs undoubtedly to Adam Smith. . . . [As] political economy its coverage [of the *Wealth of Nations*] is wide, ranging from an exhibition of the essential structural relationships of an exchange economy practicing the division of labour, to the economic functions of the state and the claims of taxation. But, as the title itself implies, the central focus is on development—what makes the *Wealth of Nations* greater or less."[59]

Agreeing with this latter view, Hollander sums up his findings on the *Wealth of Nations:* "The object of the work was ultimately to define the necessary conditions for rapid economic development in contemporary circumstances and Smith's treatment of the price mechanism must accordingly in the final resort, be considered with this end in view."[60] This, of necessity, implies that in Adam Smith the theory of allocation has a special role connected with the accumulation of surplus. Hollander adds weight to this suggestion when he goes on to say, "It is, in brief, not merely the elaboration of the mechanisms of resource allocation which requires attention, but also the particular uses to which the analysis was put. . . ."[61]

It has recently been noted by R. D. Collison Black that economists today are finding "more of value in [Smith's] contribution than did their predecessors of fifty and even a hundred years ago."[62] Black suggests that this remarkable revival of interest can be partly explained by the change in perspective which has occurred:

. . . for the standpoint from which the majority of economists today are accustomed to view Smith's contribution is that of the economics of growth and development. Seen from there, it naturally appears more sensible and significant than when it is viewed from the angle of a static theory of value and distribution of the neo-classical type.[63]

* The School of Lausanne, referred to by Lord Robbins, was founded by Léon Walras. "School of Lausanne" is thus a term for Walrasian allocation theory. See chapter 6.

In appraising this characteristic of Smith's work it is crucial to stress our distinction between two sorts of general equilibrium model (and, therefore, two sorts of *allocation*): (1) a model in which resources are given, i.e., parametric, and the object of the analysis is to show how these given resources are allocated; and (2) a model in which (variable) amounts of commodities are being produced and allocated as inputs to yield more of the same commodities, in order to maximize surplus. Observe that in both types of model a concept of allocation would play a role. However, it will become increasingly evident as we proceed that the role played by allocation is very different in each case. The first model, where resources are simply given, and the whole economic problem is seen as that of allocating them among alternative uses, is, in effect, the model developed by Walras and the neoclassics (as we show in chapters 5 and 6). But this is not what "allocating" means for Smith. In the *Wealth of Nations* the problem is to produce the right quantities of the various input commodities, and to allocate them in such a way as to encourage growth.

Hollander summarizes his view of the nature and role of capital in Smith by saying that, "Capital is *primarily* subsistence goods whereas machinery, tools, raw materials (and skills) are simply more complicated forms."[64] On this view, the rate of accumulation of surplus depends on the choice of the right input mix, and on the allocation of these produced inputs (wage goods, tools, machinery) in the employment of productive labor (engaged upon the production of commodities which can be used to produce more commodities so as to maximize the accumulation of capital). This is a model in which allocation plays the second of the two roles which we have been at pains to distinguish.

Thus, we recognize the just claims of those who stress Smith's contribution to the development of "allocation" theory, but nevertheless point out that it was in the allocation of *surplus output* and not of "given resources" that Smith was interested: a dynamic theory in which the role of the freely operating market is to allocate the surplus available as capital stock so as to put in motion the greatest quantity of productive labor. The reader will recall that the discussions of allocation theory by Richard Cantillon, by Quesnay, and by Turgot, all concerned the allocation of *surplus output*. This is, above all, true of Smith who is concerned throughout the *Wealth of Nations* with that allocation of surplus output which will generate the maximum accumulation of capital.

As early as chapter VI of Book I, the distinction between the use of the surplus for growth and its use for luxury consumption is clearly made, and the concept of the trade-off between accumulation and consumption is set out:

But there is no country in which the whole annual produce is employed in maintaining the industrious. The idle everywhere consume a great part of it, and according to the different proportions in which it is annually divided between those two different orders of people, its ordinary or average value must either annually increase, or diminish, or continue the same from one year to another.[65]

It is fundamental to Smith's view about the behavior of wages over time that "as capital accumulates, most workers will become better off, and they will continue to become better off for so long as accumulation is able to continue."[66] The importance of capital accumulation in keeping wages above bare subsistence through continual increases in the demand for labor is vividly described in chapter VIII of Book I: "It is not the actual greatness of national wealth, but its continual increase, which occasions a rise in the wages of labour."[67] And, again, "The liberal reward of labour, therefore, as it is the necessary effect, so it is the natural symptom of increasing national wealth."[68] It should be borne in mind that, for Smith, even "subsistence" does not mean bare biological survival:

In Great Britain the wages of labour seem, in the present times, to be evidently more than what is precisely necessary to enable the labourer to bring up a family. In order to satisfy ourselves upon this point it will not be necessary to enter into any tedious or doubtful calculation of what may be the lowest sum upon which it is possible to do this.[69]

Furthermore, Smith, and later Ricardo, look to capital accumulation, as it proceeds, to occasion short-run changes in demand which will tend to keep pushing wages something above even the customary long-run subsistence level.[70]

In chapter XI of Book I, we find a clear statement of the concept of surplus in agriculture:

But land, in almost any situation, produces a greater quantity of food than what is sufficient to maintain all the labour necessary for bringing it to market, in the most liberal way in which that labour is ever maintained. The surplus too, is always more than sufficient to replace the stock which employed that labour, together with its profits. Something, therefore, always remains for a rent to the landlord.[71]

Here Smith's way of using the concept of subsistence is vividly illustrated, and the role of the agricultural surplus in making capital accumulation possible is precisely stated:

But when by the improvement and cultivation of land the labour of one family can provide food for two, the labour of half the society becomes sufficient to provide food for the whole. The other half, therefore, or at least the greater part of them, can be employed in providing other things. . . .[72]

Thus, Smith accepted and emphatically carried on the deeply sound insight of physiocracy to the effect that capital accumulation is impossible without an agricultural surplus.

In Book II, entitled, "Of the Nature, Accumulation, and Employment of Stock," the theme of capital accumulation positively thunders out. The division of labor, we are told, is intimately related to the accumulation of stock:

In that rude state of society in which there is no division of labour, in which exchanges are seldom made, and in which every man provides everything for himself, it is not necessary that any stock should be accumulated or stored up beforehand. . . .[73]

And so:

As the accumulation of stock must, in the nature of things, be previous to the division of labour, so labour can be more and more subdivided in proportion only as stock is previously more and more accumulated.[74]

This fundamental characteristic of Smith's concept of capital accumulation has been tellingly analyzed in the recent paper by W. A. Eltis, already cited.[75]

In chapter I of Book II, Smith distinguishes capital stock into fixed and circulating, making it plain that he fully understands the need for both kinds of capital in agriculture as well as in manufacturing industry, treating both kinds of enterprises as identical capitalist undertakings. We are far from physiocracy:

In a great iron-works, for example, the furnace for melting the ore, the forge, the slitt-mill, are instruments of trade which cannot be created without a very great expense. . . . That part of the capital of the farmer which is employed in the instruments of agriculture is a fixed; that which is employed in the wages and maintenance of his labouring servants, is a circulating capital.[76]

The notion, sometimes put forward, that capital in Smith can be treated simply as a quantity of corn for wages and seed is totally refuted by a perusal of this section.[77] Yet, curiously enough, the view that Adam Smith in the *Wealth of Nations* was dealing with capitalist industry has been denied. Samuel Hollander notes, in his recent work on Smith, that "There is to be found in the secondary literature the widely-held view that Smith's preoccupation in discussing the industrial sector was with domestic handicrafts, where workers were often self-employed, and in any event not maintained by a master from another *class* but rather from another generation.'' [78] Hollander marshalls a mass of detailed evidence to disprove this. He shows that ''Smith entered into a highly sophisticated analysis of the effect of scale of *industry* upon the degree of division of labor practiced at the plant. This in itself is eloquent testimonial to the fact that factory organization was to Smith's mind well established and calling for detailed analysis.'' [79] He adds that, ''Further evidence that Smith's analytical structure was largely designed for factory, rather than domestic, organization may be drawn from the discussion of 'profits'.'' [80] New support for this view of Smith has been offered in a recent contribution by R. M. Hartwell, who argues that ''Adam Smith was aware of the economic changes occurring during his lifetime, which coincided with the background and beginnings of the industrial revolution. . . .'' [81]

Again, in chapter II of Book II, Smith stresses the importance of fixed capital for both agriculture and manufacturers. [82] It is typical that though the chapter is called ''Money,'' it should be used to discuss the relations of money to capital stock and its accumulation. A paper currency would not require the diversion to the purchase of gold or silver of stock which could be used for capital accumulation. Then, in chapter III of this book, we find the great treatment of productive and unproductive labor: ''Thus the labour of a manufacturer adds, generally, to the value of the materials which he works upon, that of his own maintenance, and of his master's profit. The labour of a menial servant, on the contrary, adds to the value of nothing. . . . A man grows rich by employing a multitude of manufacturers: He grows poor by maintaining a multitude of menial servants.'' [83] Manufacturer, as the reader will have noted, is used here in its original sense of a *worker* in industry. Cannan, in a footnote in his edition, points out that one will only get rich by employing manufacturers if the latter are employed to produce commodities for *sale,* and not luxuries for the rich man's own consumption. Likewise, one will only grow poor by employing menial servants when they are for one's own comfort, not if one is, for example, an innkeeper. And, indeed, it must be admitted that Smith does not quite capture the distinction he needs in all cases. But it is fairly clear that Smith intends labor to be thought of as productive if and only if it is devoted to the maintenance and growth of capital, as distinct from turning out luxuries:

Both productive and unproductive labourers, and those who do not labour at all, are all equally maintained by the annual produce of the land and labour of the country. . . . According, therefore, as a smaller or greater proportion of it is in any one year employed in maintaining unproductive hands, the more in the one case and the less in the other will remain for the productive, and the next year's produce will be greater or smaller accordingly; the whole annual produce, if we except the spontaneous productions of the earth, being the effect of productive labour.[84]

Eltis has commented on Smith's distinction between productive and unproductive labor that, "There are obviously difficult borderline cases (as there are in the modern distinction between investment and consumption) and the distinction has lapsed, but it may have force in distinguishing activities which contribute to growth from those that do not."[85] He adds that, "The sole echo of Smith's distinction in modern theory is in Piero Sraffa's classically based *Production of Commodities by Means of Commodities* (1960) where goods (and presumably services) that are used as factors of production and those that are bought by workers influence the prices of other goods, the wage, the rate of profit, etc., while goods (and presumably services) that are solely consumed by non-workers do not."[86]

Of course, the fact is that some related notion is to be found in *any* modern classical reproduction system. An examination of the mathematics of any such system will reveal that there is a technology whose outputs are necessary to the reproduction of the system—to its viability. Labor devoted to producing this output is "productive"—in fact, it is "reproductive", i.e., necessary for reproduction. Labor devoted to producing, for example, carriages, which do not enter into the reproducibility of the system, is not, in this sense, productive. Intellectual historians whose historiography took for granted a general equilibrium system of the post-Walrasian, neoclassical type where, as we shall see, these ideas are without meaning, necessarily misunderstood Smith's analysis of the accumulation of capital.

Smith's concern for the accumulation of subsistence goods, of the subsistence of laborers, shows very clearly in his discussion of agricultural surplus:

As subsistence is, in the nature of things, prior to conveniency and luxury, so the industry which produces the former, ministers to the latter. The cultivation and improvement of the country, therefore, which affords subsistence, must, necessarily, be prior to the increase of the town, which furnishes only the means of conveniency and luxury. It is the surplus produce of the country only, or what is over and above the maintenance of the cultivators, that constitutes the subsistence of the town, which can therefore increase only with the increase of this surplus produce.[87]

As always, the emphasis is on allocation of surplus so as to maximize growth. Thus he contrasts the primitive use of the agricultural surplus during feudal times to feed retainers, with its later use to buy manufactures, which leads to growth:

In a country which has neither foreign commerce, nor any of the finer manufactures, a great proprietor, having nothing for which he can exchange the greater part of the produce of his lands which is over and above the maintenance of the cultivators, consumes the whole in rustick hospitality at home. If this surplus produce is sufficient to maintain a hundred or a thousand men, he can make use of it in no other way than by maintaining a hundred or a thousand men.[88]

Smith's grasp of the surplus in manufacturing comes out vividly in his analysis of the way in which the latter is used to pay for foreign wars:

No foreign war of great expense or duration could conveniently be carried on by the exportation of the rude produce of the soil. . . . . It is otherwise with the exportation of manufactures. The maintenance of the people employed in them is left at home, and only the surplus part of their work is exported.[89]

Thus, the theme of surplus and accumulation pervades Smith's discussion of colonies, of foreign wars, of everything pertaining to the wealth of a nation. He speaks of a balance:

. . . very different from the balance of trade, and which, according as it happens to be either favourable or unfavourable, necessarily occasions the prosperity or decay of every nation. This is the balance of the annual produce and consumption. If the exchangeable value of the annual produce . . . exceeds that of the annual consumption, the capital of the society must annually increase in proportion to this excess.[90]

And, in discussing America and the East Indies, he writes:

The most advantageous employment of any capital to the country to which it belongs, is that which maintains there the greatest quantity of productive labour, and increases the most the annual produce of the land and labour of that country.[91]

Thus he attacks the monopoly of the colony trade on the grounds that it diverts stock from uses in which growth would be greater. The monopoly artificially raises the rate of profit, and merchants gain. "But as it obstructs the natural increase of capital, it tends rather to diminish than to increase the sum total of the revenue which the inhabitants of the country derive from the profits of stock. . . ."[92]

Summing up his case against mercantilist restrictions, Smith argues: "The mercantile stock of every country . . . naturally seeks, if one may say so, the employment most advantageous to that country."[93] And so, "All the different regulations of the mercantile system, necessarily derange more or less this natural and most advantageous distribution of stock."[94] Thus, his whole attack on mercantilism can be seen in terms of the misallocation of surplus to which the policy leads, thereby reducing the accumulation of capital.

In his treatment of physiocracy, which he describes as "this liberal and generous system,''[95] and which "with all its imperfections, is, perhaps, the nearest approximation to the truth that has yet been published upon the subject of political economy . . . ,''[96] Smith's main criticism centers on the physiocratic mistake about the role of manufactures in the accumulation process: "The capital error of this system, however, seems to lie in its representing the class of artificers, manufacturers and merchants, as altogether barren and unproductive."[97] So, in his eyes, the cardinal sin of the physiocrats is to favor agriculture in a way which leads to the misallocation of surplus, thus defeating their own ends:

These systems, therefore, which preferring agriculture to all other employments, in order to promote it, impose restraints upon manufactures and foreign trade, act contrary to the very end which they propose, and indirectly discourage that very species of industry which they mean to promote.[98]

It is the same with his discussion of the physiocratic policy proposal of a single tax on land—his whole concern is that the progress of agriculture and the accumulation of capital not be hindered.[99] And, indeed, this is true of his discussion of taxation in general. Thus, taxes on ground-rents are approved of, since they do not interfere with production and output: "The annual produce of the land and labour of the society, the real wealth and revenue of the great body of the people, might be the same after such a tax as before,''[100] And this point of view shows especially clearly throughout his discussion of "Taxes upon Profit or upon the Revenue arising from Stock."[101]

Finally, when he comes to discuss taxes on wages, we find that these are ordinarily shifted to the consumer, since wages are supposed to be at the then appropriate subsistence level: *

The demand for labour, according as it happens to be either increasing, stationary, or declining; or to require an increasing, stationary, or declining population, regulates the subsistence of the labourer, and determines in what degree it shall be, either liberal, moderate, or scanty . . . while the demand for labour and the price of provisions, therefore, remain the same, a direct tax upon the wages of labour can have no other effect than to raise them somewhat higher than the tax.[102]

With splendid consistency, he concludes:

If direct taxes upon the wages of labour have not always occasioned a proportionable rise in their wages, it is because they have generally occasioned a considerable fall in the demand for labour. The declension of industry, the decrease of employment for the poor, the diminution of the annual produce of the land and labour of the country, have generally been the effects of such taxes.[103]

---

* Recall that this does not mean bare physical survival.

How to increase, not diminish, the annual produce—that is always the question for Smith. Thus, it is again with a tax upon the necessities of life: he believes this operates "exactly in the same manner as a direct tax upon the wages of labour."[104] And it is the fact that they cannot be shifted which enables Smith to distinguish taxes on luxuries, even the luxuries of the poor.[105]

As the book draws to a close, Smith reiterates the unique consequences of the use of surplus for capital accumulation: a complete departure from the characteristic earlier practice of using it to feed retainers.[106] He recalls that "Land and Capital Stock are the two original sources of all revenue both private and publick,"[107] and goes on to remind us that land is largely a produced capital good.[108] Thus, the allocation of surplus to capital accumulation lies at the heart of Smith's whole account of the emergence of capitalism out of the previous phase of history. Deep concern with human progress illuminates all of Smith's writings, from beginning to end, and as has been recently remarked, "It is known for example that he lectured on the 'progress of society' while in Edinburgh between 1748 and 1751. . . ."[109] Dugald Stewart reported that Smith:

followed the plan that seems to be suggested by Montesquieu; endeavouring to trace the gradual progress of jurisprudence, both public and private, from the rudest to the most refined ages, and to point out the effect of those arts which contribute to subsistence, and to the accumulation of property, in producing correspondent improvements or alterations in law and government.[110]

It is perhaps unnecessary to add, for anyone acquainted with the breadth and humanity of Smith's mind, that for all his correct insistence on the crucial importance of the accumulation of capital in the period in which he lived, he never fell into the vulgar error of imagining that economic growth was costless in human terms. As has recently been well said:

Smith believed that, to a large extent, nature speaks to history in the language of economics, and that the broad course of history so instructed is probably toward an easier, more cultivated, more rational and secure life for the generality of mankind. At the same time, he imagined that the advance of civilization was synchronous with the generation of a tremendous industrial mob, deprived of nearly every admirable human quality. Civilization is not an unqualified good, or more accurately, it comes at a price.[111]

The Uniform Rate of Profit

As we have now seen, the *Wealth of Nations* masterfully develops and brings to a climax Smith's earliest theme: the allocation of surplus to capital accumulation. With respect to the dual of physical surplus—namely, profit—however, the *Wealth of Nations* breaks quite new ground, both for Smith, and for the history of economic analysis. In the report of the *Lectures on Jurisprudence,* published by Cannan, LJ(B), and in the "Early Draft" of the *Wealth of Nations,* the term profit does occur. But it was possible for Ronald Meek to observe of these manuscripts:

The amount of 'profit' received is variously visualized as being dependent upon the degree of risk involved, the amount of good luck experienced, the strength of the monopoly position enjoyed, or the quantity and quality of labour performed—nowhere is it clearly visualized as varying according to the amount of stock employed.[112]

Thus, the view of profit in Cannan's version of the *Lectures* and in the "Early Draft" does not differ substantially from that of Turgot in the *Reflections.* Turgot's capitalists were "industrious," and, while they were described as receiving "profits," these profits were not clearly distinguished from the wages of management, or from the interest on the finance they provided. Smith, as we know, had finished his lecturing in Glasgow long before Turgot's *Reflections* appeared in print, and had reached the view of profits which we have seen reported in LJ(A). Clearly, when they met, Smith had already gone further than Turgot on the issue of profits, *before* going to France. Indeed, it is possible that Smith's early thoughts on profits influenced Turgot's position as presented in the *Reflections.* Our interest, however, is in Smith's fully *mature* theory of profits, which is set out in detail for the first time in the first edition of the *Wealth of Nations.*

In Smith's mature theory, it is not the least the point that capitalists should be "industrious." What is at issue is that the capitalists use their stock in setting to work industrious people. In return, Smith's capitalists "receive, over and above the return of their paid-out costs and interest on their capital at the normal rate, a *net* income, profit, which is, as it were, exuded by the capital-labour relationship, and which bears a regular proportion not to the effort, if any, which they expend, but, to the value of the capital they have invested."[113]

For Smith, profit is the reflection in prices of the physical surplus which can be generated in each sector. Given that capitalists are free to invest their stock where they please, Smith expects profit to be extracted at a normal or usual rate throughout the economy, in proportion to the amount of stock invested. To show this duality between surplus and profit a little notation is very helpful, but a warning must be issued first. We cannot give any adequate formalization of Smith's rich picture of capital accumulation. To mention only the most obvious point, accumulation is being accelerated, in the *Wealth of Nations,* by continual extensions of the division of labour. As the scale of output increases in a sector, certainly a sector devoted to manufacturing, returns are increasing more than proportionately. This feature of Smith cannot be captured by our simple models which assume *constant* returns to scale in production.

We can, however, adapt the corn and iron model first introduced in chapter 2 so that it will exhibit the *single feature* of Smith's theory with which we are at the moment concerned: the duality between surplus in the quantity relations and a uniform rate of profit in the price relations. Let us then consider an alternative way of closing the model introduced in chapter 2, in a somewhat Smithian spirit. We do this through a specification of how the surplus is used in accumulating larger stocks of corn and iron in each sector of the economy. This particular allocation of surplus can be represented by introducing, in each sector, a *rate of growth:* a percentage, written g_C in the corn sector and g_I in the iron sector, by which the allocations of corn and iron increase through time. On the assumption that this growth in the means of production absorbs the *entire* surplus, we write:*

$$a_{CC} Y_C(1 + g_C) + a_{CI} Y_I(1 + g_I) = Y_C \tag{1}$$

$$a_{IC} Y_C(1 + g_C) + a_{II} Y_I(1 + g_I) = Y_I \tag{2}$$

Of course, Smith was aware that there was luxury consumption which, as we have seen, was the point of his famous distinction between productive and unproductive labor. His disapproval of unproductive labor shows that he wished to see the economy approximate as closely as possible to a condition of maximum growth. Assuming, however, that luxury goods absorb some of the output of both sectors in their production (but not for present purposes specifying these production processes in detail) we may write down the case where there is some growth but also some consumption of surplus in each sector as follows:

$$a_{CC} Y_C(1 + g_C) + a_{CI} Y_I(1 + g_I) = (1 - \lambda_C) Y_C \tag{3}$$

$$a_{IC} Y_C(1 + g_C) + a_{II} Y_I(1 + g_I) = (1 - \lambda_I) Y_I \tag{4}$$

Luxury consumption of corn and iron is measured, respectively, by $\lambda_C Y_C$ and $\lambda_I Y_I$. The values of g_C and g_I in these equations will, of course, be less than in equations (1) and (2).

*In *long run* equilibrium a state of *un*balanced growth such that $g_C \neq g_I$ is inconsistent with a linear (constant returns to scale) technology. In our more complete discussion in chapter 11 we therefore assume balanced growth.

In the *Wealth of Nations,* Smith is quite explicit in stating that industrial profits are a reflection of surplus and arise, not from any labor of management, but out of a social relation between propertyless labor and the capitalist class:

As soon as stock has accumulated in the hands of particular persons, some of them will naturally employ it in setting to work industrious people, whom they will supply with materials and subsistence, in order to make a profit by the sale of their work, or by what their labour adds to the value of the materials.[114]

Indeed, Smith is perfectly clear about what he means by profit:

The Profits of stock, it may perhaps be thought, are only a different name for the wages of a particular sort of labour, the labour of inspection and direction. They are, however, altogether different, are regulated by quite different principles, and bear no proportion to the quantity, the hardship, or the ingenuity of this supposed labour of inspection and direction. They are regulated altogether by the value of the stock employed, and are greater or smaller in proportion to the extent of this stock.[115]

Thus, not only did Smith recognize the generation of surplus throughout industry, but he clearly saw its relation to a uniform rate of profit on stock. As has been remarked by Samuel Hollander, a characteristic element of Smith's work "is his extension of physiocratic doctrine to allow for the generation of surplus value in *all* sectors."[116] Seeing physical surplus as possible only in the agricultural sector, the physiocrats had naturally conceived of a disposable "revenue" only in the form of rent. For Smith all sectors were capable of yielding a physical surplus and all sectors must offer the capitalist, if he is to commit his stock to them, a uniform rate of profit on that stock.

We can represent this fundamental feature of Smith's theory in our little model as follows. Writing P_C and P_I for the price of a unit of corn and the price of a unit of iron, respectively, then, if the rate of profit were zero—if corn and iron were sold at cost—the price equations would be:

$$P_C a_{CC} + P_I a_{IC} = P_C \qquad (5)$$
$$P_C a_{CI} + P_I a_{II} = P_I \qquad (6)$$

It is shown in chapter 12 that for these equations to hold, surplus would have to be zero. Thus, it follows that if surplus exists, prices must exceed cost, giving rise to profit. Equations (5) and (6) must therefore be written as inequalities:

$$P_C a_{CC} + P_I a_{IC} < P_C \qquad (7)$$
$$P_C a_{CI} + P_I a_{II} < P_I \qquad (8)$$

The price relations for a simple classical model with surplus become equations again when we introduce a rate of profit, r. Formally, r measures the ratio of profit to the value of capital stock in each sector—which was exactly Smith's concept. In per-unit terms, the value of capital stock is the value of the commodities used up in producing a unit of output (in sustaining the productive laborers and providing them with the materials and equipment they need to produce a unit of output). This value is measured by the sums on the left-hand sides of inequalities (7) and (8). Profit per unit of output is the excess of price over capital value (per unit of output). The price relations of the model are thus written:

$$(P_C a_{CC} + P_I a_{IC})(1 + r) = P_C \tag{9}$$

$$(P_C a_{CI} + P_I a_{II})(1 + r) = P_I \tag{10}$$

so that:

$$r = \frac{P_C - P_C a_{CC} - P_I a_{IC}}{P_C a_{CC} + P_I a_{IC}} = \frac{P_I - P_C a_{CI} - P_I a_{II}}{P_C a_{CI} + P_I a_{II}}$$

which is the ratio of profit to capital in each sector.

When we turn to Smith's many discussions of profit in the *Wealth of Nations,* we see again and again the clarity and force with which he held the theory we have just formalized in our simple model. Thus, speaking of the natural and market price of commodities, he tells us that if anyone sells a commodity:

at a price which does not allow him the ordinary rate of profit in his neighbourhood, he is evidently a loser by the trade; since by employing his stock in some other way he might have made that profit.[117]

That a price will normally include, in addition to cost, profit at some normal rate,* is made quite explicit:

Though the price, therefore, which leaves him this profit, is not always the lowest at which a dealer may sometimes sell his goods, it is the lowest at which he is likely to sell them for any considerable time; at least where there is perfect liberty, or where he may change his trade as often as he pleases.[118]

In chapter X of Book I, speaking of wages and profits in the different employments of labor and stock, he tells us that:

* Smith made it quite clear in the *Wealth of Nations* that profit would tend to be equalized among trades in the long run. He had no theory, however, of the determination of what this rate would be. Providing a theory of how the rate of profit is determined was to be one of Ricardo's great contributions. See chapter 4.

The whole of the advantages and disadvantages of the different employments of labour and stock must, in the same neighbourhood, be either perfectly equal or continually tending to equality. If in the same neighbourhood, there was any employment evidently either more or less advantageous than the rest so many people would crowd into it in the one case, and so many would desert it in the other, that its advantages would soon return to the level of other employments.[119]

Smith shows a clear understanding of the circumstances which can make profits diverge, in the short run, from the uniform rate. These divergences have no bearing, he in effect argues, in a model of long-run equilibrium:

The establishment of any new manufacture, of any new branch of commerce, or of any new practise in agriculture, is always a speculation, from which the projector promises himself extraordinary profits. These profits sometimes are very great, and sometimes, more frequently, perhaps, they are quite otherwise; but in general they bear no regular proportion to those of other trades in the neighbourhood. If the project succeeds they are commonly at first very high. When the trade or practise becomes thoroughly established and well known, the competition reduces them to the level of other trades.[120]

Thus, the short-run gains due to uncertainty have nothing to do with what Smith means by the rate of profit, which is a phenomenon of long-run equilibrium. Aside from these short-run phenomena, profits may differ even in the long run owing to differences in the "agreeableness or disagreeableness of the business. . . ."[121] However, Smith remarks, "In point of agreeableness or disagreeableness, there is little or no difference in the far greater part of the different employments of stock."[122] So, profits differ little on this account, and, furthermore:

The apparent differences, besides, in the profits of different trades, is generally a deception arising from our not always distinguishing what ought to be considered as wages, from what ought to be considered as profit.[123]

Thus, specially skilled management, or entrepreneurship is appropriately seen as getting a wage, which is not a part of the rate of profit.

Smith is perfectly aware that government policies can cause profits to diverge from the normal rate. He is always at pains to point out that the uniform rate of profit will be approximated only in so far as an economy approaches to his concept of the system of natural liberty.[124]

The role of the uniform rate of profit in Smith's analysis of the allocation of surplus output is perhaps most clearly shown in his attack on bounties:

Bounties, it is allowed, ought to be given to those branches of trade only which cannot be carried on without them. But every branch of trade in which the merchant can sell his goods for a price which replaces to him, with the ordinary profits of stock, the whole capital employed in preparing and sending them to market, can be carried on without a bounty. . . . . Those trades only require bounties in which the merchant is obliged to sell his goods for a price which does not replace to him his capital, together with the ordinary profit; or in which he is obliged to sell them for less than it really costs him to send them to market. The bounty is given in order to make up this loss, and to encourage him to continue, or perhaps begin, a trade of which the expense is supposed to be greater than the returns, of which every operation eats up a part of the capital employed in it, and which is of such a nature, that if all other trades resembled it, there would soon be no capital left in the country.[125]

These trenchant phrases are echoed in a letter of January 3, 1780, published for the first time in The Glasgow Edition of the *Correspondence*. Smith advocates measures for increasing the public revenue without laying new burdens on the people: "The first is a repeal of all bounties upon exportation . . . our merchants ought not to complain if we refuse to tax ourselves any longer in order to support a few feeble and languishing branches of their commerce."[126] Thus, in equilibrium, where inputs and outputs have the composition that maximizes the desired growth of output, *each sector earns the ordinary profits of stock* (without the need for bounties). The duality between surplus and profit could hardly be more clearly expressed.

The Last Years

About two years after the publication of the *Wealth of Nations,* Smith was offered the preferment of being a commissioner of his Majesty's Customs in Scotland. This brought ease and affluence, but it probably hindered his finishing his projected tasks. He moved to Edinburgh in 1778, to take up office, and there remained for the rest of his life with his mother, and his beloved cousin, Jane Douglas, who now took charge. Then, in 1784, his mother died, and Jane Douglas followed her to the grave in 1788. Stewart, who knew whereof he wrote, tells us that:

They had been the objects of his affection for more than sixty years; and in their society he had enjoyed, from his infancy, all that he ever knew of the endearments of a family. He was now alone, and helpless. . . .[127]

Smith now declined rapidly. He had been in poor health, though still eager for the society of his remaining friends, as we see from a letter of February 8, 1788, published for the first time in the *Correspondence:*

Though nothing can be more tempting than the company you propose I should dine with to-morrow; yet the state of my health, the coldness of the weather, and my fear of bringing back some of my old complaints; by venturing to dine at so great a distance, oblige me to beg you would excuse me. It is a great mortification to me; but necessity must be submitted to.[128]

Smith died on July 17, 1790. A few days before his death, he gave orders that all his manuscripts, except the few posthumously published as essays, be destroyed.

The quantity and price relations of the classical system, as we would say today, were now set forth. Profit appeared as the dual of surplus, and long-run equilibrium would require that it be earned at a uniform rate throughout industry. The fundamental importance of agricultural surplus to all economic development had been given due credit, while the errors of physiocracy in attributing the creation of surplus wholly to agriculture had been removed.

Smith had replaced the archaic classes of the physiocrats—peasant and self-employed artisan (who owned his tools and his working capital)—by the significant classes of modern capitalism: propertyless wage earners and capitalists who owned and controlled the means of production. Smith, however, had provided no theory as to what determined the *level* of the profits which were earned at a uniform rate throughout industry. This was to be the great task of Ricardo.

Notes

1. Cited by Dugald Stewart in "Account of the Life and Writings of Adam Smith, LL.D.," in Joseph Black and James Hutton, eds., *Essays on Philosophical Subjects by the Late Adam Smith, LL.D.,* printed for T. Cadell Jun., and W. Davies (successors to Mr. Cadell), London, 1795, facsimile by University Microfilms, Ann Arbor, Michigan, 1967, p. ix.
2. David Ricardo, *Principles of Political Economy and Taxation,* John Murray, London, 1817. All our citations will be from Piero Sraffa, ed., *The Works and Correspondence of David Ricardo,* Cambridge University Press, 1951–73. For the present quotation, see Vol. I, p. 6.
3. Lord Robbins of Claremarket, *The Theory of Economic Development in the History of Economic Thought,* Macmillan, London, 1968, p. 9.
4. William Robert Scott, *Adam Smith as Student and Professor,* Glasgow University Publications, xlvi, 1937. Reprinted by A. M. Kelly, New York, 1965, pp. 7–8.
5. *Ibid.,* p. 18.
6. Lady Antonia Fraser, *Mary Queen of Scots,* Weidenfeld and Nicolson, London, 1969. Reprinted by Panther Books, London, 1970, pp. 399–429.

7. Ernest Campbell Mossner and Ian Simpson Ross, eds., *The Correspondence of Adam Smith* (The Glasgow Edition of the Works and Correspondence of Adam Smith, Vol. VI), Oxford at the Clarendon Press, 1977, p. vii.

8. John Rae, *Life of Adam Smith,* Macmillan, London, 1895. Reprinted with an introduction by Jacob Viner by A. M. Kelly, New York, 1965, p. 34.

9. Jacob Viner, "Guide to John Rae's Life of Adam Smith," in Rae, *Life of Adam Smith,* p. 5.

10. Stewart, "Account of the Life of Smith," p. xiii.

11. *Ibid*.

12. Smith, *Essays on Philosophical Subjects,* pp. 113–94.

13. Scott, *Adam Smith,* p. 46.

14. *Ibid.,* p. 51.

15. *Ibid.,* p. 56.

16. Stewart, "Account of the Life of Smith," p. lxxxi.

17. *Ibid*.

18. Scott, *Adam Smith,* p. 56. See also pp. 113–4.

19. Smith, Letter 70, *Correspondence,* p. 89.

20. Smith, *The Theory of Moral Sentiments,* Andrew Millar, London, 1759; D. D. Raphael and A. L. Macfie, eds. (The Glasgow Edition, Vol. I), Oxford, 1976.

21. Smith, *Lectures on Justice, Police, Revenue, and Arms, Delivered in the University of Glasgow by Adam Smith,* ed. Edwin Cannan, Oxford at the Clarendon Press, 1896; R. L. Meek, D. D. Raphael, and P. G. Stein, eds., *Lectures on Jurisprudence* (The Glasgow Edition, Vol. V), Oxford, 1978.

22. Smith, *An Inquiry into the Nature and Causes of the Wealth of Nations,* A. Strahan and T. Cadell, London, 1776. All our citations will be from R. H. Campbell, A. S. Skinner, and W. B. Todd, eds., The Glasgow Edition, Vol. II, Oxford, 1976, and will be given according to the original divisions, with the paragraph numbers of The Glasgow Edition. The equivalent page numbers of the Cannan edition, Modern Library, New York, 1937 will immediately follow in parentheses.

23. Cannan, "Introduction," to Smith, *Lectures on Justice and Arms,* p. xxii–xxiv.

24. *Ibid.,* p. xxviii.

25. Smith, *Lectures on Jurisprudence,* p. 498. In references to LJ(B), we shall first cite the page numbers of The Glasgow Edition, Vol. V, and then, in parentheses, the page numbers of Cannan, ed., *Lectures on Justice and Arms,* which in this case is (181).

26. *Ibid.,* p. 503 (191).

27. *Ibid.,* p. 508 (199).

28. *Ibid.,* pp. 513–14 (208–9).

29. *Ibid.,* p. 514 (210).

30. *Ibid.,* pp. 519–20 (220).

31. *Ibid.,* p. 521 (222).

32. *Ibid.,* pp. 522–26 (224–30).

33. *Ibid.,* p. 527 (233).

34. *Ibid.,* p. 530 (239).

35. *Ibid.,* p. 535 (246).

36. Smith, *Lectures on Jurisprudence,* p. 34; editors' italics. This is a reference to LJ(A).

37. *Ibid.,* p. 343; our italics.

38. *Ibid.,* p. 357.

39. *Ibid.,* p. 363.

40. Scott, *Adam Smith,* p. 317.

41. Cannan, "Introduction," p. xxxi.

42. Smith, "Early Draft," p. 562. In references to the "early Draft" we shall give first the page reference to The Glasgow Edition, Vol. V, and then the page of Scott, *Adam Smith,* in parentheses which in this case is (322).

43. *Ibid.,* p. 563 (326–7).

44. *Ibid.,* p. 564 (328).

45. *Ibid.,* p. 566 (331).

46. Scott, *Adam Smith,* p. 173.

47. Stewart, "Account of the Life of Smith," p. lii.

48. *Ibid.,* p. lii.

49. Sir Harold Nicholson, *The Age of Reason,* Constable, London, 1960; Panther Books, London, 1971, p. 297.

50. Smith, Letter 194, *Correspondence,* pp. 233–4.

51. Rae, *Life of Smith,* p. 192.

52. Smith, Letter 194, *Correspondence,* pp. 233–4.

53. Stewart, "Account of the Life of Smith," p. lvii.

54. Smith, Letter 82, *Correspondence,* pp. 101–2.

55. Stewart, "Account of the Life of Smith," p. ix.

56. Samuel Hollander, *The Economics of Adam Smith,* University of Toronto Press, 1973, p. 19.

57. Robbins, *An Essay on the Nature and Significance of Economic Science,* Macmillan, London, 1935, pp. 68–9; cited by Hollander, *The Economics of Smith,* p. 20.

58. Hollander, *The Economics of Smith,* p. 20, n. 53.

59. Robbins, *The Theory of Economic Development in the History of Economic Thought;* cited by Hollander, *The Economics of Smith,* p. 20, n. 64.

60. Hollander, *The Economics of Smith,* p. 307.

61. *Ibid.*

62. R. D. Collison Black, "Smith's Contribution in Historical Perspective," in Thomas Wilson and Andrew S. Skinner, eds., *The Market and the State, Essays in Honour of Adam Smith,* Oxford at the Clarendon Press, 1976, p. 61.

63. *Ibid.*

64. Hollander, *The Economics of Smith,* p. 155; Hollander's italics.

65. Smith, *Wealth of Nations,* I.vi.24 (54).

66. W. A. Eltis, "Adam Smith's Theory of Economic Growth," in Andrew S. Skinner and Thomas Wilson, eds., *Essays on Adam Smith,* Oxford at the Clarendon Press, 1975, p. 439.

67. Smith, *Wealth of Nations,* I.viii.22 (69).

68. *Ibid.,* I.viii.27 (73). See the whole passage, I.viii.15–I.viii.31 (68–74).

69. *Ibid.,* I.viii.28 (74).

70. *Ibid.*, I.viii.28–I.viii.45 (74–83).
71. *Ibid.*, I.xi.b.2 (146). See also I.xi.b.34–I.xi.b.41 (159–60).
72. *Ibid.*, I.xi.e.7 (163).
73. *Ibid.*, II.intro.1 (259).
74. *Ibid.*, II.intro.3 (260).
75. Eltis, "Adam Smith's Theory of Economic Growth," pp. 426–54.
76. Smith, *Wealth of Nations,* II.i.9–10 (263).
77. *Ibid.*, II.i.8–II.i.28 (263–7).
78. Hollander, *The Economics of Smith,* p. 95, n. 1; Hollander's italics. See, further, the literature cited there.
79. *Ibid.*, p. 105. Hollander's italics.
80. *Ibid.*, pp. 105–6.
81. R. M. Hartwell, "Comment," in *The Market and the State,* pp. 33–41.
82. Smith, *Wealth of Nations,* II.ii.1–II.ii.7 (270–1).
83. *Ibid.*, II.iii.1 (314).
84. *Ibid.*, II.iii.3 (315). The whole of chapter iii is relevant.
85. Eltis, "Adam Smith's Theory of Economic Growth," p. 434.
86. *Ibid.*, p. 435, n. 10.
87. Smith, *Wealth of Nations,* III.i.2 (357).
88. *Ibid.*, III.iv.5 (385).
89. *Ibid.*, IV.i.30 (413).
90. *Ibid.*, IV.iii.c.15 (464).
91. *Ibid.*, IV.vii.c.35 (566).
92. *Ibid.*, IV.vii.c.59 (577–8).
93. *Ibid.*, IV.vii.c.86 (593).
94. *Ibid.*, IV.vii.c.89 (596).
95. *Ibid.*, IV.ix.24 (636).
96. *Ibid.*, IV.ix.38 (642).
97. *Ibid.*, IV.ix.29 (638–9).
98. *Ibid.*, IV.ix.49 (650).
99. *Ibid.*, V.ii.c.7–27 (782–8).
100. *Ibid.*, V.ii.e.10 (795–6).
101. *Ibid.*, V.ii.f.1–14 (798–803).
102. *Ibid.*, V.ii.i.1 (815).
103. *Ibid.*, V.ii.i.3 (817).
104. *Ibid.*, V.ii.k.5 (822).
105. *Ibid.*, V.ii.k.6–9, 43–4 (823–4, 838–9).
106. *Ibid.*, V.iii.1 (859).
107. *Ibid.*, V.iii.53 (879).
108. *Ibid.*, V.iii.54 (879–80).
109. Andrew S. Skinner, "Adam Smith: an Economic Interpretation of History," in *Essays on Adam Smith,* p. 154.
110. Stewart, cited by Skinner, "Adam Smith: an Economic Interpretation," p. 154.
111. Joseph Cropsey, "Adam Smith and Political Philosophy," in *Essays on Adam Smith,* p. 151.

112. Ronald L. Meek, *Studies in the Labour Theory of Value*, 2nd ed., Lawrence and Wishart, London, 1973, p. 47.
113. Meek, *Turgot on Progress, Sociology, and Economics*, Cambridge University Press, 1973, p. 33. Meek's italics.
114. Smith, *Wealth of Nations*, I.vi.5 (48).
115. *Ibid.*, I.vi.6 (48).
116. Hollander, *The Economics of Smith*, p. 318. Hollander's italics.
117. Smith, *Wealth of Nations*, I.vii.5 (55).
118. *Ibid.*, I.vii.6 (56). See further I.vii.30 (62).
119. *Ibid.*, I.x.a.1 (99).
120. *Ibid.*, I.x.b.43 (115).
121. *Ibid.*, I.x.b.34 (111).
122. *Ibid.*
123. *Ibid.*
124. *Ibid.*, I.x.c.1–63 (118–43).
125. *Ibid.*, IV. v.a.2 (472).
126. Smith, Letter 203, *Correspondence*, p. 245.
127. Stewart, "Account of the Life of Smith," p. lxxxvii.
128. Smith, Letter 303, *Correspondence*, p. 334.

4

The Full Flowering: Nineteenth Century Classical English Political Economy

> Mr. Ricardo seemed as if he had dropped from another planet.
>
> LORD BROUGHAM[1]

> It is not worth our while to stay to describe the way in which the inner-circle Ricardians, James Mill, De Quincey, and McCulloch, handled Ricardo's theory of value and the spurious problems it created. But it will be convenient . . . to consider with the utmost brevity some essentials of the doctrine of Ricardo's only great follower, Karl Marx.
>
> JOSEPH A. SCHUMPETER[2]

The great contribution of David Ricardo (1772–1823) was a theory of the *rate* of profit. Smith had understood the tendency for profits to become uniform in the long run in competitive industry; but he had no theory as to what governed the level at which they would settle. Smith had been unclear as to the nature of rent and its role in the theory of distribution; Ricardo gave a precise analysis of the division of the total produce of society into rents, wages, and profit.

The primary sources for the life of Ricardo are, in most respects, much richer than those for Adam Smith. Thanks, in part, to the dramatic discovery of a locked metal box in July 1943 at Raheny, county Dublin, we possess a remarkably extensive and complete Ricardo correspondence, so that Sraffa could write:

It is perhaps unique in economic literature for the writings, letters and speeches of one thinker to have such unity of subject matter (as is the case with Ricardo) that, although his works and correspondence are extant almost complete, they admit of publication virtually in their entirety as being all of them of interest to the economist.[3]

In one way, however, the biographical situation resembles that for Smith: once again there is a short Memoir, in this case written by one of Ricardo's brothers (probably Moses Ricardo[4]) upon which virtually all subsequent biography (until the writings of Piero Sraffa) has been based. Indeed, as Sraffa has remarked, "Every subsequent biographer, from McCulloch onwards, has drawn almost exclusively upon it for the earlier part of Ricardo's life."[5]

Unfortunately, unlike Dugald Stewart's Memoir of Adam Smith, the brief sketch of Ricardo's life is both restrained and defensive in tone. It begins with the statement that, "In the early history of Mr. Ricardo's life there is nothing, the relation of which would be likely to excite either attention or interest."[6] After this discouraging beginning, some hint of what is really at issue begins to show in a passage in which the author points out that Ricardo did not receive a classical education:

It is not true, however, as has been more than insinuated, that Mr. Ricardo was of very low origin, and that he had been wholly denied the advantages of education; a reflection upon his father which he by no means deserved. The latter was always in affluent circumstances, most respectably connected, and both able and willing to afford his children all the advantages which the line of life for which they were destined appeared to require.[7]

This passage, and the whole sketch of Ricardo's life from which it comes, became more intelligible in the light of facts discovered in the present century. It appears from hitherto unpublished material, which was printed for the first time by Sraffa, that Moses Ricardo had been engaged in collecting material for a memoir of Ricardo until he was discouraged by Ricardo's children, who did not wish the family history dug up since (as was remarked by a contemporary), "They are now people of fortune and of some consequence, and landed gentry. . . ."[8] It must be remembered that in the early nineteenth century, before the passing of Parliamentary Reform, when the bourgeoisie was only beginning its great struggle for power in England, a newly landed family had many reasons for wishing to use the entrée which its landed estates bestowed upon it, to enter the still dominant landlord class. They could not be expected to look with favor upon the publishing of their great father's mercantile activities, however brilliant, or honorable, these might have been.

Thus, we owe to the present-day researches of Piero Sraffa, aided by the "ready cooperation"[9] of Ricardo's modern descendants, the information that Ricardo's family left Spain and emigrated to Amsterdam in the late seventeenth, or early eighteenth, century where they were established in the Sephardic community. Ricardo's grandfather "was a stock broker and in that capacity took part in the drawing up of new rules for dealing in options on the Amsterdam Bourse in 1739."[10] Ricardo's father, Abraham, was also a stockbroker in Amsterdam, but emigrated to London where the Memoir notes that:

being a man of good natural abilities, and of the strictest honour and integrity, [he] made a corresponding progress; acquiring a respectable fortune, and possessing considerable influence within the circle in which he moved.[11]

This was no exaggeration: Sraffa notes that Abraham Ricardo "at his death left a fortune which was valued for probate at £45,000." [12]

David Ricardo's mother, Abigail Delvalle, came of a family long established in the Sephardic community in England, but their fortune disappeared around 1811, and eventually "most of the Delvalle uncles and aunts came to be a charge on Ricardo . . ." [13]

Young David Ricardo was sent to Holland for part of his education, which is not surprising, given the importance of that country as a financial center, and the fact that much of his father's business was connected with it. Fairness of dealing, and a scrupulous concern for giving due weight to an opponent's arguments, intellectual honesty, and the love of truth, were always to be outstanding characteristics of the mature Ricardo. Perhaps it is not wholly fanciful to see the influence upon his natural disposition of a Dutch mercantile culture famous for its honesty and careful dealing.

The novelist, Maria Edgeworth, writing from Ricardo's estate, Gatcomb Park, a couple of years before his death, noted that:

We had delightful conversation, both on deep and shallow subjects. Mr. Ricardo, with a very composed manner, has a continual life of mind, and starts perpetually new game in conversation. I never argued or discussed a question with any person who argues more fairly or less for victory and more for truth. He gives full weight to every argument brought against him, and seems not to be on any side of the question for one instant longer than the conviction of his mind on that side. It seems quite indifferent to him whether you find the truth, or whether he finds it, provided it be found. [14]

The Rise of the Capitalist Class

Adam Smith had been the last major figure of classical political economy to be wholly a man of the eighteenth century Enlightenment.* It was in many ways an intellectually progressive circle, but its base was in land, and in the liberal professions which served (as did the arts) the landed class. Smith had analyzed brilliantly the emergent industrial capitalism of his day. But he was not a merchant, and it would never have occurred to him to see the great issues of policy through the eyes of tradesmen, who, he felt, neither were nor ought to be the rulers of mankind.

By the time David Ricardo began to write, on the other hand, members of the capitalist class were making their bid to become the rulers of Britain. And Ricardo, for all his election to Brooks's Club in 1818 at the proposal of the

_____
*Marx, as we shall see, spent his childhood and early youth in the last rays of the German Enlightenment.

two Whig Magnificos, Lord Essex and Lord Holland,[15] and for all his parliamentary distinction and landed estates, had risen to political, intellectual, and social prominence out of the capitalist class. He was one of the first great leaders of British opinion of whom this could be said. And, of course, it was said.

It is important, therefore, to see clearly in what sense Ricardo supported this new class, and felt impelled to defend its interests, and in what sense he did not. Schumpeter remarks with very proper disapproval that some people have "interpreted Ricardo as a representative of the 'monied interest' and as inspired by a 'hatred' of the landowning class."[16] Schumpeter's position on this matter has received massive support from the work of Piero Sraffa. Sraffa, having quietly demolished in detail the argument that Ricardo's writings on currency supported a "bear" interest with which he was supposedly identified,[17] sums up his findings:

> We can now evaluate the relative importance of the main types of property in which Ricardo had invested: landed estates, £275,000; sums lent on mortgage, £200,000; French stocks, £140,000. This distribution, which remained virtually unaltered between 1819 and 1823, illustrates Ricardo's statement in Parliament that 'it would puzzle a good accountant to make out in which side his interest predominated' with respect to currency policy.[18]

Ricardo began at the age of fourteen to work for his father on the Stock Exchange, and this meant that he did not have the classical education of men like Adam Smith.* But, for all that, he never acquired any compulsive devotion to the City (meaning London's financial district and its life). Like Richard Cantillon, he had no interest in making money for its own sake, and he retired as soon as he felt his fortune made. Cantillon, of course, had roots in the old county families, but Ricardo, who did not have such roots, proceeded to grow them for himself. Sraffa remarks that, "Ricardo . . . brought up his sons to be country gentlemen, and as for himself had no craving for the bustle of the City and viewed financial success as a means of retirement into the country, to the quiet pursuit of his 'favourite science'."[19] He quotes Ricardo, writing in a letter when he first went to his newly acquired estate, Gatcomb Park: "I believe that in this sweet place I shall not sigh after the Stock Exchange and its enjoyments."[20]

But, however little he wanted to lead a life devoted to business, there was a rising new class in Ricardo's day in Britain, and *as a political economist,* he

---

* And later, of Karl Marx, who was a deep scholar of the Greek and Latin classics, as well as of ancient and modern philosophy and the history of letters.

had a firm opinion about it. Ricardo always assumed that the landlords, as a class, spent the surplus which they extracted as rent on high living, while the class of industrial capitalists, as a whole, saved the surplus they extracted as profits and devoted it to capital accumulation. In common with other classical economists, Ricardo saw the key importance in his day of economic development. And the pace of development depended, on his assumptions, upon how the surplus was distributed between the landlords and capitalists. Workers, in any event, got a subsistence wage, but it need not be bare physical subsistence, and might be expected to be higher in a growing economy.

Since growth depended on the division of surplus between rent and capitalists' profit, "Ricardo, rightly for his time, regards the capitalist mode of production as the most advantageous for the creation of wealth."[21] And "Ricardo's conception is, on the whole, in the interests of the *industrial bourgeoisie*, only *because*, and *in so far as*, their interests coincide with that of production or the productive development of human labour. Where the bourgeoisie comes into conflict with this, he is just as *ruthless* towards it as he is at other times towards the proletariat and the aristocracy."[22]

To be understood, Ricardo's carefully circumscribed defense of the capitalist interest must be set against the stormy background of Corn Law agitation. It needs to be remembered that during the years when Ricardo was writing, from 1810 to 1823:

there was a good deal of popular discontent and government repression. Only about two per cent of the adult male population had the right to vote for their MPs, and the middle classes of the great industrial towns of the north were not entitled to send members to Parliament. . . . There was also a great deal of economic misery in the country, which was made worse when the Corn Laws of 1815 prohibited the importation of grain in order to keep up the price of corn. . . .[23]

The manufacturers wanted cheap corn, to keep wages down and profits up, but they were without representation in a parliament dominated by the landed aristocracy. As it happened, the Corn Laws survived the Reform Act of 1832, despite the Duke of Wellington's opinion that parliamentary reform would leave Britain at the mercy of "lawyers, Physicians, and shopkeepers."[24] In the end it took the Irish Famine to sound the final doom of the Corn Laws, which were at last repealed in 1846, with the Duke of Wellington now giving its marching orders to a reluctant House of Lords. David Ricardo had been dead for 23 years.

As the urbane humanism of Adam Smith gave way to the austere logical rigor of Ricardo, the picture of classical political economy as being above all a theory of the extraction, distribution, allocation, and accumulation of social surplus under capitalist production, became yet more clearly focused. Ricardo, however, has not always been looked at from this point of view. For example, those interested may read with illumination a number of passages of sharp criticism of Ricardo in the work of distinguished neoclassics such as Frank H. Knight, and Joseph A. Schumpeter, where Ricardo is taken to task on the grounds that his theory of the distribution of the total produce of society among social classes was not derived from allocation theory of the neoclassical type, showing factor prices as equal to the factor's marginal product; but rather showed profits, for instance, emerging as a reflection of surplus. Against this, Frank Knight insisted that "a sound distribution theory is hardly more than a corollary or footnote to an exposition of the mechanism by which resources are apportioned among different uses. . . ."[25] And Schumpeter wrote that production was nothing but "a combination, by purchase, of requisite and scarce services. In this process each of the requisite and scarce services secures a price and the determination of these prices is all that distribution or income formation fundamentally consists in."[26]

Commenting on these views, Hollander notes that they might be to the point if it could be shown that Ricardo was a neoclassical allocation theorist. However, "That this is so is by no means certain. To the extent that Ricardo was in fact developing an alternative 'basic theory'—whereby distribution and value are treated *separately*—the view of Knight and Schumpeter according to which his approach is 'non-scientific' and in error is seriously misleading."[27] In fact, Ricardo, taking over the classical tradition in the form in which he had inherited it from Adam Smith, was critically developing an essential part of that tradition, the first coherent theory of the rate of profit.

The Rate of Profit—Prelude to the Ricardo-Malthus Correspondence

Ricardo's earliest explorations of the notions of surplus and profit are to be found in his correspondence with his intimate friend, Thomas Robert Malthus (1766–1834), which began in 1811, immediately after their first meeting. Nowhere could one find a stronger case (hardly even in the letters of Léon Walras) for the view that private correspondence, and other biographical sources, can be of vital importance in the writing of intellectual history. As was remarked by Lord Keynes, "This friendship will live in history on account of its having given rise to the most important literary correspondence in the whole development of Political Economy."[28]

When they met, Ricardo was just beginning to publish, while Malthus's

Essay on Population, whose first edition appeared in 1798, had made him a passionately debated author throughout the country. Unlike the Marquis de Mirabeau, however, Malthus was never to become an uncritical disciple, and the principal value of his contributions to the correspondence, from the point of view of the core of classical theory, probably lies in the way his criticisms continually force Ricardo to state his position more precisely.

Sir William Petty, it will be recalled, sought a par between land and labor. Since he saw land in terms of its annual produce, one might say he sought a par between corn and labor. He seems to have had some inkling that the surplus could be measured either as a quantity of corn or as a quantity of labor. The physiocrats saw surplus only in agriculture, but they did not normally express it literally as a quantity of corn: confounding quantity with price relations, they express it as "revenue," i.e., in terms of money. Smith, who saw surplus throughout industry, and understood its dual, profit, never developed a fully articulated theory as to how surplus should be measured, or the rate of profit determined. David Ricardo, in his time, tried out both the possibilities hinted at by Petty: he considered the implications of measuring surplus, and therefore profit, in terms of physical quantities of produce; and he also considered measuring surplus in terms of quantities of labor embodied. The first approach appears fairly early in his correspondence.

From 1810, when the surviving correspondence begins, until 1813, Ricardo is almost exclusively concerned with monetary questions. Then there appear the first of the long series of letters dealing with profits, and the evaluation of surplus. In a letter written to Malthus on August 17, 1813, for example, Ricardo, in speaking of profits, uses the phrase "my theory."[29] Before Sraffa's edition, these letters of 1813 had been attributed to 1810, with the effect, as Sraffa remarks, "of advancing by three years the formation of Ricardo's theory of profits."[30]

From the letters of 1813, however, everyone is agreed that Ricardo was deeply concerned with maintaining the claim that the profits of the farmer regulate the profits of all other trades. To see the overwhelming policy importance of this claim to Ricardo, it is essential to understand the reasons for his opposition to laws restricting the free import of corn. If foreign corn was excluded, and population continued to grow, progressively poorer parcels of English land would have to be taken into cultivation. Competition for the better land among capitalist farmers would then enable the landlords to extract as rent sums representing the extra productivity of the superior land. Progressively more of what had been the profits of the farmer would be extracted as rent. Since Ricardo believed that the landlords consumed the surplus and that capitalist farmers used it for accumulation, this process would put a brake upon the progress of society. Moreover, he argued correctly that the rising costs of producing the subsistence wage would force down the profits in all other trades, thus inhibiting the accumulation of capital. Ricardo, following Smith, assumed that in the long run competition would ensure a uniform rate of profit. He further believed, however, that he could prove that farming profits were independent of influences from the industrial sector which, on the other hand, would find its profit inexorably adjusted to that ruling in agriculture.

In this context the pure corn model may be seen as a brilliant simplification. Ricardo (rightly) believed that the things left out did not substantially affect his conclusions. In a model which has both agricultural and industrial sectors, suppose that the agricultural sector produces only corn and uses only corn as an input. (There are no plows!) Suppose, on the other hand, that the industrial sector uses both manufactured inputs and corn. The rate of profit in farming is then the ratio of corn surplus net of rent to necessary corn input. Observe that this is a pure number, being a ratio of quantities of the same thing, and therefore unaffected by changes in the relative prices of other commodities, in particular, of industrial commodities. In this model, therefore, competition would, in the long run, make the rate of profit in industry equal to that in farming. Since the profits of the farmer would be independent of the fluctuations of relative price, the profit in industry would have to move into line with that in agriculture.

As we shall shortly see in our survey of the Ricardo-Malthus correspondence, Malthus was to concentrate his attacks on the simplifications built into this pure corn model of profits. Agriculture requires manufactured inputs (plows, etc.) and the real wage has manufactured components: clothes, furniture, soap, etc. Now, Ricardo never denied these facts, and indeed often refers to the existence of manufactured necessities, i.e., manufactured components of the real wage. He had, however, reason to believe that the admission of these complications would not destroy (though they would necessarily complicate) his theory. The point is this: Ricardo believed that, simply because of the scarcity of first-rate land, agriculture was the unique branch of production which operated under conditions of increasing cost (diminishing returns to land). Broadly speaking, industry, on the other hand, could be assumed to operate under conditions of constant cost. Hence, as population rose and demand for necessities increased, *manufactured* necessities could be supplied in increased quantities at constant prices. *Agricultural* necessities, on the contrary, could only be supplied at rising prices. Thus, the rising real wage (reflecting the rising costs of subsistence) would be overwhelmingly the result of rising agricultural prices—exactly the result of the simple corn model. Malthus's criticisms of the latter, however, progressively drove Ricardo to seek a theory of value: a theory, that is, of relative prices.

The Early Correspondence

It has been suggested by Piero Sraffa that the pure corn model of profits was probably Ricardo's position in the lost "papers on the profits of capital" of March, 1814,[31] and that this continued to be his position up to and including the *Essay on the Influence of a Low Price of Corn on the Profits of Stock,*[32] which appeared about February 24, 1815. The most recent statement of this position is by John Eatwell[33] in a discussion with Samuel Hollander.[34]

Ricardo and Malthus did not, of course, set out their arguments in terms of formal models, in the manner characteristic of modern theory. Indeed, much of the argument in the correspondence revolves around special situations, especially in the case of Malthus. As early as August 17, 1813 the cause of changes in the rate of profits is already being described by Ricardo, writing to Malthus, as "the question between us."[35] Ricardo admits that for a long period, since the commencement of the Napoleonic Wars:

> there has been an increased rate of profit, but it has been accompanied with such decided improvements of agriculture both here and abroad,—for the French Revolution was exceedingly favorable to the increased production of food, that it is perfectly reconcileable to my theory. My conclusion is that there has been a rapid increase of Capital which has been prevented from showing itself in a low rate of interest by new facilities in the production of food.[36]

By March 8, 1814, in any event, Ricardo is writing to his friend Hutches Trower:*

> that in short it is the profits of the farmer which regulate the profits of all other trades,—and as the profits of the farmer must necessarily decrease with every augmentation of Capital employed on the land, provided no improvements be at the same time made in husbandry, all other profits must diminish and therefore the rate of interest must fall. To this proposition Mr. Malthus does not agree.[38]

Although Ricardo is quite clear from the beginning about the dominant role of agricultural profits, he nowhere explicitly states the basis on which this must rest in the case of the pure corn model, namely, that input and output are

---

* Sraffa remarks of Hutches Trower (1777–1835), who was a stock broker, like Ricardo, that "he is only remembered because of this correspondence."[37]

both corn. "The rational foundation of the principle of the determining role of the profits of agriculture," Sraffa remarks, ". . . is never explicitly stated by Ricardo." [39] Sraffa adds that, "The nearest that Ricardo comes to an explicit statement on these lines is in a striking passage in a letter of June, 1814; 'The rate of profit and of interest must depend on the proportion of the consumption necessary to such production.' " [40] Significantly enough, Ricardo continues to Malthus, in the letter just cited, "This is a repetition you will say of the old story, and I might have spared you the trouble of reading at 200 miles distance what I had so often stated to you as my opinion before, but you have set me off, and must now abide the consequences." [41]

Perhaps stronger (though indirect) confirmation that Ricardo was thinking simply in terms of corn at this stage is to be found in a letter to Malthus of July 25, 1814. Here Ricardo writes that, "the price of all commodities must increase if the price of corn be increased." [42] This supposition, which was that of Adam Smith, is, of course, flatly inconsistent with the labor theory of value adopted in Ricardo's later work. Malthus eventually drove Ricardo out of the pure corn model and landed him in the problem of "value." In terms of the labor theory of value, Ricardo was to say in his later work that agricultural profits govern those of other trades because the prices of agricultural products rise (due to increased labor cost with less fertile lands) while all other prices (where labor cost is unchanged) remain constant. Certainly Malthus, in a letter written to Ricardo only eleven days after that just cited, appears to have interpreted his friend as holding a corn theory of the rate of profit, although Malthus points out that it may only be a rough approximation: "In no case of production, is the produce exactly of the same nature as the capital advanced. Consequently we can never properly refer to a material rate of produce. . . . It is not the particular profits or rate of produce upon the land which determines the general profits of stock and the interest of money." [43]

Then Ricardo wrote to Malthus, from Gatcomb Park, on September 16, 1814: "I agree with you that when capital is scanty compared with the means of employing it, from whatever cause arising, profits will be high," and added, "I am led to believe that the state of the cultivation of the land is almost the only great permanent cause. There are other circumstances which are attended with temporary effects of more or less duration, and frequently operate partially on particular trades. The state of production from the land compared with the means necessary to make it produce operates on all, and is alone lasting in its effects." [44] Malthus, in his reply of October 9, 1814, appears initially sympathetic to the corn theory, for he writes:

You seem to think that the state of production from the land, compared with the means necessary to make it produce, is almost the sole cause which regulates the profits of stock, and the means of advantageously employing capital. After what I have written on the subject of food and population I can hardly be supposed not to allow a very great effect to so very great a cause.[45]

He still has reservations, however:

It appears to me that nearly all which can be safely advanced respecting the dependence of profits on the state of the land is, that the facility of acquiring food, and particularly the possession of a great quantity of good land is the main cause of high profits, . . . and that the difficulty of acquiring food is the main cause of low profits. . . .[46]

In differentiating his own point of view (to which a ratio of *values* is essential), Malthus does not fully accept Ricardo's produce ratio as determining the rate of profit: "It is not the *quantity* of produce compared with the expenses of production that determines profits (which I think is your position) but the exchangeable value or money price of that produce, compared with the money expense of production."[47] Ricardo, replying on October 23, 1814, appraises with some irony the apparent differences between them: "You, instead of allowing *the facility of obtaining food to be almost the sole cause of high profits,* think it may be safely said to be the main cause, and also a difficulty of acquiring food the main cause of low profits."[48] And again, on December 18 of that year, Ricardo writes to Malthus: "accumulation of capital has a tendency to lower profits. Why? because every accumulation is attended with increased difficulty in obtaining food, unless it is accompanied with improvements in agriculture; in which case it has no tendency to diminish profits."[49]

Ricardo nevertheless admits quite freely in the letter just quoted that the rate of profit may also be affected by the prices of the manufactured wage goods: "I admit at the same time that commerce, or machinery may produce an abundance and cheapness of commodities, and if they affect the price of those commodities on which the wages of labor are expended they will so far raise profits . . ."[50] Evidently, Ricardo was as well aware as Malthus that the admission of manufactured commodities into the wage modifies the pure corn model.

The Essay on Profits

About February 24, 1815, Ricardo published his famous contribution to the public debate about the proposed restrictions upon the importation of corn, the *Essay on the Influence of a Low Price of Corn on the Profits of Stock.* Here we are told that:

Profits of stock fall because land equally fertile cannot be obtained, and through the whole progress of society, profits are regulated by the difficulty or facility of procuring food. This is a principle of great importance, and has been almost overlooked in the writings of Political Economists. They appear to think that profits of stock can be raised by commercial causes, independently of the supply of food.[51]

In the *Essay,* calculations are expressed in corn.* As Sraffa remarks, "The numerical examples in the *Essay* reflect this approach; and particularly in the well-known Table which shows the effects of an increase of capital, both capital and the 'neat produce' are expressed in corn, and thus the profit per cent is calculated without need to mention price."[52] As Sraffa has pointed out, Malthus took the "Corn Model" aspect of Ricardo's *Essay* very seriously, choosing to attack just this feature of the work. Thus, Malthus wrote to Francis Horner† on March 14, 1815:

On the supposition which is generally allowed, that in a rich and progressive country, corn naturally rises compared with manufactured and foreign commodities, will it not follow that, as the real capital of the farmer which is advanced does not consist merely in raw produce, but in ploughs wagons threshing machines etc: and in the tea sugar clothes &c.: used by his labourers, if with a less quantity of raw produce he can purchase the same quantity of these commodities, a greater quantity of raw produce will remain for the farmer and landlord, and afford a greater surplus from the land for the maintainance and encouragement of the manufacturing and mercantile classes.[53]

He continues in the same letter:

The fault of Mr. Ricardo's Table which is curious, is that the advances of the farmer instead of being calculated in corn, should be calculated either in the actual materials of which the capital consists, or in money which is the best representation of a variety of commodities.[54]

Pressure from Malthus was obliging Ricardo to find a theory of prices—a theory of relative values—in which to express his theory of profits. Thus, for all its concentration on corn, hints of the labor theory of value, which was used by Ricardo in the *Principles,* can be seen here and there in the *Essay.* Sraffa describes how this labor value theme runs parallel with the corn theory:

Parallel with this ran another theme in the development of Ricardo's thought. At first he had subscribed to the generally accepted view that a rise in corn prices, through its effect upon wages, would be followed by a rise of all other prices. He had not regarded this view as inconsistent with his theory of profit so long as the latter had

---

* Strictly, in wheat. In Ricardo's England "corn" was a normal term for wheat.
† Francis Horner (1778–1817) was one of the founders of the *Edinburgh Review* and the chairman of the Bullion Committee of 1810.

been expressed in its primitive 'agricultural' form. The conflict between the two however was bound to become apparent in the degree to which he groped towards a more
general form of his theory, since the supposed general rise of prices obscured the
simple relation of the rise of wages to the fall of profits.[55]

Sraffa goes on to remark that, "Already in the *Essay on Profits,* although
his general presentation is still in the 'agricultural' form, he repudiates the accepted view in a footnote."[56] Here Ricardo had written, "It has been thought
that the price of corn regulates the prices of all other things. This appears to
me to be a mistake."[57] It will be recalled that we have used Ricardo's
previous endorsement of the position that the price of corn would govern all
other prices as evidence that he could not, while holding this view, have yet
thought through the implications of a coherent labor theory of value. Sraffa
adds that, "Elsewhere in the *Essay,* in connection with this question, there are
passages which foreshadow his full theory of value and already link it with
the theory of profits."[58] He cites Ricardo:

The exchangeable value of all commodities rises as the difficulties of their production
increase. If then new difficulties occur in the production of corn, from more labour
being necessary, whilst no more labour is required to produce gold, silver, cloth, linen
&c. the exchangeable value of corn will necessarily rise, as compared with those
things.[59]

And, again, further on in the *Essay on Profits:*

A fall in the price of corn, in consequence of improvements in agriculture or of importation, will lower the exchangeable value of corn only,—the price of no other commodity will be affected. If, then, the price of labour falls, which it must do when the
price of corn is lowered, the real profits of all descriptions must rise.[60]

The wage rate falls, so profit rises.

The Later Correspondence

Fighting against the proposed Corn Laws with all he had at hand, Ricardo was
bringing up new forces. The situation in the country was indeed desperate.
Writing to Malthus from London on March 9, 1815, Ricardo told his friend:

The opposition to the bill is more formidable than I expected, but they appear so determined in the house of Commons that I suppose it will finally pass. I regret that the
people should have proceeded to acts of riot and outrage. I am too much a friend to
good order to wish to succeed through such means, besides that I am persuaded that
they hurt rather than promote the object which they and I have in view.[61,*]

* Sraffa notes that there were riots in London on March 6, 7, and 8, and that the Bill was passed
in the House of Commons on March 10.

In this very letter Ricardo is wrestling with problems which bear on the labor-value approach to prices:

I would indeed rather modify what I have said concerning the stationary state of the prices of commodities, under all variations in the price of corn. . . . I made no allowance for the altered value of raw material in all manufactured goods; they would I think be subject to a variation in price not on account of increased or diminished wages, but on account of the rise or fall in the price of the raw produce which enters into their composition and which in some commodities cannot be inconsiderable.[62]

This shows Ricardo working on the relations between his (corn) theory of profits and his emerging (labor value) theory of relative prices. Malthus had persuaded Ricardo of the necessity of a theory of value—of relative prices—to supplement his theory of distribution (the corn theory) and Ricardo was now providing it. For instance, on April 21, 1815, Ricardo is insisting to Malthus that:

It appears to me that my table is applicable to all cases in which the relative price of corn rises from more labour being required to produce it, and under no other circumstances can there be a rise, however great the demand may be, unless commodities fall in value from less labour being required for their production.[63]

The whole argument of the letter is in labor-value terms. Certainly, this is how Malthus read it, in writing his opposition, on May 5, 1815: ". . . I cannot help thinking that you are fundamentally wrong in measuring the rate of profits by the facility of production. For what in fact is meant by facility of production? It is that a day's labour instead of producing two measures of corn, cloth and cotton will produce four."[64]

Things are now moving rapidly towards the writing of what was to be Ricardo's definitive statement of his labor theory of value: the *Principles*. Already in a letter to the French economist, Jean-Baptiste Say,* of August 18, 1815, Ricardo is saying of his *Essay on Profits* (a copy of which he had sent to Say) that, "Mr . Mill wishes me to write it over again more at large. I fear the undertaking exceeds my power."[65] We are thus alerted to the commencement of discussions on what was to become the manuscript of the *Principles*. In the development of this work, another of Ricardo's correspondents, James Mill,† becomes noteworthy. Throughout the period up to the completion of Ricardo's great work in 1817, Mill is to be found continually encouraging his

---

* Jean-Baptiste Say (1767–1832), author of the *Traite d'Èconomie Politique* (1803) and other works, met Ricardo at Gatcomb Park in 1814, and in Paris in 1817 and 1822, and corresponded.
† James Mill (1773–1836), Ricardo's intimate friend from 1810 on, was author of a *History of British India,* and contributor to the reviews. Mill's eldest son was the economist and philosopher, John Stuart Mill.

friend, while Ricardo equally often expresses his doubts of ever succeeding. It begins on August 23, 1815, when Mill writes to Ricardo, ". . . my friendship for you, for mankind, and for science, all prompt me to give you no rest, till you are plunged over head and ears in political economy." [66]

Ricardo replies a week later, "If you could witness the small progress which I make in writing on the subject which I have most considered you would be convinced of your error. . . ." [67] But the determined Mill is nevertheless writing to Ricardo on October 10 of that year, demanding "some account of the progress you have been making in your book. I now consider you as fairly pledged to that task." [68] Ricardo, struggling away, significantly comments to Mill on December 30 that, "I know I shall be soon stopped by the word price. . . ." [69] As Sraffa has observed, Ricardo is now facing "the necessity for a general solution of the problem. . . ." [70] As he wrote to his old friend, Malthus, on February 7, 1816, "If I could overcome the obstacles in the way of giving a clear insight into the origin and law of relative or exchangeable value I should have gained half the battle." [71] As early as April 28 of that year Malthus was to write, expressing the feeling that Ricardo had swerved a little from the right course by "determining all prices by labour. . . ." [72] Labor values, however, were to be the best approximation Ricardo could find. Thus, he wrote to Malthus to tell him of the virtual completion of his manuscript on January 3, 1817: ". . . I have resolutely persevered till I have committed every thing to paper that was floating in my mind. There are a few points on which there is a shadow of difference between my present and my past opinions, but they are not those on which we could not agree." [73]

Praising Ricardo's decision to use the labor theory of value despite its shortcomings, Mill told him, commenting on the manuscript of the *Principles,* in a letter of November, 1816, "Your explanation of the general principle that quantity of labour is the cause and measure of exchangeable value, excepting in the cases which you except, is both satisfactory, and clear." [74]

Ricardo of the Principles

By the time the *Principles of Political Economy and Taxation* first appeared in 1817, [75] Ricardo was adopting a clearly labor-value approach to the characterization of surplus. Returning to another tradition with roots in Petty and Cantillon, he was expressing surplus in terms of embodied labor: the total labor embodied in output minus the total labor embodied in the necessary inputs. For this purpose, Ricardo proceeded in the *Principles* to translate all inputs into the number of hours of labor they represented, and likewise translated outputs into a number of hours of embodied labor. He had been reading the *Wealth of Nations,* however, and the role he assigned to embodied labor cannot be understood without some analysis of his position vis à vis Adam Smith.

Ricardo begins his chapter "On Value" by sorting out his differences from Smith. In his famous example of deer and beaver hunters, Smith had argued that it was only in an early and rude state of society that products would exchange in proportion to the labor time embodied in them. "In this state of things, the whole produce of labour belongs to the labourer; . . . [whereas as] soon as stock has accumulated in the hands of particular persons, [these latter will demand a profit for the use of the stock, so that] the value which the workmen add to the materials therefore, resolves itself in this case into two parts, of which the one pays their wages, the other the profits of their employer upon the whole stock of materials and wages which he advanced." [76] For Smith, the existence of *wages,* of a payment to labor less than simply the value of its whole product, seemed to destroy the validity of a labor-embodied theory of value. Not so for Ricardo. Of his historic chapter "On Value" Marx was to write:

In the style which runs through the whole of his inquiry, Ricardo begins his book by stating that the determination of the value of commodities by labour-time is *not* incompatible with *wages,* in other words with the varying compensation paid for that labour-time or that quantity of labour. From the very outset, he turns against Smith's confusion between the determination of the value of commodities by the relative *quantity of labour* required for their production and the *value of labour* (or the compensation paid to the labourer). [77]

Ricardo, insisting that Adam Smith "so accurately defined the original source of exchangeable value," [78] stoutly denied that this definition holds, as Smith had believed, only for the early and rude state of society before the accumulation of stock and the appropriation of land. After all, if the existence of capital as such were to interfere with products being exchanged in proportion to the labor embodied, it could do so even in the society of hunters, where *some* capital, "though possibly made and accumulated by the hunter himself, would be necessary to enable him to kill his game." [79] And so the value of the deer and beaver would be regulated "not solely by the time and labour necessary to their destruction, but also by the time and labour necessary for providing the hunter's capital. . . ." [80]

Most important of all, the later division of society into social classes could not upset the validity of the analysis of value: "all the implements necessary to kill the beaver and deer might belong to one class of men, and labour employed in their destruction might be furnished by another class; still their comparative prices would be in proportion to the actual labour bestowed, both on the formation of the capital, and on the destruction of the animals."[81]

Sraffa remarks that, "It has come to be a widely accepted opinion about Ricardo that in subsequent editions he steadily retreated under pressure of his critics from the theory of value presented in edition 1."[82] Since what Lord Robbins has called the "masterly and illuminating"[83] refutation of this claim in Sraffa's "Introduction" to Ricardo's *Principles,* and the new evidence first presented there, little need be said. It will suffice to point out that, in Ricardo, the labor theory of value does not mean that the only cost of production is labor. Since Ricardo never held this view, there could be no question of his retreating from it. It is enough to quote Ricardo's letter to Mill, of December 28, 1818, printed for the first time in the Sraffa edition. Here Ricardo remarks that Adam Smith thought that:

as after stock was accumulated, a part went to profits, that accumulation, necessarily, without any regard to the different degrees of durability of capital, or any other circumstance whatever, raised the prices or exchangeable value of commodities, and consequently that their value was no longer regulated by the quantity of labour necessary to their production. In opposition to him I maintain that it is not because of this division into profits and wages . . . that exchangeable value varies. . . .[84]

Exchangeable value, he continued, would vary, in any stage of society "owing only to two causes: one the more or less quantity of labour required, the other the greater or less durability of capital:—that the former is never superceded by the latter, but is only modified by it."[85]

In Section IV of his chapter, "On Value," which is specifically devoted to these issues, Ricardo remarks that he had assumed so far that the weapons used in deer and beaver hunting were durable and cost the same amount of labor. In any state of society, however, this may well not be so: "the tools, implements, buildings and machinery employed in different trades may be of various degrees of durability, and may require different portions of labour to produce them."[86] In some trades the capitalist mainly supplies wage goods, in others his capital is mainly spent on machinery and buildings. This situation was later to be described by Marx as being one where the organic composition of capital differed from one sector of the economy to another. But, for any price reflecting a positive rate of profit, differing organic composition of capital between sectors entails abandoning either the uniformity of the rate of profit or the proportionality of price to embodied labor.

The capitalist must pay a price for the raw materials and equipment he uses up in production equivalent to its total labor cost if prices are to be proportional to labor values. Suppose that in iron production the materials, etc. cost 90 hours of embodied labor, while the direct labor of the iron workers embodies 20 hours per unit of iron output. Then the per-unit price of iron must be the equivalent of 110 hours of labor if it is to reflect the total embodied labor. So, if the hours of labor embodied in producing the workers' subsistence for 20 hours is 10 hours, the wage for 20 hours of labor is the equivalent of 10 hours of labor. The per-unit profit in the iron sector must therefore be the equivalent of 10 hours of labor. This is a *rate* of profit of 10% on the assumption that the wage is paid at the beginning of the period of production.

Now, if a unit of *corn* embodies 110 hours of labor, there will be a uniform rate of profit throughout industry only if the profit rate in corn is the equivalent of 10 hours of labor per unit of output. But suppose that in corn production the equipment etc. bought by the farmer is only the equivalent of 50 hours of labor per unit of corn output. The other 60 hours embodied in per-unit output are current labor in farming. With a uniform real wage, this means that the direct labor cost of per-unit output is 30 hours, so profit, if it is to reflect labor values, must be at a rate equivalent to 30 hours per unit of corn output. The rate of profit is $30/80 = 37.5\%$. Clearly, this is inconsistent with the requirement that there be a uniform rate of profit on the total (money) value of capital (again, including the wage which is paid in advance). Hence where what Marx was later to call the organic composition of capital differs between sectors, prices proportional to embodied labor are inconsistent with a uniform rate of profit.*

Ricardo (like Marx after him) rightly insisted that, under competition, capitalism would tend in the long run to a uniform positive rate of profit. Capital would move out of an industry with an abnormally low rate, and into an industry with a high rate. Thus, the supply of one commodity would shrink, and that of the other would grow. This would in turn force the price of the former up and the price of the latter down. But, this positive rate of profit will be inconsistent with labor-value prices except on the drastic assumption of uniform organic composition of capital. From the first edition of the *Principles* to the end of his life, Ricardo clearly saw and explicitly faced this fact (as has been definitively shown by Sraffa in his "Introduction" to the *Principles*). Ricardo recognized that the reflection of values in prices would be "modified" as a

---

* For Marx's analysis of the problem of differing organic compositions of capital in different sectors making a uniform rate of profit inconsistent with labor-value prices, see pp. 106–8. See also the analysis of the price relations of a classical model in chapters 12 and 13, and the discussion in chapter 15 where the concept of embodied labor is made explicit in terms of direct and indirect labor requirements per unit of output.

result; hence his search for a standard of value, upon which he was engaged in the last months before his death.

Marx, fully understanding Ricardo's problem, never expected prices to be proportional to labor values. The point, for Marx, of expressing output and input as quantities of embodied labor was to have a way of analyzing the extraction of surplus under capitalist production, and of laying bare the unique social relations of the capitalist phase of history. Ricardo, who took the institutions of capitalism for granted, did not therefore develop this idea which belongs instead to the mature work of Marx.

The Relations of Rent, Wages, and Profits

Adam Smith had treated the appropriation of land as another factor which led values to depart from proportionality to embodied labor. Ricardo thus turned in his great Chapter II, "On Rent," to the question, "whether the appropriation of land, and the consequent creation of rent, will occasion any variation in the relative value of commodities, independent of the quantity of labour necessary to production."[87] Rent he defined as "that proportion of the produce of the earth, which is paid to the landlord for the use of the original and indestructible powers of the soil."[88] Thus, a payment for the use of capital improvements embodied in a farm was not rent in his sense. He then clearly states the principles on which rent is paid:

Thus, suppose land—No. 1, 2, 3,—to yield, with an equal employment of capital and labour, a net produce of 100, 90, and 80 quarters of corn. In a new country, where there is an abundance of fertile land compared with the population, and where therefore it is only necessary to cultivate No. 1, the whole net produce will belong to the cultivator, and will be the profits of the stock which he advances. As soon as population had so far increased as to make it necessary to cultivate No. 2, from which ninety quarters only can be obtained after supporting the labourers, rent would commence on No. 1; for either there must be two rates of profit on agricultural capital, or ten quarters, or the value of ten quarters must be withdrawn from the produce of No. 1, for some other purpose. . . . In the same manner it might be shown that when No. 3 is brought into cultivation, the rent of No. 2 must be ten quarters, whilst the rent of No. 1 would rise to twenty quarters. . . .[89]

It would be the same if a second or third dose of capital were applied to the first class of land, yielding a progressively declining return. The landlord could extract the extra yield from the first and second doses of capital, "for there cannot be two rates of profit."[90] The important point for Ricardo's theory of value is that, "In this case, as well as in the other, the capital last employed pays no rent."[91]

On Ricardo's assumptions, the vital conclusion follows:

The reason then, why raw produce rises in comparative value, is because more labour is employed in the production of the last portion obtained, and not because a rent is paid to the landlord. The value of corn is regulated by the quantity of labour bestowed on its production on that quality of land, or with that portion of capital, which pays no rent. Corn is not high because a rent is paid, but a rent is paid because corn is high. . . .[92]

Returning to Smith's argument, Ricardo then remarks:

Adam Smith, therefore, cannot be correct in supposing that the original rule which regulated the exchangeable value of commodities, namely, the comparative quantity of labour by which they were produced, can be at all altered by the appropriation of land and the payment of rent. Raw material enters into the composition of most commodities, but the value of that raw material, as well as corn, is regulated by the productiveness of the portion of capital last employed on the land, and paying no rent; and therefore rent is not a component part of the price of commodities.[93]

Having thus corrected Smith's mistake over rent, Ricardo accepted Smith's distinction between short-run market (demand and supply) prices and long-run, natural (cost of production) prices, and agreed that long-run wages are governed by the subsistence requirements of the laborer.* Ricardo was then ready to set out his final argument as to what determined the rate of profit.

To simplify his exposition, Ricardo assumed the value of money constant so that every variation in price will reflect variation in the value of the relevant commodity. He then sets out his theory:

We have seen that the price of corn is regulated by the quantity of labour necessary to produce it, with that portion of capital which pays no rent. We have seen, too, that all manufactured commodities rise and fall in price, in proportion as more or less labour becomes necessary to their production. Neither the farmer who cultivates that quantity† of land, which regulates price, nor the manufacturer, who manufactures goods, sacrifice any portion of the produce for rent. The whole value of their commodities is divided into two portions only: one constitutes the profits of stock, the other the wages of labour.[95]

Thus, it follows inescapably that profits will vary inversely with wages. Ricardo then considers the effect of rising corn prices:

But suppose corn to rise in price because more labour is necessary to produce it; that cause will not raise the price of manufactured goods in the production of which no additional quantity of labour is required. If, then, wages continued the same, the profits

---

*But not by bare physical subsistence: "The friends of humanity cannot but wish that in all countries the labouring classes should have a taste for comforts and enjoyments. . . ."[94]
† Sraffa notes: "Eds. 1–2 read 'quality', which seems more appropriate."

of manufacturers* would remain the same; but if, as is absolutely certain, wages should rise with the rise of corn, then their† profits would necessarily fall.[96]

He then draws the logical conclusion that, "profits depend on the quantity of labour requisite to provide necessaries for the labourers, on that land or with that capital which yields no rent."[97]

As population grew, and poorer and poorer lands had to be taken into cultivation (if foreign corn were excluded), the rate of profit must progressively fall in agriculture, and, in the long run, throughout industry. This, in turn, must threaten the accumulation of capital, and those wages above the natural level which were a consequence of growth and for which the "friends of humanity" must wish.

Ricardo had faithfully carried out the project announced in the famous passage with which the *Principles* began:

The produce of the earth—all that is derived from its surface by the united application of labour, machinery, and capital, is divided among three classes of the community; namely, the proprietor of the land, the owner of the stock of capital necessary for its cultivation, and the labourers by whose industry it is cultivated. . . .

To determine the laws which regulate this distribution, is the principal problem in Political Economy: much as the science has been improved by the writings of Turgot, Stuart, Smith, Say, Sismondi, and others, they afford very little satisfactory information respecting the natural course of rent, profit, and wages.[98]

This claim was just. Ricardo was the only thinker in the whole development of the classical tradition from Petty on to have a clear theory of distribution. Smith had blocked out the basic structure of classical theory; he had seen the existence of surplus throughout industry, and of its dual, profit: but he had no theory as to how the rate of profit was determined. Ricardo disentangled profit from rent, and showed how the rate of profit depended on the real wage, which was principally affected by the cost of food.

The vivid light cast by Ricardo's analysis on the problem of distribution under capitalism was, in the classical tradition, never quite extinguished. Meanwhile, he had prepared the way for Marx.

Karl Marx, The Last Great Nineteenth Century Classic

Karl Heinrich Marx (1818–1883) in his maturity was very much a man of the nineteenth century, but his childhood and youth were warmed by the last rays of the Enlightenment. To begin with, he had the same thorough classical edu-

* Sraffa notes: "Ed. 1 does not contain 'of manufacturers'."
† Sraffa notes: "Ed. 1 does not contain 'their'."

cation as that eighteenth century gentleman, Adam Smith. And then, the ancient and elegant little city of Trier, set in the vineyards of the Mosel valley, steeped in history from Roman times, had been annexed to France by Napoleon's bayonets, and "governed long enough in accordance with the principles of the French Revolution to be imbued by a taste for freedom of speech and constitutional liberty uncharacteristic of the rest of Germany." [99] David McLellan, Marx's most recent full-scale biographer in English, remarks of the High School of Trier, which Marx attended, that, "The liberal spirit of the Enlightenment had been introduced into the school by the late Prince Elector of Trier. . . ." [100] Eleanor Marx, the youngest daughter, writes in a letter about an intimate friend of Marx's father, the Baron von Westphalen, who was to be a great influence on the young Marx, and ultimately his father-in-law:

[Marx] never tired of telling us of the old Baron von Westphalen and his surprising knowledge of Shakespeare and Homer. The baron could recite some of Homer's songs by heart from beginning to end and he knew most of Shakespeare's dramas by heart in both German and English. In contrast to him, Moor's* father—for whom Moor had a great admiration—was a real eighteenth century 'Frenchman.' He knew Voltaire and Rousseau by heart just as the old Westphalen did Homer and Shakespeare. Moor's astonishing versatility was due without doubt to these 'hereditary' influences. [101]

The fact is that the Age of Enlightenment came to Germany long after its noon day had passed in France or Britain, and lingered there into the nineteenth century, so that Marx, though born in 1818 when Ricardo was writing work that bore the utterly nineteenth century stamp of British industrial capitalism, grew up in surroundings and among men that would not have seemed strange to the Marquis de Mirabeau. Cultivated Germans were thinking in French and living in the eighteenth century after England—and even France— had moved into the age of iron. As Sir Harold Nicolson has remarked, "It was not until 1813, when Madame de Staël published her highly intelligent work *De L'Allemagne,* that German Letters became in any manner fashionable." [102]

Meanwhile, the young Marx, having been grounded in the classical languages, and polished with the rationalism of the French *Philosophes* by his father, was to be filled "with enthusiasm for the romantic school" [103] by his long intellectual walks with the Baron von Westphalen. It appears that the baron also "interested Marx in the personality and work of the French utopian socialist Saint-Simon." [104] Thus, a leading theme of Marx's mature life emerges, though it is a long time yet before we hear the themes of classical political economy.

---

* Among his intimates Marx was called "Moor."

As McLellan remarks, the influence of the Romantic Movement stimulated in Marx by Ludwig von Westphalen, was heightened by his year at the University of Bonn. The story has all the typical trappings of drinking scenes, a little dueling, much writing of poetry. It was inspired no doubt by the romantic separation from Jenny von Westphalen, with whom, before Marx left for Bonn, there had been a declaration of love. "A new world," Marx writes in the famous letter to his father, "had just begun to exist for me, the world of love that was at first drunk with its own desire and hopeless."[105] Heinrich Marx had quickly decided to transfer his son to the University of Berlin where the atmosphere was much more sober and scholarly. It worked. Here the wild youthful romantic flame burned down into a white heat of intellect. Studying to the peril of his health, Marx acquired mastery of German philosophy to the point it had reached at Berlin, where Hegel, until his death in 1831, had held the chair.

The Young Hegelian movement, which Marx now joined, has some importance for us as it offers an explanation of the long time it took before Marx began to see the anatomy of society as being contained in political economy. Hegel's philosophy, deeply conservative, not to say absolutist in its surface message, yet rested on a method—the method of dialectic, which in young rebellious minds could be fundamentally corrosive of all absolutes. But since this critical method began within philosophy itself, it was natural for the Young Hegelians also to begin their criticism of orthodox beliefs with attacks on philosophical and religious orthodoxy. Attacking religious absolutism, in the Germany of their day, led naturally to attacking political absolutism. Economic issues lay in wait. Thus Marx's doctoral dissertation showed him as a student of ancient philosophy, and (in its critical aspects) as a student of Hegel. But in both the dissertation and his other first writings he was iconoclast enough to have difficulty obtaining an academic appointment, without even broaching political economy. In fact, as Marx himself tells us:

In the year 1842–43, as editor of the *Rhenische Zeitung,* I first found myself in the embarrassing position of having to discuss what is known as material interests. The deliberations of the Rhenische Landtag on forest thefts . . . caused me in the first instance to turn my attention to economic questions.[106]

The serious study of classical political economy shows itself, and Ricardo's name appears for the first time, in the manuscripts which Marx wrote in the late summer of 1844, in Paris. [107] These were not published until this century, when they became known as the "Economic and Philosophical Manuscripts," or "Paris Manuscripts." But it was with the *Poverty of Philoso-*

phy,[108] which Marx wrote in French, and published in Brussels and Paris in July, 1847, that his lifelong devotion to Ricardo's analysis of surplus as a quantity of embodied labor first appeared.[109] Now there is heard once more the great theme of surplus which was first sounded in the work of Sir William Petty.

"Ricardo shows us the real movement of bourgeois production, which constitutes value,"[110] wrote Marx in *The Poverty of Philosophy.* His treatment of Ricardo shows him by this point a master of the Ricardian analysis.[111] And that at a time when, as Friedrich Engels remarks, "Marx had never yet been in the reading room of the British Museum."[112] When Marx crossed the English Channel in August, 1849, the scene was set.

Now began about twenty years during which, despite the interruptions caused by bitter quarrels with political opponents, agonizing family problems, wretched poverty accentuated by mismanagement,[113] and the distractions of journalism, Marx produced the great series of works in which he took up the core issues of classical political economy, which, for him, were above all those which had been analyzed by Ricardo.

Between October 1857 and March 1858 he had filled a series of seven notebooks with work on political economy. These were lost in circumstances which are still mysterious, and only published in a limited edition in two volumes in 1939 and 1941.[114] The first complete English translation did not appear until 1973. It has been claimed that, "The *Grundrisse* * challenges and puts to the test every serious interpretation of Marx yet conceived."[115] The notebooks reveal vividly, almost as a private journal might, Marx's long struggle against what to him was invalid or mystifying in the thought of the two great intellectual influences on his life, Hegel and Ricardo: "The *suspension* of Hegel and of Ricardo—the demolition of what was metaphysical, mystical in their doctrines, the preservation of the rational cores—is a struggle with which Marx is occupied throughout the pages of the seven notebooks."[116] Here Marx is ready for the first time to pick up the great theme of surplus where Ricardo had left it. The difficulty in the idea, he writes, "shows itself in those modern English economists who accuse Ricardo of not having understood the surplus, the *surplus value* . . . whereas, among all the economists, Ricardo alone understood it. . . ."[117]

Less than two years after the composing of the *Grundrisse,* in *A Contribution to the Critique of Political Economy,* which he published in 1859, Marx added, "Ricardo analyses bourgeois economy, whose deeper layers differ es-

* These workbooks are customarily referred to by scholars by the first word of the German title given to their first edition.

sentially from its surface appearance, with such theoretical acumen that Lord Brougham could say of him: 'Mr. Ricardo seemed as if he had dropped from another planet'.''[118] Holding consistently this view of Ricardo's eminence, it was natural for Marx in *Capital,* Volume I to construct as a starting point what might be called the pure Ricardian model. In this way he could show first precisely how he took his departure from it. Now, we already know the model that would have suited Ricardo perfectly. It would be a model where one could assume that all commodities exchanged at prices which were *exactly* proportional to the amount of labor embodied in each good. We have also been made aware by Sraffa that Ricardo, from the first edition of his *Principles,* knew that in the real world this proportionality of prices to labor values would be modified. So it should not surprise us to see Marx, in Volume I of *Capital,* constructing a model where Ricardo's theory would work perfectly, without the need for modification, and all commodities would exchange at prices exactly proportional to the quantities of embodied labor.

Marx's purpose is to show how, in the model most favorable to Ricardo, surplus is extracted in the process of production. No one is cheated: every commodity, including labor-power, exchanges for a price exactly proportional to the amount of labor necessary to produce it. Surplus value arises simply because the value of labor-power (the hours of work socially necessary to produce the worker's subsistence wage—his ''corn,'' as it were) is less than the value of the product of labor (the hours of work embodied in what the laborer produces in the whole of his working day). All this can be expressed in labor values in the simple model of Volume I. As we know, however, Marx was well aware of what a special case this model was by the time he was writing the *Grundrisse,* in the winter of 1857–58, ten years before he published Volume I of *Capital.* Thus, we learn in the *Grundrisse* that *''A general rate of profit* as such is possible only if the rate of profit in one branch of business is too high and in another too low; i.e. that a part of the surplus value—which corresponds to surplus labour—is transferred from one capitalist to the other.''[119] And he continues:

> The capitalist class thus to a certain extent distributes the total surplus value so that, to a certain degree, it [shares in it] evenly in accordance with the *size* of its capital, instead of in accordance with the surplus values actually created by the capitals in the varous branches of business . . . This is realized [realisiert] by means of the relation of prices in the different branches of business, which fall *below* the *value* in some, rise *above* it in others.[120]

Ricardo, it will be recalled, had seen quite clearly that he could not consistently postulate labor-value prices *and* a uniform rate of profit in industries "containing different proportions of the various forms of capital." [121] But there could be no question of giving up the tendency to a uniform rate of profit. It was of the essence of classical political economy from Smith all the way to Marx to insist that, given time and freedom to enter or leave an industry, competition among capitalists would lead to uniformity of profit rates. Ricardo as we know always took the view that this mechanism would *modify* relative values. He did not see it as one form of a systematic divergence of embodied labor values from prices. Marx, of course, always took the view that prices diverge systematically from labor values. In the manuscript later called *Theories of Surplus Value* and written between 1861 and 1863* he states precisely his position vis à vis Ricardo:

> Therefore [Ricardo] further concludes these differences affect the "relative values" when wages rise or fall. He should have said on the contrary: Although these differences have nothing to do with the values as such, they do, through their varying effects on profits in the different spheres, give rise to average prices or, as we shall call them *cost-prices* which are different from the values themselves and are not directly determined by the values of the commodities but by the capital advances for their production plus the average profit. [122]

In an important letter of the same period (Marx to Engels in Manchester, August 2, 1862), Marx sets out in full the manner in which the maintenance of a uniform rate of profit causes prices to diverge systematically from values. [123] Marx developed the sophisticated models of this theory in Volume III of *Capital*. This was finished in rough form (the only version ever written) well before Volume I was given to Meissner of Hamburg to print. Then, in July, 1865 Marx wrote to Engels:

> there are still three chapters to write to complete the theoretical part (the first three books). Then there is still the fourth book to write—the historico literary one. . . . But I cannot make up my mind to send anything off until I have the whole thing in front of me. [124]

Volumes II and III had to be put together by Engels from the rough draft, after Marx's death in March, 1883. But rough or not there is no question of the systematic divergence of prices from labor values in Volume III. The "prices of production" which then became *central* to the analysis are, as Marx points out, the long-run "natural" prices of the whole classical tradition—above all of Smith and Ricardo. The capitalist no longer obtains for his commodity a price proportional to the labor embodied in it, neither does he

---

*This draft of 1861–63 is the first and only draft of the manuscript which we know today as *Theories of Surplus Value*.

have to pay his worker a wage proportional to the labor value of the latter's means of subsistence. He pays a wage which covers the price of production of the wage goods, and sells his product for its price of production, a price representing its cost of production plus the uniform rate of profit in the economy.[125] Surplus is still extracted, but one cannot use labor values directly to show this. If one wishes to show the relation between labor values and prices of production it is necessary to transform the one into the other. Since we shall not use labor values in our analysis of the extraction of surplus in this book, it would lead us too far off our course to attempt at this point a treatment of the solutions to what has come to be called the *transformation problem*.[126]

Leaving this issue on one side, we turn to the part of Marx's mature work which carries to new heights of development that great classical theme with which we are concerned: the extraction, distribution, and accumulation of surplus. This development is to be found in a part of *Capital* which, until recently, has not been given its due weight in the critical literature: the schemes of simple and extended reproduction in Volume II.

Simple Reproduction and Extended Reproduction

Already in Volume I of *Capital,* Marx shows his understanding of the concept of viability as a necessary property of the dynamic general equilibrium of the production of commodities by means of commodities:

> Whatever the form of the process of production in a society, it must be a continuous process, must continue to go periodically through the same phases. A society can no more cease to produce than it can cease to consume. When viewed, therefore, as a connected whole, and as flowing on with incessant renewal, every social process of production is, at the same time, a process of reproduction.
> The conditions of production are also those of reproduction. No society can go on producing, in other words, no society can reproduce, unless it constantly reconverts a part of its products into means of production, or elements of fresh products. . . .[127]

Marx's notion of "simple reproduction," however, is not that of a society whose technology is *barely viable*. He makes it clear from the very first time he discusses the idea that what he intends is a society where physical surplus is produced, but where this is not devoted to accumulation of capital—i.e., there is no growth, only luxury consumption of the surplus. The society he has in mind is capitalist, and therefore surplus-value is extracted. He adopts the physiocratic term "revenue" to stand for surplus-value when the physical form into which the capitalist class chooses to cast the surplus is luxury consumption.[128] He then remarks that, "If this revenue serve the capitalist only as a fund to provide for his consumption, and to be spent as periodically as it is gained, then, *ceteris paribus,* simple reproduction will take place."[129]

The concepts of viability, physical surplus, luxury consumption, and the accumulation of capital are made quite clear:

> The annual production must in the first place furnish all those objects (use values) from which the material components of capital, used up in the course of the year, have to be replaced. Deducting these there remains the net or surplus-product in which the surplus-value lies. And of what does this surplus-product consist? Only of things destined to satisfy the wants and desires of the capitalist class, things which, consequently, enter into the consumption-fund of the capitalists? Were that the case, the cup of surplus-value would be drained to the very dregs, and nothing but simple reproduction would ever take place.

> To accumulate it is necessary to convert a portion of the surplus-product into capital. But we cannot, except by a miracle, convert into capital anything but such articles as can be employed in the labour-process (i.e., means of production), and such further articles as are suitable for the sustenance of the labourer (i.e., means of subsistence). Consequently a part of the annual surplus-labour must have been applied to the production of additional means of production and subsistence, over and above the quantity of these things required to replace the capital advanced.[130]

He assumes that the economy is closed,[131] and that the additional labor-power necessary for accumulation will be available:

> For this the mechanism of capitalist production provides beforehand, by converting the working-class into a class dependent on wages, a class whose ordinary wages suffice, not only for its maintenance, but for its increase. It is only necessary for capital to incorporate this additional labour-power . . . with the surplus means of production comprised in the annual produce, and the conversion of surplus-value into capital is complete. From a concrete point of view, accumulation resolves itself into the reproduction of capital on a progressively increasing scale.[132]

Marx now sends one to Volume II for his detailed analysis.[133] He begins by praising Quesnay's *Tableau Économique* for its picture of simple reproduction.[134] It will be recalled that the *Tableau* depicts a projected estimate of the *end result* of a period of growth and transformation of French agriculture. In the economy analyzed in the *Tableau* itself, all surplus is being treated as revenue, and devoted to luxury consumption. After a detailed discussion of Adam Smith and other predecessors, Marx sets up his own model.

At the outset, he adopts certain simplifying assumptions which are convenient, but not necessary:

> It is furthermore assumed that products are exchanged at their values and also that there is no revolution in the values of the component parts of productive capital. The

fact that prices diverge from values cannot, however, exert any influence on the movements of the social capital. On the whole, there is the same exchange of the same quantities of products, although the individual capitalists are involved in value-relations no longer proportional to their respective advances and to the quantities of surplus-value produced singly by every one of them. As for revolutions in value, they do not alter anything in the relations between the value-components of the total annual product, provided they are universally and evenly distributed.[135]

This is an extremely important passage. Marx states that he is going to assume that products are exchanged at their labor values—that prices are everywhere proportional to labor values. And, in fact, he retains this assumption until the analysis of Volume III. We have already discussed the implications of assuming proportionality between labor values and prices in dealing with Volume I. Marx immediately goes on to make a most interesting claim, namely, that even if prices *did* diverge from values, this could not exert any influence on the movement of social capital: "there is the same exchange of the same quantities of products. . . ."[136]

We remarked in our discussion of physiocracy that the *Tableau Économique,* while manifestly concerned with questions of viability and the disposition of surplus output, ran in terms of current prices, and tended to confuse what we would now call the price relations and quantity relations of the model. Whereas, to use modern terminology, the interdependent requirements upon the input-output coefficients of a model of general equilibrium which have to do with whether the technology is viable, can be set up and discussed solely in terms of the quantity relations of the model, without bringing in the price relations. It is hard to resist the impression that Marx, in the passage we are discussing, is in effect saying that the viability of an economy can be studied in abstraction from both price and value relations (which, it has recently been suggested, form a "dual duality"[137] to the quantity relations of the Marxian model). We shall find, however, that when Marx comes to set out his model, quantities of inputs and outputs appear, not in physical terms, but valued at current (labor value) prices. Superficially, this could be confusing in the way in which the *Tableau Économique* can be, through the intrusion of pricing considerations into what is in effect a statement of quantity relations. In Marx's case, however, the figures (in pounds or francs) can be translated into hours of embodied labor. Given the technology, these quantities of labor can then be translated into quantities of physical inputs and outputs. So one can arrive quite naturally at the quantity relations of Marx's model.

Marx sets up what he calls a two-department model: "The total product, and therefore the total production, of society may be divided into two major departments."[138] Since it is of some importance to us to decide exactly how to interpret these departments, we quote in detail Marx's own description of them:

I *Means of Production,* commodities having a form in which they must, or at least may, pass into productive consumption.
II *Articles of Consumption,* commodities having a form in which they pass into the individual consumption of the capitalist and the working-class.[139]

Clearly, this is a picture of production by means of produced inputs. Department I produces means of production for itself and for department II. Department II produces articles of consumption for the subsistence needs of its own workers and the workers of department I, and also luxury consumption for the capitalists of both departments. Marx recognizes that "a part of the products of II is capable of entering into I as means of production,"[140] and instances the case of seed in agriculture. As he had remarked in Volume I:

Every object possesses various properties, and is thus capable of being applied to different uses. One and the same product may therefore serve as raw material in very different processes. Corn, for example, is a raw material for millers, starch-manufacturers, distillers, and cattle-breeders. It also enters as raw material into its own production in the shape of seed; coal, too, is at the same time the product of, and a means of production in, coal mining.[141]

In each sector, Marx tells us, the capital consists of two parts, variable capital and constant capital. The variable capital is the labor-power, and is represented by the wage—a bundle of commodities necessary for subsistence. The constant capital is the means of production. Here we are forced to introduce a simplification, and thus to fail to represent Marx's original treatment adequately: he divided constant capital into "*fixed* capital, such as machines, instruments of labour, buildings, labouring animals, etc., and *circulating* constant capital, such as materials of production; raw and auxiliary materials, semi-finished products, etc."[142] We limit ourselves in this book, however, to capital goods which all wear out in one period of production—say, a year.* So our model of Department I, which simply turns out machines which wear out in a year, does not do justice to the complexity of Marx's picture. Subject to this simplification, we can represent the "means of production" of Department I, without departing from the limitations of our own analytical structures, used later in the book.

Although he is studying viability and physical surplus, Marx does not (as

---

* This is done to avoid complications relating to joint production.

we have noted) set out his scheme of simple reproduction directly in physical quantity units, as is done in the quantity relations of a modern general equilibrium model of the production of commodities by means of commodities. The units are expressed in figures which, we are told, "may indicate millions of marks, francs, or pounds sterling." [143] In this Marx is following the lead of Quesnay, whose *Tableau* shows the distribution of the total produce of the society, expressed in *money*.

Here we shall first reproduce Marx's actual scheme, and then suggest how a simple model of a viable economy may be derived from it. In the scheme, "c stands for constant capital, v for variable capital, and s for surplus-value, assuming the rate of surplus-value s/v to be 100 per cent," [144] Marx's scheme of simple reproduction may be set out as follows:

I   Production of Means of Production:
    Capital   4,000c + 1,000v   = 5,000
    Commodity-Product   4,000c + 1,000v + 1,000s = 6,000

II Production of Articles of Consumption:
    Capital   2,000c + 500v   = 2,500
    Commodity-Product   2,000c + 500v + 500s   = 3,000 [145]

We are now to "examine the transformations necessary on the basis of simple reproduction, where the entire suplus-value is unproductively consumed, *and leave aside for the present the money circulation that brings them about.* . . ." [146] Thus, it is, as we would nowadays express it, the *quantity* relations of the model which concern us. Marx makes three points:

1) The 500v, representing wages of the labourers, and 500s, representing surplus-value of the capitalists, in department II, must be spent for articles of consumption. But their value exists in articles of consumption worth 1,000, held by the capitalists of department II, which replace the advanced 500v and represent the 500s. Consequently the wages and surplus-value of department II are exchanged within this department for products of this same department. Thereby articles of consumption to the amount of $(500v + 500s) = 1,000$, drop out of the total product. [147]

The 500v, we may represent as consumption goods needed to produce consumption goods, i.e., as $a_{22}Y_2$, where a_{22} is the requirement of department II goods in their own production, per unit of output, and Y_2 is the level of output. (For obvious typographical reasons, we use Arabic numbers in place of Roman numerals for subscripts.) The 500s likewise can be treated as part of the luxury consumption of department II goods, written in our notation as $\lambda_2 Y_2$, where, it will be recalled, λ_2 is our notation for the fraction of a gross output devoted to luxury consumption. Marx now tells us that:

2) The 1,000v plus 1,000s of department I must likewise be spent for articles of consumption; in other words, for products of department II. Hence they must be exchanged for the remainder of this product equal to the constant capital part, 2,000c. Department II receives in return an equal quantity of means of production, the product of I, in which the value of 1,000v + 1,000s of I is incorporated. Thereby 2,000 IIc and (1,000v + 1,000s) I drop out of the calculation.[148]

Marx's 1,000v of department I is the wage of labor in the capital goods sector, which may be treated as the technically given requirement of department II goods in the production of department I goods $a_{21}Y_1$. His 1,000s of department I is luxury consumption of department II goods by the department I capitalists, which must be counted as the remaining part of $\lambda_2 Y_2$, the luxury goods produced by the consumption goods sector. There does not appear a separate fraction, λ_1, in the capital goods sector (to multiply Y_1) because of Marx's assumption that department I produces only means of production, and not directly consumable commodities (luxury goods or wage goods).

Meanwhile, department II receives in return from the capital goods sector the 2,000c: the means of production it needs. This is our $a_{12}Y_2$, the input of department I goods in the production of Y_2. Finally, we are told:

3) There still remain 4,000 Ic. These consist of means of production which can be used only in department I to replace its consumed constant capital, and are therefore disposed of by mutual exchange between the individual capitalists of I. . . .[149]

These means of production are the capital goods input into the production of capital goods, written in our notation as $a_{11}Y_1$.

The resulting version of the quantity relations which we have constructed for Marx's model are two equations, one for each of his departments:

I   production of means of production:

$$a_{11}Y_1 + a_{12}Y_2 = Y_1 \tag{1}$$

II   production of articles of consumption:

$$a_{21}Y_1 + a_{22}Y_2 = (1 - \lambda_2)Y_2 \tag{2}$$

Marx goes on to remark that:

Category II of the annual production of commodities consists of a great variety of branches of production, which may, however, be divided into two great sub-divisions by their products:

a) Articles of consumption, which enter into the consumption of the working-class and, to the extent that they are necessities of life . . . also form a portion of the consumption of the capitalist class.

b) Articles of *luxury,* which enter into the consumption of only the capitalist class and can therefore be exchanged only for spent surplus-value, which never falls to the share of the labourer.[150]

To bring this subdivision into our model we need to expand it by bringing back the output of luxury commodities Y_X, which we called "carriages" in our discussion of physiocracy in chapter 2. Since it is reasonable to suppose that these luxury commodities require inputs of means of production as well as labor-power, the capital goods sector must now be run on a large enough scale to provide the necessary input $a_{1X} Y_X$, where a_{1X} is the input of department I goods per unit of output of luxuries Y_X. Thus, part of the surplus is now being taken in the form of capital goods used in making luxury commodities, so that less of the surplus can be taken in the form of department II goods (λ_2 must be reduced). Furthermore, of the remaining surplus of department II goods, not all can be consumed directly—some are needed for the input into production of "carriages" $a_{2X} Y_X$. We may then write the quantity relations, expanded to include manufactured luxuries:

$$a_{11} Y_1 + a_{12} Y_2 + a_{1X} Y_X = Y_1 \tag{3}$$
$$a_{21} Y_1 + a_{22} Y_2 + a_{2X} Y_X = (1 - \lambda_2) Y_2 \tag{4}$$

Marx now tells us of his picture of the accumulation of capital, or reproduction on an *extended* scale:

The difference is here only in the form of the surplus-labour performed, in the concrete nature of its particular useful character. It has been expended in means of production for Ic instead of IIc, in means of production of means of production instead of means of production of articles of consumption. In the case of simple reproduction it was assumed that the entire surplus-value I is spent as revenue, hence in commodities II. . . . In order that the transition from simple to extended reproduction may take place, production in department I must be in a position to fabricate fewer elements of constant capital for II and so many the more for I.[151]

In other words, the amount of capital goods being used to produce commodities for direct luxury consumption and for the capital goods input into "carriages," must be reduced by an amount which represents the growth of the capital goods industry.

In order to grow, however, the economy needs to remove some of its surplus from direct luxury consumption and from providing the wage input into "carriages," and devote it instead to the wage needs implicit in growth. As Marx writes, "Hitherto we have been dealing only with additional constant capital. Now we must direct our attention to a consideration of the additional variable capital."[152] He describes the production of variable capital—the wage goods input into growth:

> Consequently, just as I has to supply the additional constant capital of II out of its surplus-product, so II likewise supplies the additional variable capital for I. II accumulates for I and for itself, so far as the variable capital is concerned, by reproducing a greater portion of its total product, and hence especially of its surplus-product, in the shape of necessary articles of consumption.[153]

This is the increased output of wage goods needed to produce capital goods for the economy's growth. Marx writes: "let us suppose that both I and II accumulate one half of their surplus-value. . . ."[154] We can represent a growth rate, g, in our notation as follows:

$$(a_{11} Y_1 + a_{12} Y_2 + a_{1x} Y_X)(1 + g) = Y_1 \tag{5}$$

$$(a_{21} Y_1 + a_{22} Y_2 + a_{2x} Y_X)(1 + g) = (1 - \lambda_2) Y_2 \tag{6}$$

where, in each equation, g times the first sum in parentheses measures accumulation of department I goods and department II goods, respectively. It should be noted that we are (for convenience) following our usual practice of representing growth as some fraction, g, of *total input requirements,* and not as Marx did, of the surplus.

With his treatment of simple and extended reproduction, Marx had laid part of the vital foundation of the modern theory of classical general equilibrium. His treatment of general equilibrium is dynamic in character, and shows the whole circular process of the production of commodities by means of commodities, and of the accumulation of capital. When blended with the mathematical methods of Léon Walras and Abraham Wald (whose systems lacked, however, the dynamic properties of Marx's), this theory pointed toward Neumann and Sraffa. In the later work of Marx, classical English political economy had thus reached its final nineteenth century expression.

Notes

1. Cited by Karl Marx, *Zur Kritik der Politischen Oekonomie,* Franz Duncker, Berlin, 1859, Marx/Engels *Werke,* Band 13, Dietz Verlag, Berlin, 1964. Our citations are from S. W. Ryazanskaya, trans. and Maurice Dobb, ed., *A Contribution to the Critique of Political Economy,* International Publishers, New York, 1970, p. 20.
2. Joseph A. Schumpeter, *History of Economic Analysis,* Oxford University Press, New York, 1954, pp. 595–6.
3. Piero Sraffa, ed., in collaboration with Maurice Dobb, *Works and Correspondence of David Ricardo,* Cambridge University Press, 1951–73, Vol. I,

p. vii. Subsequent references will be preceded by the editor's name where we are referring to his "Introduction," and to other remarks or notes; and by Ricardo's name where we are referring to the original works and correspondence.

4. Sraffa, *Works and Correspondence,* Vol. X, pp. 14–5.

5. *Ibid.,* p. 16.

6. *Ibid.,* p. 3.

7. *Ibid.,* p. 4.

8. *Ibid.,* p. 16; from the hitherto unpublished manuscript diary of J. L. Mallet.

9. *Ibid.,* p. 16.

10. *Ibid.,* p. 19.

11. *Ibid.,* p. 3.

12. *Ibid.,* p. 25.

13. *Ibid.,* p. 28.

14. *Ibid.,* pp. 168–9.

15. *Ibid.,* p. 50.

16. Schumpeter, *History of Economic Analysis,* p. 470.

17. Sraffa, *Works and Correspondence,* Vol. X, pp. 91–104.

18. *Ibid.,* pp. 102–3.

19. *Ibid.,* p. 90.

20. *Ibid.*

21. Marx, *Theorien über den Mehrwert,* Teil II, Dietz Verlag, Berlin, 1959. Our citation is from the translation, *Theories of Surplus Value,* Part II, Progress Publishers, Moscow, 1963, p. 117.

22. *Ibid.,* p. 118. Marx's italics.

23. Jaspar Ridley, *Lord Palmerston,* Constable, London, 1970; Panther Books, 1972, p. 77.

24. Elizabeth, Countess of Longford, *Wellington: Pillar of State,* Weidenfeld and Nicolson, London, 1972; Panther Books, London, 1973, p. 343.

25. Frank H. Knight, "The Ricardian Theory of Production and Distribution," *Canadian Journal of Economics and Political Science,* Vol. I, 1935; reprinted in Knight, *On the History and Method of Economics,* University of Chicago Press, 1956, p. 42.

26. Schumpeter, *History of Economic Analysis,* p. 567.

27. Samuel Hollander, *The Economics of Adam Smith,* University of Toronto Press, 1973, p. 14.

28. Lord Keynes, *Essays in Biography,* Macmillan, New York, 1933, p. 137; cited by Sraffa, *Works and Correspondence,* Vol. VI, p. xiii.

29. Ricardo, *Works and Correspondence,* Vol. VI, p. 95.

30. Sraffa, *Works and Correspondence,* Vol. VI, p. xxi.

31. Sraffa, "Introduction" to *Works and Correspondence,* Vol. I, pp. xxi–xxii.

32. Ricardo, *Works and Correspondence,* Vol. IV, pp. 9–41.

33. John Eatwell, "The Interpretation of Ricardo's *Essay on Profits,*" *Economica,* N.S. 42, 1975, pp. 182–7.

34. Hollander, "Ricardo's Analysis of the Profit Rate, 1813–15," *Economica,* N.S. 40, 1973, pp. 260–82; and "Ricardo and the Corn Profit Model: Reply to Eatwell," *Economica,* N.S. 42, 1975, pp. 188–202.

35. Ricardo, *Works and Correspondence,* Vol. VI, p. 94.
36. *Ibid.,* pp. 94–5.
37. *Ibid.,* p. xxiii.
38. *Ibid.,* p. 104.
39. Sraffa, *Works and Correspondence,* Vol. I, p. xxxi.
40. *Ibid.,* p. xxxii. The letter quoted is to be found *ibid.,* Vol. VI, p. 108.
41. Ricardo, *Works and Correspondence,* Vol. VI, p. 109.
42. *Ibid.,* p. 114.
43. *Ibid.,* pp. 117–8.
44. *Ibid.,* p. 143.
45. *Ibid.,* pp. 139–40.
46. *Ibid.,* p. 140.
47. *Ibid.,* pp. 140–1. Malthus's italics.
48. *Ibid.,* p. 144. Our italics.
49. *Ibid.,* p. 162.
50. *Ibid.* On manufactured necessities, see also *ibid.,* pp. 194, 212–3, 234.
51. Ricardo, *An Essay on the Influence of a Low Price of Corn on the Profits of Stock; shewing the Inexpediency of Restrictions on Importation: with Remarks on Mr. Malthus' Two Last Publications,* etc., John Murray, London, 1815, in *Works and Correspondence,* Vol. IV, p. 13, n.
52. Sraffa, "Introduction" to *Works and Correspondence,* Vol. I, p. xxxii.
53. Malthus, in Sraffa, *Works and Correspondence,* Vol. VI, p. 187.
54. *Ibid.,* pp. 187–8.
55. Sraffa, "Introduction" to *Works and Correspondence,* Vol. I, p. xxxiii.
56. *Ibid.*
57. *Ibid.*
58. *Ibid.*
59. Ricardo, *Works and Correspondence,* Vol. IV, p. 19.
60. *Ibid.,* pp. 35–6.
61. *Ibid.,* Vol VI, p. 180.
62. *Ibid.,* p. 179.
63. *Ibid.,* p. 220.
64. *Ibid.,* p. 224.
65. *Ibid.,* p. 249.
66. *Ibid.,* p. 252.
67. *Ibid.,* pp. 262–3.
68. *Ibid.,* p. 309.
69. *Ibid.,* p. 348.
70. Sraffa, "Introduction" to *Works and Correspondence,* Vol. I, p. xxxiv.
71. Ricardo, *Works and Correspondence,* Vol. VII, p. 20.
72. *Ibid.,* p. 30.
73. *Ibid.,* p. 115.
74. *Ibid.,* p. 98.
75. Ricardo, *On the Principles of Political Economy and Taxation,* London, John Murray, 1817, in *Works and Correspondence,* Vol. I.
76. Adam Smith, *An Inquiry into the Nature and Causes of the Wealth of Nations,*

Oxford at the Clarendon Press, 1976, I.vi.4–5, Cannan, ed., pp. 47–8. For full reference, see chapter 3, note 22.

77. Marx, *Theories of Surplus Value,* Part II, p. 395. Marx's italics.

78. Ricardo, *Works and Correspondence,* Vol. I, p. 13.

79. *Ibid.,* pp. 22–3.

80. *Ibid.,* p. 23.

81. *Ibid.,* p. 24.

82. Sraffa, "Introduction" to *Works and Correspondence,* Vol. I, p. xxxvii.

83. Lord Robbins of Claremarket, *Robert Torrens and the Evolution of Classical Economics,* Macmillan, London, 1958, p. 61, n. 1.

84. Ricardo, *Works and Correspondence,* Vol. VII, p. 377.

85. *Ibid.*

86. *Ibid.,* Vol. I, p. 30.

87. *Ibid.,* p. 67.

88. *Ibid.*

89. *Ibid.,* pp. 70–1.

90. *Ibid.,* p. 72.

91. *Ibid.*

92. *Ibid.,* p. 74.

93. *Ibid.,* pp. 77–8.

94. *Ibid.,* p. 100.

95. *Ibid.,* p. 110.

96. *Ibid.,* pp. 110–11.

97. *Ibid.,* p. 126.

98. *Ibid.,* p. 5.

99. David McLellan, *Karl Marx His Life and Thought,* Macmillan, London, 1973, p. 2.

100. *Ibid.,* p. 9.

101. Eleanor Marx-Aveling, letter to Wilhelm Liebknecht, cited in *Reminiscences of Marx and Engels,* Foreign Languages Publishers, Moscow, n.d., p. 130.

102. Sir Harold Nicolson, *The Age of Reason,* Constable, London, 1960, p. 331.

103. Eleanor Marx-Aveling, *Die Neue Zeit,* May 1883, p. 441; cited in McLellan, *Karl Marx,* p. 15.

104. McLellan, *Karl Marx,* p. 16.

105. Karl Marx, Letter to his Father, in David McLellan, ed. and trans., *Karl Marx: Selected Writings,* Oxford University Press, 1977, p. 6.

106. Marx, *Contribution to the Critique of Political Economy,* pp. 19–20.

107. The Paris Manuscripts were first published in Karl Marx and Friedrich Engels, *Historisch Kritische Gesamtausgabe,* Marx Engels Verlag, Berlin, 1932. There is a complete English translation in T. Bottomore, ed., *K. Marx, Early Writings,* McGraw-Hill, New York, 1964.

108. Karl Marx, *La Misère de la Philosophie,* A. Franck, Paris, and C. G. Vogler, Brussels, 1847. Our citations will be from *The Poverty of Philosophy,* International Publishers. New York, 1963.

109. McLellan, *Karl Marx,* p. 162, n. 3.

110. Marx, *The Poverty of Philosophy,* p. 49.

111. See the treatment of Ricardo *ibid.*, pp. 44–51, 123–4, 156–60, 213.

112. Friedrich Engels, "Preface to the First German Edition," *The Poverty of Philosophy*, p. 9.

113. That there really was mismanagement is argued by McLellan, *Karl Marx*, pp. 262–66.

114. Marx, *Grundrisse der Kritik der Politischen Oekonomie*, Foreign Languages Publishers, Moscow, Vol. I, 1939, Vol. II, 1941. This title was given to the notebooks by their first editors at the Institute of Marxism-Leninism. Our citations are from Martin Nicolaus, trans., *Karl Marx's Grundrisse Foundations of the Critique of Political Economy*, Vintage Books, New York, 1973.

115. Nicolaus, "Foreword" to *Karl Marx's Grundrisse*, p. 7.

116. *Ibid.*, p. 42. Nicolaus's italics.

117. Marx, *Grundrisse*, p. 326. Marx's italics.

118. Marx, *Contribution to the Critique of Political Economy*, p. 61.

119. Marx, *Grundrisse*, p. 435. Marx's italics.

120. *Ibid.*, pp. 435–6. Marx's italics. The implications of the divergence of prices from labor values are analyzed in detail on pp. 432–43; and also, with specific references to Ricardo, on pp. 547–54.

121. Marx, *Theories of Surplus Value*, Part II, p. 174.

122. *Ibid.*, p. 175.

123. Marx to Engels, *Ausgewälte Schriften in 2 Banden*, Dietz Verlag, Berlin, 1952. Our citation is from the partial translation, *Karl Marx and Frederich Engel's Selected Correspondence*, Progress Publishers, Moscow, 1955, pp. 129–31.

124. Marx to Engels, cited by McLellan, *Karl Marx*, p. 338.

125. Marx, *Das Kapital, Kritik der Politischen Oekonomie*, Vol. III, ed. F. Engels, Meissner, Hamburg, 1894. Our citations are from the English translation, *Capital*, Vol. III, Progress Publishers, Moscow, 1971. In the present context, see especially pp. 154–72.

126. Without discussing the relationship between the Marxian Average Commodity (*Capital*, Vol. III, pp. 173–4) and the Sraffian Standard Commodity, and the bearing of this upon the solution to the transformation problem, one cannot achieve a satisfactory analysis of the link between values and prices in Marx. It will be seen that such a discussion requires technical apparatus which we have not so far developed. An up-to-date introduction to the issues is provided in John Eatwell, "Controversies in the Theory of Surplus Value: Old and New," *Science and Society*, 1975, pp. 281–303; and "Mr. Sraffa's Standard Commodity and the Rate of Exploitation," *Quarterly Journal of Economics*, November, 1975, pp. 543–55.

127. Marx, *Das Kapital, Kritik der Politischen Oekonomie*, Vol. I, Meissner, Hamburg, 1867. Our citations are from *Capital*, Vol. I, Progress Publishers, Moscow, n.d.; see p. 531.

128. *Ibid.*, p. 554 and n. 2.

129. *Ibid.*, p. 532.

130. *Ibid.*, p. 544.

131. *Ibid.*, p. 544, n. 1.

132. *Ibid.*, p. 545.

133. *Ibid.*, p. 554.
134. Marx, *Das Kapital, Kritik der Politischen Oekonomie,* Vol. II, ed. F. Engels, Meissner, Hamburg, 1893. Our citations are from *Capital,* Vol. II, Progress' Publishers, Moscow, 1967; p. 363.
135. *Ibid.*, pp. 397–98.
136. *Ibid.*
137. Michio Morishima, *Marx's Economics, A Dual Theory of Value and Growth,* Cambridge University Press, 1973, pp. 1–9.
138. Marx, *Capital,* Vol. II, p. 399.
139. *Ibid.*
140. *Ibid.*, p. 525.
141. *Ibid.*, Vol. 1, p. 177.
142. *Ibid.*, Vol. II, p. 400. Marx's italics.
143. *Ibid.*, p. 401.
144. *Ibid.*
145. *Ibid.*
146. *Ibid.* Our italics.
147. *Ibid.*, pp. 401–2.
148. *Ibid.*, p. 402.
149. *Ibid.*
150. *Ibid.*, p. 407. Marx's italics.
151. *Ibid.*, pp. 500–501.
152. *Ibid.*, p. 505.
153. *Ibid.*, p. 521.
154. *Ibid.*, p. 511.

5

The Founding of Neoclassical Allocation Theory

> Jevons' *Theory* is the . . . . first modern book on economics, it has proved singularly attractive to all bright minds newly attacking the subject;—simple, lucid, unfaltering, chiselled in stone where Marshall knits in wool.
>
> LORD KEYNES[1]

> . . . I yield to no one in the honour I give to Menger.
>
> SIR JOHN HICKS[2]

We have treated Marx as the last great figure in the tradition of classical political economy.* It is natural to see him in this light today, insofar as his economics is at issue (and that is our concern here). But it must be remembered that his work was not known to the immediate followers of Ricardo, and therefore could play no role in keeping the Ricardian insights alive, correcting them, or developing them, during the years from Ricardo's death in 1823 until virtually the end of the nineteenth century. As far as keeping the classical tradition alive during those years is concerned, the mantle of David Ricardo fell upon lesser men, and the light was gradually extinguished. Rather as the British army after the death of the Duke of Wellington retained in atrophied form only the great duke's defects, and not his brilliant leadership, so the classical school after Ricardo preserved with the well meaning devotion of the unoriginal only his weaknesses; and, under increasing fire, gave up just those positions which he had conquered and which it was vital to preserve. By the last quarter of the nineteenth century, it had reached a state of "fatty degeneration."[3]

Thus, the core concept of classicism from Sir William Petty to David Ricardo,† the concept of surplus, fades from view in the British literature, only to reappear half way through the twentieth century. On the continent of Europe, however, it was never wholly lost to sight. Engels brought out Volume III of *Capital* in 1894, and it was only a few years later that the Russian

---

* The last great figure before, that is to say, the revival of classical theory in the twentieth century.

† And to Marx, of course, but, as we have noted, his work was read too late to keep the Ricardian tradition alive.

mathematical economist, V. K. Dmitriev, took some vital first steps toward a satisfactory solution of Marx's transformation problem in his *Essais Économiques,* published in 1898.[4] He was also possibly the first to defend Ricardo's theory against the criticism of Léon Walras.[5] Then, in 1906, Ladislaus von Bortkiewicz (1868–1931), building on the work of Dmitriev, produced the first thoroughgoing solution to the transformation problem.[6] And, in the 1930's, John von Neumann began his path-breaking work on an expanding economy—a strictly classical study of the accumulation of surplus.[7]

Meanwhile, in England, Piero Sraffa had begun in the 1920's to write his *Production of Commodities by Means of Commodities,*[8] which was not to appear in print until so much later. By 1953, with Joan Robinson's article, "The Production Function and the Theory of Capital,"[9] the classical theme was heard once more in England. However, between 1871 and the 1930's, a highly special new version of the theory of allocation had come to be the overwhelming preoccupation of economists in Britain, on the Continent of Europe, and elsewhere. To this we must now turn.

Classical Allocation Theory versus Neoclassical Allocation Theory

Allocation, understood as the problem of how to allocate surplus output so as to maximize growth and the accumulation of capital, had always been important to classical political economy. From the work of Richard Cantillon on, it is made quite clear by the classical theorists that a problem arises *only* over the allocation of the surplus. For them, allocation meant deciding how the surplus was to be divided between the accumulation of capital and luxury consumption. The composition of the surplus corresponding to this division, and the corresponding stock of capital goods that enter into production, then follow from the requirements of technology (including subsistence).

The basic policy proposal of the physiocrats was that the net product should be devoted to the development of large-scale capitalist agriculture. Only after this had been accomplished would they be content that the now larger surplus should be wholly allocated to luxury consumption. When one turns to the *Wealth of Nations,* it is to find continual stress on the importance of removing those mercantilist restrictions which were holding up the accumulation of capital. An essential aspect of Smith's doctrine of natural liberty is that it would result in stock being so allocated as to maximize growth. Ricardo's distribution theory, again, was written specifically to show that the Corn Laws must lead to rising rents (given a growing population) and thus to the allocation of an increasing proportion of the surplus to luxury consumption by landlords, thereby choking off accumulation of capital. And all of Marx's mature work shows that the historic role of the bourgeoisie is not simply to extract surplus—other classes in other periods of history had done that—but rather to allocate it to the accumulation of capital.

The classical economists would never have entertained the idea of constructing an economic theory where inputs are an arbitrary job lot of "resources," treated (to use modern language) as *parameters,* since the allocation of such a set of given resources would not have been recognized by them as the essential economic problem. For them, questions of allocation arise in connection with the reproduction of surplus, and with the maximization of future surplus.

During the 1870's, however, a school of thought, emerging from several quite independent beginnings, focused attention on just that problem which would not have concerned the classics—the allocation of a set of parametric inputs—and regarded it as the central issue for economic analysis. In their initial models these writers, among whom Léon Walras in his work on general equilibrium is the outstanding master, presented the problem of allocation in a pure-exchange model where production is not treated. When production is introduced in their more developed models, it appears as a kind of exchange. This treatment of allocation in terms of exchange theory is characteristic of what has come to be known as neoclassical economics. Kenneth Arrow and David Starrett have well described the point of view of the founders of neoclassical economics:

> The great founders of the neo-classical school, Carl Menger, W. S. Jevons, and Léon Walras . . . took as an expository point of departure a model which was the polar opposite of the classical, the model of pure exchange. They recognized the importance of production, but Menger and Jevons especially put stress on the notion of exchange as expressing the essence of the economic system: production to some extent appeared merely as an indirect way of exchanging initial holdings.[10]

As Arrow and Starrett remark, it was a feature of classical economics that consumers' demand played a comparatively minor role. In neoclassical theory, on the other hand, consumers' demand is strikingly important. Commenting on this contrast they point out:

> If a classical model of production is completed by adding a system of demand relations, the prices are determined purely by technological or cost considerations. Then the quantities are completely determined by the demands at these prices. In a model of pure exchange, the direction of causation is almost completely reversed. The total

quantities of the goods are given; the demand conditions determine the prices as that set that will cause demand to equal the given supply for all goods.[11],*

So it turns out that demand relations can be embedded in a classical system of reproduction without giving that system neoclassical characteristics. Thus, it is only in terms of their theories of production and allocation that the two schools are to be distinguished. Once this is understood, the original departure of the founders of neoclassical economics shows much more clearly. It was not simply their use of utility theory,† or the demand theory derived from it, that made them so different. But we must examine their views in detail for this to become fully evident.

William Stanley Jevons—the Lonely Hunter

William Stanley Jevons (1835–1882) is described by Lord Keynes as coming from a family which "belonged to the class of educated non-conformists, who, without academic connections, made up, in the first half of the nine-teenth century, the intelligentsia of Liverpool, Manchester, Leeds and Birmingham, [and] became the backbone of Bentham's foundation (in 1826) at University College, London, and of Owens College, Manchester (founded in 1846)."[12] The reader accustomed to thinking of the industrial north of England in the mid-nineteenth century as wholly composed of dark satanic mills, may be interested to note that, while Jevons's father was (appropriately for the time and place) an iron merchant, his mother was a poetess, and *her* father, though a solicitor and banker by profession, was an historian and author who found time to write a *Life of Lorenzo de Medici* among other learned works. He was also noted as a social reformer, and for his work toward the abolition of the slave trade.[13]

R. D. Collison Black and Rosamond Könekamp suggest that Jevons owed his predisposition toward the study of economics to his Liverpool childhood and London youth:

In Jevons's youth poverty and its attendant problems were worse in Liverpool than in any other city. . . . But it was in London in the early fifties that the problems of the growth of towns coupled with rising prosperity were present in all their magnitude. . . . Major cholera epidemics occurred in 1849 and 1854. . . . Charles Dickens threw his strength into a personal campaign for sanitary reform. In his novels the Lon-

---

* The argument of Arrow and Starrett should be re-examined after studying the price relations of neoclassical and classical models, discussed in chapters 9, 12, and 13.
† On utility see pp. 129–31; also chapter 6, pp. 147, 150; and chapter 10, pp. 250–55.

don poor were made real in scenes in *Oliver Twist* (1838) and *Bleak House* (1853). Jevons was influenced by Dickens's writings.[14]

They point out that it was Jevons's habit, as his *Journal* shows, to take long walks through the poorest parts of London. T. W. Hutchison also remarks on Jevons's tendency "to go for long walks through the poorest parts of the Dickensian London of the early fifties."[15] Thus the seventeen-year-old Jevons records in his journal:

I have long had a curiosity about the dark passages and arches between the Strand and the river; . . . I went on Friday. The first thing I saw worth mentioning was the 'dark arches' under the Adelphi but the first time I only looked in and was afraid of going further. . . . There were some women in them then, and I read a little time ago in the newspaper of some women who were found almost starved in them.[16]

And later in the same entry, he adds:

It was some time however before I found any of the wretched places I have heard so much of. One narrow lane, was the worst I think, that I ever saw; almost every house had a dirty piece of paper in the patched and dirty window, with, 'Lodging for single men' at 2d or 3d a night.[17]

Jevons notes with enthusiasm the wide new roads that here and there were being cut through the worst parts, revealing what had lain behind. His early interest in economics seems to have centered on the growth and conditions of towns, especially London.[18] Later, from Australia, where he wrote much on the subject, some of it published as "Social Cesspools of Sidney" in 1858, he remarks: "That man who can witness all the phases of a city unmoved, and uninterested, is himself a criminal. . . ."[19] The similarity of the tone of Jevons's social observation with certain great passages in *Capital* and with Friedrich Engels' *The Condition of the Working Classes in England*,[20] is so striking that one could sandwich a passage from Jevons between a couple of those of Marx or Engels without any sharp change of feeling or style being obvious.

It should never be forgotten that the England (and Europe in general) of late mature classical economics was still exposing its gaunt features to the young eyes of the founders of neoclassicism—the conditions of which the classics wrote had not vanished from the face of the earth. Their models, however, were different. As we shall shortly see, the formal arguments of Jevons, Menger, and Walras start, not from social classes in the relations of production, but from isolated maximizing individuals who are endowed with given stocks of goods which they trade with each other. The concept of class is given no analytical role to play in these models.*

What was probably the most crucial turning point in the life of the young Jevons now came when, at the age of eighteen, he left University College, London before finishing his degree, to take a job as assayer at the Mint, in Sidney, Australia. He did this simply because his family was in financial difficulties, and he stayed in Australia for five years, deliberately saving up money on which he was to live when he returned to finish his university work, and to wait for the establishment of his intellectual reputation. The point about Australia was his isolation and loneliness there. Of course, all the evidence we have suggests that Jevons could have made a desert of isolation out of the center of London, but one cannot help feeling that the habit of inwardness, almost Kirkegaardian in its intensity, was *established* during the formative Australian years.

We can see this from his correspondence, but above all from his amazing *Journal.* Lord Keynes, who had not seen the complete text when he wrote his biographical essay on Jevons, yet thought the extract then published by Jevons's wife to be "of the highest interest both in itself and for the light which it casts on his nature." [21] Black and Könekamp, in introducing their edition of the *Papers and Correspondence of William Stanley Jevons,* with the complete text of the *Journal,* describe this as "an intimate and even a moving document." [22] Indeed, Jevons leaps out at the reader of those pages, stark and exposed, all masks, all protective outer skin stripped off. In the best tradition of the fatally flawed hero of the Romantic Rebellion, he is at one moment tormented by his loneliness, at another glorying in it.

In a letter written from Sidney to his sister Henrietta, on August 4, 1858, Jevons reveals his "Australian" philosophy:

> Now I very much fear that a gay unsettled life is just what would rub off from your mind many buds of truth of which I have caught a glimpse. . . . No one can rise above the common level if he do not cherish within him an almost secret soul to animate and guide him. Partial solitude is necessary to earnest thoughts. I might give many instances to prove this; I will only notice one which is closely applicable viz. Charlotte Brontë, who had few or no friends except her sisters and lived in a quiet retired home. [23]

The comparison with that other darkly brilliant North of England Victorian family is not absurd. Jevons's sister, Lucy, wrote in her diary when she was

---

*The distinction between landlords and the rest of society no doubt plays a role in Walras's social thinking, but classes play no analytical role in his mathematical model of general equilibrium.

fifteen years old, "In Stanley I see the dawning of a great mind."[24] And Jevons even had a brother, Roscoe, who echoes the tragic Branwell Brontë. Black and Könekamp write that "a streak of tragedy runs through the Jevons family history—of which Jevons's own accidental death is an instance. And Jevons carried a secret burden from early youth. Roscoe became insane at the age of about eighteen, shortly after his mother's death, and never recovered. It was this loss which drove Jevons to work with such remorseless passion. Roscoe was a poet who showed brilliant promise as chemist and mathematician. Unfortunately his poems and diaries, which meant so much to Jevons, have not survived."[25]

In his *Journal* for May 23, 1864, Jevons describes reading his dead brother's verses: "I have hardly perhaps read them all, for I can hardly bear to read much at a time. But the more I read the more I am convinced that he was as great in soul as he was good."[26] Anyone who studies the surviving evidence of Jevons's inner life will not be surprised that, for all the scenes of Dickensian London through which he had moved as a youth, he made the isolated individual the center of his thought.

The Economic Writings

In the solitude of his Australian period, Jevons recollected the doctrines of the great lecturer on mathematics and logic he had heard at University College, London, Augustus De Morgan. It was to seek out De Morgan again that he returned to University College.[27] The notion, characteristic of much twentieth century work influenced by mathematical logic, of a fundamental unity of science, under the rule of mathematics, was already strikingly apparent in Jevons's approach to all science. It was in turn to dictate his approach to economics. Thus appears what was to be a salient characteristic of neoclassical economics—the effort to give its fundamental principles mathematical form. Of the three founders, only Menger held aloof from this, and subsequent development has tended to follow Walras, and to some extent Jevons.

According to a letter to his brother, Herbert, of June 1, 1860, Jevons had arrived in the previous few months at what he had no doubt was *"the true theory of economy* so thorough-going and consistent, that I cannot now read other books on the subject without indignation."[28] The theory was, he added, entirely mathematical in principle. By 1862 Jevons had his core of pure theory ready to present. (In the previous year or so he had also been doing, and publishing, work on statistics, chemistry, and meteorology.) In September, 1862, Jevons sent two papers to the British Association, one an applied study of industrial fluctuations, and the other his "Notice of a General Mathematical Theory of Political Economy." The papers were read, but neither was printed in full, although summaries were included in the Report of the Association for 1862. The "Mathematical Theory of Political Economy" got about a page. (Four years later it was finally published in the *Statistical Journal*.[29]) As the year 1862 ended, Jevons confided to his Journal that it had seen his theory "offered to a Learned Society (?) and received without a word of interest or belief."[30]

Jevons's first book, which was on an issue in applied economics, was much better received: *The Coal Question: An Inquiry Concerning the Progress of the Nation and the Probable Exhaustion of Our Coal Mines*.[31] The very title conveys the startling thesis of the book. Lord Keynes, who admitted that the book was "most brilliantly and engagingly written,"[32] nevertheless did not consider it one of Jevons's best works. He argued (with evidence[33]) that Jevons was determined upon a *succès de scandale,* and decided that Jevons's conclusions about the exhaustion of Britain's coal reserves "were influenced, I suspect, by a psychological trait, unusually strong in him, which many other people share, a certain hoarding instinct, a readiness to be alarmed and excited by the idea of the exhaustion of resources."[34] Certainly the readiness to be alarmed by the idea in question is one which, since then, probably many people increasingly share. What is undoubtedly true is that Jevons, during his own lifetime, had a much wider reputation for his work as an applied economist, statistician, and logician, than for his original contribution to pure economic theory. The latter, in its mature form, was published in 1871: *The Theory of Political Economy*.[35]

It has been observed that, "From his earliest studies Jevons saw pure economic problems as optimum-allocation problems,"[36] and indeed he had written to this effect as early as February 28, 1858, in a letter to his sister, Henrietta, in which, after some charming reflections on society, affection, and music—"Music is always to me the same, a condition of my existence, a part of me,"[37]—Jevons writes, "I am glad you found Political Economy tolerable. . . . You will perceive that *Economy,* scientifically speaking, is a very contracted science; it is in part a sort of vague mathematics which calculates the causes and effects of man's industry and shows how it may best be applied."[38] In the *Theory of Political Economy* Jevons spelled out this "very contracted science," already outlined in his paper of 1862, in words that foreshadowed the development of neoclassical theory. He begins with the maximizing activity of the individual, then proceeds to the theory of pure exchange. He is well aware that in reality industry is in a condition of perpetual change:

> If we wished to have a complete solution of the problem in all its natural complexity, we should have to treat it as a problem of dynamics. But it would surely be absurd to attempt the more difficult question when the more easy one is yet so imperfectly within our power. It is only as a purely statistical problem that I can venture to treat the action of exchange. Holders of commodities will be regarded not as continuously passing on these commodities in streams of trade, but as possessing certain fixed amounts which they exchange until they come to equilibrium.[39]

The classical attempt to depict the production of commodities by means of commodities was to be abandoned and the science contracted in search of mathematical rigor. Jevons as always in his public (and private) writings was utterly honest about what he planned to do, and about its limitations. Walras, as we shall see, was to exhibit just these same qualities.

In the older secondary sources the concept of utility was always given star billing as the distinguishing characteristic of the work of Jevons and the other founders of neoclassicism. We have already seen reason to doubt this view. It is certainly true that Jevons (at least) sometimes wrote hedonistic passages. Back in September, 1856, while still in Australia, he had entered in his *Journal:*

> I regard man in reality as essentially selfish, that is as doing everything with a view to gain enjoyment or avoid pain. This self interest is certainly the main-spring of all his actions.[40]

He goes on to point out that it is not his intention that self interest be narrowly interpreted: "It is by the quality of those pleasures which he is continually seeking and by the causes of pain he equally flies from that he is to be judged. It is quite possible that one of his chief pleasures may be to see another person happy."[41] Hedonism, as a philosophical doctrine, is of course an ancient one with its roots in classical Greece. Whether or not Jevons consistently subscribed to this philosophical position, it will be our contention that this makes no essential difference to his mathematical theory of political economy since hedonism can be eliminated from that theory without changing either its mathematical structure or its economic content.

The core of Jevons's theory is the theory of exchange, which requires not less than two individuals* endowed with given stocks of commodities, any

---

* Jevons, unlike Walras, fails to distinguish the two-person, two-commodity case from the case of many persons and commodities.

part of which may be offered in trade. But, on Jevons's own account, any objective which one of these agents seeks to maximize through exchange *counts* as maximizing utility. So the philosophical content of the concept "utility" plays no role in the economic argument. Jevons's theory of the exchange of given stocks will have the same structure and economic implications if we describe the individuals involved simply as maximizing an objective function, whose nature is left unspecified, and is their own business. It is a truism of modern neoclassical mathematical economics that whatever a consumer (or household) maximizes counts as maximizing utility. Whenever the consumer's preferences can be represented by a real valued function, one calls this a utility function simply out of *gravitas*. If this is true, as everyone knows it is, of today's neoclassical theory, the same generous interpretation can be put on Jevons's utility functions. Hutchison has noted that:

> It is interesting to speculate as to how Jevons would have met the powerful criticisms of hedonist and utilitarian psychologizing which two or three decades later were to be levelled at his form of marginal utility analysis.[42]

Hutchison apparently thought that, on the whole, Jevons "might well have been ready to accept [it]."[43]

All that was essential to Jevons's theory of pure exchange was the assumption that the consumers or households were in a position to make marginal changes in their holdings of commodities. They would then exchange so as to achieve that allocation which of all feasible allocations would result in the maximization of their objective. Jevons was making precisely this point when he wrote (using, of course, his term "utility"), "a person procures such quantities of commodities that the final degrees of utility[*] of any pair of commodities are inversely as the ratios of exchange of the commodities."[44] Evidently, this is a pure theory of the exchange of given stocks, and is quite independent of the concrete nature of the motives or desires of the individual households. The theory describes a mechanism which operates whatever the parties to the exchanges are in fact maximizing. As has been well said:

> Jevons's marginal utility analysis posed the allocation problem for the individual consumer, and formulated the maximizing solution . . . it was to be some time before the firm's allocation problems were generally solved on parallel lines to those of the household. But the marginal utility theory of value provided the archetype of a 'microeconomic' maximizing allocation problem, capable of a pure and simple mathematical formulation, and using the concept of the marginal unit to formulate a precise

---

*Jevons always spoke of the "final degree of utility," but for convenience, we shall use the later, now familiar, term "marginal utility."

maximizing solution . . . what was important in marginal utility was the adjective rather than the noun.[45]

Referring to these views of Hutchison, Maurice Dobb has remarked that, "Some have, indeed, actually identified the change introduced by Jevons with attention to the conditions of 'allocation'."[46] Mark Blaug, again citing Hutchison, writes: "The significance of marginal utility theory was that it provided the archetype of the general problem of allocating given means with maximum effect."[47] And R. D. Collison Black sums up his findings on Jevons by saying that, "my contention is that Jevons was really setting out to establish the core of our subject as a science of economizing behaviour. . . ."[48]

As Hutchison and others have pointed out, Jevons confined his theory of allocation to the exchange of given stocks of *goods*. He did not develop it to include the allocation of given resources to the production of commodities, which was to be typical of later neoclassicism. Thus, it can be said that Jevons "only really completed one half of the marginal revolution or evolution. . . . He did not work out the corresponding formula for the producer buying producers' goods or services from their owners."[49]

Jevons drowned at the age of 46 in August of 1882. He never had true recognition for the core of his economic theory, but he had tasted a brief eminence for his manifold contributions to statistics, applied economics, logic, and other sciences, and he had held two chairs: at Owens College, Manchester; and at University College, London. In May, 1866, he confided to his *Journal:* "The last week or two I have had enough of newspaper fame. I know it is no slight thing to be quoted in the Budget of a Minister* when he announces a change in the policy of the country he leads. But what poor mortals we are. I feel as if I would readily give it all for a few kind words from a loving girl."[50] In December 1867, Jevons married Harriet Ann Taylor, a daughter of the founder of the *Manchester Guardian*. Thus, in his last years of happiness, as in his early beginnings, he was, as Lord Keynes has remarked, very much part of that characteristic type of North Country life of which Manchester is a center.

Carl Menger: His Excellency

Having noted that Jevons left the core of neoclassical allocation theory half completed, Hutchison writes, "one of the most important contributions of

* Gladstone. Our footnote.

Menger's contemporary work was that it straightway applied the same allocation analysis to producers' goods and services as it did to consumers' goods
and services. . . .''[51] But this took place against a very different background, the Vienna of 1871, and at the hands of a very different man from the
lonely Jevons.

Carl Menger (1840–1921) was anything but obscure. To Friedrich von
Wieser, who left the fullest account of him, Menger was, above all, the
founder of the Austrian School. And, as has been well said by Erich Streissler
and W. Weber:

> Coming from Wieser, this is almost a dynastic pronouncement, the characterization
> of Menger as a ruling monarch, the description of a man who, by virtue of his office
> and by the force of his personality, *imperio et auctoritate,* dominated a group of out-
> standing scholars and public men. The extraordinary thing about his school is its out-
> standing social success.[52]

Streissler (the present holder of the chair at the University of Vienna which
was once Menger's) and Weber add, speaking of the founder of the Austrian
School:

> Menger, Böhm-Bawerk, and Wieser were all of them Excellencies (and even Life
> Members of the Upper House of Parliament)—at a time when to become an Ex-
> cellency was a rare honour, hardly to be achieved by anyone not born to it. Wieser and
> Böhm-Bawerk were both of them cabinet ministers . . . Menger himself did not hold
> office; his social position was attained in another way. He was one of the tutors of the
> Crown Prince Rudolf and even later appears to have retained some influence on the
> Prince.[53]

Truly, the dark lonely streets of Jevons's Victorian Manchester and London
have faded from view, to be replaced by the bright plumage of Vienna as that
city lay basking in the late afternoon sun of the Austro-Hungarian Empire: a
scene bright with a rainbow of uniforms, light as good champagne, with the
chill of approaching night ever so faintly felt behind the warmth of its mel-
ody.

"Menger, unlike Jevons and Walras, did not begin by claiming to be a
'revolutionary' . . . ,''[54] Streissler and Weber tell us. He never needed to
feel an outsider, to fight for recognition against an entrenched local establishment. He simply thought of himself as developing a tradition until, later, the
German Historical School (who were opposed to theory) rejected or ignored
his work. Then, and then only, he became a controversial writer. On the other
hand, it would be a great mistake to imagine that Carl Menger founded the
great Austrian School, as it were, effortlessly. Being well connected at court

and in society no doubt made life pleasant. One has only to read the Jevons *Papers and Correspondence* or the Marx-Engels *Correspondence* to see vividly how poverty, loneliness, and neglect can corrode a thinker's peace. Connections bring their consolations, but they will accomplish more than that only if the society in which one moves contains the great minds of the day *in one's field*. For Mirabeau, being at Versailles meant the entrée to Quesnay's society. For Adam Smith, making the Grand Tour meant meeting the French physiocrats and Turgot. For Ricardo, London meant the society of James Mill, of Robert Malthus, of the whole circle that was to form the Political Economy Club, and, by no means least, the House of Commons in the early days of the anti-Corn Law agitation: a brilliant intellectual society in which, according to Marx, the greatest tournaments of classical political economy took place.

With the utmost respect for the charm and polish of Vienna, it was a backwater of economic science until Menger, "this hickory of a man."[55] by sheer force of character had built it up and found disciples. "[The University of Vienna] was by no means ideal, both because there was no local tradition in the subject, let alone one that commanded the attention of the world, and because the future lawyers and civil servants who formed his audience were but mildly interested in what he had to say."[56]

Menger was born on February 28, 1840, in part of what is now Poland; the son of a lawyer, Anton Menger Edler von Wolfergruen, "he came from an old family of Austrian craftsmen, musicians, civil servants and army officers."[57] After studying at the Universities of Vienna and Prague, he took his doctor's degree at the University of Cracow in 1867. Then followed a few years of journalism and work in the press department of the Austrian Civil Service. But he was only thirty-one when, in early 1871, the book appeared upon which his reputation as an original economic theorist securely rests: his *Principles of Economics*.[58] This secured Menger the appointment as lecturer (*privatdocent*) in economic theory at the University of Vienna in 1872. One year later he became associate professor (*professor extraordinarius*). Then, after a few years as tutor to Crown Prince Rudolf of Austria, during which they traveled through England, France, Germany, and Switzerland, Menger was appointed full professor (*professor ordinarius*) at Vienna in 1879. He was now reigning monarch of Austrian economic theory. True, he had as yet no kingdom—there was no Austrian School. But he promptly set about creating one. And, of course, if there was no living tradition in Austria, neither did he have powerful rivals. He had almost unlimited authority over the recruitment of academic teachers of economic theory. Even the doctoral course was confined to students who had made their mark and had become close intimates, so:

how much more so for the *Habilitation,* the final 'degree' admitting to academic teaching! It was therefore usual in the *Habilitationschrift* to quote the Master copiously, to paraphrase him, and if He liked the variations on His theme, even to dedicate the finished work to Menger.[59]

The cohesiveness of the Austrian School as it developed was not *just* a matter of common social background: "all the Austrians being lawyers (or rather jurists), most of them closely connected with the civil service, and about half of them nobles. . . ."[60] It was the influence, "or perhaps better the grip of Menger which enforced cohesion. Menger, even more than the founder of a school was the apex of a social system!"[61]

Menger's Principles

Like Jevons, and the like the whole neoclassical tradition which was to follow, Menger takes as his starting point the maximizing individual. He then sets out the theory of exchange between such individuals, and only brings in production toward the end of his book. Nevertheless Menger's treatment has certain special characteristics which distinguish him sharply from both Jevons and Walras. For one thing, his account of the maximizing consumer avoids all use of the differential calculus and eschews even such notions as continuous change and divisibility without limit. George Stigler has argued that, "It seems clear that Menger is thinking in terms of small, finite quantitative changes, and not of infinitesimals."[62] Stigler comments that Menger "probably had no mathematical training."[63]

Menger's son Karl, the distinguished mathematician, has countered by suggesting that the formulation of maximizing in finite terms in the *Principles* was deliberate, and not due to ignorance:

The Austrian formulation of decreasing marginal utility is more general since it is valid even if there are places where the formulation does not admit a second derivative and its graph has no curvature, whereas at such places the mathematical formulation fails to assert anything.[64]

Streissler also has noted that:

[Menger] came from a mathematically minded family so that the explanation of his behavior by lack of mathematical training does not really hold water. Rather, the then prevalent mathematics, calculus, was useful only in the description of equilibrium situations, and Menger was not interested in these.[65]

It is hard to see how a reader of the Menger-Walras correspondence could continue to believe that Menger stayed away from the use of mathematics simply as a result of ignorance. Writing to Walras on June 28, 1883,[66] Menger argues that in economics the mathematical method is a method of exposition, of demonstration, not a method of actual research. Whereupon Walras, who treats Menger's comments on mathematics with complete respect, replies in a modestly argued letter of July 2.[67] Nothing in this exchange of letters could give support to the idea that Walras believed Menger incompetent to argue the case for or against the use of mathematics in economics.

It has been argued in recent years, however, that Menger differs from Jevons and Walras in much more fundamental ways than over the use of mathematics. So much so that it is being increasingly questioned whether Menger is best regarded as one of the founders of neoclassicism at all. Menger's real concern, so this argument runs, is with the detailed study of various aspects of an economy which is always *out of equilibrium*. His theory, it is contended, is dynamic and not static, and involves the rejection of the perfect foresight assumption characteristic of neoclassical economics. He rejects even the standard simplification of assuming a single ruling equilibrium price in a market.[68] Streissler, for example, contrasts the unique properties of Menger and the Austrian school with those of neoclassicism, insisting that for the neoclassical school the essence of the economic problem was:

. . . to search for the conditions under which given productive services were allocated with optimal results among competitive uses, optimal in the sense of maximizing consumers' satisfaction. This ruled out consideration of the effects of increases in the quantity and quality of resources, as well as the dynamic expansion of wants—effects that the classical economists had regarded as the *sine qua non* of improvements in economic welfare. I would add that by the very logic of the maximization problem, all true neoclassical economics is economics under certainty, the static framework of analysis being closely linked to the plausibility of the implied assumption of full information. Finally, marginalism in its essence is a decision theory; in the language of mathematical programming it focuses on the objective function first, on the choice variables second, and on the restraints not at all.[69]

In this passage, it may be remarked, Streissler gives a precise account of exactly the view of neoclassical economics which we are adopting in this book. He adds that:

In all these senses the Austrians were not marginalist. Or, to put this central thesis of my article more cautiously, marginalism was not the essence of their endeavour. . . . Marginalism is introduced in the middle of Menger's *Grundsätze* [*Principles*], but it is for this very reason not central to, not the keystone of, this very logical construction.[70]

Not only was Menger the great founder of the Austrian school, Streissler points out, but, "Menger embodied the unique Austrian tradition, and he was the least marginalist of all the Austrians. *The farther his pupils escaped him, the more marginalist they became . . .*" [71]

It is true that Menger repeatedly refers to uncertainty in his *Principles* and, as Streissler remarks:

> Menger had incorporated into his founding volume practically all the ideas which make the application of the marginal calculus difficult and hazy; and by his express refusal to recognize a unique and determinate market price he even discarded the main prop that supports marginalism. . . . His economics in its substantive content was disequilibrium economics. [72]

Deep and interesting questions are thus posed, but any further discussion of the reinterpretation of Menger and the Austrian school cannot be entered into in this book. Our concern is with the core characteristics of what became neoclassical economics, and with Menger only insofar as he possessed these characteristics. And, despite the other strands that can be found in his theory, it did in fact possess such neoclassical properties: certain concepts essential to later neoclassicism are fully and clearly stated for the first time in Menger's *Principles*. Above all there is the distinction between factors of production (goods of higher order) and commodities (goods of lower order), and the argument that the factors derive their value from the value of the commodities which are produced by their use. This entails the characteristic neoclassical theory of "distribution" among the "factors" of the total income resulting from production, together with a theory of the allocation of the given factors.

There were the outlines of such a theory in Jevons's preface to the second edition of his *Theory of Political Economy,* [73] but only in Menger's *Principles* was this outline filled in. As has been pointed out by K. W. Rothschild, "Among these fathers [of marginal analysis] it was certainly Menger who was most acutely aware of the distributional implications of the new theoretical approach. . . . If Menger's analysis is to be criticized it is along lines that apply equally to contemporary models of the neoclassical school." [74] The classical analysis of distribution in terms of the rent of land, the profits of stock, and the subsistence wage disappear from view and Menger offers the single concept of goods of higher order. These play the role of the familiar neoclassical factors of production: given resources whose value is imputed to them from the value of the consumer's goods they produce. Thus, Menger states categorically, "the value of goods of higher order will depend under all circumstances on the expected value of goods of lower order." [75] Indeed, as

Rothschild has said, "If utility was to be regarded as the *sole* cause of factor costs, the scarcity of the factors had to be taken as given. Only in this way could their values be made a pure imputation problem. Classical theory, on the other hand, had—with the exception of land—never assumed such constancy of factor supplies."[76] Rothschild claims that Menger's abandonment of the land, labor, and capital of classical economics in favor of generalized goods of higher order, factors, "was a first-class analytical achievement; yet it pushed into the background a distinction between the different positions of the various socio-economic classes (land owners, capitalist, workers) in the distribution process."[77]

Whatever we may feel about this move as an analytical achievement, we can all agree with Rothschild's estimation of its consequences. George Stigler took the same view as to what constituted Menger's specific contribution to neoclassical distribution theory. Unlike Rothschild, however, he regarded the neoclassical treatment, in terms of given factors, which begins with Menger, as superior in every way to the classical treatment:

> Prior to Menger no satisfactory theory of distribution had emerged. The classical view was one of the division of income between social classes: Smith and his followers never confronted the problem of how a given product may be imputed to the resources which cooperate in its production nor did they consider distribution as a value problem or discuss the pricing of productive services. Menger was the first economist to raise this question, and moreover, to suggest the proper manner of answering it.[78]

The case for the view that Menger—whatever else he may have been—was one of the founders of the neoclassical school has surely never been better put. The fascinating hints to be found throughout Menger's work as to the importance of historical time and the uncertainty that is its necessary concomitant, may eventually be fruitful. It is certainly true that the Austrian school (witness the work of Neumann and Morgenstern) had never ceased to be haunted by the problem of uncertainty. But, the historical fact is that Menger's work was an important component in the development of those models which indisputably characterize the core of neoclassical theory. In Jevons's *Theory of Political Economy* the ghosts of the classical social classes still faintly linger. In Menger's *Principles* they have been completely exorcised. Goods of lower order (commodities) are produced by means of goods of higher order (given resources) and the economic problem consists simply in the allocation of these resources.

With Jevons and Menger there is a clear break with the classical tradition. Jevons places the maximizing individual at the center of the picture and gives a mathematical account of the allocation of given stocks of commodities among trading individuals. Menger does not use the mathematical method, but he adds the other half of the picture: the theory of production by means of given resources. It remained for the third great founder of neoclassicism, Léon Walras, to present pure economic theory in terms of a general equilibrium model. Then the structure of neoclassical economics, in a form still recognizable today, was essentially complete.

Notes

1. Lord Keynes of Tilton, *Essays in Biography,* Macmillan, London, 1933. Our citation is from *The Collected Writings of John Maynard Keynes,* Vol. X, Macmillan for The Royal Economic Society, London, 1972, p. 131.
2. Sir John Hicks, "The Austrian Theory of Capital and its Rebirth in Modern Economics," in J. R. Hicks and W. Weber, eds., *Carl Menger and the Austrian School of Economics,* Oxford University Press, 1973, p. 190.
3. The phrase, "fatty degeneration of classical economics," is used by N. Annan in his biography of Sir Leslie Stephen, and cited by T. W. Hutchinson, *A Review of Economic Doctrines 1870–1929,* Oxford University Press, 1953, p. 10, n. 1.
4. V. K. Dmitriev, *Economicheskei ocherki,* 1898; trans. *Essais Économiques,* 1904; reprinted in Editions du Centre de la Recherche Scientifique, Paris, 1968.
5. See Maurice Dobb, "The Sraffa System and Critique of the Neo-classical Theory of Distribution," *De Economist,* Vol. 118, 1970, pp. 347–62; reprinted in E. K. Hunt and Jesse G. Schwartz, *A Critique of Economic Theory,* Penguin Books, Middlesex, England, 1972.
6. Ladislaus von Bortkiewicz, "Wertrechnung und Preisrechnung im Marxschen System," *Archiv für Sozialwissenschaft,* 1906, 1907; and "Zür Berichtigung der grundlegenden theoretischen Konstruktion von Marx im dritten Band der Kapital," *Jahrbücher für Nationaloekonomie und Statistik,* 1907; trans. "Value and Price in the Marxian System," *International Economic Papers,* No. 2, 1952, pp. 5–60.
7. John von Neumann, "Über ein Ökonomisches Gleichungs-System und eine Verallgemeinerung des Browerschen Fixpunktsatzes," in Karl Menger, ed., *Ergebnisse eines Mathematischen Kolloquiums,* No. 8, 1935–6, published 1937; trans. "A Model of General Economic Equilibrium," *Review of Economic Studies,* Vol. 13, 1945–6, pp. 1–9.
8. Piero Sraffa, *Production of Commodities by Means of Commodities, Prelude to a Critique of Economic Theory,* Cambridge University Press, 1960.
9. Joan Robinson, "The Production Function and the Theory of Capital," *Review of Economic Studies,* 1953, pp. 81–111; reprinted in *Collected Economic Papers,* Vol. II, Basil Blackwell, Oxford, 1975, pp. 114–31.
10. Kenneth J. Arrow and David A. Starrett, "Cost and Demand-Theoretic Approaches to the Theory of Price Determination," in *Carl Menger and the Austrian School of Economics,* p. 133.

11. *Ibid.*, p. 133.
12. Keynes, *Collected Writings,* Vol. X, p. 109.
13. For these and other fascinating biographical details on Jevons, see *ibid.,* pp. 109–60. See also R. D. Collison Black and Rosamond Könekamp, eds., *Papers and Correspondence of William Stanley Jevons,* Vol. I, *Biography and Personal Journal,* Macmillan, London, 1972. Subsequent references to the *Papers and Correspondence* will be preceded by the editors' names where we are referring to their text, and by Jevons's name where we are referring to his writings.
14. Black and Könekamp, *Papers and Correspondence,* Vol. I, p. 16.
15. Hutchison, *Economic Doctrines,* pp. 32–33.
16. Jevons, *Papers and Correspondence,* Vol. I, p. 67.
17. *Ibid.*, p. 68.
18. Black and Könekamp, *Papers and Correspondence,* Vol. I, p. 17.
19. Cited in Hutchison, *Economic Doctrines,* p. 33.
20. Friedrich Engels, *Die Lage der arbeitenden Klasse in England,* Otto Wigand, Leipzig, 1845; trans. *The Condition of the Working Class in England,* Progress Publishers, Moscow, 1973.
21. Keynes, *Collected Works,* Vol. X, p. 149.
22. Black and Könekamp, *Papers and Correspondence,* Vol. I, p. 1.
23. Jevons, *Papers and Correspondence,* Vol. II, p. 337.
24. Black and Könekamp, *Papers and Correspondence,* Vol. I, p. 13.
25. *Ibid.*, p. 7.
26. Jevons, *Journal* in *Papers and Correspondence,* Vol. I, p. 194.
27. Black and Könekamp, *Papers and Correspondence,* Vol. I, pp. 15–16.
28. Jevons, *Papers and Correspondence,* Vol. II, p. 410. Jevons's italics.
29. Jevons, "Notice of a General Mathematical Theory of Political Economy," *Statistical Journal,* Vol. XXIX, June 1866.
30. Jevons, *Papers and Correspondence,* Vol. I, p. 188.
31. Jevons, *The Coal Question: An Inquiry Concerning the Progress of the Nation and the Probable Exhaustion of Our Coal Mines,* Macmillan, London, 1865.
32. Keynes, *Collected Writings,* Vol X, p. 112.
33. *Ibid.*, pp. 113–7.
34. *Ibid.*, p. 117.
35. Jevons, *The Theory of Political Economy,* Macmillan, London, 1871.
36. Hutchison, *Economic Doctrines,* pp. 35–6.
37. Jevons, *Papers and Correspondence,* Vol. II, p. 319.
38. *Ibid.*, p. 321. Jevons's italics.
39. Jevons, *Theory of Political Economy,* p. 319.
40. Jevons, *Papers and Correspondence,* Vol. I, p. 133.
41. *Ibid.*
42. Hutchison, *Economic Doctrines,* p. 42.
43. *Ibid.*
44. Jevons, *Theory of Political Economy,* p. 139.
45. Hutchison, *Economic Doctrines,* p. 16.
46. Maurice Dobb, *Theories of Value and Distribution Since Adam Smith,* Cambridge University Press, 1973, p. 174.

47. Mark Blaug, *Economic Theory in Retrospect*, Richard D. Irwin, Homewood, Ill., 1968, p. 299.
48. R. D. Collison Black, "W. S. Jevons and the Foundation of Modern Economics," in R. D. Collison Black, A. W. Coats, and Craufurd D. W. Goodwin, eds., *The Marginal Revolution in Economics, Interpretation and Evaluation*, Duke University Press, 1973, p. 106.
49. Hutchison, *Economic Doctrines*, p. 44.
50. Jevons, *Papers and Correspondence*, Vol. I, p. 206.
51. Hutchison, *Economic Doctrines*, p. 44.
52. E. Streissler and W. Weber, "The Menger Tradition," in *Carl Menger and the Austrian School of Economics*, p. 226.
53. *Ibid.*
54. *Ibid.*, p. 228.
55. Joseph Schumpeter, *History of Economic Analysis*, Oxford University Press, 1954, p. 827.
56. *Ibid.*
57. F. A. von Hayek, "Introduction" to *The Collected Works of Carl Menger*, Vol. I, *Grundsätze der Volkswirtschaftslehre*, The London School of Economics and Political Science Series of Reprints of Scarce Tracts in Economic and Political Science, no. 17, 1934, p. x.
58. Carl Menger, *Grundsätze der Volkswirtschaftslehre*, Erster Allgemeiner Theil, Braumüller, Vienna, 1871; trans. *Principles of Economics*, Free Press, Glencoe, Ill., 1950.
59. Erich Streissler, "To what extent was the Austrian School Marginalist?" in *The Marginal Revolution in Economics*, p. 162.
60. *Ibid.*, p. 163.
61. *Ibid.*
62. George J. Stigler, *Production and Distribution Theories: The Formative Period*, Macmillan, New York, 1941, p. 147.
63. *Ibid.*
64. Karl Menger, "Austrian Marginalism and Mathematical Economics," in *Carl Menger and the Austrian School of Economics*, p. 40.
65. Streissler, "To what extent . . . Marginalist?" p. 174.
66. Carl Menger to Léon Walras, in William Jaffé, ed., *Correspondence of Léon Walras and Related Papers*, Vol. I, North-Holland, Amsterdam, 1965, p. 768.
67. Walras to Menger, *ibid.*; see further, Menger to Walras, *ibid.*, Vol. II, pp. 2–6.
68. These questions of time and uncertainty are raised by Sir John Hicks in "Some Questions of Time in Economics," in Anthony M. Tang, Fred M. Westfield, and James S. Worley, eds., *Evolution, Welfare, and Time in Economics, Essays in Honor of Nicholas Georgescu-Roegen*, Lexington Books, Lexington, Mass., 1976, pp. 135–51. See also the symposium *Carl Menger and Austrian Economics, Atlantic Economic Journal*, Vol. VI (September 1978) for other papers, including one by the present authors, concerned with the re-interpretation of Menger.
69. Streissler, "To what extent . . . Marginalist?" p. 160.
70. *Ibid.*, p. 161.

71. *Ibid.,* p. 163. Streissler's italics.
72. Streissler, "To what extent . . . Marginalist?" pp. 172–3. See further, Streissler and Weber, "The Menger Tradition," pp. 226–32.
73. Jevons, *Theory of Political Economy,* 2nd ed., Macmillan, London, 1879, pp. xliv–li.
74. K. W. Rothschild, "Distributive Aspects of the Austrian Theory," in *Carl Menger and the Austrian School of Economics,* p. 208.
75. Menger, *Principles,* p. 124; cited by Rothschild, "Distributive Aspects," p. 214.
76. Rothschild, "Distributive Aspects," p. 216.
77. *Ibid.,* p. 217.
78. Stigler, *Production and Distribution,* p. 152.

6

Walrasian General Equilibrium Theory

> His system of economic equilibrium, uniting, as it does, the quality of "revolutionary" creativeness with the quality of classic synthesis, is the only work by an economist that will stand comparison with the achievements of theoretical physics.
>
> JOSEPH SCHUMPETER[1]

> It has rarely been pointed out that the general equilibrium theory was formulated independently and simultaneously by Walras and Marx. . . .
>
> MICHIO MORISHIMA[2]

Marie Esprit Léon Walras: as French as Racine

Individual components of neoclassical theory had been sketched more or less adequately by Jevons and Menger, but they had not been assembled into a complete system of general equilibrium, and set out clearly in a mathematically consistent form. This task was an important part of the life-work of Léon Walras (1834–1910). Schumpeter has written of Walras that, "The simple greatness which lies in unconditional surrender to one task is what strikes us when we look back today on this scholarly life."[3] He added that, "The external events of this life are quickly told."[4] But now that we have the unbelievably rich *Correspondence of Léon Walras and Related Papers,*[5] edited by William Jaffé, Schumpeter's conclusions may be doubted.

The correspondence of Walras offers weighty evidence for Jaffé's well-known thesis that the intimate biography of a thinker is highly relevant to the scholarly understanding of his creative work. To let Jaffé speak for himself, in selecting letters for publication:

> . . . it was found neither possible nor desirable to eschew or slur over all references to the private lives of Léon Walras and his more noteworthy correspondents. To bowdlerize the letters . . . would defeat an important purpose of this publication, which is to reveal what lies beneath the surface of Walras's scientific achievement and its reception by his contemporaries.[6]

No grey, uneventful life emerges from the warm letters Walras wrote to Célestine Aline Ferbach,* with whom he apparently lived from 1858, when she was twenty-three and he twenty-four, until their marriage in 1869.[8] And, above all, as we shall see in due course, Walras, isolated from daily contact with men of his own intellectual caliber in Lausanne, lived a rich mental life in his correspondence with virtually every great economist of his day.

Born on December 16, 1834 to Antoine-Auguste Walras and Louise Aline de Sainte Beuve, at Evreux, between Rouen and Paris, Léon Walras, as Hutchison remarks, "intellectually and temperamentally was to a quite exceptional extent the son of his father, and very devoted to him and his ideas."[9] Like Marx, who was devoted both to his father and to that other father-figure of his childhood and youth, the Baron von Westphalen, Walras offers no confirmation of Freudian theories of Oedipal conflict. Marx, however, does not appear to have derived any of his specifically *economic* ideas from fatherly influence, whereas Walras unquestionably did. Hutchison remarks:

> There is surely no parallel in political economy for the intellectual relationship between father and son, which held between Auguste and Léon Walras. The son followed out with the closest loyalty both the spirit and most of the technical details and definitions of his father's work.[10]

Léon Walras is described by Hutchison as "the son of an economist"[11] but this description could mislead a modern reader. In fact, Auguste Walras was a teacher of philosophy and rhetoric, and an educational administrator. The father thought and wrote on economics, but it was in the course of investigations into the philosophical foundations of the concept of property that Auguste Walras was led to the concept of *rareté*, which may best be translated as "scarcity." In scarcity the senior Walras saw the foundation both of property and of economic value. Deep in the idea of scarcity lay the seed of neoclassical allocation theory, and it was to be Léon Walras's role to draw it out and bring it to final flower in his theory of general equilibrium.

The interest of Léon Walras in economic theory had been aroused when he was fourteen years old, by having his father read from one of his own manuscripts that land and its services had an intrinsic value resulting from their utility combined with their limited supply.† All his life Léon Walras was to

---

* "A bientôt mon chéri mignon; je t'embrasse mille et mille fois ici en attendant mieux."[7]
† ". . . la terre et son service avaient une valeur intrinsèque provenant de leur utilité combinée avec la limitation de leur quantité."[12]

follow his father in regarding the private ownership of land (together with private ownership of monopolies) as the great source of social injustice and maldistribution. Another ten years were to pass, however, before the son made his final commitment to economic theory. In the meantime he had made two attempts to get into the École Polytechnique, and met the failure which, as Schumpeter remarks, we would expect of one whose preparation consisted of "studying Descartes and Newton."[13] He then attempted, equally unsuccessfully, to study at the École des Mines. Alas, as Jaffé remarks, "Neither the study nor the career of engineering suited the bohemian temperament of his youth."[14]

Walras admits with charming frankness that engineering held no joys for him and that he happily returned to literature, philosophy, history, literary and art criticism, and political economy and social science.* It is highly significant that he should link "political economy" with "social science," and with "literature, philosophy, history, literary and art criticism"—the things he loved. Walras was, from his earliest youth to the end of his life, an intellectual of the later days of the Romantic period, and the Walrasian critic forgets this at his peril. This is especially so since Walras's entire private correspondence shows him to have been intellectually all of a piece—his most abstract and technical work was an expression of his most intimately personal ideals of social justice. Walras never had a compartmentalized mind: all of his work expresses the aspirations of the whole man. His mathematical general equilibrium theory exhibits, in its perfectly competitive equilibrium, his social ideals; and mathematical abstractions could be of passionate import for him, just as for Jevons, whose private correspondence and journal show the same wholehearted devotion to *his* ideals. We should never forget, however, that Walras's formal schooling had been mainly in the natural sciences and mathematics, and this was available to him when, later, he needed it.

Finally, his novels and journalistic ventures having yielded him less than success, he was persuaded by his father in 1858 to devote himself entirely to the development of a scientific economics. As we know, this concentration on economics would not mean to either father or son any abandonment of the effort to express their social ideals in abstract form. Indeed, Walras has left what Hutchison quite correctly calls "a characteristically glowing account of

---

* "Mais me trouvant dépourvu de toutes espèces de gôut pour les détails techniques de l'art de l'ingénieur, ... [je] revins avec ardeur aux études litéraires en vue de compléter mes connaissances en philosophie, en histoire, en critique de la literature et de l'art, en économie politique et en science sociale."[15]

the moment of this almost religious conversion.''[16] Walras writes in his auto-
biography of his dedication to political economy:

In that respect, the most decisive hour of my whole life took place one summer evening in 1858 when, during a walk in the valley of the Gave du Parc, my father insisted
energetically that there remained two great tasks for the nineteenth century: to put
finishing touches to the writing of history and to begin laying the foundations of social
science. . . . The second, which had preoccupied him throughout his life, touched
him much more deeply. He insisted on this with a conviction which he passed on to
me. And thus it happened that standing in front of the gate of a farm called *Les
Roseux,* I promised him to abandon literature and art criticism and consecrate myself
entirely to the continuation of his work.[17]

The spirit of these passionate lines belongs as much to the Romantic Movement as does the famous last letter to his father of Karl Marx. Walras had been
called to his destiny. He carried with him the concept of scarcity.

The Pure Economics

Aided by his father, Walras wrote in Paris, in 1859, his first work on economics, which he describes as his refutation of the doctrines of Proudhon.
Already he had the idea to found a pure and applied economics in mathematical form.* Then, in July, 1860, he took part by some happy destiny in an international conference on taxation at Lausanne. There he made an influential
friend, Louis Ruchonnet, and through him was in due course appointed to the
chair of political economy founded at the Académie de Lausanne in 1870. It
was to be the only chair Walras ever held, but it gave him the peace and secu-
rity he needed to do his life's work.

Hutchison remarks on Walras that, ''His first writings on *L'Économie politique et la justice* (1860), and *L'Idéal social* (1867), were essays in the philosophy of social reform, hardly likely to advance him to the semiofficial academic posts of the Second Empire. . . .''[19] Again, one is strongly reminded
of the personality of the young Marx, up to the publication of his first mature
piece of economic analysis, the *Poverty of Philosophy*—also, as the reader
will recall, an attack on the theories of Proudhon. And one is again given notice that the decision to devote his life to the development of a scientific economics was not in the least regarded, by either Walras or his father, as imply-

* ''j'eus l'intuition d'une économie politique pure et appliquée à créer dans la forme mathématique.''[18]

ing the abandonment of social philosphy. The part of his work which Walras could present as a mathematical system of general equilibrium was never seen by either father or son as the only important part of his writings.

Walras's inability to find a chair in France—whether caused by his writings on social justice or not—certainly was a lifelong source of bitterness to him. Walras always saw himself as French, even after he had spent many years in Switzerland. He tried to publish in the *Journal des Économistes* in 1859, but he describes conditions in political economy in France as utterly miserable. He paints the picture of an inbred orthodoxy as it has seldom been painted before or since, an orthodoxy which "by various arguments, often contradictory, always bad, presents the existing social order as a *nec plus ultra* sufficient for humanity till kingdom come."*

On August 16 and 23, 1873, Walras entered the lists with his "daring paper,"[21] "Principles of a Mathematical Theory of Exchange."[22] His colors were now flying: the transformation of pure economics into a mathematical science. He was ignored. For us, however, two concepts stand out, strikingly linking the two founders of neoclassicism who favored the mathematical method, Jevons and Walras: first, that the prime task was to cast into mathematical form whatever *part* of the science it was feasible to handle in this way;† and, second, that it was the pure theory of exchange that would yield to this treatment first.

In the proceedings of the Academy, Walras's paper was listed among communications "des savants étrangers," despite the fact that, as Jaffé remarks, Walras "was as much a Frenchman as the academicians, though he did come from a foreign professorial post in Lausanne to deliver his paper."[23] As Schumpeter has well said, history has mercilessly judged the Academy: "It has become long since manifest who was being judged when the Académie des Sciences Morales et Politiques rejected his work."[24] This view into the future was not available to Walras. He wrote to Célestine Aline, now his first wife:

> Of all the members of the Institute, one alone understood me; but he was precisely the one for whom my words were intended, J. J. Garnier. He saw very clearly that my effort was serious and has accepted my work for the *Journal des Économistes*. . . .[25]

---

*"en vertue d'arguments variés, souvent contradictoires, et toujours mauvais, nous donne le régime social actuel comme un *nec plus ultra* susceptible de suffire à l'humanité jusqu'à la consummation des siècles."[20]
†Not, remember, that Walras ever suggested that the part of the theory which could be translated into mathematics at that time (or later) was the only important part.

Walras had already asked Garnier to publish, not just his short paper to the Academy, but the first 60 pages[26] of his forthcoming great work, the *Elements of Pure Economics.*[27]

It may be noted that in the first edition of Walras's *Elements* the relevant pages dealt with the theory of exchange of two commodities.[28] If Walras was to excerpt something from his opus, it was the *simplest,* most fundamental case of the theory of *exchange* that he chose. In the brief paper he read before the Academy the same approach ruled. Walras's object was to render as much of pure economics as possible a rigorous mathematical science; so naturally he started with what he regarded as the simplest part: the pure, static, theory of the exchange of two commodities. In the "Principles of a Mathematical Theory of Exchange," he describes the complexities involved in attempting a static theory of the allocation of a *given* set of productive resources. He concludes that the problem must be handled in two stages, in the first of which production is not considered. The problem is then reduced to one which Walras describes as, "Given certain quantities of commodities, to formulate a system of equations of which the prices of the commodities are the roots."[29] As Jaffé comments, "This is what the mathematical theory of exchange is all about."[30]

This point of view also shows in Walras's treatment of marginal utility in his "Mathematical Theory of Exchange," and again in the *Elements,* so that Jaffé may justly remark:

> It is this, more than anything else, which distinguishes Léon Walras from his corevolutionaries and which made him, rather than Jevons or Menger, the favorite ancestor most frequently honored in the latest developments of economic theory since the 1930's. . . . From the very start, Léon Walras introduced his marginal utility theory immediately into his analysis of market price determination without considering it in any other context. His whole attention was focussed on market phenomena and not on consumption.[31]

Thus, it is the *marginal* adjustment (not the utility as such) that matters; Walras is interested in the attainment of equilibrium in the market—in the pure theory of exchange.

General Equilibrium: The Elements

We have the authority of Schumpeter for giving star billing, among the founding works of the neoclassical school, to the *Elements* of Léon Walras. And this view has recently been echoed by Kenneth Arrow and Frank Hahn, who give it as their opinion that:

> The full recognition of the general equilibrium concept can be attributed unmistakably to Walras . . . though many elements of the neoclassical system had been worked out independently by W. Stanley Jevons and by Carl Menger.[32]

Walras, described by Schumpeter as having been French "in the same sense in which Racine's plays . . . are characteristically French,"[33,*] was, as we have seen, without honor in his own country. However, by 1949 Schumpeter could claim that "it would be hard to find a theorist who does not acknowledge Walras' influence. . . ."[34] The central role of Walras's *Elements* is well expressed by Arrow and Hahn. They consider the claim that Adam Smith should be regarded as a founder of general equilibrium theory, and add that:

> . . . later systematic expositors of the classical system, such as Ricardo, Mill, and Marx, whose work filled in some of Smith's logical gaps, can all be regarded as early expositors of general equilibrium theory. In some ways, Marx came closer in form to modern theory in his scheme of simple reproduction (*Capital,* Vol. II), studied in combination with his development of relative price theory (Vols. I and III), than any other classical economist. . . .[35]

They then proceed to isolate a special sense in which they believe none of these writers had a *true* general equilibrium theory. This resulted from certain special classical assumptions about the supply of inputs. Now, as the reader will recall, we have seen that classical economists, such as Cantillon or Smith, do have a general equilibrium theory—a theory of allocation—*in a sense*. This theory, however, is not about the attainment of general equilibrium in the allocation of *given resources* to alternative uses. It is, on the contrary, a theory of the allocation of surplus output, of produced commodities—a theory of growth in the making. Classical allocation theory describes how commodities available today are allocated as inputs, so as to give the surplus produced in the next period the exact composition appropriate to the output desired by the capitalists. It is a theory of the optimal input mix rather than of the optimal allocation of given factors in the production of outputs. Arrow and Hahn sum up their argument:

*Odette de Mourgues writes of the great French dramatist, Jean Racine (1639–1699), "The simple and noble outline of a Greek column is the result of mathematical calculation, and the same is true of the architecture of a Racinian tragedy," *Racine, or the Triumph of Relevance,* Cambridge University Press, 1967, p. 138.

Thus, in a certain sense, the classical economists had no true theory of resource allocation. . . . It is in this context that the neoclassical theories emerged about 1870, with all primary resources in the role that land alone had had before.[36]

They add in a note that, "The classical failure to see clearly the allocational nature of the economic problem has been most forcefully argued by F. H. Knight."[37] As will be recalled from chapter 4, Knight attempted to interpret Ricardo as a neoclassical allocation theorist.

Leaving aside for the moment what the classical economists understood by allocation, it is certainly clear that the views of Arrow and Hahn are in complete agreement with our characterization of a neoclassical theory as one in which inputs are treated as *given* resources—*parameters* of the model.*
And it is, as Arrow and Hahn point out, *this* concept of general equilibrium which was first systematically developed by Walras:

> The economic system is made up of households and firms. Each household owns a set of resources, commodities useful in production or consumption, including different kinds of labor. For any given set of prices, then, a household has an income from the sale of its resources and, with this income, it can choose among all alternative bundles of consumer goods whose cost, at the given prices does not exceed the household's income.[38]

The development of this sort of allocation is seen at its purest in the *Elements* of Walras.

The *Elements* does not begin, however, with the theory of the allocation of *resources*. After some preliminary discussion in Part I of the nature of economic theory, Part II discusses the theory of exchange of two commodities for each other.[39] We are then introduced in Part III to the generalization of the theory of pure exchange to the case of several commodities.[40] It is not until page 211 that the theory of production is introduced, and we move from the theory of the exchange of goods from given stocks held by the trading parties to the expanded theory, where it is shown how these goods are themselves produced by the exchange of the services of the given resources in return for claims to income. In all, in the first edition, we are still in the theory of pure exchange for 211 out of 459 pages.[41] "Thus far," Walras writes, "we have left out of consideration the fact that commodities are products which result from the combination of productive factors such as land, men and capital goods."[42]

The detailed architecture and formal expression of Walras's analysis, even in the case of pure exchange which Jevons treated, is massive beside Jevons.

---

* On parameters in a model, see chapter 7.

But in essence the principles are the same. Walras assumes that the total *stocks* of goods in the hands of the participants in exchange are given. We begin with the exchange of two commodities for each other. Walras applies "the term *effective offer* to any offer made . . . of a definite amount of a commodity at a definite price."[43] He applies "the term *effective demand* to any such demand for a definite amount of a commodity at a definite price."[44]

Walras establishes in great detail what he calls *"the law of effective offer and effective demand or the law of the establishment [or emergence] of equilibrium prices* in the case of the exchange of two commodities. . . ."[45] This law is stated in the following way:

> . . . *given two commodities, for the market to be in equilibrium with respect to these commodities, or for the price of either commodity to be stationary in terms of the other, it is necessary and sufficient that the effective demand be equal to the effective offer of each commodity. Where this equality does not obtain, in order to reach equilibrium prices, the commodity having an effective demand greater than its effective offer must rise in price, and the commodity having an effective offer greater than its effective demand must fall in price.*[46]

Walras now goes behind these offers and demands and presents his account of how his individual economic agents will arrive at them. Again, assuming two commodities,

> . . . *each holder attains maximum satisfaction of wants . . . when the ratio of the intensities of the last wants satisfied [by each of these goods], or the ratio of their* raretés, *is equal to the price. Until this equality has been reached, a party to the exchange will find it to his advantage to sell the commodity the* rareté *of which is smaller than its price multiplied by the* rareté *of the other commodity and to buy the other commodity the* rareté *of which is greater than its price multiplied by the* rareté *of the first commodity.*[47]

Walras has explicitly considered from the beginning the case where there are arbitrarily many traders; he is assuming perfect competition among traders, i.e., no single trader can by his actions influence the price, and traders cannot form coalitions that would have this effect. In this he was far ahead of his time. He now turns to the case of many goods. Here again the condition of "maximum satisfaction," he points out,

> . . . always consists in the attainment of equality between the ratio of the *raretés* of any two commodities and the price of one in terms of the other, for otherwise it would be advantageous to make further exchanges of these commodities for each other.[48]

Thus the demand, and the offer, of any commodity is a function, not simply of the price of that commodity, but of the prices of all commodities.

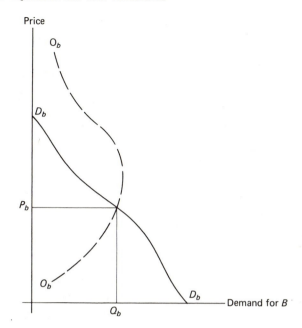

Figure 6-1. Equilibrium offer and demand for a commodity B.

In Appendix I, which first appeared in the third edition of the *Elements,* Walras shows the equilibrium of offer and demand for a single good geometrically. Somewhat simplified and transposed,* his idea is as follows. The heavy curve in Fig. 6-1 [49] is the demand for B, labelled D_b, which Walras assumed would be negatively sloped throughout its length.[50] The dotted curve O_b is the offer curve for B, which cuts D_b at the point of equilibrium. Quantity Q_b is sold at price P_b.

Only when he has completed the theory of the pure exchange of given stocks of many commodities among many traders under competition, does Walras finally introduce production. "Capital," for him, is made up of a job lot of durable resources. The value of a given capital good—a piece of land, a machine—results from the services it yields:

I define *fixed capital,* i.e., *capital* in general, just as my father did in his *Théorie de la richesse Social* (1849), as all durable goods, all forms of social wealth which are not used up at all or are used up only after a lapse of time. . . .[51]

---

*We beg forgiveness from Walrasian scholars for having transposed the axes, putting price on the vertical, as is the usual practice.

All nondurable goods, on the other hand, all goods which are used up immediately, "every scarce thing which does not outlast its first use,"[52] he classified as *income* ("revenue"). Nowhere does the influence of Auguste Walras show more strikingly—the latter had written almost the same words.[53]

Walras explicitly insists that, while some goods may be treated either as capital or income (a tree may bear fruit or be cut for fuel), capital is quite distinct from *stocks*. "Capital should not be confused with stocks which are aggregates of income accumulated in advance for eventual consumption. Wine in the cellar, wood in the shed and raw materials in the store room are stocks."[54] This passage vividly warns us that we are in a model totally different from the classical one. Commodities are going to be produced, not by means of the same commodities, but by means of the services yielded by fixed capital goods, assumed as *given* in the model.

Pursuing his distinction between capital and income, Walras designates "all those incomes which consist in the uses made of capital by the name of services."[55] There are consumers' services—the shelter of a house, the service of a lawyer—and there are *productive* services: "Our special concern is with the study of the transformation of production services into products."[56] Again, he stresses that capital (say, land) and its services are to be distinguished from "fertilizers, seeds and standing crops."[57] The special feature of his analysis is the treatment of raw materials as "income goods." Walras is quite explicit about this:

Income, by definition, does not outlast its first use. The very instant it renders a service, it passes out of existence; technically speaking, it is *consumed*. Bread and meat are eaten; wine is drunk; oil and wood are burned; fertilizers and seeds are put in the soil; metals, lumber and textile fibres are worked up; fuels are consumed.[58]

The problems to which this approach gives rise are not our present concern,* which is simply to make Walras's view clear: "Capital goods, by definition, do outlast their first use. As they render the successive services for which they are suited, capital goods serve their purpose: technically speaking, they *produce*."[59] So in Walras's model production is by means of the services of capital goods, not by means of commodities in the sense of produced inputs. Commodities (income goods) are seen as produced, but not in their turn producing. It follows that, when we look at the technology of his model the same things will not appear as inputs and as outputs: inputs are amounts of the services of the capital goods, outputs are quantities of income goods.

* In chapters 8 and 9 we discuss certain generalizations of neoclassical allocation theory in which the presence of produced factors of production (capital goods) creates certain anomolous results in the analysis of equilibrium prices.

Income goods can only be *sold;* capital goods can be *hired out* to someone who uses their services. Walras tells us, ''The hiring out of a capital good is the alienation of the service of that capital good. This definition is based entirely on the distinction between capital and income and is fundamental.''[60] There is a *services market:* ''Here land-owners, workers and capitalists appear as sellers, and entrepreneurs as buyers of the various productive services, i.e. land-services, labour and capital-services.''[61] The other market, of course, is the *products market:*

> Here the entrepreneurs appear as sellers, and the land-owners, labourers and capitalists as buyers of products. These products are exchanged, like services, with the aid of a *numéraire* and in accordance with the mechanism of free competition.[62]

In a stunningly modern passage, Walras characterizes the whole system of general equilibrium:

> Equilibrium in production, which implies equilibrium in exchange, can now be easily defined. First, it is a state in which the effective demand and offer of productive services are equal and there is a stationary current price in the market for these services. Secondly it is a state in which the effective demand and supply of products are also equal and there is a stationary current price in the products market. Finally, it is a state in which the selling prices of products equal the costs of the productive services that enter into them. The first two conditions relate to equilibrium in exchange; the third to equilibrium in production.[63]

We shall have much occasion to recollect this passage. Walras continues in a vein which, again, will be central to our exposition of neoclassical allocation theory:

> Assuming equilibrium, we may even go so far as to abstract from enterpreneurs and simply consider the productive services as being, in a certain sense, exchanged directly for one another, instead of being exchanged first against products, and then against productive services.[64]

Walras's mathematical model is always strictly static, with no uncertainty and therefore no role for an ''entrepreneur'' in the rich sense of Knight or Schumpeter. There is simply the matter of so combining the productive services as to reflect the demands of consumers. Later in this book we shall use the term ''producing agent'' to designate this operation (which could in principle be performed by a computer) so as to avoid possible confusion which might arise through the use of a term like ''entrepreneur.''

Walras is entirely consistent with the formal properties of his model when he insists that in a state of equilibrium in production, ''entrepreneurs make neither profit nor loss.''* At equilibrium, in his model, there can be no speculative gains or losses due to uncertainty since there is no uncertainty in the model. (Walras was perfectly aware that in the real world, where uncertainty rules, such gains and losses occur.) Nor could there be "profit," in the sense of classical political economy, as a component of Walrasian equilibrium prices. Rather, the equilibrium price of a commodity is composed simply of the payments necessary to elicit the per-unit input requirements of the given resource services used up in its production.

It was a matter of importance to Walras that in competitive equilibrium all incomes generated in his model were in respect of payments for factor "services." Walras believed that if "land services" were not privately owned, and if monopoly were eliminated, the results would come as close as dynamic, uncertain, real-life ever can to the timeless, perfect-knowledge governed, competitive equilibrium of his mathematical model. Error lies imminently in wait for the interpreter of this mathematical model who forgets Walras's total social philosophy. This philosophy, largely inherited from his father, as we have seen, gave special importance to the removal of private ownership of land and other sources of monopoly income. This was because these exclusive rights prevented a system of incomes equal (in *numeraire*) to the value of "factor services" rendered in a perfectly competitive market where transactions at nonequilibrium prices are ruled out (since these would generate receipts above or below factor cost). Thus, only competitive prices were consistent with the Walrasian ideal of distributive justice. That "profit" in the sense of a uniform return on the quantity of "stock" used up does not appear in the price relations of the Walrasian model is therefore no accident— for Walras it was one of its most important features. He does not mean to imply, however, that the owners of capital goods (capitalists) do not receive rents for supplying the services of their capital goods. On the contrary, their rents appear at equilibrium as part of the *cost* of the commodity, and not at all as the reflection in the price relations of surplus in the quantity relations. No such surplus appears, as we shall see, in the Walrasian quantity relations, and so nothing properly called "profit" can appear as its dual. Thus, the "capitalist" who in Walras is quite separate from the "entrepreneur" does not play the role that he plays in classical theory. The capitalist simply rents capital goods, and receives a payment equal to their relative scarcity.†

Walras had special reasons for constructing his model in the way he did. But certain of its properties remained highly characteristic of post-Walrasian

---

* "Les entrepreneurs ne font ni bénéfice ni perte." [65]
† On relative scarcity, see chapter 9, especially the concluding section.

(neoclassical) general equilibrium theory although Walras's successors did not have his social philosophical reasons for assigning these properties to their model. We shall find it to be an essential aspect of post-Walrasian theory that the entrepreneur has a tendency to melt away.* The capitalist, too, has been dethroned from the role which he plays in classical theory. A striking contrast will thus emerge from an examination of the formal structure of classical and neoclassical models, to which we devote subsequent chapters. But, for the moment, we simply recall that, in classical economics, the capitalist is a far from unimportant figure; and profit, received at a uniform rate on the value of capital in equilibrium, is a main focus of analysis.

Returning to Walras, as Schumpeter remarks, "it is clear that in Walras' thought the households were really the agents that, both as buyers of products and as sellers of services, determine the economic process."[66] The households, maximizing their satisfactions, determine what shall be the composition of output and thereby influence relative prices. One sees at once the great importance of the role played by consumers' choices in the new structure, in contrast with their much less important role in classical theory. On the other hand, social classes play no analytical role in the mathematical structure of the Walrasian model,† since the main actors are individual resource-owning households who derive incomes from the sale of resource services and spend these incomes on commodities—i.e., consumer's goods and services since the purchase of any new capital goods is not allowed to alter the resource parameters within Walras's main (static) model. Producers thus act simply as agents for resource-owning households, transforming given factor services into consumption goods.

In order to sketch in the formal structure of Walrasian theory, we consider the quantity relations of a typical model. These take the form of resource constraints which merely state that the use made of any particular resource (including the use, if any, by the owners of the resource) is limited by the (given) available supply of its services. For simplicity, we construct a model for the theory in which there are just two resource services and two sectors of production to which these services can be allocated.‡ Let the resources in this

---

* In particular, see the discussion of prices in chapter 9.
† As we have seen, however, in their broader social theory, the Walrases, father and son, regarded landlords as forming a separate social class whose existence interferes with the attainment of distributive justice.
‡ Walras assumed fixed amounts of n productive services, used to produce m finished products, for arbitrary, finite n and m. We shall consider these more complicated cases when we come to generalize the model developed in chapters 8 and 9, but here the exposition is simplified by taking $n = 2$ and $m = 2$.

two-sector model be labor and land; and the products they produce, rice and wheat. We then follow Walras in referring to "labor-services" and "land-services" as flows of productive factor services during a certain period in which production takes place. Walras tells us that "the quantities of productive services used are equal to the quantities effectively offered."[67] This implies that resource constraints must be written as equations:

available labor-services = labor-services used in rice production
                                + labor-services used in wheat production

available land-services = land-services used in rice production
                                + land-services used in wheat production

Walras, in fact, always assumed that all available factor services would be fully used up, since, otherwise, a factor might receive no reward for its services,* which violates one of the ideal requirements of his model as a description of distributive justice. In his more complicated model, where there are many resources and many commodities, part of the given supply of, say, land-services may be held back by its owner(s), and directly used by the resource owner(s) instead of being offered on the market. But, again, the *assumption* is that the given supplies of factor services are all used up, whether by a buyer or by their owners. Thus, quantity relations are written here as equations.

The per-unit input requirements, i.e., the amount of labor-services and land-services needed to produce a unit of rice, or a unit of wheat, are called by Walras the "coefficients of production" ("coefficients de fabrication"). He writes: "We are evidently assuming the coefficients . . . to be determined *a priori.*"[68] He was well aware that this was a simplification. Thus, the argument abstracts from variable inputs, as the first edition makes clear, for greater simplicity, supposing that the coefficients are among the givens and not the unknowns of the problem.† This assumption is removed only when Walras turns to the question of decisions to accumulate capital, which he regards as a problem strictly separate from static general equilibrium theory.

Walras thus ruled out technical choice in his standard model. It is a further implication of his structure that returns to scale are constant: the input requirements for two units of output are simply twice those for one unit,

---

*On this important point concerning the analytical structure of post-Walrasian theory, see chapter 9.
†"Nous en faisons abstraction, pour plus de simplicité, en supposant que les coefficients ci-dessus figurent parmi les donnés et non parmi les inconnues du problème."[69]

etc.[70] We therefore assume fixed per-unit input requirements, independent of the scale of output, and write, following standard modern notation,* a_{LR} for the amount of labor-services needed to produce a unit of rice, and a_{LW} for the amount of labor-services needed to produce a unit of wheat. Since "land" also begins with "L", we shall call it by its Latin name, Terra, and write the per-unit requirements of Terra-services in the production of rice and wheat as a_{TR} and a_{TW}, respectively.

The number of units of rice production is a variable in our simple Walrasian model; likewise, the number of units of wheat production. These will be indicated by the symbols Y_R and Y_W, respectively. The total labor-service requirement in production is then written as the sum of two terms: labor-services required to produce Y_R units of rice $a_{LR}Y_R$; plus labor-services required to produce Y_W units of wheat $a_{LW}Y_W$. Similarly, total land-services needed to produce Y_R and Y_W is the sum of $a_{TR}Y_R$ and $a_{TW}Y_W$. Each of these terms is simply the *per unit* factor service requirement multiplied by the level of production, a variable. Given the available supply of labor-services L and land-services T, resource constraints are now written in notation as:

$$L = a_{LR} Y_R + a_{LW} Y_W \tag{1}$$
$$T = a_{TR} Y_R + a_{TW} Y_W \tag{2}$$

For the moment, we leave open the question as to whether or not these equations have a solution consistent with the given data (factor supplies and technical coefficients) and the (as yet unspecified) demand functions. What *is* important is to notice that the concept of surplus output is not defined in this model: Y_R and Y_W simply use up the available factor services, and the dynamic question of reproducibility does not arise.

Turning to the price relations: when there are only two-factor services there can be only two components in the definition of factor cost, and therefore only two possible sources of income. And, with only two commodities specified, there are only two cost–price relationships to consider: one for the rice sector and one for the wheat sector, each expressing the equilibrium condition, as Walras saw it, that price must *equal* unit factor cost:

unit labor cost in rice production + unit land cost in rice production
= price of a unit of rice

unit labor cost in wheat production + unit land cost in wheat production
= price of a unit of wheat

---

* We shall not attempt to reproduce Walras's exact notation in our model.

Introducing notation, unit labor cost in the rice sector is simply the unit labor requirement in the production of rice a_{LR} times the wage rate W_L, or $a_{LR} W_L$; while unit land cost in rice production is $a_{TR} W_T$ where W_T is the rental rate for land services. Similarly, in the wheat sector unit costs for the services of labor and land are $a_{LW} W_L$ and $a_{TW} W_T$, respectively. The fact that the same symbols are used to measure factor prices, regardless of the sector of production, means that the same value is placed on each unit of any given factor service irrespective of the commodity being produced. Thus, W_L and W_T may be interpreted as *competitive* prices for labor-services and land-services, an interpretation which was important to Walras. Using this notation, Walras's price equations are written:

$$a_{LR} W_L + a_{TR} W_T = P_R \tag{3}$$
$$a_{LW} W_L + a_{TW} W_T = P_W \tag{4}$$

where P_R and P_W are, respectively, the price of a unit of rice and the price of a unit of wheat. All prices, W_i, $i = L, T$ and P_j, $j = R, W$, are positive.

Again, we leave aside the question of finding solutions to the price equations. But what does stand out is the fact that, just as there is no surplus in the quantity equations (1) and (2), there is no profit in the dual price equations (3) and (4). At equilibrium, prices are exactly equal to the sum of unit-factor costs. This property of Walras's model—the absence of surplus in the quantity relations and profit in the their dual—will remain characteristic of the post-Walrasian, or neoclassical models with which we shall be later concerned. It must immediately be noted, however, that a number of other, highly important characteristic features of Walras's work were not retained by the general equilibrium theorists who came after him and who must, for that reason, be described as post-Walrasian. Above all, they quite lacked his social philosophy, and they endeavored to pry loose his mathematical model of general equilibrium from the world view in which it was embedded. It is questionable whether the results have always been happy. Be this as it may, we shall of necessity be concerned with that mathematical theory of general equilibrium, conveniently described as post-Walrasian, which has in fact become the intellectual core of neoclassicism, whatever its rights to the name of Walras.

We may note right away one respect in which post-Walrasian theory departs in a quite specific technical way from the original. It was observed by later theorists that one needed to be able to allow, in a general equilibrium system, for a situation in which the whole given supply of a factor service is not fully used up; and for the case of a product whose cost exceeds its price (and is therefore not produced).* The original system was thus adapted to allow for these possibilities by writing the quantity and price relations as weak inequalities:

$$L \geq a_{LR} Y_R + a_{LW} Y_W \qquad (1)'$$

$$T \geq a_{TR} Y_R + a_{TW} Y_W \qquad (2)'$$

$$a_{LR} W_L + a_{TR} W_T \geq P_R \qquad (3)'$$

$$a_{LW} W_L + a_{TW} W_T \geq P_W \qquad (4)'$$

$$W_i \geq 0 \qquad P_j \geq 0 \qquad i = L, T \qquad j = R, W$$

This extension of the original Walrasian system was first made by Abraham Wald. Oskar Morgenstern had introduced Wald to a Viennese banker called Schlesinger who had intuitive ideas on the subject.[72] The original arguments of Wald were made in a seminar in Vienna presided over by Karl Menger (the son of the founder of the Austrian School) in 1934.[73]

In later chapters we shall follow the modern, post-Walrasian practice of writing the quantity and price relations as weak inequalities. The point for us is that such a model is in fact a mature neoclassical model, with the appropriate framework to be compared with those fundamentally different structures which we have described as mature classical models.

Decisions to Accumulate versus the Coda †

It is sometimes suggested (a recent instance will be found in a work of Michio Morishima)[74] that a theory of the accumulation of capital is to be found in Walras's *Elements,* as an integral part of his standard general equilibrium model. The question here is not whether a theory of intertemporal general equilibrium, involving growth, can (with more or less validity) be grafted onto a post-Walrasian model. Rather, the question before us is one of historical fact. Did Walras embody a theory of capital accumulation and dynamic change in his standard general equilibrium model?

To this, the answer, on the evidence, must surely be no. The general equilibrium system developed carefully and explicitly by Walras in the body of his

---

* These points are further developed in chapters 8 and 9. It may be noted that Walras was not unaware of "corner" solutions to his model in which one or more relations would be satisfied only as strict inequalities. These cases are discussed by Walras in connection with the pure theory of exchange.[71]

† This term has been used by William Jaffé to characterize the role of Walras's discussion of a progressive economy at the end of the *Elements.*

Elements is a model of the timeless allocation of a set of given resources so as to satisfy given consumers' preferences at a moment in time, given technology, with instantaneous production and a complete absence of uncertainty. Unidirectional time plays no role in the model, and the concepts of reproducibility and surplus are without definition, as is the dual concept of the classical rate of profit.

It is only at the end of the *Elements,* in what Jaffé calls its Coda, that Walras goes beyond mere decisions to accumulate and raises the problem of the effects of actual accumulation. It is true that in the main body of the *Elements,* before reaching the Coda, Walras discusses what would happen if the system were to be brought to the brink of becoming dynamic through some individuals making *decisions* to accumulate: reducing their consumption so as to have savings left for acquiring additional capital goods. However, as Jaffé has pointed out to us,* this discussion of capital formation (théorie de la capitalisation) is a theory of decisions to accumulate, not a theory of the effects and working of accumulation. It depicts an economy on the *verge* of expansion, not the ongoing dynamics of a growing economy. As far as his formal general equilibrium model is concerned, Walras always remained faithful to the original assumptions upon which its whole character depended, such as that of given, invariant resources of all kinds including capital goods. He was well aware that decisions to accumulate capital *once carried out* would introduce dynamic characteristics inconsistent with his original system. Hence, he confined himself rigorously to a consideration of *decisions to accumulate* introduced, among the other decisions, into his timeless model, but without their historical consequences being followed up. Walras, in effect, treated only the situation *before* new capital goods have arrived to play a part in the economy. In this he perhaps showed a more sensitive understanding of the powers and limits of a general equilibrium theory of the allocation of given resources than has been demonstrated by some of the more recent devotees of such models.

In any event, it was as a theory of the allocation of *given* resources that post-Walrasian general equilibrium theory entered the mainstream of neoclassical economics and exerted its influence on the development of the most characteristic neoclassical structures.

One cannot leave Walras without pointing out once more that the general equilibrium model, known today as "Walrasian," formed for him barely one

---

* In private correspondence, and in an unpublished paper, "Further Neglected Aspects of Léon Walras's Theoretical Writings," given to the History of Economics Society, University of Toronto, May, 1978.

of the three parts into which he saw the whole of economics divided. Alas, he never completed whole treatises on the other two parts, but his collected papers were published in two volumes whose titles suggest the scope he would have given to the other two parts: *Études d'économie sociale (Théorie de la répartition de la richesse sociale)* [75] and *Études d'économie politique appliquée.* [76] His attempt to expand even his pure theory so as to carry it to the edge of the question of accumulation (whatever we may say of its success) shows that he would never have been satisfied that mathematical economics, having solved the problem of pure exchange, and production by means of given resources, should remain content.

The post-Walrasian model of general equilibrium, as adapted by Wald, has been much refined mathematically since Walras wrote, and sophisticated proofs have been offered to show that it possesses certain properties. But the bare bony structure of what has come to be the standard theory of resource allocation is in fact in Walras's *Elements,* and with his work neoclassical allocation theory was already mature.

Walras corresponded with virtually every notable economist of his time, and, in the end, recognition of the central role of his work flowed in to him. Jevons was the first British economist to reply: "It is satisfactory to me to find that my theory of exchange," he wrote to Walras on May 12, 1874, "which, when published in England, was either neglected or criticized, is practically confirmed by your researches." [77] And Walras wrote warmly to Menger, saying that they had posed the same problem and had set about its resolution by the same method.*

Neoclassical Allocation Theory and the Marginal Revolution

The work of Jevons, Menger, and Walras in the 1870's is often referred to as the "marginal revolution," and we have ourselves on occasion used the term "marginal" to characterize the new allocation theory. Leaving aside for the moment the legitimacy of describing the emergence of neoclassical theory as a "revolution," we must say a few words about the appropriateness of using the notion of marginal analysis—of the analysis of very small changes—as a characteristic of neoclassical economic theory.

It must be remembered that there had been "a type of analysis, long met with in English political economy, which consisted in centering attention on

---

* "Nous nous sommes évidemment posé le même problème, Monsieur; et nous avons évidemment entrepris de la résoudre par la même méthode. . . ." [78]

the circumstances at the 'margin of cultivation.' ''[79] Summarizing a tradition going back to Thomas Robert Malthus and David Ricardo, John Stuart Mill had written that "many of the most important lessons in political economy are to be learned at the extreme margin of cultivation."[80] This consideration—that the classical economists had paid considerable attention to marginal changes in methods of production (primarily in agriculture)—makes us reluctant to emphasize "marginal productivity" as the *differentia specifica* of neoclassical analysis.

Then there is the fact that Jevons barely hinted at the theory of marginal productivity, and that Walras first mentions it in his *Elements* in the postscript to Appendix III, first published in the *third* edition of 1896. As we know from the researches of William Jaffé,[81] the Italian mathematical economist, Enrico Barone, had sent Walras an unpublished paper stating the calculus version of marginal productivity theory. Only Walras's French translation of Barone's paper survives. Barone had written to Walras about marginal productivity on September 20, 1894,[82] and Walras wrote his agreement in a letter to Barone of October 23, 1895.[83] But this was rather late in the day, and Walras was in retirement, though very active. The great structure of the *Elements* through three editions had not depended on the calculus version of marginal productivity theory as presented by Barone; Walras's equilibrium model was characterized instead by fixed technical coefficients, as we have seen. As Jaffé has written, "One thing is clear: Léon Walras neither invented nor ever said he invented the marginal productivity theory."[84]

Finally, to identify neoclassical allocation theory with the calculus version of marginal productivity theory can lead to considerable confusion in the interpretation of certain very modern debates. Rather, the distinctive use of the concept of the margin that identifies, in a fundamental sense, the essence of a neoclassical, Walrasian, model is the interpretation of prices as marginal valuations. In particular, as the reader will see clearly in chapter 9, factor prices in neoclassical theory, the prices paid for the productive services of the various given resources, are interpreted as measures of the *marginal change* in the value of production that would occur if a small *increment* of the corresponding factor service became available. It is in this sense that *marginalism* is an essential element in our analysis of neoclassical theory. Incidentally, one finds here another way of expressing one of the reasons why surplus does not enter as an analytical category in neoclassical theory. Besides the fact that resources are *given,* there is also the fact that the services of these given factors have values, in the theory, which can be interpreted to mean that not a single *marginal* unit of any factor with a positive value can be withdrawn without forcing a *reduction* in the value of production.

The objectives and point of view of Walras differed fundamentally from those of later neoclassical general equilibrium theorists. With the work of Abraham Wald, however, the stage was set: post-Walrasian theory had begun. The bare bones of its present-day form were thus established so that the subsequent development of neoclassical theory need not be further discussed by the use of historical methods. The theory is too close to us for such an approach. Instead, our treatment will be presented analytically in chapters 8, 9, and 10.

In the meantime we turn to a preliminary sketch of the structure of the analytical arguments that we shall employ in giving formal expression to those concepts of economic theory whose historical development we have thus far been describing.

Notes

1. Joseph Schumpeter, *A History of Economic Analysis,* Oxford University Press, New York, 1954, p. 827.
2. Michio Morishima, *Marx's Economics, A Dual Theory of Value and Growth,* Cambridge University Press, 1973, p. 1.
3. Joseph Schumpeter, *Ten Great Economists from Marx to Keynes,* George Allen and Unwin, London, 1952, p. 74.
4. *Ibid.*
5. William Jaffé, ed., *Correspondence of Léon Walras and Related Papers,* Vols. I, II, III, North-Holland, Amsterdam, 1965. Subsequent references will be preceded by the editor's name where we are referring to his notes and preface, and by Walras's name where we are referring to the original correspondence and papers.
6. Jaffé, *Correspondence,* Vol. I, Preface, p. ix.
7. Walras, *Correspondence,* Vol. I, p. 68.
8. Jaffé, *Correspondence,* Vol. I, p. 28, n. 3.
9. T. W. Hutchison, *A Review of Economic Doctrines,* Oxford University Press, 1962, p. 199.
10. *Ibid.,* p. 199, n. 1.
11. *Ibid.,* p. 199.
12. Léon Walras, "Un initiateur en économie politique: A. A. Walras," *Revue du Mois,* 6 (1908), p. 181, cited by Richard S. Howey, "The Origins of Marginalism," in R. D. Collison Black, A. W. Coats, and Craufurd D. W. Goodwin, eds., *The Marginal Revolution in Economics, Interpretation and Evaluation,* Duke University Press, Durham, N.C., 1973, p. 23.
13. Schumpeter, *Ten Great Economists,* p. 75.

14. William Jaffé, tr., Walras, *Elements of Pure Economics, or The Theory of Social Wealth,* Richard D. Irwin, Homewood, Ill., 1973, p. 5.
15. Walras, "Notice Autobiographique," in *Correspondence,* Vol. I, p. 2.
16. Hutchison, *Economic Doctrines,* p. 199.
17. Walras, *Correspondence,* Vol. I, p. 2. Our translation.
18. *Ibid.*
19. Hutchison, *Economic Doctrines,* p. 201.
20. Walras, *Correspondence,* Vol. I, p. 3.
21. Jaffé, "Léon Walras's role in the 'Marginal Revolution' of the 1870's," in *The Marginal Revolution in Economics,* p. 115.
22. Léon Walras, "Principe d'une théorie mathématique de l'exchange," *Séances et travaux de l'Académie des Sciences morales et politiques,* January, 1874.
23. Jaffé, "Léon Walras's role," p. 114, n. 3.
24. Schumpeter, *Ten Great Economists,* p. 76.
25. Walras, *Correspondence,* Vol. I, p. 329. Our translation.
26. *Ibid.,* pp. 318–9, 332–4.
27. Walras, *Éléments d'économie politique pure,* L. Corbaz, Lausanne, 1874. All citations will be from the definitive translation by William Jaffé, *Elements of Pure Economics.*
28. See Jaffé, *Correspondence,* Vol. I, p. 319, n. 3.
29. Walras, cited by Jaffé, "Léon Walras's role . . . ," p. 115.
30. Jaffé, "Léon Walras's role. . . ." p. 115.
31. *Ibid.,* p. 118.
32. Kenneth J. Arrow and F. H. Hahn, *General Competitive Analysis,* Holden-Day, San Francisco, 1971, p. 31.
33. Schumpeter, *History of Economic Analysis,* p. 828.
34. *Ibid.,* p. 829.
35. Arrow and Hahn, *General Competitive Analysis,* p. 2.
36. *Ibid.,* p. 3.
37. *Ibid.,* n. 1.
38. *Ibid.,* p. 3.
39. Walras, *Elements,* pp. 83–149.
40. *Ibid.,* pp. 153–207.
41. *Ibid.,* Collation of editions, pp. 609–10.
42. *Ibid.,* p. 211.
43. *Ibid.,* p. 84. Walras's italics.
44. *Ibid.,* p. 85. Walras's italics.
45. *Ibid.,* pp. 105–6. Walras's italics.
46. *Ibid.,* p. 106. Walras's italics.
47. *Ibid.,* p. 125. Walras's italics.
48. *Ibid.,* p. 164.
49. *Ibid.,* adapted and simplified from the figure on page 469.
50. *Ibid.,* p. 466.
51. *Ibid.,* p. 212. Walras's italics.
52. *Ibid.*
53. *Ibid.,* see the striking passage cited on p. 525, n. 4.

54. *Ibid.*, p. 213.
55. *Ibid.*
56. *Ibid.*, p. 214.
57. *Ibid.*, p. 217.
58. *Ibid.*, p. 220. Walras's italics.
59. *Ibid.* Walras's italics.
60. *Ibid.*, p. 222.
61. *Ibid.*, pp. 222–3.
62. *Ibid.*, p. 223.
63. *Ibid.*, p. 224.
64. *Ibid.*, p. 225.
65. *Ibid.*
66. Schumpeter, History of Economic Analysis, p. 1011.
67. Walras, *Elements*, p. 240.
68. *Ibid.*, p. 240.
69. *Ibid.*, Collation of editions, p. 582. n. f.
70. *Ibid.* On these properties of Walras's model, see Translator's Notes, p. 527, n. 3.
71. Walras, *Elements*, §§ 80, 89, 128, 129. See also Michio Morishima, *Walras's Economics, A Pure Theory of Capital and Money*, Cambridge University Press, 1977, pp. 13–14.
72. Arrow and Hahn, *General Competitive Analysis*, p. 9.
73. *Ergebnisse eines Mathematischen Kolloquiums*, Heft 6, March, 1934. See also Heft 7, November, 1934. Wald's results concerning Walras's equations were summarized in *Zeitschrift für Nationalökonomie*, 7, 1936, pp. 637–70; trans. "On Some Systems of Equations of Mathematical Economics," *Econometrica*, Vol. 19 (1951), pp. 368–403.
74. Michio Morishima, *Walras's Economics*.
75. Walras, *Études d'économie sociale (Théorie de la répartition de la richesse sociale)*, Rouge, Lausanne, 1896; ed. G. Leduc, Rouge, Lausanne and Pichon, Paris, 1936.
76. Walras, *Études d'économie politique appliquée (Théorie de la production de la richesse sociale)*, Rouge, Lausanne, 1898; ed. G. Leduc, Rouge, Lausanne and Pichon, Paris, 1936.
77. Jaffé, *Correspondence*, Vol. I, p. 393.
78. *Ibid.*, p. 771. See further Richard S. Howey, "The Origins of Marginalism," in *The Marginal Revolution in Economics*.
79. Howey, "The Origins of Marginalism," p. 33.
80. John Stuart Mill, *Principles of Political Economy*, 1848, Vol. II, p. 234; cited by Howey, "The Origins of Marginalism," p. 34.
81. William Jaffé, "New Light on an Old Quarrel: Barone's Unpublished Review of Wicksteed's Essay on the Coordination of the Laws of Distribution and Related Documents," *Cahiers Vilfredo Pareto Revue Européene D'Histoire des Sciences Sociales*, 3, 1964, Librairie Droz, Geneva.
82. Walras, *Correspondence*, Vol. II, pp. 619–21.
83. *Ibid.*, pp. 643–44.
84. Jaffé, "Old Quarrel," p. 89.

7

Models of General Equilibrium Theory

> First let us be aware that there exists at present no universal system of economic theory. . . . Even in sciences which are far more advanced than economics, like physics, there is no universal system available at present.
>
> JOHN VON NEUMANN AND OSKAR MORGENSTERN [1]

> A model which took account of all the variegation of reality would be of no more use than a map at the scale of one to one.
>
> JOAN ROBINSON [2]

> In the analysis of economic forms, moreover, neither microscopes nor chemical reagents are of use. The force of abstraction must replace both.
>
> KARL MARX [3]

In presenting the historical development of classical and neoclassical theories of general equilibrium, we have sketched certain models beginning with the simplest of all, a one-sector corn model. It must not be thought, however, that simplicity in a model is something to be sought only for pedagogical purposes: one-sector models are to be found in quite sophisticated literature, and the two-sector model flourishes like the green bay tree. Thus, all economic models (including the most modern and mathematical) are, of necessity, abstractions from the reality around us—they are never intended to be complete and accurate *descriptions*.

A useful analogy suggested by Joan Robinson[4] is provided by a map. The traveler, of course, always has a perfect map before him, the actual world, complete in every detail and always up to date. But it is useless in guiding him from one town to the next. For that purpose he needs a "model" of the reality, and preferably one that is small enough to be folded up and placed in his pocket. A good model is one that abstracts from all the details that are unnecessary for the purpose of solving the problem at hand. In order to get from one town to the next by car, the motorist's map need indicate only the locations of towns and the main roads that connect them. Secondary roads, as long as they are distinguishable from main roads, can be ignored. What is more, only the general direction of these main roads need be shown. A map for a hiker, on the other hand, needs to show precisely the minor sideroads and trails which are of no importance to a motorist, not to speak of mountain paths, impossible except on foot. In this way a good model is constructed to suit a particular purpose. For predicting the weather, a road map is of no use; a better model would be a photograph taken from a satellite.

Economic models are also constructed with a particular problem in mind, or from a particular perspective on a particular class of problems. Our purpose thus far has been to establish, on the basis of a reading of the history of economic analysis, that there are two sharply distinct traditions in the theory of general equilibrium. We now focus on modern formulations of the two theories with a view to further clarification of the difference between classical models of surplus and accumulation and neoclassical models of the allocation of given resources. In this we find it useful to emphasize the distinction between *variable* and *parameter,* an understanding of which greatly facilitates the analysis and interpretation of any model.

A variable is determined by the relationships that characterize a model; a parameter is constant within a model, although it can take on different values within a given class of models. This difference reveals an aspect of the methodology of economics which is fundamental to all our arguments, both historical and analytical. Imagine a totally alien society about which one has been given certain information that describes its economic aspects. *All* the information is given. The observing economist, however, will assume that certain relationships exist among the data and that, in some sense, these relationships identify cause and effect. Thus, the problem in setting up a model of the economy in question is to decide what elements it is helpful to treat as exogenous, and what elements are to be taken as *dependent* on these exogenous factors. The solution to the problem is entailed in the construction of a model. We shall therefore use the word *parameter* to refer to what is regarded as given or exogenous *in a model;* and the word *variable* to refer to what is regarded as endogenous, or determined by the model's relationships.

A simple illustration of the modelling problem clarifies this distinction. Suppose one has, as a picture of reality, the data contained in an actual photograph of an automobile smashed against a wall. A model constructed to explain the observed phenomenon could, in principle, have two entirely different structures: one in which the wall is a given parameter and in which the car is a variable which has run into it; and the other, a model in which the car, like a parameter, is standing still and is hit by a moving variable, the wall. Of course, experience suggests that only the first model is helpful in explaining the phenomena (and in predicting future events of the same kind), and so the choice of models is clear. Unfortunately, choosing models with a view to understanding economic systems of production and exchange is never as easy.

Outline of a Model for the Pure Theory of Exchange

To introduce the role of parameters and variables in an economic model, we follow Walras in considering a simple system in which the only important relationships are those of exchange.

As we have seen, theories of allocation and exchange have existed in some form at least since the time of Richard Cantillon. It is characteristic of the presentation of exchange by the classical economists, however, that they never analyzed the trading of consumer's goods in abstraction from the technical and social conditions under which these goods were themselves produced. In Adam Smith's work, for example, the study of the process of exchange is inextricably bound up with the allocation of surplus output to produce a greater surplus in the future. It was not until the neoclassical period, and the work, above all, of Léon Walras, that a theory of pure exchange was developed—*pure* in the sense that all the interdependent relations of production were abstracted from, i.e., were outside the theory. Indeed, it may be regarded as an essential feature of the tradition of which Walras was a great founder, that many of its important concepts can be presented in models that abstract altogether from the theory of production. Certainly this is true of much of the *Elements* where relations of production were kept outside the theory by endowing the trading parties with given stocks of goods to exchange—*quantities* which then appeared among the essential *parameters* of any model for this theory.

We shall continue to argue, in light of the structure of modern classical and neoclassical models, that one of the salient characteristics of post-Walrasian theory is the development of not simply a theory of allocation (all the classical economists had this), but rather a theory of pure exchange in the sense discussed above. In order to see the role played by this theory in neoclassical economics it is important to come to terms with its essential nature. It is for this purpose that we now turn to consider an exemplary situation which is widely used to illustrate the principles of the post-Walrasian theory of pure exchange; namely, R. A. Radford's well-known essay on exchange in a prisoner-of-war camp,[5] from which the essential elements of a pure exchange economy can be extracted.*

---

* Ironically, even in the P.O.W. camp as described by Radford, capitalist relations of production, the sale of labor-power, and financial speculation arose. It is indeed as hard to find a real life ex-

The important activity in an exchange model of the prisoner-of-war camp is the trading of various items received by each prisoner from the Red Cross. In this story there is no production; the bundles of goods simply arrive periodically. The economic problem is to establish rates of exchange between various goods traded by prisoners to their mutual advantage. These rates of exchange determine the purchasing power of each prisoner's initial bundle of goods. One item, such as cigarettes, can perform the function of a medium of exchange, a kind of money, in terms of which all other items are valued.[6] The cigarette price of a razor blade divided by the cigarette price of a chocolate bar determines the number of chocolate bars needed to purchase a razor blade, etc. When these prices are known each prisoner can decide what, if anything from his initial bundle, he wishes to exchange in the "market place."

This interpretation of the prisoner-of-war camp provides a clear illustration of a pure exchange economy. Expressed in terms of a formal model, it would have certain parameters; namely, the total quantities of each good sent by the Red Cross, the initial distribution of goods among the prisoners (their initial bundles), and the tastes or preferences of each prisoner for the different goods.* These "data" may be assigned arbitrary values so that, although constant in a particular model, they may change from one model to another and so define a class of pure exchange models. The determined variables are the quantities consumed of each good by each prisoner after all trades have taken place (the final allocations), and the price of each good (in terms of cigarettes) associated with these trades. The model itself is a set of relationships among the variables and parameters that yields an *equilibrium* solution in terms of the variable prices and quantities, a solution that has two important properties.

First, at the prices or rates of exchange determined by the model, each prisoner is engaged in just those trades with the other prisoners that he finds advantageous: his final bundle of goods is at least as preferred as the initial one received. Secondly, when all trades are added up, there is no excess demand for any good. In other words, all the individual offers of each particular good, when taken together, are equal to the sum of the individual demands for that commodity including what each prisoner has kept for himself from his own Red Cross parcel. Now, it is not at all obvious that such ratios of exchange, i.e., prices, should even exist. It is a function of the theory to show that, given various assumptions concerning the parametric structure of the model, a set of equilibrium prices and quantities *can* be established. (This is often called the "existence" problem.)

ample of a pure exchange economy as it is to find real life situations which fit any simple model, classical or neoclassical.

* On representing "tastes" by a real valued utility function, see chapter 10.

In the formal statement of a post-Walrasian pure exchange model, of which we have given only the barest outline, abstraction from the real problem of exchange occurs in various ways. Perhaps the most important abstraction is the notion of a *single set of prices* applying simultaneously to all transactions and to all transactors.* In real life this is never the case except in certain highly organized markets—even the stock exchange, which Walras referred to in his analysis, lists "bid" and "ask" prices for its securities. Thus, Radford, in his account of the actual mechanism of exchange in a prisoner-of-war camp noted that trade would occasionally proceed on a somewhat *ad hoc* basis with some prisoners ending up paying more than others for the same things. Despite this problem, the abstraction involved in speaking of a single set of prices *may* not be misleading if the purpose of the analysis lies in showing that all the transactors can, in principle, benefit from trade.† But, if the problem is to explain the *process* by which prices are formed, it would be misleading to suppose that all trades take place at the *same* set of prices. Here is an example of how the interpretation of a model and the uses to which it can be put depend upon its formal structure.

Neoclassical Allocation Theory: An Extension of the Pure Theory of Exchange

The neoclassical approach to the analysis of economies in which production takes place consists essentially in a sophisticated elaboration of the pure exchange model,[7] an approach which Walras himself initiated. The scope of the analysis is thus widened to include production relationships but these are, in effect, treated formally as relationships of exchange.

In a *pure* exchange model we have seen that the individual agents are endowed with a particular, initial bundle of goods, and with given preferences for *all* the goods that may conceivably enter into trade. In the extended allocation model, however, the endowment of goods is replaced by an endowment

---

* Remember that Menger was unwilling to make this assumption even though he is regarded as one of the three founders of the modern neoclassical tradition.

† If every trade is motivated simply by the desire to obtain a bundle of goods, the components of which are preferred to those of the bundle already obtained (rather than for the purpose of speculating on the future purchasing power of its constituent commodities), then no prisoner can be worse off as a result of trade when the "market period" has ended. But the advantage that any particular prisoner gains from engaging in trade does depend on how prices are established in the market, that is to say, on whether transactions take place at various prices during the market period or at just one set of equilibrium prices for which there is no unsatisfied demand *relative to the initial endowments*. Again, see Radford's discussion of speculation and the holding of stocks of commodities by certain prisoners.

of resource inputs, while preferences are defined over the set of commodity outputs produced with these inputs (and over the inputs where these are directly consumable). Producing agents are introduced into the analysis to act as intermediaries among the resource owners *qua* consumers. The role of producers is simply to coordinate the transformation of inputs into outputs (in the most efficient manner possible), responding, as it were, to the "price signals of the market place" where consumers make known their preferences for particular commodities. In the model, however, both producers and consumers are conceived as responding to a single set of equilibrium prices—prices for which there is no excess demand for either inputs or outputs.

There are more parameters in the formal structure of an allocation model than in a pure exchange model. These given data include the total quantities of resources or factor services (in place of the total quantities of tradeable commodities in the pure exchange model); the distribution of ownership of resources among consuming agents; the technology for transforming inputs into outputs (a parameter not present in the pure exchange model); and the tastes or preferences of consuming agents for produced commodities or directly consumable inputs. The variables determined by a neoclassical allocation model include the quantities of factor services allocated to the production of each commodity, and the quantities of each commodity (and of factors where these are consumed) allocated to each consumer. There are also relative prices or rates of exchange associated, first of all, with the purchase of factor services by producing agents (thus determining the incomes of resource owners), and secondly, with the expenditure on final commodities by consumers (which determines the receipts of producers). These ratios of exchange* ensure that there is no excess demand anywhere in the system and, as we shall see in chapter 9 on the price relations of a neoclassical model, that there is no excess of receipts over costs on the part of any producing agent.

The neoclassical allocation model is widely used as the basis for an interpretation of the circular flow of income and expenditure in actual systems of interdependent markets. "Households" are identified with the model's consuming agents, and they are also the owners of the given resources. The model's producing agents are interpreted as "firms." In "factor markets" households, as resource owners, supply factor services, while in "commodity markets" they demand final outputs. The other parties to these transactions

---

* Prices can be measured in terms of some particular commodity (recall the cigarette prices of the P.O.W. camp), or in terms of money, but, in any case, it is the *ratio* of two prices that determines the purchasing power of one commodity or factor service in terms of another. Such ratios are what the theory determines. See chapters 9 and 10.

are firms who act as intermediaries among the households, demanding factor services and supplying final outputs.

Despite its greater complexity, the allocation model is very much like the *pure* exchange model of the prisoner-of-war camp. In each case, individual agents form an economy on the basis of their mutual interest in the benefits of trade. In the simpler case it is possible to trade goods directly; in the more complicated model it is not. The exchange of factor endowments is indirect because it is the factor services which produce the consumable commodities. Production must be taken into account, but this should not obscure the fact that when a neoclassical allocation model is used to analyze a capitalist economy, it treats the indirect exchange of given resources for commodities, through a production process, as strictly analogous to the exchange of given stocks of goods in a model of pure exchange. But a treatment of production in terms of the allocation of given means among alternative uses is static, and it presents a sharp contrast with classical analysis where the focus is on *re*production as a dynamic process, and where the physical stock of (produced) inputs is *not* a parameter but a variable which is related to the size of the social surplus.

Classical Theories of Surplus and Accumulation and The Role of Social Class

The classical theory of surplus and the accumulation of capital was originally written when capitalism was replacing feudalism, and was the work of men whose primary interest lay in explaining the nature of this historical development. Models for the theory were set within a period of history in which one social class had acquired ownership of the means of production, while another class owned only its labor-power which it had to sell if it was to survive. Ian Steedman writes in his analysis of Marxian theory:

> All labour is performed by workers, characterized by their familiar 'double freedom', the freedom *to* offer their labour power to whichever capitalist they choose and the freedom *from* ownership of any land or produced means of production. Workers are thus freely mobile between industries but the only thing they have to sell is their capacity to work.[8]

In a classical model, moreover, it is assumed that technology has developed to the stage where it is possible to produce a social surplus. The purpose of the theory is neither to prove the existence of a surplus (any society that rises above subsistence evidently has some surplus), nor to prove the existence of a particular class structure (any capitalist economy has this structure). Rather, the purpose of the theory is to exhibit the special *historical* form assumed by the surplus under capitalism: to show how the generation, extraction, and distribution of surplus depends on the social (class) and technical relationships of capitalist production; and to show how this distribution affects the division of the surplus between capital accumulation and luxury consumption,* thereby affecting the development of the economy.

In neoclassical theory, on the other hand, incomes are derived, not on the basis of class relationships in production, but from the scarcity value of factor services owned by independent households. Incomes are therefore determined, once scarcity values are determined, by the given pattern of ownership of resources. As Dobb remarks:

. . . an initial distribution of income [factor endowments] between individuals is implicit in the general pricing-process, in the sense that it must be included as one of the determinants of the structure of demand from which all prices (including prices of productive factors) are derived; the whole pricing process being relative to this postulated distribution. A theory of distribution, in other words, if it is conceived as a theory of derived prices of productive services or factors, cannot be independent of initial income distribution as essential premise.[9]

A conception of society as a group of independent households is a natural corollary to the view that economic relationships are essentially those of exchange of given endowments (of goods in a pure exchange model, of factor services in an allocation model). No analytical importance is attached to the existence of social class, despite the fact that endowments may be very uneven. At first glance, the neoclassical theory has therefore appeared to some as universal since it can allow for any given distribution of property rights. Thus, a medieval manor is as legitimate a context within which to apply the neoclassical theory of resource allocation as a modern, capitalist economy (although, in the former, exchange ratios would have to be interpreted as "shadow prices" where markets did not exist). When used as a conceptual framework for an analysis of capitalism, the theory subsumes all class distinctions within the parameters defining resource endowments of the various households. "Workers," if they are to be identified, are those who sell "labor services" of all kinds; "landlords" sell "land services;" "rentiers"

---

* Recall the use of λ_j, $j = C,I$ and g in our sketch of certain two-sector classical models. These symbols were used to give formal expression to the division of the surplus between consumption and the accumulation of capital. Consumption can then be further disaggregated to show how the surplus is utilized in making "carriages" (see pp. 36–7, 114) or, more generally, "nonbasics" (see pp. 337–40).

sell the "services of finance;" and "capitalists" sell the "services of machines" they own. An individual resource owner, however, depending on his resource endowment, may be all these things at once. The social categories, "worker," "landlord," "rentier," and "capitalist," are, in neoclassical analysis, irrelevant.

The existence of a social structure was, for the classical economists, fundamental to their theories of surplus and the accumulation of capital. Property in the means of production implied control of the process by which a surplus is extracted. The capitalists' decisions regarding expenditure of profits determines the composition of output in the form of the social surplus: either as investment goods or as consumption goods absorbed by the capitalist class.*

In a model where commodities are produced by means of commodities, surplus is defined as the gross output of commodities minus those used up in the process of production. Since the notion of surplus is at least implicit in *any* picture of an ongoing (capitalist) economy, it is therefore all the more remarkable that it is not an explicit category in neoclassical theory. The reason, however, is simple. Surplus is only defined in a model in which, among the outputs, there are commodities used as inputs into further production. If, instead, all resources are treated analytically as if they were primary nonproduced factors of production (in the manner of Walras), the question of defining a surplus or net output simply cannot arise. Moreover, to admit the concept of surplus would imply that capital is no longer a parameter, but instead a variable stock of produced means of production to be determined within the model as a result of an ongoing process of investment.

To discover the size and composition of the physical stock of capital in a classical model, it is necessary to know what counts as replacement of the means of production. This raises questions about technology and about the nature of society which must be answered before such a model can be constructed. The classical economists were quite aware of the problem of defining subsistence as a component of the means of production. Their normal attitude toward it was succinctly expressed by David Ricardo:

It is not to be understood that the natural price of labour, estimated even in food and necessaries, is absolutely fixed and constant. It varies at different times in the same country, and very materially differs in different countries. It essentially depends on the habits and customs of the people. . . . Many of the conveniences now enjoyed in an English cottage would have been thought luxuries at an earlier period of our history.[10]

---

* There may also be a class of landlords or of rentiers living off the accumulated financial obligations of the capitalists, but the incomes accruing to such classes can be regarded as paid out of profits, at least as a first approximation.

Joan Robinson, in considering how surplus arises in certain preindustrial economies, put it this way:

> It is impossible precisely to define a surplus of production over the necessities of subsistence, because it is impossible precisely to define subsistence. Needs, as we know only too well, grow with the means to satisfy them. All the same, in any society there is some notion of a distinction between daily bread and something extra—for a guest, for a feast or for tribute to whom tribute is due.[11]

Neoclassical economists have taken this difficulty in defining subsistence to be a major stumbling block in the classical approach. If subsistence is imprecise, then surplus cannot be defined. This criticism, however, ignores three points. First, subsistence in classical theory is an historically relative concept. One readily grants that it is a simplifying abstraction to fix the exact quantities of goods and services that make up subsistence consumption on the part of workers. Having done so, however, one can then work out the logical implications of the subsistence assumption in terms of the possibilities for extraction and accumulation of surplus. In this way, subsistence requirements take on the role of a parameter in classical theory which can be altered in a manner appropriate to the relevant historical setting.

Secondly, whatever the difficulties inherent in the classical approach, the structure of *neo*classical theory does not avoid the subsistence problem,* which simply arises in an indirect and often unnoticeable way.† Thus, in the solution to a neoclassical model one finds that there is nothing to ensure that all resource owners have positive incomes—the prices of particular factor services can be zero.‡ Although it has been said in defense of the theory that the concept of equilibrium does not lay claim to any normative properties, any model of exchange is incoherent if some of the participants have nothing to consume. In order for neoclassical equilibrium to be meaningful it must tacitly be assumed that every resource owner receives at least a subsistence income.[12]

Finally, as we will show in chapter 13, wages can be treated as variable in a model which nevertheless describes the production and extraction of surplus, and the accumulation of capital. The belief that difficulties in defining subsistence are fatal to classical theory but not to neoclassical theory therefore has no foundation.

---

* See chapter 10 for a discussion of the problem of zero incomes in neoclassical theory.
† Unnoticeable in models where technology admits of continuous substitution among factors, but very noticeable in linear models of the type used in this book.
‡ Walras assumed all prices would be positive (for reasons connected with his broader social philosophy), but see the post-Walrasian analysis of prices in chapter 9.

Outline of the Structure of a Model
of Surplus and Accumulation

The history of economic analysis shows clearly that the structure of models in which the concepts of surplus and accumulation can be analyzed must differ sharply from that of models for the theory of the allocation of given means among alternative uses. As a prelude to our formal development we consider these differences in terms of the parameters and variables that enter into the structure of a classical model.

Technology is a parameter, but the relationship between inputs and outputs is different from that in neoclassical theory. Instead of a "one-way street" from given factors to final outputs, there is a circular flow of production of commodities by means of commodities. As we have seen in our discussion of one- and two-sector classical models, the list of outputs and the list of inputs contain the same physical things. It is the resulting circular flow of production that allows one to define surplus and to give formal expression to the trade-off between accumulation and "luxury" consumption. Included in the technical specifications of production is a second parameter, the subsistence wage, already discussed. We shall always include the commodity components of subsistence in the input–output coefficients even in models where the wage rises above subsistence.

A third parameter of a classical model specifies some aspect of the composition of output. We shall consider two cases. In one the proportions of gross output consumed by the capitalists are fixed, an assumption consistent with the austere classical formulation of Neumann.[13] In the other case the rate of accumulation is a parameter, whereas the proportions of gross output consumed are variables determined by the given preferences of capitalists (or of capitalists and workers in models where the wage rises above subsistence).*

Finally, since a classical model lacks "given resources," the absolute scale of production must be fixed by treating as a fourth parameter either the number of units of gross output (following an appropriate "normalization"), or the number of units of employed labor.† This choice has implications for the way in which the model is interpreted.

The variables determined in a classical model depend, of course, on the

---

* Compare the various treatments of demand in classical theory at the end of chapters 11, 12, and 13.

† We shall generally follow the former procedure so that the number of laborers employed is a variable, on the assumption that it is never greater than the supply. In a technical sense, however, absolute size plays little role in our analysis since returns to scale are constant. See chapters 8 and 11 on this aspect of technology which is common to all our models, classical and neoclassical.

particular list of parameters chosen. In the model of chapters 11 and 12 where the wage is a subsistence parameter, no variable wage enters into the analysis. The variables that are determined include relative prices and the rate of profit. Given the proportions of gross outputs consumed by the capitalists, the rate of accumulation is treated as a variable in chapter 11. Then, in chapter 12 we reverse this procedure by fixing the growth rate and showing how demand for "luxury" consumption is determined by capitalists' preferences. In each case the composition of the stock of produced inputs and the composition of the flow of gross and net output are also variables.

In chapter 13 the variable wage (over and above subsistence) is a further variable. In determining it we add to the parameters a specification of savings behavior. Workers' preferences for consumption goods, as well as the capitalists', are shown to affect the composition of demand which, in turn, influences the composition of gross and net output and of the means of production, all of which are variables in a classical model (in contrast to the given resources of neoclassical theory).

We have presented the neoclassical theory of resource allocation as an extension of the pure theory of exchange. Models for the theory therefore imply that relationships of exchange among owners of given factors are the essential market relationships from which all else follows. Identifying the parameters and variables of neoclassical theory brings out this fact. Resources and technology define supply conditions; preferences and factor ownership define demand conditions. Variable quantities and prices are then determined by a general equilibrium of supply and demand. According to this view the distribution of income is a reflection of the relative intensity of demand for the factors of production and therefore of the preferences of resource owners for final goods and services. The behavior of producing agents certainly enters into the arguments, but in the system as a whole these agents are intermediaries in an exchange among resource owners *qua* consumers.

In the group of models labelled classical the basic parameters can be summed in terms of the technical and social relations of production. Technology is given from outside the model and is specified in terms of a circular flow of reproduction. Variable prices and quantities are then determined by the particular social structure imposed on these technical relationships. In a model with a subsistence wage, for example, prices and the rate of profit emerge solely from technical relationships which incorporate subsistence, and are independent of the composition of the surplus. The form of the surplus is determined by the decisions of capitalists regarding accumulation and consumption of surplus output. In more complicated models with a variable wage these results emerge again, but in a modified form.

Notes

1. John von Neumann and Oskar Morgenstern, *Theory of Games and Economic Behavior,* Princeton University Press, 1944; paperback ed., Wiley, New York, 1967, p. 2.
2. Joan Robinson, *Essays on the Theory of Economic Growth,* Macmillan, London, 1962, p. 33.
3. Karl Marx, *Das Kapital, Kritik der Politischen Oekonomie,* Vol. I, Meissner, Hamburg, 1867; trans. *Capital,* Vol. I, Progress Publishers, Moscow, n.d., p. 19.
4. Joan Robinson, *Essays,* p. 33. Professor Robinson refers to Lewis Carroll's *Sylvie and Bruno.*
5. R. A. Radford, "The Economic Organization of a P.O.W. Camp," *Economica,* New Series, Vol. XII (1945), pp. 189–201.
6. *Ibid.,* p. 190–91.
7. For a modern example, in the context of the most advanced mathematical formulations of neoclassical theory, see Hukukaine Nikaido, *Introduction to Sets and Mappings in Modern Economics,* American Elsevier, New York, 1970, pp. 268–72.
8. Ian Steedman, *Marx after Sraffa,* New Left Books, London, 1977, p. 16. Steedman's italics.
9. Maurice Dobb, *Theories of Value and Distribution Since Adam Smith: Ideology and Economic Theory,* Cambridge University Press, 1973, p. 34.
10. David Ricardo, *On the Principles of Political Economy and Taxation,* John Murray, London, 1817; ed. Piero Sraffa in collaboration with Maurice Dobb, *Works and Correspondence of David Ricardo,* Cambridge University Press, Vol. I, 1951, pp. 96–7.
11. Robinson, *Freedom and Necessity,* Pantheon Books, New York, 1970, p. 25.
12. For a brief discussion of the mathematical problems that arise when incomes of certain resource owners are zero, see Kenneth J. Arrow, "General Economic Equilibrium: Purpose, Analytic Techniques, Collective Choice," *American Economic Review,* Vol. 64 (1974), p. 267.
13. John von Neumann, "A Model of General Economic Equilibrium," *Review of Economics Studies,* Vol. 13 (1945–46), pp. 1–9. For a full reference see chapter 1, note 2.

8

The Neoclassical Theory of Resource Allocation: Quantity Relations

> If we take the famous definition, given so many years ago by Lord Robbins—"the relationship between ends and scarce means that have alternative uses"—economics, in that sense, is very well covered by linear theory.
>
> SIR JOHN HICKS[1]

The theory of the allocation of given resources among alternative uses provides the analytical foundation for much of neoclassical microeconomics. Indeed, it is no exaggeration to say that all standard microeconomic models are particular cases of the allocation of given resources: in consumption theory, for example, a given income is allocated among purchases of given commodities at given prices in order to maximize a utility index; in production theory, a given cost outlay is allocated among the purchases of given factor services at given prices in order to maximize the value of output. More important to our analysis, however, is the fact that the various parts of neoclassical microeconomics are intended to fit together in a logical and coherent fashion, that is to say, within a theoretically consistent framework of *general* equilibrium. And, remarkably, this framework is itself another model for the theory of the allocation of given resources, although a more complicated one than those typical of the constituent parts of microeconomics. In this and the next two chapters we develop the basic principles of neoclassical allocation theory using a simple two-sector model of general equilibrium which, in all important respects, is a direct descendant of the model first set forth by Walras in his *Elements*. Thus, we shall often invoke exactly those assumptions made by Walras concerning, for example, fixed production coefficients; although, in other respects, the model takes into account modern developments which have removed certain formal inconsistencies in Walras's formulation.* The model is therefore post-Walrasian.

---

*We say *formal* since the inconsistencies relate to the mathematical structure of the theory, a structure which forces one to allow for unemployment of resources and (as a consequence) zero prices for certain factor services (see chapter 9). Recall that Walras ruled out these possibilities since he was interested in equilibria consistent with the underlying social philosophy he shared with his father.

The restrictions we impose on the analytical structure are chosen expressly for the purpose of bringing into a clear light those characteristics of neoclassical theory which we regard as fundamental. This involves a judgment as to what constitute the essential elements in the neoclassical explanation of prices, incomes, the employment of resources, and the distribution of output. To succeed in exposing these elements, a simple model must be made of strong materials since it is to bear a considerable interpretational weight. To draw a comparison with another field of scientific inquiry, consider the problem of explaining the basic principles of mechanics. One approach would be to illustrate these principles with the aid of a simple pulley and lever device; another would be to use as a model a complicated piece of construction equipment made up of a whole system of pulleys and levers. The simple model has the advantage of isolating basic concepts, but it is clearly not meant to narrow the application of the theory to simple devices. On the contrary, a consideration of the simple case is only an aid to understanding how more complicated systems function. Here, we are in essentially the same position. A simple model for the theory of resource allocation is used to elucidate principles, but one must always bear in mind that this model is, in the words of Sir John Hicks, "mainly interesting because it can be generalized." [2]

Parameters and Variables

As we remarked in the preceding chapter, the construction of a model entails a distinction between parameters, exogenous to the model, and variables, determined endogenously by the relationships of which the model is composed. It is convenient to group the parameters of a neoclassical allocation model under two headings: those relating to conditions of supply and those relating to conditions of demand. Under the first heading are two categories of data:

(1) the available quantities of various resources yielding factor services in production;
(2) the technology of production specifying the ways in which factor services are transformable into final outputs.

Since factor services are measured as flows within a given time period, while resources are measured as stocks, it must be assumed either that the flows are the given data, or, if only the stocks are given, that the technical link between stocks and flows is fully specified. Under the heading of demand are two further categories of exogenous data:

(3) the preferences of consuming agents for the various final products specified in the technology as well as for any directly consumable resources;
(4) the pattern of ownership among consuming agents of the given factors of production.

In our analysis it is also convenient to have the variables divided into two groups. On the one hand, there are quantities; namely,

(1) the allocations of factor services to different technical processes, and hence the outputs of various final commodities;
(2) the allocations of outputs to the various resource owners who are the model's consuming agents.

On the other hand, there are two sets of relative prices or ratios of exchange associated with these allocations of inputs and outputs:

(3) factor prices measuring the relative values of the different factor services;
(4) commodity prices measuring the relative values of various final outputs.

The intended interpretation of neoclassical allocation theory depends fundamentally on the meaning attached to the parameters that enter into its structural relationships. To begin with, the category "resources" is to be broadly interpreted as including every possible type of input or factor service. One should think therefore in terms of a completely disaggregated list, a sort of "who's who" of different items, all specified in particular physical terms. Each of the following would therefore qualify as a "resource":

(a) a pool of oil of a given quality known to exist at a particular location beneath the earth's surface;
(b) a civil engineer with a particular range of talents acquired through education and experience;
(c) a diesel engine complete with detailed specifications concerning its horsepower, fuel consumption, maintenance requirements, etc.*

---

* In specifying the characteristics of a resource it is implicitly assumed that these characteristics can be known with certainty. However, one might well ask of our list of factors: Is there really a pool of oil in the location specified? Does the engineer really have the abilities attributed to him? Is the diesel engine actually going to perform as specified, or is it about to fall apart unexpectedly? These questions are not addressed in standard treatments of allocation theory and we therefore proceed on the assumption that all the data parametric to any model for the theory are known with certainty.

It may also be noted here that the list of resources evidently cannot be given independently of the technology of production which defines inputs in relationship to outputs.

It is conventional to distinguish the so-called primary (nonproduced) inputs of land and labor from inputs of "capital" that embody the services of primary factors utilized in previous time periods. The pool of oil would fall under the heading of land; the engineer, under the heading of labor; and the diesel engine, under "capital." On the other hand, it might easily be said that each of these inputs (and, indeed, any input) is, strictly speaking, a *produced* means of production. A geological process, and a process of discovery, produced the oil; a process of education and training produced the engineer; and a process of investment of other inputs produced the diesel engine. Thus, the question arises as to whether the distinction between produced and nonproduced inputs needs to be made more precise before the argument can proceed.

The answer is simple. In a model of neoclassical allocation theory it is of no importance to distinguish inputs on the basis of the process by which they came into being. It does not matter that the diesel engine was produced in anticipation of a profit on its operation, or that the engineer acquired an education in anticipation of the future market value of engineering services; while nature (though not the drillers of oil wells) produced the oil independently of the conditions of the marketplace. Indeed, the *only* historical fact that has any bearing on the analysis is that a given quantity of resources has come into existence and is now available at a point in time to be used in ways that may or may not have been anticipated when these resources were produced. Formally, this is expressed in the treatment of the supply of resources or factors of production as a parameter of the neoclassical model—a given list of inputs with an essentially *arbitrary* composition. Thus, the categories land, labor, and "capital" are only descriptive; they have *no analytical significance* in static allocation models.* They *may* be used as convenient headings under which to group the factors of production; but they cannot be thought of in classical terms as implying any particular social organization of production or class division, since social class has no role in the analytical structure of neoclassical theory.

Technology, the second parameter, is best thought of in neoclassical theory as a book of recipes listing all the known methods for combining factors of production to yield alternative goods and services.† As such, the technology

---

*This becomes even more clear in the context of multiperiod, and in that respect dynamic models of resource allocation, where the concept of "capital" as produced inputs naturally arises, but where allocation at every point in time (whether handled discretely or continuously) is still conceived of in static terms—as the allocation of *given* resources.

†"Outputs," "commodities," "goods," and "goods and services," are used interchangeably in our discussion of neoclassical theory. In particular, "goods" can always be read "goods and services" although we generally associate the word "services" with factors of production. In any case, wherever we give descriptive content to our models, outputs are always particular products such as rice and wheat.

does not specify the particular methods that will characterize an equilibrium solution to the allocation problem, nor does it say anything concerning the list of commodities that are produced (as opposed to those for which output is zero). Technology is just a list of possible transformations of inputs into outputs.

The analogy with a book of recipes implies that the transformation of inputs into outputs is a *one-way* flow from factors to final goods and services, unlike the technology of classical theory in which commodities are produced in order to be used in the reproduction of themselves and other commodities. It is important to understand, however, that in taking this view, neoclassical theory does not deny the reproducibility of the means of production. It simply takes no account of this reproducibility in its analysis of prices and quantities.* The interpretation of technology as a one-way flow, suspended in time, is therefore closely tied to the parametric representation of inputs as given resources. Thus, the flow of services of a diesel engine may enter as a factor input into certain technical processes, but it is immaterial to the theory's treatment of production that the engine itself is the result of a previous investment of resources as opposed to a free gift of nature, dropping, as it were, from Heaven! And, insofar as there *are* free gifts of nature, like oil in the ground, it is *not* the unknown, finite quantity in existence that is a parameter of an allocation model, since the only parts of this quantity relevant to a technical process are those already discovered. In all cases, then, the one-way flow from factors to final outputs in the specification of technology is a mirror image of the treatment of resources as given parameters of the problem, irrespective of the way in which they have come into existence.

Turning now to the demand-related parameters of neoclassical allocation theory, we may interpret the given preferences of consuming agents for various goods and services to mean that the theory does not require an explanation of how consumers' tastes are formed (although it does not preclude explanation on the basis of advertising, peer group pressure, etc.). In formal models, preferences are represented in a variety of ways, but regardless of the particular formulation, they have the same essential role: to show how the resulting pattern of demand for different goods and services (given the other parameters of the model) affects the composition of output, and, indirectly, the distribution of income. This is perhaps the most remarkable aspect of the theory since it provides the analytical basis for the notion that consumers are "sovereign" in a freely competitive market economy—that they decide what

---

* Again, this is all the more clear in multiperiod models for the theory where outputs of one period may become factors in the next period. The point is simply that *within* each period the analysis proceeds *as if* it were concerned with a static allocation problem, isolated in time.

goods (or, more correctly, what *quantities* of goods*) will be produced by casting "monetary votes" in the marketplace. For this reason, producing agents can only be interpreted as intermediaries acting in a way that is consistent with the wishes of consumers, a point of view adopted by Schumpeter in his discussion of Walras.† Moreover, the choices of consumers, insofar as they affect prices in the model, serve to establish a relationship between the demand for final outputs and the *relative scarcity* of the different factors that are inputs in production. This relationship between the composition of output and what Hicks has called the *differential intensity* of the various constraints on output[3] provides the basis for the neoclassical theory of factor prices, and thus of the distribution of income, given the ownership of factors which is the remaining parameter of the theory.

Owing to the parametric treatment of factor ownership,‡ it has been claimed that neoclassical theory, when applied to the analysis of market economies, is neutral with respect to the existence of social class. The theory is meant to apply irrespective of the class structure (since factor ownership may be specified in any manner whatever) and, in that sense, the analysis is taken to be classless. This is surely a striking proposition, implying that a *single* analytical framework can be adapted to comprehend the essential elements of a wide variety of economic systems. Thus, the logical structure of the relationships among parameters and variables would be exactly the same in a model of an economy of independent families (each with its own means of production specified to some particular task) and in a model of a capitalist economy in which ownership of the means of production is concentrated in the hands of one social class which hires the labor services of another. The theory differentiates the two cases simply by altering the specification of the pattern of ownership of the given factors. Of course, a different pattern of ownership will, in all likelihood, alter the solution to the allocation problem i.e., the prices and allocations of inputs and outputs, since a different distribution of ownership alters the relative importance of the preferences (for commodities) of various resource owners. But any shift in ownership, however drastic, would not alter the way in which the model is constructed.

---

*Quantities only since preferences for final outputs (and any consumable resources) are not defined independently of technology and factor supplies which specify the menu of goods and services available for consumption. Thus, *in the theory,* consuming agents cannot demand anything that is not already on this list of outputs (and consumable inputs); and so their only influence is on the *quantities* and not the *qualities* of goods produced.

†See above, p. 155.

‡The interdependence of parameters is again apparent since factor ownership cannot be specified without knowing what the factors are and this, in turn, depends on the specification of technology.

More to the point, however, is not the doubtful claim that all class structures are encompassed by neoclassical theory through changes in the specification of factor ownership (not all neoclassical economists would subscribe to this[4]), but rather that this is the *only* way in which class relationships can possibly impinge on the analysis. Thus, factor ownership, the sole expression of class distinctions in neoclassical theory, can affect *demand* and thus the terms of exchange among factors and commodities, which are the fundamental relationships of the theory. But different social relationships will in no way affect the analysis of production.

Resources and Factor Allocations

The first set of relationships to be satisfied in a neoclassical allocation model are resource constraints, which state that the use made of any given factor service cannot exceed its available supply. The sum of the *variable* allocations of a particular factor of production to the different processes of production cannot exceed its *parametrically* given supply. For purposes of illustration we take up the model introduced in chapter 6 in which there were two inputs: labor services and land services, and two outputs, rice and wheat. Recall that the land is assumed to be of uniform quality and that each unit of labor is equally well suited to cultivating either crop so that there is no need to distinguish different types of land or to consider various categories of labor.*

Given factor supplies and the technology of production, resource constraints, one for labor services and one for land services, define the set of *alternative feasible outputs* of rice and wheat. Certain fundamental characteristics of neoclassical theory become starkly evident in a model in which technology is very simple, and it is for this reason that we follow Walras in assuming that inputs of labor and land are given as fixed per-unit requirements in each process of production.† Recalling our earlier notation and abbreviations,‡ we define technology in a two-sector model by a pair of processes, one for each commodity: (a_{LR}, a_{TR}); (a_{LW}, a_{TW}). Thus:

---

* Some resources *are* specific in the sense that they have only one use. For example, a deposit of iron ore is useful only in the production of iron, so that its allocation to different uses degenerates into a trivial problem. To prevent this from happening in the present model, it is assumed that each resource has alternative uses. This is not, however, an essential feature of the analysis and, presently, we consider a model in which some inputs are used in only one process. See Figure 8-6, and the discussion pertaining to it.

† In chapter 14 less restrictive assumptions on technology are introduced and the results of the theory reinterpreted.

‡ See p. 157.

$$\mathbf{A} = \begin{bmatrix} a_{LR} & a_{LW} \\ a_{TR} & a_{TW} \end{bmatrix}$$

forms a 2 x 2 matrix of coefficients with per unit labor requirements in the first row and per unit land requirements in the second row, the columns corresponding to outputs. Each row of coefficients is used in defining a resource constraint in which factor allocations are written as the product of the relevant per-unit factor requirement multiplied by the level of production of the corresponding output, Y_R and Y_W in the case of rice and wheat. We then have:

$$L \geq a_{LR} Y_R + a_{LW} Y_W \qquad \text{labor constraint} \tag{1}$$

$$T \geq a_{TR} Y_R + a_{TW} Y_W \qquad \text{land constraint} \tag{2}$$

where L and T measure the given supplies of labor services and land services; and $a_{ij} Y_j$, $i = L, T, j = R, W$ measure the allocations of factor i to sector j.* Resource constraints (in any neoclassical allocation model) state the relationship between parametric factor supplies (L, T) and variable outputs (Y_R, Y_W) consistent with a given technology $\mathbf{A}$. Outputs that satisfy the constraints are said to be *feasible*. Since outputs must be nonnegative, the formal statement of the *feasible set of outputs* is complete only upon adding the pair of nonnegativity conditions:

$$Y_R \geq 0 \qquad Y_W \geq 0 \tag{3}$$

A question of interpretation now arises. Since constant returns to scale have been assumed (i.e., that a given percentage change in all factor inputs results in an equal percentage change in any given output), it follows that there is nothing in the theory to determine the *scale of operation* of the producing unit. We shall therefore speak of sectors of production without recourse to the distinction between firms and industries. In the present chapter, this causes no difficulty, but in the next chapter on prices the producing unit must be regarded as small enough to take prices as given.

A numerical example illustrates the general proposition that a list, or vec-

---

*At this point it is convenient to clear up a possible source of confusion concerning units of measurement. Resources of labor and land are needed during some particular period of time, the time period for which the allocation problem is defined, say, a year. Thus, L and T measure the supply of labor services per year and land services per year. The symbols, Y_R and Y_W, on the other hand, measure flows of output over the same period in, say, bushels per year. The coefficients, a_{ij}, are then ratios of factor services per year to output per year, in which case the time dimension cancels out. In our discussion, we will usually drop the reference to time altogether referring to *flows* of factor services and *flows* of output simply as factor services and outputs, respectively.

tor, of outputs is feasible if and only if it does not use up more than the available supply of *all* factor services; while, on the other hand, it is infeasible if it requires more than the available supply of *at least one* of the factors of production. In the two-sector model, let there be a total of 120 units of labor services and 96 units of land services for use in both sectors; and the technology matrix **A** is specified as follows:

$$\mathbf{A} = \begin{bmatrix} a_{LR} & a_{LW} \\ a_{TR} & a_{TW} \end{bmatrix} = \begin{bmatrix} 6 & 2 \\ 3 & 4 \end{bmatrix}$$

Resource constraints are therefore written:

$$120 \geq 6Y_R + 2Y_W \tag{1$'$}$$

$$96 \geq 3Y_R + 4Y_W \tag{2$'$}$$

A given composition of output will be indicated by the ordered pair (Y_R, Y_W). It is feasible if both (1)$'$ and (2)$'$ are satisfied subject to condition (3), and infeasible if any one of these constraints is violated.

A diagram of the feasible set of outputs is easily constructed since each resource constraint can be represented by a set of points with coordinates (Y_R, Y_W) in a Euclidean space where the horizontal axis measures rice production and the vertical axis, wheat production. Consider the labor constraint. For nonnegative outputs, there is some quantity of rice that requires the total supply of labor services in its production, given the technical coefficient a_{LR}. In our example, this is $Y_R = 20$ since $a_{LR} Y_R = 6 \times 20 = 120$ units of labor, the available supply. This may not be a feasible output—it is impossible to tell without taking into account the supply of land services and their requirement in rice production—but, for the moment, we are considering only labor as a constraint on production. In general, the output of rice that would use up the given supply of labor is L/a_{LR}, for any values of L and a_{LR}, and, in that event, the output of wheat would be zero. By the same reasoning, the output of wheat that requires the total supply of labor services is $Y_W = L/a_{LW}$, since $a_{LW} Y_W = 2 \times 60 = 120 = L$, a given parameter. Whether or not this level of wheat production is feasible (we have not taken into account the land requirement), rice production will necessarily be zero when the total supply of labor is allocated to the wheat sector.

In Figure 8-1 the two points just considered are marked off along the horizontal and vertical axes as: $(Y_R, Y_W) = (L/a_{LR}, 0) = (20, 0)$ and $(Y_R, Y_W) = (0, L/a_{LW}) = (0, 60)$. A straight line joining them as the slope:

$$-(L/a_{LW})/(L/a_{LR}) = -a_{LR}/a_{LW} = -3$$

Along this line is a third point $(Y_R, Y_W) = (16, 12)$ for which the labor requirement is again just equal to the total supply of labor services:

$$a_{LR} Y_R + a_{LW} Y_W = (6 \times 16) + (2 \times 12) = 96 + 24 = 120$$

Thus, a shift in the composition of output from, say, (20, 0) to (16, 12), releases labor from the rice sector, where output falls by 4 units, in exactly the amount needed in the wheat sector, where output increases by 12 units. The trade-off of 3 units of wheat per unit of rice is dictated by the technology of production which states that a unit of rice requires three times the labor needed to produce a unit of wheat. Using the symbol Δ to denote change, we have for any movement along the labor constraint:

$$\Delta Y_W / \Delta Y_R = - a_{LR}/a_{LW} = -3 \tag{4}$$

The associated reallocations of labor between the two sectors maintain full employment of labor services, barring shortages of any other inputs.

In general, the interpretation of the line joining $(L/a_{LR}, 0)$ to $(0, L/a_{LW})$ is

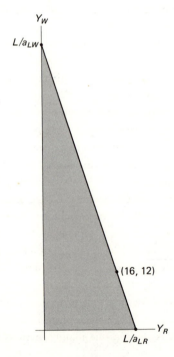

Figure 8-1. Labor constraint, given $L = 120$, $a_{LR} = 6$, $a_{LW} = 2$.

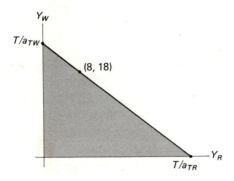

Figure 8-2. Land constraint, given $T = 96$, $a_{TR} = 3$, $a_{TW} = 4$.

that of a *boundary* of a set of points measuring nonnegative outputs of rice and wheat that do not violate the labor constraint, (1). Points along the line are called *limit points,* outputs that require the total supply of labor services and satisfy (1) as an equation.* Points above the line define outputs that require a labor input greater than the given supply and are therefore infeasible; while points below the line, but still in the nonnegative quadrant, require less than the available labor supply. The shaded area in Figure 8-1, including its boundaries, is thus a graph of the set of points, (Y_R, Y_W), that satisfy (1) and (3).

The concept of resource constraint in neoclassical allocation theory is general because all factors of production are handled in exactly the manner just described. No input, or group of inputs, has logical priority over any other. Thus, in analyzing the land constraint, all we need do in our discussion of the labor constraint is replace L, a_{LR}, and a_{LW} with T, a_{TR}, and a_{TW}, respectively. Briefly, then, limit points along the straight line, in the nonnegative quadrant, joining $(T/a_{TR}, 0) = (32, 0)$ and $(0, T/a_{TW}) = (0, 24)$ indicate various outputs of rice and wheat for which the available supply of land services, T, is fully utilized. One such point in our example is $(Y_R, Y_W) = (8, 18)$, indicated in Figure 8-2, which can be verified by substituting these values into (2). Any movement along this line releases land services from one sector in exactly the amount needed by the other sector, thereby yielding a technologically determined trade-off:†

---

* These points satisfy the labor constraint as an equation, written in standard form as: $Y_W = -(a_{LR}/a_{LW}) Y_R + L/a_{LW}$. In our example, $Y_W = -3Y_R + 60$. Note $a_{LW} \neq 0$.
† The boundary of the land constraint, written as a linear equation in standard form is: $Y_W = -(a_{TR}/a_{TW})Y_R + T/a_{TW}$. In our example, $Y_W = -.75Y_R + 24$. Note that $a_{TW} \neq 0$.

$$\Delta Y_W / \Delta Y_R = -a_{TR}/a_{TW} = -.75 \tag{5}$$

As before, points above the line are infeasible since they require a total allocation of land in excess of the parameter T, while points below the line but still in the nonnegative quadrant require a total input of land that is less than the given supply. The shaded area in Figure 8-2, including its boundaries, is a graph of the points that satisfy (2) and (3).

We now construct a diagram to show feasible and infeasible outputs in our example by superimposing the set of points in the shaded area of Figure 8-1 onto the set of points in the shaded area of Figure 8-2, thereby obtaining an intersection of points, the darkly shaded area in Figure 8-3. This is the set of nonnegative feasible outputs satisfying both resource constraints. In particular, $y_0 - y_5$ are all feasible* since they belong to the darkly shaded area, and, for that reason, are possible solutions to the allocation problem: y_0 illustrates the case where neither factor is fully utilized; y_1 and y_2 are points where all the land but not all the labor is required to sustain the corresponding outputs; y_4 and y_5 are points where all the labor but not all the land is needed; and y_3 indicates the one output in our example requiring the total supply of both factor services.† Points $y_6 - y_8$, on the other hand, are representative of infeasible outputs. In the lightly shaded area containing y_6 there is enough labor but not enough land; in the area containing y_7 the opposite is true; and at y_8, in the unshaded area, outputs require more than the available supply of *both* factors of production.

The diagram just constructed shows clearly how post-Walrasian analysis of the relationship between inputs and outputs differs from the original Walrasian formulation. Thus, the solution to (1) and (2), written as equations in the manner of Walras, restricts the composition of output in the two-input, two-output model to the single point y_3; whereas in the modern formulation, (1)–(3) define a whole set of feasible outputs of which y_3 is only a particular case. That y_3 is the point of full utilization of factors does not mean that it is the best point—consuming agents in the model may be rice eaters, unfamiliar

---

* Lower case y, usually with a subscript or superscript label, will always indicate a point in commodity space, in the present case, with two coordinates (Y_R, Y_W). Thus, we write, for example, $y_3 = (16, 12)$.

† The *uniqueness* of the point y_3 (given its existence, the conditions for which are discussed presently), follows from our Walrasian assumption that coefficients in production are fixed. In chapter 14, on the other hand, we allow for more than one coefficient matrix, **A**, and, as a result, there is a range of outputs rather than a single point where both factors are fully utilized. It should be noted that in certain standard presentations of the two-sector neoclassical allocation model, technology is so represented (by "well-behaved" production functions) that *all* limit points of the feasible set of outputs fully utilize both factors of production. This, however, is a special case that diverts attention from some of the more interesting aspects of the theory.

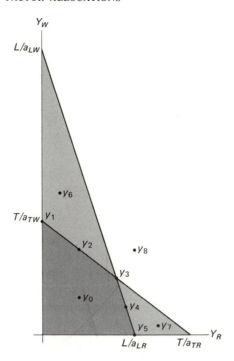

Figure 8-3. Feasible set of outputs as an intersection of resource constraints, given $(L, T) = (120, 96)$, $(a_{LR}, a_{TR}) = (6, 3)$, $(a_{LW}, a_{TW}) = (2, 4)$. The coordinates (Y_R, Y_W) of the indicated points are: $y_0 = (8, 8)$; $y_1 = (0, 24)$; $y_2 = (8, 18)$; $y_3 = (16, 12)$; $y_4 = (18, 6)$; $y_5 = (20, 0)$; $y_6 = (4, 30)$; $y_7 = (25, 2)$; $y_8 = (20, 18)$.

with wheat, in which case y_5 might be "best". Hence, there is no *a priori* rationale in the analysis for restricting output to y_3. In any case, it is not certain that the point of intersection of the two constraints (where each is satisfied as an equation) is even meaningful since it may well have a negative coordinate. Finally, there is the further difficulty that would arise if, say, three or more constraints were drawn as in Figure 8-6. In that case it would be fortuitous if all the lines defining outputs that use up all of each factor happened to intersect in a single point—Walras's *equations* might therefore be inconsistent, i.e., have no solution. Of course, this is interesting—overdetermined systems often are—since it shows the error of *assuming* that it will always be possible to utilize fully all factor services in a neoclassical allocation model.

These and other aspects of Walras's original formulation were the subject of important papers written in the 1930's, culminating in the work of

Abraham Wald and the fundamental contributions of John von Neumann and Oskar Morgenstern.[5] New results in the field of linear programming in the 1950's complemented this earlier work and made possible the most recent systematic accounts of the theory of resource allocation. Our model, though simple, is closely linked to this earlier work.

Some Generalizations

Certain generalizations of the two-sector model deserve attention simply because they may not be obvious. We will consider the effects of differences in the parameters defining factor supplies and the technology of production. At the same time, we will take up the problem of defining a necessary (but not sufficient) condition for full employment of both factors of production in the two-sector model. We then go on to consider the feasible set of outputs in models with more than two inputs and more than two outputs.

Our analysis has not depended on the particular values assigned to the parameters of the model: L, T, and the elements of $\mathbf{A}$.* Given the other parameters, a larger value for T, for example, would simply shift the land constraint away from the origin without changing its slope. This shift would alter the feasible set of outputs, moving the point of full employment of both factors up and to the left along the labor constraint.† In Figure 8-4 the supply of land services is so great *relative* to the supply of labor services that the labor constraint lies entirely "inside" the land constraint. There is then no feasible composition of output, or allocation of resources, that would fully utilize the land—the land constraint is never binding. (To illustrate the opposite case in which it is impossible to employ all the available labor services, simply reverse the labels of the factors.)

A necessary condition for the simultaneous full employment of both factors of production is that the two lines representing the boundaries of the resource constraints intersect at a point where both outputs are nonnegative.‡ This requires that the ratio of labor to land in the economy as a whole, L/T, is

---

* One restriction is necessary to ensure that the feasible set of outputs is *bounded*: it cannot be the case that all the coefficients in a process of production are zero, i.e., that an output can be produced without any input of factors. This is a standard assumption.

† Up and to the left rather than down and to the right because the labor constraint is steeper with respect to the horizontal axis than the land constraint, i.e., $a_{LR}/a_{LW} > a_{TR}/a_{TW}$, given our assumption that rice is the relatively labor-intensive product, i.e., $a_{LR}/a_{TR} > a_{LW}/a_{TW}$. Reversing these inequalities would cause the point of full employment of both factors, y_3, to shift down and to the right along the labor constraint for higher values of T.

‡ The results in this paragraph require the simultaneous solution to a pair of linear equations. See the appendix to this chapter on Cramer's Rule, a convenient method of solution.

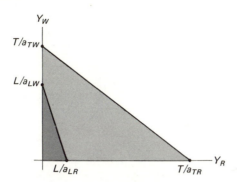

Figure 8-4. A nonbinding land constraint, given $(L, T) = (32, 96)$, $(a_{LR}, a_{TR}) = (6, 3)$, $(a_{LW}, a_{TW}) = (2, 4)$.

neither greater than the ratio of labor to land in the production of the labor-intensive product (rice) nor less than the corresponding ratio in the production of the land-intensive product (wheat). Given $a_{LR}/a_{TR} > a_{LW}/a_{TW}$, it must be the case that:

$$a_{LR}/a_{TR} \geq L/T \geq a_{LW}/a_{TW} \qquad (6)$$

Thus, as long as the aggregate factor ratio lies between the sectoral factor ratios, there is always some weighted average of the sectoral ratios (the weights being determined by the composition of output) such that the total supply of both factor services will be fully utilized.

A change in the technical coefficients will also result in a change in the feasible set of outputs. Thus, a *lower* value for either rice-sector coefficient *reduces* the rate at which wheat must be given up to obtain more rice along the boundary of the relevant constraint; and, in the same way, a lower wheat-sector coefficient reduces the rate at which rice must be given up to obtain more wheat along the relevant boundary. (See Figures 8-1 and 8-2 and equations (4) and (5).) It is also possible to consider the effect, in terms of the feasible set of outputs, of *variable* production coefficients within each sector. This raises a number of complications not relevant to our main line of argument.*

* As we point out in chapter 14, however, the treatment which follows immediately of a model with two factors and three commodities can be *interpreted* as allowing for variable coefficients just so long as two of the three outputs are regarded as physically homogeneous but differentiated according to their process of production. In effect, variation in the coefficients of production is already covered in this chapter's *m* factor, *n* commodity model discussed below, where a separate commodity label is attached to every process in every sector. Chapter 14's analysis simply brings out certain effects of variable coefficients not immediately obvious in the formulation adopted here.

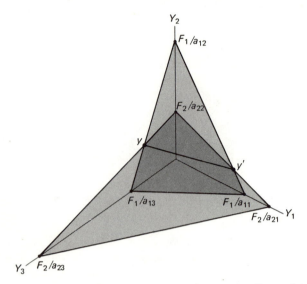

Figure 8-5. Feasible set of outputs in a two-factor three-commodity model, given (F_1, F_2) = (150, 120), (a_{11}, a_{21}) = (5, 3), (a_{12}, a_{22}) = (3, 6), (a_{13}, a_{23}) = (7.5, 2). The coordinates (Y_1, Y_2, Y_3) of the indicated points are: y = (0, 200/13, 180/13) and y' = (180/7, 50/7, 0) where the two resource constraints are satisfied as equations.

The model may also be generalized by increasing the number of inputs and/or outputs in the resource constraints. To show the effects of adding products while holding constant the number of factors, we construct a three-commodity model in which two factors, F_1 and F_2 (measuring total supplies), are allocated to three sectors, Y_1, Y_2, and Y_3. There are still two resource constraints but in each case a sum of three terms defines the total factor allocation. Thus:

$$F_1 \geq a_{11} Y_1 + a_{12} Y_2 + a_{13} Y_3 \tag{7}$$

$$F_2 \geq a_{21} Y_1 + a_{22} Y_2 + a_{23} Y_3 \tag{8}$$

$$Y_j \geq 0 \quad j = 1,2,3 \tag{9}$$

In a coordinate space of three dimensions, one for each product, the graph of each resource constraint is a set of points in the nonnegative orthant bounded by a plane. Their intersection, illustrated by the darkly shaded area in Figure 8-5, defines the feasible set of outputs that simultaneously satisfies (7)–(9).

Alternatively, the effect of adding factors without changing the number of products is shown in the following constraints for a model with five inputs and two outputs:

$$F_1 \geq a_{11} Y_1 + a_{12} Y_2 \tag{10}$$

$$F_2 \geq a_{21} Y_1 + a_{22} Y_2 \tag{11}$$

$$F_3 \geq a_{31} Y_1 + a_{32} Y_2 \tag{12}$$

$$F_4 \geq a_{41} Y_1 + a_{42} Y_2 \tag{13}$$

$$F_5 \geq a_{51} Y_1 + a_{52} Y_2 \tag{14}$$

$$Y_j \geq 0 \quad j = 1,2 \tag{15}$$

A graph of the feasible set is given in Figure 8-6. In the diagram the third factor of production is "plentiful" in the sense that there is no feasible output that requires the total given supply F_3. This input might be water available in large amounts (to both sectors) from an unpolluted river. The fourth and fifth factors are also noteworthy since F_4 does not restrict the output of Y_2 (the boundary of the constraint is a vertical line which never intersects the Y_2 axis); while F_5 does not restrict the output of Y_1 (the boundary of the constraint is horizontal). These are inputs with only one use so that there is no possibility of allocating them to alternative uses. For example, if Y_1 is rice and Y_2 is wheat as in our earlier model, F_4 may be rice seed and F_5, wheat

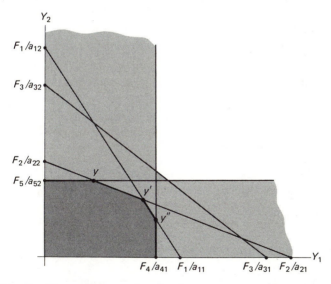

Figure 8-6. Feasible set of outputs in a five-factor two-commodity model, given $(F_1, F_2, F_3, F_4, F_5) = (66, 120, 108, 36, 12)$, $(a_{11}, a_{21}, a_{31}, a_{41}, a_{51}) = (3, 3, 3, 2, 0)$, $(a_{12}, a_{22}, a_{32}, a_{42}, a_{52}) = (2, 8, 4, 0, 1)$. The coordinates (Y_1, Y_2) of the indicated points are: $y = (8, 12)$, $y' = (16, 9)$, $y'' = (18, 6)$.

seed. Thus, a_{42} and a_{51} are both zero so that the boundaries of constraints (13) and (14) in the positive quadrant are simply constants: $Y_1 = F_4/a_{41}$ and $Y_2 = F_5/a_{52}$.

The interpretation just given illustrates a point made earlier in our discussion of resources in neoclassical theory. Recall that factor inputs are not differentiated according to the *process* which produced them—all are simply given. We may therefore interpret the plentiful factor F_3 as a "free gift of nature," in contrast to factors F_4 and F_5, the two types of seed which are forms of "capital" accumulated from previous harvests. This distinction does not, however, have any effect on the way in which the inputs enter into the analytical structure of the theory. On the other hand, treating all inputs in the same manner—as given factors—does not *deny* that the supply of produced inputs is a result of past decisions to invest in the means of production. Rather, the point is simply that insofar as the theory is concerned, this fact does not have any bearing on the analytical representation of the feasible set of outputs; and, as chapter 9 will show, this has implications for the way in which prices are analyzed.

Finally, we may write down resource constraints for a model with an arbitrary numbers of factors m, and an arbitrary number of final commodities n. Using ellipses to indicate omitted terms:*

$$F_1 \geq a_{11} Y_1 + a_{12} Y_2 + \ldots + a_{1n} Y_n$$
$$F_2 \geq a_{21} Y_1 + a_{22} Y_2 + \ldots + a_{2n} Y_n$$
$$\vdots \qquad \vdots \qquad \vdots \qquad \qquad \vdots \qquad \qquad (16)$$
$$F_m \geq a_{m1} Y_1 + a_{m2} Y_2 + \ldots + a_{mn} Y_n$$
$$Y_j \geq 0 \qquad j = 1, \ldots, n$$

The interpretation of these constraints is meant to be as general as the allocation problem under consideration requires. Thus, each factor of production,

---

* In the notation of matrix algebra, inequalities (16) are more compactly written as $F \geq AY$, $Y \geq 0$, where $F = \{F_1, F_2, \ldots, F_m\}$, $Y = \{Y_1, Y_2, \ldots, Y_n\}$ are column vectors, and A is a matrix of coefficients $\| a_{ij} \|$ in which $i = 1, \ldots, m$ is the row number, and $j = 1, \ldots, n$ is the column number of the entry, a_{ij}. Postmultiplication of a matrix A by a column vector Y is the operation in which the column vector is turned counterclockwise on its side and then multiplied, element by element, with the corresponding entries in a given row of the matrix. These products are summed and the procedure is repeated sequentially for each row. The result is itself a column vector of sums to be compared with the corresponding elements of F, using the relation, $\geq$. This procedure, it should be noted, is meaningful if and only if the number of elements in Y is equal to the number of columns in A, and the number of elements in F is equal to the number of rows in A.

F_i, $i = 1, \ldots, m$, and each output, Y_j, $j = 1, \ldots, n$ can have units of measurement specified not only in terms of *physical,* but also *temporal* and *spatial* characteristics. The implied distinctions are indicated in remarks of Gerard Debreu which preface his famous study of general equilibrium:

. . . wheat available now and wheat available in a week play entirely different economic roles for a flour mill which is to use them. Thus a good at a certain date and the same good at a later date are *different* economic objects, and the specification of the date at which it will be available is essential. Finally wheat available in Minneapolis and wheat available in Chicago play also entirely different economic roles for a flour mill which is to use them. Again, a good at a certain location and the same good at another location are *different* economic objects, and the specification of the location at which it will be available is essential. In the case now discussed a *commodity* is therefore defined by a specification of all its physical characteristics, of its availability date, and of its availability location. As soon as one of these three factors changes, a different commodity results.[6]

On factor services, Debreu gives this interpretation of the theory:

The first example of an economic *service* will be human labor. Its description is that of the task performed; thus one has the labor of a coal miner, of a truck driver, of a member of some category of teachers, of engineers, of draftsmen, of executives, etc. (all including any further specification necessary for a complete description). When one adds date and location one has again a well-defined [factor of production].[7]

One may conclude from these remarks on the meaning of commodities and factors that the neoclassical theory of resource allocation is intended to provide a framework of analysis appropriate to a very wide range of problems. Again, Debreu sums up the case:

By focusing attention of change of dates one obtains, *as a particular case* of the general theory of commodities . . . , a theory of saving, investment, capital, and interest. Similarly by focusing attention on changes of locations one obtains *as another particular case* of the same general theory, a theory of location, transportation, international trade and exchange.[8]

Thus a *single* framework of analysis is offered as the basis for solving all problems of allocation. In particular, there is no suggestion of any fundamental distinction between classical and neoclassical theories of general equilibrium which, we submit, is substantiated not only by the historical record, but also by the mathematical structure of modern analysis. Indeed, the purpose of our juxtaposition of various chapters on neoclassical and classical theory is to contrast these structures in as simple a context as possible, while still giving expression to the fundamental concepts of each theory. Even at this stage, however, the methodological contrast is becoming apparent. In neoclassical theory a sharp distinction between factors of production and final products is essential. When this is not possible in terms of *physical* characteristics (recall the seed which is an input and an output in the five-factor, two-commodity model) the distinction is introduced by a definition in terms of temporal and/or spatial characteristics. Wheat seed as an input occurs at one time and place; wheat seed as an output occurs at another time and place. In the analysis all inputs can therefore be treated *as if* they were given "primary" (nonproduced) factors of production. This aspect of the theory has important implications for the way in which the distribution of the total product is explained, as we show in the next chapter. It also presents a sharp contrast with the structure of classical theory.

Opportunity Cost—A Fundamental Principle

The quantity relations of a neoclassical allocation model give expression to a fundamental principle of the theory: the concept of *opportunity cost*. It is a principle which arises naturally in a model where inputs of factors and technology are parameters. Thus, given a feasible set of outputs (or production possibilities set) one may ask how much of one commodity must be given up, through a *reallocation* of resources, to obtain more of a second commodity? In other words, what is the opportunity cost of the second commodity in terms of the first?

In the two-factor, two-commodity model, opportunity cost at a point such as y_0 in Figure 8-3, where neither resource is fully utilized, is *zero* for both commodities since, as long as both labor and land are underutilized, the output of rice (wheat) can be increased without decreasing the output of wheat (rice). On the other hand, at a *limit point* of the feasible set at least one of the factors of production is fully utilized so that, even though there may be an excess supply of the other factor, the composition of output cannot be shifted in the direction of more rice (wheat) without giving up a certain amount of wheat (rice). Opportunity cost at such points is therefore positive.

The graph of the feasible set of outputs in Figure 8-3 illustrates the concept of opportunity cost. First of all, there are points such as y_2 and y_4 where both commodities are produced but just one constraint is binding. Opportunity cost is measured there by the ratio of per-unit factor requirements of the fully utilized factor, i.e., by the absolute value of the slope (or the reciprocal of the slope) of the relevant constraint. Along the boundary of the land constraint in our example opportunity cost is $a_{TR}/a_{TW} = 3/4$ unit of wheat per unit of rice, or $a_{TW}/a_{TR} = 4/3$ units of rice per unit of wheat; while, along the boundary of the labor constraint, it is $a_{LR}/a_{LW} = 3$ units of wheat per unit of rice, or $a_{LW}/a_{LR} = 1/3$ unit of rice per unit of wheat. In each case a movement along a binding constraint *toward* the point of full employment of both factors (a movement toward y_3) requires an allocation of the less than fully utilized factor to the expanding sector which *exceeds* the amount released from the contracting sector. This creates no problem, however, since the non-binding constraint remains "slack" up to the point where both resources are fully utilized. Thus, in our example, a shift in the composition of output from $(Y_R, Y_W) = (4, 21)$ to $(Y_R, Y_W) = (12, 15)$ releases 12 units of labor and 24 units of land from the wheat sector but requires 48 units of labor and 24 units of land to be allocated to the rice sector. The extra 36 units of labor are drawn from the previously unemployed labor since only 66 units of the given supply, $L = 120$, were required at the initial point, $(Y_R, Y_W) = (4, 21)$. By the same reasoning a shift in the composition of output from $(Y_R, Y_W) = (19, 3)$ to $(Y_R, Y_W) = (17, 9)$ maintains full employment of labor while bringing into cultivation 18 units of previously unused land.

It is now a simple matter to analyze the remaining points in Figure 8-3. At y_1 and y_5 only one resource constraint is binding,* and only one commodity is produced. At y_1 it is still possible to measure the opportunity cost of rice in terms of what by the ratio a_{TR}/a_{TW} since only land is fully utilized. The cost of additional wheat, on the other hand, is no longer the reciprocal slope, a_{TW}/a_{TR}, since rice production is already zero and cannot be reduced further. The opportunity cost of wheat is therefore assigned the value, plus infinity, to indicate that the output of wheat cannot be increased through any further reallocation of resources. At y_5, the situation is reversed: the opportunity cost of wheat is the absolute value of the reciprocal slope of the labor constraint, a_{LW}/a_{LR}, while the cost of additional rice, already a maximum, is assigned the value, plus infinity.

Finally, at y_3 both constraints are binding and both commodities are produced. In the direction of more rice production, however, *only* labor remains fully utilized so that a_{LR}/a_{LW} units of wheat per unit of rice measures the opportunity cost ratio; while, in the direction of additional wheat, only land remains fully utilized so that a_{TW}/a_{TR} units of rice per unit of wheat is the opportunity cost ratio. This double value is characteristic of all such corners. In a two-commodity model with more than two factors, for example, opportunity cost is measured in exactly the same manner as in the case of two factors. Thus, in Figure 8-6, at y the opportunity cost of Y_1 is a_{21}/a_{22}, a positive, fi-

---

* Formally, a second constraint is binding at y_1, namely, $Y_R = 0$; and similarly at y_5, $Y_W = 0$.

nite number; but for Y_2 it is infinite since the output of Y_2 is already a maximum. At y' the opportunity cost ratios are a_{11}/a_{12} and a_{22}/a_{21} for Y_1 and Y_2, respectively; and at y'' they become plus infinity for Y_1, now a maximum, and a_{12}/a_{11} for Y_2. At intermediate points between these corners, on the other hand, the opportunity cost of one commodity *is* the reciprocal value of the opportunity cost of the other.*

In our two-factor, two-commodity model it is assumed that the ratio of labor to land in the rice sector exceeds the corresponding ratio in the wheat sector: $a_{LR}/a_{TR} > a_{LW}/a_{TW}$. This means that a movement in the direction of more rice production is a shift toward the relatively labor-intensive product. Now, if there exist unemployed laborers (at feasible points such as y_2 along the land constraint), it is always possible (in moving toward y_3) to add labor to the factors released from the wheat sector and so make the overall mix of factors appropriate to the production of rice. In that event, *all* the land released from the relatively *land* intensive-sector (wheat) can be put into cultivation in the relatively *labor* intensive sector (rice). However, as soon as the unemployed units of labor are used up (at y_3), it becomes necessary to give up *more* wheat than before in order to obtain the factors needed to produce a given increment of rice. This increase in opportunity cost occurs because all the labor required to produce the additional rice must now come from the land-intensive sector. As a result, some of the land released from that sector is left uncultivated since there is no other way to alter the ratio of released inputs to make it appropriate to the rice-sector technology. (If factor proportions, i.e., the ratios, a_{Lj}/a_{Tj}, $j = R, W$, were *variable* the situation would be less rigid. See chapter 14 for details.)

Increasing opportunity cost, an important aspect of neoclassical allocation models, arises in the two-sector model owing to the relative positions of the resource constraints, as determined by the supply parameters: L, T, and A. In general, whenever linear constraints intersect at a point in the strictly positive quadrant, opportunity cost jumps discretely at that point: in our example, from $a_{TR}/a_{TW} = 3/4$ to $a_{LR}/a_{LW} = 3$ units of wheat per unit of rice at (Y_R,

---

* With more than two *commodities* the measure of opportunity cost is a little more complicated since the boundary of feasible outputs along any resource constraint is no longer characterized by a single slope (and its reciprocal). Thus, in Figure 8-5, there are three slopes (and their reciprocals) determined by the lines of intersection of the boundary of each resource constraint with the coordinate planes: a_{11}/a_{12}, $a_{11}a_{13}$, and a_{12}/a_{13}, $i = 1,2$, although, in each case, it is evident that only *two* of these ratios are independent. At a feasible point where *only* factor i is fully utilized, the opportunity cost of commodity j in terms of commodity k is a_{ij}/a_{ik}, $i = 1,2$, $j,k = 1,2,3$, $j \neq k$. The same ratios apply at limit points where two resource constraints are binding except that the relevant factor, i, is the one whose constraint is binding in the direction of the coordinate axis along which commodity j is measured, i.e., the commodity whose output is increasing.

$Y_W) = (16, 12)$. Notice, however, that a model is easily constructed in which only one constraint is binding at limit points of the feasible set of outputs, as in Figure 8-4, in which case opportunity cost is constant.*

We have now shown how the simplest two-sector model for the neoclassical theory of resource allocation, stripped to its bare essentials, gives clear expression to the concept of opportunity cost. It is a concept defined solely with reference to certain *physical* characteristics of production, namely, the quantities of resource inputs available together with the technical requirements of these inputs in the production of outputs. The theory thus isolates opportunity cost as a principle common to all economic models in which questions arise concerning the allocation of given resources among alternative uses. In the next chapter we link this notion of physical cost to prices for factor services and for final commodities.

Appendix to Chapter 8

A NECESSARY CONDITION FOR THE FULL EMPLOYMENT OF RESOURCES, AN ILLUSTRATION OF CRAMER'S RULE

In a two-input, two-output model the possibility of full employment of both factors of production is assured if and only if the resource constraints, written as equations, have a solution, (Y_R, Y_W), in the nonnegative quadrant. It is convenient to have a standard method of solution of a pair of linear equations in two variables which we now illustrate as a special case of Cramer's Rule. For this purpose, (1) and (2) are written as equations in matrix form:

$$\begin{bmatrix} L \\ T \end{bmatrix} = \begin{bmatrix} a_{LR} & a_{LW} \\ a_{TR} & a_{TW} \end{bmatrix} \begin{bmatrix} Y_R \\ Y_W \end{bmatrix} \tag{A1}$$

This notation indicates that the vector on the left-hand side is equal, item-by-item, to the vector on the right-hand side formed by postmultiplying the matrix $\mathbf{A}$ by the column vector $\{Y_R, Y_W\}$.†

Cramer's Rule states that the variables Y_R and Y_W are found by forming ratios of certain determinants involving L, T, and the elements of $\mathbf{A}$:

*Constant opportunity cost has relevance for our development of the contrast between classical and neoclassical theories of general equilibrium since, *on a neoclassical interpretation,* classical models of the type we consider in subsequent chapters exhibit *constant* opportunity cost. Whether or not this interpretation is valid (and, strictly speaking, it should not be admitted since inputs are *not* parametric in classical models) the important point is that prices do not bear the relationship to opportunity cost, however defined, in a classical model that they characteristically do in a neoclassical model. Compare chapters 9 and 12.

† See the note on p. 196 for a description of postmultiplication.

$$Y_R = \frac{\begin{vmatrix} L & a_{LW} \\ T & a_{TW} \\ \hline a_{LR} & a_{LW} \\ a_{TR} & a_{TW} \end{vmatrix}}{}\qquad Y_W = \frac{\begin{vmatrix} a_{LR} & L \\ a_{LR} & T \\ \hline a_{LR} & a_{LW} \\ a_{TR} & a_{TW} \end{vmatrix}}{} \qquad (A2)$$

Note that in the matrix in each numerator the column of coefficients that is replaced by the vector of factor supplies corresponds to the variable being solved for. A determinant is simply an operation performed on a matrix which, in the 2×2 case, entails subtracting from the product of the diagonal elements the product of the off-diagonal elements. Thus (A2) becomes:

$$Y_R = \frac{a_{TW}L - a_{LW}T}{a_{LR}a_{TW} - a_{LW}a_{TR}} \qquad Y_W = \frac{a_{LR}T - a_{TR}L}{a_{LR}a_{TW} - a_{LW}a_{TR}} \qquad (A3)$$

Cramer's Rule can be verified by solving for either Y_R or Y_W in (1), written as an equation and substituting this into (2), also written as an equation. But the rule is simpler and less likely to result in error: Write the equations as (A1); place the determinant of the coefficient matrix in the denominator of each ratio in (A2); and place the determinant of the coefficient matrix with the column corresponding to the variable being solved for containing, instead of coefficients, the list of left-hand side parameters, in the numerator of each ratio in (A2). Then carry out the indicated operations. (This and other equivalent procedures are carefully explained in Jean E. Draper and Jane S. Klingman, *Mathematical Analysis, Business and Economic Applications,* Harper and Row, New York, 1972, pp. 590–1.)

Returning to the problem of ensuring the existence of a point of full employment of both factors in our model, since $a_{LR}/a_{TR} > a_{LW}/a_{TW}$, by assumption, it follows that $a_{LR}a_{TR} - a_{LW}a_{TR} > 0$ in (A3). Hence, $Y_R \geq 0$ if and only if $L/T \geq a_{LW}/a_{TW}$; and $Y_W \geq 0$ if and only if $L/T \geq a_{LR}/a_{TR}$. Both outputs are nonnegative if and only if $a_{LR}/a_{TR} \geq L/T \geq a_{LW}/a_{TW}$, condition (6) in the text. (If the relative factor ratios are reversed, with wheat the labor-intensive product then of course, these last inequalities are also reversed. On the other hand, in the special case of equal factor ratios, the ratio of factor supplies must also have this value in order for feasible nonnegative outputs to fully utilize both factors of production, but then *all* limits points of the feasible set are full-utilization points since the constraints are *congruent.*)

Notes

1. Sir John Hicks, "Linear Theory," in *Surveys of Economic Theory,* Vol. III, *Resource Allocation,* St. Martin's, New York, 1967, p. 111. The quotation is from Lord Robbins, *On the Nature and Significance of Economic Science,* Macmillan, London, 1932, p. 15.
2. Hicks, "Linear Theory," p. 81.
3. On this interpretation of resource constraints, see *ibid.,* p. 111.
4. See, for example, Frank Hahn, *The Share of Wages in the National Income: An Enquiry into the Theory of Distribution,* Wiedenfeld and Nicolson, London, 1972, p. 2.
5. The works referred to in our text are cited by Kenneth J. Arrow and Frank Hahn, *General Competitive Analysis,* Holden-Day, San Francisco, 1971, pp. 8–11. In particular, see Abraham Wald, "Über einige gleichungssysteme der mathematischen Oekonomie," *Zeitschrift für Nationalökonomie,* Vol. 7 (1936), pp. 637–70; trans. "On some systems of equations of mathematical economics," *Econometrica,* Vol. 19 (1951), pp. 368–403; and John von Neumann and Oskar Morgenstern, *Theory of Games and Economic Behavior,* Princeton University Press, 1944, 1947.
6. Gerard Debreu, *Theory of Value, An Axiomatic Analysis of Economic Equilibrium,* Wiley, New York, 1959, pp. 29–30. Debreu's italics.
7. *Ibid.,* pp. 30–1. Debreu's italics.
8. *Ibid.,* p. 32. Debreu's italics.

9

The Neoclassical Theory of Resource Allocation: Dual Price Relations

> . . . a sound distribution theory is hardly more than a corollary or footnote to an exposition of the mechanism by which resources are apportioned among different uses. . . .
>
> FRANK H. KNIGHT[1]

There is a fundamental duality between quantities and prices in models of general equilibrium. In neoclassical theory this duality finds expression in terms of two sets of inequalities. Given the technology of production, resource constraints, as we have seen, link *quantities* of inputs and outputs. In this chapter, a set of price constraints are shown to establish a dual link between relative prices of inputs and outputs, given the same technology. Our purpose is to interpret this duality by showing that feasible prices (prices that satisfy the constraints) are associated with efficient allocations of resources.

In neoclassical theory, a particular composition of output and corresponding allocation of resources is efficient if it is feasible and at least one resource constraint is binding, i.e., satisfied as an equation. Any such point is a possible candidate for the solution to the problem of allocating given resources among alternative sectors of production. Clearly, *in*feasible points cannot be solutions, and, on the other hand, if no constraint is binding so that no factor is fully utilized, the allocation problem as such does not arise—more of all commodities can be produced with the given technology and the given supply of factors. It is for this reason that, in analyzing efficient allocation, interior points of the feasible set of outputs must be ignored.

Putting the matter another way, *efficient* allocations are those allocations for which opportunity cost and the related concept of relative factor scarcity are defined. Since commodity prices and factor prices are intimately connected with opportunity cost and factor scarcity, we may go a step further and say that *efficient allocations are those allocations that can support a system of equilibrium factor and commodity prices.*

Prices as Rates of Exchange

The relevance of prices, insofar as neoclassical allocation theory is concerned, lies in their determining the exchange value of one commodity or factor service in terms of another. For this reason, only *ratios* of prices, or *relative* values, enter into the analysis. Thus, if the nominal or money price of rice in the two-sector model is $P_R = \$6$ per unit, and the nominal or money price of wheat is $P_W = \$4$ per unit, it follows that to obtain 1 unit of rice one must give up 1.5 units of wheat, a rate of exchange that is measured by the relative price, $p = P_R/P_W = \$6/\$4 = 1.5$ units of wheat per unit of rice, a ratio of quantities. (The reciprocal ratio, $1/p = P_W/P_R = \$4/\$6 = 2/3$ unit of rice per unit of wheat, measures the relative price of *wheat* in terms of *rice*.) Since the same result obtains at nominal prices, $P_R = \$150$ and $P_W = \$100$, or $P_R = 75\cent$ and $P_W = 50\cent$, or, for that matter, *any* pair of nominal prices such that $P_R/P_W = 1.5$, it follows that there is an arbitrary element of scale in such prices that does not affect rates of exchange between commodities, or between factors, or between factors and commodities. It is removed from the analysis by always defining prices in relative terms. We shall therefore refer only to p and its reciprocal, $1/p$, when speaking of commodity prices. In the same way, the purchasing power of the nominal wage for labor services W_L and the nominal rental for land services W_T will always be expressed in terms of either wheat or rice. In particular, $w_L = W_L/P_W$ and $w_T = W_T/P_W$ measure the purchasing power of the wage rate and the rental rate in terms of wheat, while $w_L/p = W_L/P_R$ and $w_T/p = W_T/P_R$ measure it in terms or rice.

Since relative prices are ratios of quantities, any such ratio can be represented graphically by the slope of a straight line in a coordinate space in which the quantities are measured along the axes. Two such lines with slopes measuring different values of p are drawn through an arbitrary point, $(Y_R, Y_W) = (3, 4)$ in the relevant commodity space in Figure 9-1. Each line has a negative slope, indicating that to obtain more of one commodity requires giving up some amount of the other.* In one case the relative price of rice is 2 units of wheat per unit of rice, or 1/2 unit of rice per unit of wheat. The *value* of the given point can then be measured in terms of either commodity. As a quantity of rice, it is the given amount of rice, 3 units, plus the rice value of

---

* This assumes that both prices are positive. If one price were zero the "price line" would have either a zero slope (when the price of rice is zero), or an infinite slope (when the price of wheat is zero). Negative prices are not defined in our model so that the "price line" never has a positive slope; nor is the situation defined where both prices are zero.

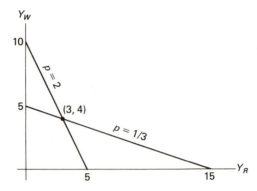

Figure 9-1. Price lines through a given output.

the given amount of wheat, which is 4 units times 1/2 unit of rice per unit of wheat, for a total value of $3 + 2 = 5$ units of rice. This is given by the intercept of the "price line" with the rice axis. The wheat value of (3, 4), on the other hand, is 4 units of wheat plus 6 "wheat units worth of rice," given $1/p = 2$, for a total of 10 units of wheat, the intercept of the price line with the wheat axis.

In the second case the slope of the price line indicates $p = 1/3$ or $1/p = 3$ so that the value of (3, 4) is either 15 units of rice or 5 units of wheat. Clearly, the same physical output can have a range of different values depending on the relative price ratio, values which are always measured in terms of each commodity by the intercepts of the price line drawn through the given point. In general, the "flatter" the price line with respect to a given axis, the lower the exchange value of the commodity measured along that axis, and the higher the value of any given output in terms of that commodity.

In Figure 9-2 it is evident that for a *given* price ratio, any combination of

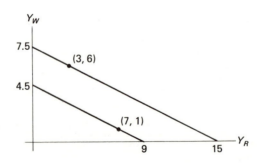

Figure 9-2. Different values holding relative price constant.

rice and wheat that lies along a price line *further* from the origin (along any ray) has a higher value in terms of either commodity than that of any combination of rice and wheat that lies along a price line *closer* to the origin. In the diagram, (3, 6) is worth more than (7, 1) when $p = 1/2$ despite the apparent ambiguity that arises when one bundle contains more rice and the other more wheat.* It follows that, for a given price ratio, a feasible output with a maximum value can always be found by placing a price line with the correct slope in a position that is as far away from the origin as possible while still containing at least one point that belongs to the feasible set.

Prices, Opportunity Cost, and the Supply Correspondence

With the aid of a price line we construct the relationship between commodity prices and outputs that must be satisfied to obtain a maximum value of production V where:

$$V = p Y_R + Y_W \tag{1}$$

In this equation of the price line, P_R and P_W are assigned particular values, thereby fixing p. Value maximizing outputs (Y_R, Y_W) are determined, subject to the resource constraints, by maximizing V or V/p, the intercepts of equation (1) with the wheat and rice axes in the space of feasible outputs. The slope of the price line with respect to the rice axis is $-p$ as can be seen from (1) rewritten as:

$$Y_W = -p Y_R + V \tag{1}'$$

In Figure 9-3 price lines are drawn for three cases: $p < a_{TR}/a_{TW}$, $p = a_{TR}/a_{TW}$, and $a_{TR}/a_{TW} < p < a_{LR}/a_{LW}$, (The other two cases, $p = a_{LR}/a_{LW}$, and $p > a_{LR}/a_{LW}$ may be illustrated in a similar way.) At the corner, y_1, where only wheat output is positive, the point $(Y_R, Y_W) = (0, 24)$ is value maximizing for any p less than the opportunity cost of rice measured by the slope of the land constraint. This is shown by the fact that the relevant price line, when drawn through y_1, lies as far from the origin as possible while still containing at least one feasible point. Hence V is a maximum. At any other efficient point it will be found that the additional wheat obtainable by shifting factor services into the wheat sector has a value in terms of rice that exceeds the output of rice foregone. In other words, at all points where rice output is positive, the relative price of wheat exceeds its opportunity

---

* For a relative price, p, less than, equal to, or greater than 1.25, the point, (3,6), has a valuation that is, respectively, greater than, equal to, or less than the valuation of (7,1).

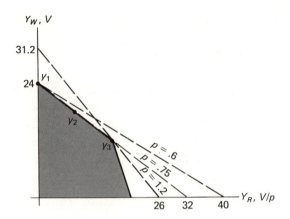

Figure 9-3. Maximum value outputs for different price ratios are measured in terms of each commodity by the intercepts V and V/p of the relevant price line with the coordinate axes.

cost.* (By the same reasoning, y_5 is value maximizing when $p > a_{LR}/a_{LW}$.)

Where relative price is equal to the opportunity cost ratio along a linear segment of limit points of the feasible set, we have a situation in which any such point is value maximizing since the price ratio does not exceed the opportunity cost ratio for either commodity. Given $p = a_{TR}/a_{TW}$ in Figure 9-3, any feasible point where the land constraint is binding (including y_1 and y_3) is value maximizing since there is no other (parallel) price line that contains a feasible output with a higher value. (The analysis for $p = a_{LR}/a_{LW}$ is similar.)

Finally, at the full employment corner, y_3, where both outputs are positive and both factors fully utilized, the corresponding outputs maximize V for any price ratio in the interval: $a_{TR}/a_{TW} < p < a_{LR}/a_{LW}$. The argument, once more, proceeds by contradiction. If the composition of output were given by a point where only *land* is fully utilized, production of rice could be increased by giving up $a_{TR}/a_{TW} = 3/4$ unit of wheat for each unit of rice obtained through a reallocation of resources. But, by assumption, the value of a unit of wheat, p, exceeds a_{TR}/a_{TW} so that total value would thereby be increased. On the

---

* Since the opportunity cost of wheat is measured by the reciprocal, absolute slope of the resource constraint that is binding, it follows that 1 unit of wheat can be obtained in place of either $a_{LW}/a_{LR} = 1/3$ units of rice (if only labor is fully utilized), or $a_{TW}/a_{TR} = 4/3$ units of rice (if land is fully utilized, and wheat production less than its maximum). But, by assumption, one unit of what is worth *more* than the larger of these numbers, since $1/p > a_{TW}/a_{TR} = 4/3$. Thus, value maximization requires that only wheat output be positive.

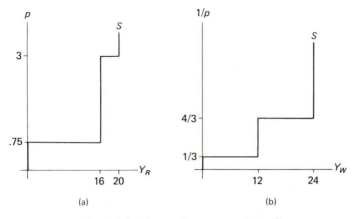

Figure 9-4. The supply correspondence S.
(a) Rice   (b) Wheat

other hand, if only *labor* were fully utilized, production of wheat could be increased by giving up $a_{LW}/a_{LR} = 1/3$ unit of rice for each additional unit of wheat. But, since the value of a unit of wheat $1/p$ is assumed to be greater than a_{LW}/a_{LR}, it follows that total value would again be increased. Thus, only the point y_3, where both factors are fully utilized, is value maximizing over the range of prices, $a_{TR}/a_{TW} < p < a_{LR}/a_{LW}$.

Summing up, we have established a relationship between commodity prices and efficient points of the feasible set of outputs by showing that for each ratio p there is a point or sets of points, $y = (Y_R, Y_W)$, such that at least one resource constraint is binding and for which the *value* of production V is a maximum. A necessary and sufficient condition for the existence of such a maximum can be stated in a manner which is independent of the number of inputs and outputs, namely, that the relative price of one commodity in terms of a second cannot exceed the opportunity cost of the first in terms of the second. This defines a supply "correspondence" * S illustrated for the two-sector model in Figure 9-4 (where the same data on resources and technology are used as in the construction of Figure 9-3). The horizontal segments of each graph (there are two since the model has two commodities) correspond to the linear segments of efficient points of the feasible set of outputs where the condition that relative price does not exceed opportunity cost is satisfied for a

---

* The graph in Figure 9-4 is a "correspondence" rather than a "function" since it is not single-valued: certain prices correspond to more than one output, and vice versa.

whole range of outputs. The vertical segments, on the other hand, correspond to the efficient corners y_1, y_3, and y_5 where the value maximizing output, for which price does not exceed opportunity cost, is unique.

Prices, Factor Costs, and Duality

By linking opportunity cost to an explicit statement of factor cost, a relationship is established between the composition of output and the relative value of factor services. This is a remarkable and distinguishing feature of models of the allocation of given resources which provides the analytical foundation for the neoclassical theory of income distribution. It is central to our development and juxtaposition of classical and neoclassical models of general equilibrium.

The connection between the quantities of goods produced and the distribution of those goods follows from the relationship between commodity prices and factor prices. On the one hand, the supply correspondence shows how commodity prices are linked to outputs, while, on the other hand, it is evident that factor prices determine the purchasing power of individual factor endowments,* which the theory takes as parametric. Our purpose, then, is to establish the relationship between commodity prices and factor prices in order to obtain a relationship between the allocation of resources and the ability of resource owners to purchase the resulting outputs. Essentially what is involved is an extension of the basic idea that lies behind the supply correspondence, namely, the requirement that relative price does not exceed opportunity cost. This is done by re-expressing opportunity cost in terms of factor cost after introducing factor prices into the analysis.

The core of the argument that follows consists in ruling out those sets of factor prices, given the commodity price ratio, which do not satisfy a condition of equilibrium, specified as the *absence of excess demand for factor services*. In this regard, producing agents, as the demanders of factor services, are given the function of maximizing net receipts from which it follows that equilibrium prices do not allow a situation in which the price of a commodity exceeds its unit factor cost.† If there were such an excess, it would be possible to increase net receipts simply by allocating additional factor services to the relevant sector of the economy, and this would entail an unsatisfied *excess*

---

* Chapter 10 contains an analysis of a consumer's *budget set*, defined by the different combinations of goods that can be purchased, given an endowment of factor services and a set of prices.
† More correctly, price cannot exceed marginal cost, but, in our linear model, marginal and average, or per-unit, cost are equal.

has as its purpose an explanation of price that is independent of social structure and, in particular, of capitalist institutions.

Relative Factor Scarcity and the Composition of Output

We return now to our main argument, concluding with a discussion of the concept of *relative factor scarcity*. Considered as the dual to opportunity cost, factor scarcity serves as the basis for an interpretation of factor price. For simplicity, the analysis is carried out only for the two-factor two-commodity model, although the same argument applies, in all important respects, to the general m-factor n-commodity model.

Perhaps the most surprising aspect of the equilibrium condition that price cannot exceed unit factor cost is the result that whenever the relative price of rice is less than or equal to the opportunity cost ratio defined by the land constraint ($p \leq a_{TR}/a_{TW}$) the value of labor services is zero; and whenever the relative price of wheat is less than or equal to the opportunity cost ratio defined by the labor constraint ($1/p \leq a_{LW}/a_{LR}$) the value of land services is zero. This presents something of a puzzle since *both* inputs are technically required in each process of production—output would be zero if the services of either factor input were withdrawn—and yet one of these factor services can have a zero value. The paradox is explained by the theory which attributes value to an input only insofar as its services would *add* to the value of output *at the margin*. This means that a factor service has value if and only if *an extra unit of it would allow the value of output to be increased,* at equilibrium prices. If so, then the factor is said to be *scarce* in relation to these prices and to the corresponding allocation of resources.

The concept of relative factor scarcity is illustrated in Figure 9-12 for the case in which $p \geq a_{LR}/a_{LW}$. The dotted lines show the effect on the feasible set of outputs of an increase in the supply of land services, from $T = 96$ to $T = 114$, holding the supply of labor services constant at $L = 120$. (Technology is the same as before.) Additional combinations of rice and wheat are now feasible which were *in*feasible before, but none is worth more than the previously value maximizing output(s). This is certainly true when $p > a_{LR}/a_{LW}$. Thus y_5 has a larger value, given the indicated price line, than any of the newly feasible outputs. It is also true when $p = a_{LR}/a_{LW}$, since all the additional feasible outputs have a value *equal to or less than* that of the initial value maximizing output (which may have been y_3 or y_5 or any intermediate point such as y_4). For this reason land services have no scarcity

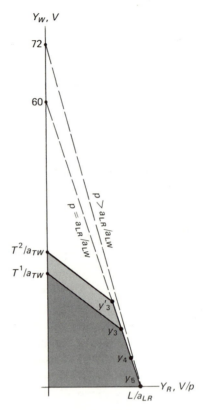

Figure 9-12. Relative scarcity of land services is zero when $p \geq a_{LR}/a_{LW}$, given $(L,$ $T^1) = (120, 96)$, $(L, T^2) = (120, 114)$, $(a_{LR}, a_{TR}) = (6, 3)$, $(a_{LW}, a_{TW}) = (2, 4)$. The coordinates (Y_R, Y_W) of the indicated points are $y'_3 = (14, 18)$; $y_3 = (16, 12)$; $y_4 = (18, 6)$; $y_5 = (20, 0)$.

value *at the margin* when $p \geq a_{LR}/a_{LW}$, since an increase in the supply of land services does not make possible any increase in the value of production.

This result is important because in our analysis of the price constraints, it is exactly over the range of prices, $p \geq a_{LR}/a_{LW}$, that the rental rate for land services w_T is zero. The rental rate therefore *measures* the relative scarcity of land services. A symmetrical case occurs when $p \leq a_{TR}/a_{TW}$. In that event, extra units of labor services do not make possible any increase in the value of output (as can be shown in diagrams similar to those in Figure 9-12), and, again, in the analysis of the price constraints, this is just the range of prices,

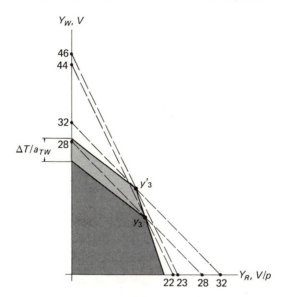

Figure 9-13. Relative scarcity of land services varies with the commodity price ratio in the interval $a_{TR}/a_{TW} \leq p \leq a_{LR}/a_{LW}$, given the data on factor supplies and technology in Figure 9-12.

$p \leq a_{TR}/a_{TW}$, for which the wage rate that satisfies these constraints is zero.*

The case in which both factor services are scarce arises when the commodity price ratio falls in the interval $a_{TR}/a_{TW} < p < a_{LR}/a_{LW}$, given an intersection of the resource constraints in the positive quadrant (i.e., given $a_{LW}/a_{TW} < L/T < a_{LR}/a_{TR}$). In Figure 9-13 two situations are considered where, again, the supply of land services has increased by a given amount (the same as in Figure 9-12). In one case the relative price ratio p is only a little less than the opportunity cost of rice along the labor constraint a_{LR}/a_{LW}, with the result that the increase in the value of output associated with an increase in the supply of land services is relatively small (2 units of Y_W or 1 unit of Y_R). In the second case, the price ratio p is only a little greater than the opportunity cost of rice along the land constraint, a_{TR}/a_{TW}, and the increase in the value of production is greater (4 units of Y_W or 4 units of Y_R).

---

* It should be noted in each of these cases that a nonbinding constraint is a sufficient but not a necessary condition for a zero factor price. Thus, the increment to the value of output made possible by an increment in the supply of land services is zero given a composition of output at y_3 in Figure 12(b) even though land *is* fully utilized. All that is necessary is that $p = a_{LR}/a_{LW}$, in which case $w_T = 0$. Similarly, the scarcity value and wage of labor services is zero when $p = a_{TR}/a_{TW}$, even though output *may* be at y_3 where labor is fully employed.

Thus, given technology and initial factor supplies, the value *at the margin* of an additional quantity of a particular factor depends on commodity prices.

It is essential to the interpretation of price that the measure of relative scarcity, or marginal value, in Figure 9-13 be exactly equal to the relevant factor price. To show this requires a formal definition of relative factor scarcity, written below as a ratio of the difference in the value of goods produced to the difference in the supply of the given factor service that makes possible this increase in value, holding prices and the supply of the other input(s) constant. Using Δ to denote difference, this ratio or *marginal product* is written:

$$\frac{\Delta V}{\Delta T} = \frac{p\Delta Y_R + \Delta Y_W}{\Delta T} \tag{31}$$

given $\Delta T > 0$, $\Delta L = 0$, and a constant p. In Figure 9-13 ratio (31) is measured graphically by the shift in the vertical intercept of the price line divided by ΔT, where ΔT is the shift in the vertical intercept of the land constraint multiplied by a_{TW}.* To show that (31) measures the rental rate for land services, simply write down the equation of Walras's Law, "value of factor services equals value of goods produced" both before and after the change in the supply of land services, and then subtract one equation from the other. Thus:

$$\begin{aligned} w_L L^2 + w_T T^2 &= p Y_R^2 + Y_W^2 \\ \text{minus: } w_L L^1 + w_T T^1 &= p Y_R^1 + Y_W^1 \\ \hline \text{equals: } \qquad w_T \Delta T &= p \Delta Y_R + \Delta Y_W \end{aligned} \tag{32}$$

where $\Delta T = T^2 - T^1 > 0$, $\Delta Y_R = Y_R^2 - Y_R^1$, $\Delta Y_W = Y_W^2 - Y_W^1$, and $\Delta L = L^2 - L^1 = 0$. It follows from (31) and (32) that:

$$\Delta V / \Delta T = w_T, \quad \text{given} \quad \Delta L = 0 \tag{33}$$

Thus, the rental rate for land services is equal to the relative scarcity or marginal product of land services. An exactly similar analysis holds for labor so that we may write:

$$\Delta V / \Delta L = w_L, \quad \text{given} \quad \Delta T = 0 \tag{34}$$

It should be noted that (33) and (34) hold only for "small" changes in T and L, respectively, where "small" means that the set of prices (p, w_L, w_T) for

---

*The vertical intercept of the land constraint is T/a_{TW}. Therefore, the difference in vertical intercepts for two values of T is $\Delta T/a_{TW}$. Multiplying this difference by a_{TW} yields ΔT.

which value is a maximum and dual cost a minimum are not altered by the change in factor supply.*

The above argument, developed within the context of an extremely simple model, gives expression to a general characteristic of neoclassical allocation theory. It shows that the relative scarcity of given resources, and the relation of scarcity to factor prices, is *implicit* the moment one defines the production problem in terms of maximizing value over the feasible set of outputs, i.e., the moment one has chosen a measure of the relative value of one commodity in terms of another. Sir John Hicks puts the matter thus:

. . . the price mechanism is something that is inherent. It did not have to be invented, or brought in from outside. It belongs.

This indeed is what was first perceived, after a fashion, by Menger and his followers; but they did not have the power of explaining, in a manner which would compel communication, the truth that they had seen. Now it has all been set down in black and white. It has been made apparent, not only that a price system is inherent in the problem of maximizing production from given resources but also that something like a price system is inherent in any problem of maximization against restraints. The imputation of prices (or "scarcities") to the factors of production is nothing else but a measurement of the *intensities* of the restraints; such intensities are always implicit— the special property of a competitive [price] system is that it brings them out and makes them visible.[18]

Hicks's imputation of prices is illustrated in Figure 9-13 where the intensity with which the given supply of land restricts production is measured by the extent to which the price line can be moved outward when the supply of land is increased. The smaller this outward movement (measured in terms of commodities by the change in the intercepts of the price line), the smaller the intensity of the land constraint. Thus, in Figure 9-12, land is not restraining output at all; whereas, in Figure 9-13, it is a binding constraint, with an intensity measured by the movement of the price line when the supply of land services is parametrically increased. The greater the intensity of the restraint, the greater the rental rate w_T, a relationship that is reflected in the dual price relations of the model. Thus, a relatively high value for wheat in terms of rice is associated with a relatively high rental rate and this is just the situation in which an increase in the supply of land services makes possible a relatively large

---

* If they were not the same it would be unclear as to which prices to use in equations (33) and (34). Note that it is easy to construct an example in which the prices *would* be different. Just imagine that the supply of land has increased to such an extent that only the labor constraint is binding at every efficient point. We would then have a situation in which w_T, for the given p, is positive before the supply of land is increased and zero after.

increase in the value of production. (The price line in Figure 9-13 is relatively flat.)

The equality of factor prices and relative factor scarcity (or the intensity with which given resources restrict production) is a property of neoclassical theory that characterizes *all* its models. It is the advantage of a simple model that the concept can be visualized graphically and given formal expression in a straightforward manner.

The analysis of the price constraints, though symmetrical in many ways to what was said about resource constraints, is inherently more subtle. The reason for this is that the analysis of prices, and the concept of duality, requires an understanding of the notion of equilibrium. We have introduced equilibrium in as natural a way as possible, starting with the supply correspondence. This relationship was shown to follow from the value-maximizing rule for producing agents, namely, that relative price cannot exceed opportunity cost. Taking explicit account of the cost of acquiring factor services led to the conclusion that, in positions of equilibrium, producing agents will receive *zero* net receipts. The theoretical justification for this is that "producing agent" refers simply to the *decision* to maximize net receipts, and, if positive net receipts are obtainable in any sector, then the "agents" will immediately attempt to allocate additional factor services to the relevant sector. An unlimited excess demand for the needed factor services (at the prevailing prices) would then materialize, and this is inconsistent with an equilibrium allocation. Equilibrium is also inconsistent with *negative* receipts—where would the excess of factor payments over the value of goods produced come from? Thus for commodities that *are* produced, price must be just *equal* to unit cost, leaving zero net receipts in all sectors. It follows that part of the solution to the allocation problem is to find out which outputs are positive (a matter not dealt with by Walras in his original formulation), just as it is necessary in the analysis of the resource constraints to find out which factors are fully utilized.

A further aspect of the analysis must also be emphasized, namely, the interdependence of quantity and price constraints when seen as dual aspects of the same problem. In an important respect this has already been established in our discussion of scarcity where it was shown that for each value of the commodity price p, there corresponds a unique pair of factor prices (w_L, w_T), which measure relative factor scarcity. But what *determines* p has not been established; we have simply considered the dual links between quantities and factor prices implicit in different, given values of p. However, since p is a variable and not a parameter, we must turn, in the next chapter, to consider a further set of equilibrium conditions sufficient to fix the commodity price ratio. This will require a specification of demand and thus a consideration of the remaining parameters of the model: preferences and factor ownership. At this stage, however, it is important to note that what we have to say about demand in chapter 10 is not independent of the foregoing analysis. Thus, on the one hand, factor prices will be shown to determine incomes, given factor ownership; while, on the other hand, consumption choices, which depend on incomes, commodity prices, and preferences, must be consistent with production decisions, which also depend on prices. In short, when the model is finally complete, it will be evident that "everything depends on everything else"—a solution to any part entails a solution to the whole. It is in this sense that the neoclassical treatment of demand establishes further links between the quantity and price relations of the theory, thereby completing a fully interdependent system in which all variables are *simultaneously* determined.

Notes

1. Frank H. Knight, *On the History and Method of Economics,* Chicago, 1956, p. 42. The passage quoted is from an article by Knight, "The Ricardian Theory of Production and Distribution," *Canadian Journal of Economics and Political Science,* Vol. I (1935), pp. 171–96.

2. For a more rigorous development, see William J. Baumol, *Economic Theory and Operations Analysis,* 4th ed., Prentice-Hall, Englewood Cliffs, N.J., 1977, pp. 127–33. In his discussion, Baumol refers to the fundamental results of David Gale, Harold W. Kuhn, and Albert W. Tucker. See, for example, their "Linear Programming and the Theory of Games," in Tjalling C. Koopmans, ed., *Activity Analysis of Production and Allocation,* Wiley, New York, 1951, pp. 317–29.

3. This was, of course, the position of Walras. Ironically, even in certain modern versions of post-Walrasian theory, in which net receipts *are* allowed to be positive in equilibrium, the resulting "profits" must somehow be assigned to the *consuming* agents. This is done by means of additional parameters that fix the share that each consumer has in the net receipts of each producing agent (subject to the condition that such shares add up to 100% for each producer). Sometimes the shares are interpreted as dividends from common stock or as the proceeds from a partnership. See, for example, Kenneth J. Arrow and F. H. Hahn, *General Competitive Analysis,* Holden-Day, San Francisco, 1971, p. 77. On this interpretation, however, the question arises as to how the shares are to be assigned. If they reflect differences in the entrepreneurial skill with which enterprises are managed then it would be more in keeping with the theme of the allocation of given resources to identify such special skills as inputs to be allocated, like any other factor service. If the shares are implicit returns to physical assets such as ma-

chinery, then, again, the ownership of such factors should be specified and the rental rate for, say, machine-services should appear as a factor price in the analysis. In short, in an allocation model, all incomes must *ultimately* be imputed to the value of some factor of production—calling any such income "profit" is just a misleading use of language.

4. The term factor price frontier was introduced by Paul Samuelson in "Parable and Realism in Capital Theory: The Surrogate Production Function," *Review of Economic Studies,* Vol. 29 (1962), pp. 193–206. Formally, a factor price frontier is the unit contour of a cost function. For further mathematical analysis, see Samuelson's "Prices of Factors and Goods in General Equilibrium," *Review of Economic Studies,* Vol. 21 (1953–54), pp. 1–20. It may be noted that a factor price frontier is a different concept from a classical wage-profit trade-off, to be discussed in chapter 13, although it is common in the literature to label both as factor price frontiers. To avoid unnecessary confusion we shall follow Sir John Hicks in drawing a sharp distinction between them. See his *Capital and Growth,* Oxford at the Clarendon Press, 1965, p. 140, n. 1.

5. The argument that follows is based on Baumol's analysis referenced above in n. 2.

6. The properties of (30), written as equations, have been the subject of much interest in the theory of international trade. For a recent discussion of the extent to which the two-factor two-commodity model *does* and *does not* exhibit properties of the general system, see R. W. Jones and J. Scheinkman, "The Relevance of the Two-Sector Production Model in Trade Theory," *Journal of Political Economy,* Vol. 85 (October 1977), pp. 909–35.

7. Gerard Debreu, *Theory of Value, An Axiomatic Analysis of Economic Equilibrium,* Wiley, New York, 1959, p. 32. Debreu's italics.

8. Tjalling C. Koopmans, *Three Essays on the State of Economic Science,* McGraw-Hill, New York, 1957, p. 105. Our italics.

9. *Ibid.,* pp. 113–4.

10. *Ibid.,* p. 114.

11. *Ibid.,* p. 115.

12. *Ibid.*

13. Avinash Dixit, "The Accumulation of Capital Theory," *Oxford Economic Papers* (New Series), Vol. 29 (1977), p. 14.

14. See Koopmans, *Three Essays,* pp. 115–21; and F. H. Hahn, *The Share of Wages in the National Income: An Enquiry into the Theory of Distribution,* Wiedenfeld and Nicolson, London, 1972, p. 5.

15. Hahn, *Share of Wages,* p. 4.

16. *Ibid.,* p. 2.

17. Koopmans, *Three Essays,* p. 120.

18. Sir John Hicks, "Linear Theory," in *Surveys in Economics Theory,* Vol. III, *Resource Allocation,* St. Martin's Press, New York, 1967, p. 111. Hicks's italics.

10

A General Equilibrium of Supply and Demand

> Prices and input-output combinations are said to be equilibrium prices and equilibrium input-output combinations if, when they rule, . . . no input or output is in excess demand.
>
> FRANK HAHN [1]

The remaining parameters of a two-factor two-commodity model of neoclassical allocation theory are consumer preferences and factor ownership. They provide the data necessary for specifying the role of demand in the determination of a general equilibrium solution for prices and quantities. This solution has one essential property: there must be no unsatisfied demand on the part of producing and consuming agents for inputs of factor services or for outputs of commodities.

The absence of excess demand defines equilibrium in all neoclassical models. Our first discussion of this concept arose in the analysis of the supply correspondence where the requirement that relative price does not exceed opportunity cost was imposed in order to ensure zero excess demand for factor services. (If price exceeded opportunity cost in any sector, there would be an excess demand for at least one factor.) The price constraints further characterize the absence of excess demand for factors by ruling out the situation in which producing agents receive profits, i.e., by restricting price to being less than or equal to unit factor cost. This analysis did not, however, imply an *equality* between supply and demand. Thus, in our interpretation of duality conditions, (7) and (8) of chapter 9, it was stated that an excess supply of any given factor requires a zero price for its services. The rationale for this is that, prior to solving the allocation problem, it is not known which factor services will be scarce, i.e., which will have positive value (just as it is not known in advance which commodities will in fact be produced). Of course, all resources in a neoclassical allocation model are in fixed supply, but, as our discussion of relative scarcity made clear, this does not imply that an extra or marginal unit of any given factor will necessarily add to the value of production.

245

An equilibrium analysis of the supply and demand for commodities requires a specification of the behavior of resource owners in their role as consumers. Central to the discussion is the concept of the budget set defining alternative consumption bundles available to each resource owner. This set of feasible choices depends on individual factor endowments (parametric to the analysis) and on prices for inputs and outputs; preferences (also parametric) determine the particular choices made. Thus, total demand for each commodity depends on consumers' tastes, prices for factors and goods, and the given distribution of resources among consumers.

A general equilibrium requires that prices for factors and commodities be such that the total demand for each commodity is not greater that its total supply. Supply, however, depends on the condition that relative price ratios do not exceed corresponding opportunity cost ratios. It follows that an equilibrium allocation of resources depends on the simultaneous solution to a whole set of relationships: resource constraints, price constraints, and the conditions of equilibrium in the supply and demand for commodities which are analyzed in this chapter.

Factor Ownership, Prices, and the Budget Set

A budget set is a set of commodity bundles, any one of which may be chosen at given prices by a consumer owning a particular endowment of factors. Let (L^h, T^h) measure the non-negative endowment of labor services and land services of a given resource owner designated by the index h where $h = 1, \ldots, s$. These s resource owners collectively own the total supply of factors.* Then, at given prices, the purchasing power of individual endowments is measured as follows. The ownership of L^h units of labor services commands a quantity of the *numeraire* wheat equal to $w_L L^h$, while the ownership of T^h units of land services has a wheat value of $w_T T^h$. The total purchasing power or "income" associated with (L^h, T^h) is therefore the sum:

$$R^h = w_L L^h + w_T T^h \tag{1}$$

which is easily converted into a rice value R^h/p after dividing factor prices by the relative price p.

Neoclassical theory is usually presented as if the pattern of ownership of factors were completely arbitrary. On this view there is no reason to assume, or to rule out, the case in which one group of resource owners has only labor

*Formally, $L = L^1 + L^2 + \ldots + L^S$; and $T = T^1 + T^2 + \ldots + T^S$.

services to offer in exchange, and another only land services; nor is there any presumption that all resource owners have equal factor endowments. In any case, the theory certainly offers no explanation of how the pattern of resource endowments gets established; it is simply treated as a parameter. It has been noticed, however, that unless some restriction on the allowable patterns of resource ownership is imposed, there is nothing in the theory to guarantee that the value of an arbitrary resource endowment will be positive. Thus, in the two-sector model, if we do not assume that each resource owner has a positive endowment of *both* factors it may well be the case that an endowment (consisting of only one factor) will have a zero value (when the corresponding factor price is zero). This possibility of zero incomes raises certain mathematical problems which are generally overcome by introducing assumptions sufficient to guarantee each consuming agent a positive income.[2] Granting these assumptions, however, leaves open the question as to whether or not a particular resource owner, acting as a consumer, has an income large enough to sustain a minimal standard of living. The theory has no standard apparatus to cover this point—indeed the concept of subsistence is rarely given any specific treatment in neoclassical theory.[3] We shall therefore follow the usual convention of assuming that the pattern of resource endowments is such that the problem of incomes below "subsistence" just does not arise, and this, of course, certainly rules out *zero* incomes.

The value of a given endowment of factors, identified with an arbitrary resource owner h, may be illustrated using prices that satisfy the constraints of chapter 9.* Letting $(L^h, T^h) = (24, 24)$ and using prices that satisfy the pair of factor price frontiers in our example, $(p, w_L, w_T) = (1.2, .1, .2)$, it follows from (1) that the purchasing power of the given endowment in terms of wheat is $R^h = 7.2$ (or $R^h/p = 6$ in terms of rice). This defines a pair of points, $(0, X_W^h) = (0. 7.2)$ and $(X_R^h, 0) = (6, 0)$ indicated along the coordinate axes in Figure 10-1. They are joined with a *budget line* having an absolute slope, $p = 1.2$ units of rice per unit of wheat, such that the coordinates of any point along this line measure positive quantities of the two commodities equal in value to the purchasing power of the given resource endowment. Such a point is $(X_R^h, X_W^h) = (3, 3.6)$ which has a wheat value of 7.2, given $p = 1.2$; and this is exactly the value of $(L^h, T^h) = (24, 24)$, given $(w_L, w_T) = (.1, .2)$.

The triangle, including its boundaries on all sides, that is formed by the

---

* In defining the value of an endowment it is not necessary to use prices that satisfy the price constraints of any particular model. We do so here because we are discussing consumption choices within the context of a general equilibrium model in which a set of price constraints must be satisfied. Throughout the following we continue with the same example where $(L, T) = (120, 96)$; $(a_{LR}, a_{TR}) = (6, 3)$; and $(a_{LW}, a_{TW}) = (2, 4)$.

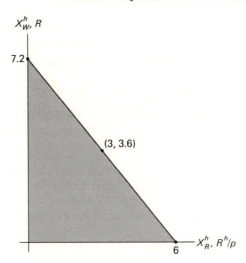

Figure 10-1. Budget line and budget set for consumer h with resource endowment $(L^h, T^h) = (24, 24)$, given $p = 1.2$, $(w_L, w_T) = (.1, .2)$.

budget line and the two coordinate axes in Figure 10-1 is called the *budget set* for consumer-resource owner h. Formally, it is the set of points $x^h = (X_R^h, X_W^h)$, satisfying:

$$R^h = w_L L^h + w_T L^h \geq p X_R^h + X_W^h \tag{2}$$

$$X_R^h \geq 0 \qquad X_W^h \geq 0 \tag{3}$$

Inequality (2) states that the wheat value of the consumer's endowment cannot be less than the amount of wheat purchased, X_W^h, plus the wheat value of the amount of rice purchased, X_R^h, while (3) simply states that these quantities are non-negative.

For any given endowment of factors there will be a different set of feasible consumption choices defined by each set of factor and commodity prices. In Figure 10-2 budget lines are drawn for five sets of prices, each satisfying the price constraints of the model.

Since the budget set for an arbitrary resource owner h includes points that do not satisfy (2) as an equation, the question arises as to the meaning of an interior point of the shaded area in, say, Figure 10-1. The only possible interpretation in the present context is that the resource owner has an *own-demand* for the factor services he might otherwise be selling, and is therefore not purchasing commodities equal in value to his endowment. It would fol-

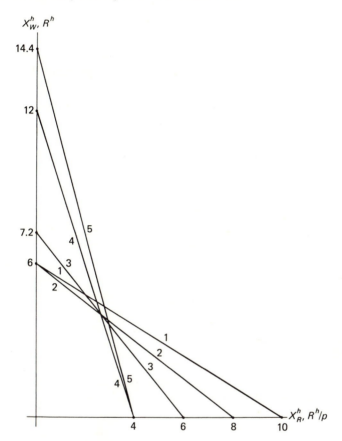

Figure 10-2. Budget lines vary with prices, given $(L^h, T^h) = (24, 24)$. The indicated lines correspond to:

	p	w_L	w_T	R^h	R^h/p
1	0.6	0.0	0.25	6.0	10
2	0.75	0.0	0.25	6.0	8
3	1.2	0.1	0.2	7.2	6
4	3.0	0.5	0.0	12.0	4
5	3.6	0.6	0.0	14.4	4

low immediately, however, that the model is incompletely specified, since own-demands imply an allocation of resources to additional activities; e.g., potential labor time allocated to leisure, or land allocated to parks (for their owners). Thus, even when there are supply functions for factor services (as, for example, when the decision regarding work versus leisure depends on the wage rate), resources are still given parameters once own-demands are recognized and added to the inputs supplied to producing agents. It does not therefore restrict the interpretation of the theory in any way to assume that resource owners consume at limit points of their budget sets. Thus, we will regard every consumer as purchasing commodities with a value *equal* to that of his resource endowment, in which case (2) becomes an equation:

$$w_L L^h + w_T T^h = p X_R^h + X_W^h \qquad h = 1, \ldots, s \qquad (4)$$

Preferences and Consumption Choices

In order to represent consumption choices formally, it is necessary to characterize preferences in some precise manner. Much time has been spent on this question during the last 40 years, particularly in the more mathematically oriented journals, and the set of assumptions strictly necessary concerning consumers' choices has been progressively weakened. It is interesting to note that, despite this, leading authorities on neoclassical general equilibrium theory, such as Arrow and Hahn in their noted work, *General Competitive Analysis,* continue to characterize preferences in such a manner as to "permit a continuous numerical representation"[4]—or what has traditionally been called a utility function. It would appear that these authors felt there was a Quixotic element in the prolonged discussion over the exact minimum assumptions necessary to characterize consumer's choice.

In our discussions of Jevons and Walras in chapters 5 and 6 we were happy to grant these authors their utility functions since we hold that what was important about neoclassical theory was that its central theme concerned the allocation of given resources. It is therefore in the same spirit that we now offer an informal account of the modern theory of consumer's choice, freely incorporating assumptions that provide sufficient structure for establishing a utility function, i.e., a continuous numerical representation of the ranking of alternative commodity bundles. (Exactly how this utility function is derived from the assumptions can be found in Arrow and Hahn.[5])

It is generally assumed in the theory of consumer's choice that individuals are able to rank in order of preference all conceivable bundles of commodities. Such bundles are represented by the coordinates of points in a space in which quantities of the different commodities are measured by real numbers along the coordinate axes. In a two-commodity model there are just two axes, and a given bundle x has two coordinates (X_R, X_W) measuring rice and wheat as in the definition of the budget set. Given arbitrary bundles x_1 and x_2, it is assumed that either x_1 is preferred or indifferent to x_2, or x_2 is preferred or indifferent to x_1. This ordering is further assumed to be transitive which means that of three bundles, x_1, x_2, and x_3, if x_1 is preferred or indifferent to x_2, and x_2 is preferred or indifferent to x_3, then x_1 is preferred or indifferent to x_3.

Next, the preference ordering is assumed to be "continuous in the sense that a strict preference between two [bundles] is not altered if either is altered by sufficiently small amounts. . . ." [6] Thus, if one bundle is preferred to another, then either can be changed slightly without affecting the ranking. The preference relation is also assumed to satisfy a convexity assumption which may be stated as follows. If x_1 is preferred to x_2 then all the points on a straight line joining x_1 and x_2 are preferred to x_2 (except for x_2 which is indifferent to itself); while, on the other hand, if x_1 and x_2 are indifferent, then all points on the straight line joining x_1 and x_2 are preferred *or* indifferent to x_1 and x_2.

Finally, it is assumed that there does *not* exist a "bliss point" which is a bundle of commodities that is preferred or indifferent to all other bundles in the set of points on which the preference ordering is defined. This is a nonsatiation assumption which means that a consumer is never in a position where more of at least one commodity would not count as an improvement.

It may be thought that some or all of the assumptions just listed are highly restrictive in the sense that the rankings of actual consumers hardly ever satisfy all the specified conditions. Of course, this is true and as we have remarked, a great deal of effort has gone into relaxing the assumptions on preferences with a view to minimizing the structure that is needed in determining a solution to the allocation problem. Within the already sparse context of a two-factor two-commodity model, a detailed examination of the different ways in which this structure can be lightened would, however, be quite artificial and irrelevant. We therefore accept the above list of standard assumptions and proceed with the analysis.

Consider any point x_0 in the non-negative quadrant of Figure 10-3. The assumptions on preferences imply that there is a numerical ranking of this point (and all other points in the non-negative quadrant) such that the set of points with the same or higher ranking has certain well defined properties. Thus, the set of points no-worse-than-x_0 has x_0 as one of its limit points, i.e., a point belonging to its boundary such that all other limit points of the shaded area have the same numerical ranking as x_0 in the consumer's utility function. These limit points define an *indifference curve*. Interior points of the shaded area are given higher rankings.

It is easy to show how the assumptions on preferences are satisfied in the

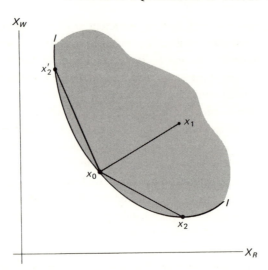

Figure 10-3. An indifference curve through x_0 is the boundary of a set of points no-worse-than-x_0.

diagram. First, all the points along a straight line joining x_0 and x_1, where x_1 is preferred to x_0 (and we know that such a point x_1 exists, given the nonsatiation assumption), are themselves preferred to x_0. Second, all the points along the straight line joining x_0 and x_2, or x_0 and x_2', where x_2 and x_2' are indifferent to x_0, are either preferred to x_0 or indifferent to it. This rules out the situation in which a line joining indifferent points passes outside the shaded area. The set of points no-worse-than-x_0 is therefore convex.

Since the initial point, x_0 in Figure 10-3, was chosen arbitrarily, we can in principle repeat the construction of an indifference curve through any point in the non-negative quadrant of the diagram. The resulting set of curves will be nonintersecting given the transitivity of the preference ordering,* and can therefore be treated as contours of a utility function. Such contours are given successively larger numerical rankings in the direction of preferred points relative to any given point.†

---

* Draw two indifference curves that *do* intersect. Consider a point on one curve strictly preferred to a point on the other; this is always possible by construction. Then, together with the point of intersection, it is easy to show that the preference ordering among the three points is *not* transitive. Therefore indifference curves cannot intersect.

† Since it is the *order* of the numerical ranking that matters, the utility function $U(x)$ that assigns numerical values to the indifference curves can be transformed by any strictly increasing function, a transformation that is order preserving. The new utility function is just as valid a representation of the preference ordering as the original function. This ordinal rather than cardinal significance means that utility functions are unique only up to transformations by strictly increasing functions.

The analysis of consumer's choice is complete once a behavioral rule is specified, namely, that a commodity bundle is chosen if and only if no other bundle in the consumer's budget set is preferred to the chosen bundle. Such a choice is illustrated in Figure 10-4 which combines part of the map of indifference curves derived from a given preference ordering with the budget set defined by a given factor endowment (L^h, T^h) and a given set of prices, (p, w_L, w_T). The choice x_0 satisfies the rule just stated and *maximizes utility* since it belongs to the most highly ranked set of indifferent points containing at least one point that belongs to the budget set.

Utility maximizing consumption choices can be described in a manner that parallels the description of value maximizing outputs, once the concept of the marginal rate of substitution has been introduced. This ratio of changes in the consumption of two commodities is measured in Figure 10-4 by the (absolute) slope of a line joining any pair of indifferent points such as x_0 and x_1. The slope of this line indicates the *rate* at which the consumer is willing to give up one commodity, wheat, to obtain another, rice, over the range of quantities given by the coordinates of the two points. If, for example, the (absolute) slope is ⅔, a sacrifice of wheat in exchange for rice in the ratio 2:3 will leave

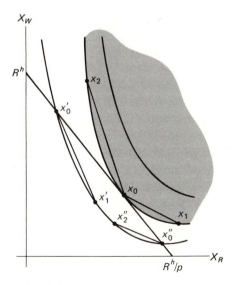

Figure 10-4. Consumption choice x_0 maximizes utility. At points x_0' and x_0'' that do not maximize utility the marginal rate of substitution is greater than relative price for at least one commodity. The absolute slopes of line segments $\overline{x_0 x_1}$ and $\overline{x_0' x_1'}$ with respect to the rice axis measure MRS_{RW}; the absolute slopes of line segments $\overline{x_0 x_2}$ and $\overline{x_0'' x_2''}$ with respect to the wheat axis measure MRS_{WR}.

the consumer just as well off as at the initial point. In considering a shift from x_0 to x_1 the usual abbreviation for the marginal rate of substitution is MRS_{RW}, the order of the subscripts indicating that rice is taking the place of wheat.

The utility maximizing point, x_0 in Figure 10-4, has the property that, relative to any indifferent point x_1 containing more rice and less wheat, MRS_{RW} is not greater than p. (In the diagram the line joining x_0 and x_1 has a smaller absolute slope than that of the budget line so that MRS_{RW} is strictly less than p.) Thus, the rate at which the consumer is willing to given up wheat to obtain rice for any movement away from the utility maximizing point cannot exceed the rate at which it is possible to carry out such an exchange given the price ratio p. This also characterizes x_2, indifferent to x_0, but containing more wheat and less rice. Again, MRS_{WR} (reversing the order of the subscripts) is not greater than the relative price of wheat, $1/p$, so that the rate at which the consumer is willing to give up rice to obtain wheat (relative to x_0) is not greater than the rate at which it is possible to do so, as measured by $1/p$.

We conclude that at any point belonging to the budget set where utility is *not* a maximum, at least one of the following conditions, both of which are necessary for such a maximum, must be violated:

$$MRS_{RW} \leq p \qquad MRS_{WR} \leq 1/p \qquad (5)$$

Thus, a shift from x_0' to x_1' in Figure 10-4 leaves the consumer's level of utility unchanged while at the same time releasing enough purchasing power to allow a further shift to x_0 which is preferred to x_1'. Utility was not a maximum at x_0' and this is just the situation in which $MRS_{RW} > p$ at x_0', violating the first inequality in (5). Similarly, a shift from x_0'' to x_2'' leaves utility unchanged while releasing enough purchasing power to permit a further shift to the preferred point x_0. The fact that x_0'' is not utility maximizing means that (5) is not satisfied since $MRS_{WR} > 1/p$ at x_0''

The condition that the marginal rate of substitution of one commodity in place of another shall not exceed the relative price of the first in terms of the second holds whatever the number of commodities in the consumption bundle. It echoes the condition in production that relative price shall not exceed opportunity cost (to ensure that the value of production is a maximum). Both rules may be combined to yield a pair of double inequalities characterizing equilibrium in production *and* consumption:

$$MRS_{RW} \leq p \leq OPP_{RW}$$
$$MRS_{WR} \leq 1/p \leq OPP_{WR} \qquad (6)$$

where OPP_{ij} is the opportunity cost of commodity i in terms of j, $i,j = R, W$. Note that (6) does not rule out *equality* of marginal rates of substitution and

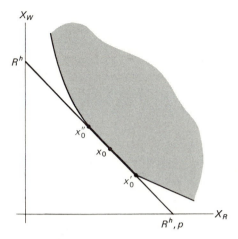

Figure 10-5. Utility maximizing choice may not be unique. There is no point in the budget set preferred to any point on the line segment $\overline{x_0' x_0''}$ so that all such points maximize utility.

relative prices illustrated in Figure 10-5 by an indifference curve containing a flat facet congruent with some range of the relevant budget line (or by an indifference curve that is tangent to the budget line). What the weak inequalities in (6) allow for is the further possibility that the indifference curve has a kink or corner at the utility maximizing point.

Consumption Choices and the Demand Function

Just as the value maximizing rule for producing agents generates a supply correspondence linking prices to efficient outputs, so the utility maximizing rule for consumers yields a demand relationship linking prices to total consumption of each commodity. This relationship is established by showing the effect of a difference in prices on the total demand of consumers. A demand function (or correspondence) is thereby constructed on the basis of *individual* choices.

To measure total demand for rice and wheat at a given set of prices, consumption choices must be added. This is illustrated for two consumers in Figure 10-6 where budget lines are drawn for the pair of factor endowments, $(L^1, T^1) = (24, 24)$ and $(L^2, T^2) = (12, 6)$, given $(p, w_L, w_T) = (1.2, .1, .2)$. Leaving out the indifference curves for simplicity, consumption choices are indicated by the pair of points, $x^1 = (X_R^1, X_W^1) = (4, 2.4)$ and $x^2 = (X_R^2, X_W^2) = (1, 1.2)$. Total demand is found graphically by drawing the parallelogram which has as two of its sides the rays joining x^1 and x^2 to the origin. The corner of

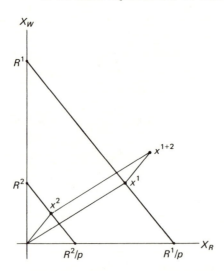

Figure 10-6. Addition of consumption choices for two consumers.

this parelleolgram opposite the origin, $x^{1+2} = (5, 3.6)$, has coordinates $(X_R^1 + X_R^2, X_W^1 + X_W^2)$ measuring the aggregate demand of the two consumers.

The choice of a third consumer, x^3, can be added to x^{1+2} in the manner just described, and so on for all consumers, until a total demand is obtained which has coordinates equal to the sums of the quantities of rice and wheat in all the individual choices. Since there are s resource owners, there are s consumers and so we write total demand as:

$$x = (X_R^1 + X_R^2 + \ldots + X_R^s, \ X_W^1 + X_W^2 + \ldots + X_W^s) = (X_R, X_W) \tag{7}$$

Since prices determine the position and slope of the budget line for each consumer, given the distribution of resource endowments, and since utility maximizing consumption choices are determined by the given set of preferences, it follows that consumption choices may be considered dependent on prices. In other words, factor ownership and "tastes" are parameters so that the only variables that remain to affect individual and total demands are factor and commodity prices which determine the purchasing power of the given endowments. The relationship between prices and consumption choices can be illustrated in a diagram similar to the one in Figure 10-6 constructed on the assumption that the resource endowments and preference orderings of the two consumers are unchanged, but that prices are now $(p, w_L \ w_T) = (.75, 0, .25)$ instead of $(1.2, .1, .2)$. In the new diagram suppose x^1 and x^2 are shifted to $(5.6, 1.8)$ and $(1.2, .6)$, respectively, so that $x^{1+2} = (6.8, 2.4)$ instead of $(5,

3.6) as in Figure 10-6. Both the slope and intercepts of the pair of budget lines are altered by the difference in prices,* while indifference curves are assumed to be unchanged.

With each variations in prices (consistent with the price constraints of the model) there will, in general, be a variation in the utility maximizing consumption choices of individual resource owners, and thus in the total demand for commodities. The resulting relationships between prices and quantities are demand functions, defined not only for individuals, but also for collections of consumers including the aggregate of all consumers. The two cases just considered yield two points on each of a pair of individual demand functions, one for rice and one for wheat.

> Consumer 1's demand for rice: $(X_R^1, p) = (4, 1.2)$ and $(5.6, .75)$
> Consumer 2's demand for rice: $(X_R^2, p) = (1, 1.2)$ and $(1.2, .75)$
>
> Consumer 1's demand for wheat: $(X_W^1, 1/p) = (2.4, 5/6)$ and $(1.8, 4/3)$
> Consumer 2's demand for wheat: $(X_W^2, 1/p) = (1.2, 5/6)$ and $(0.6, 4/3)$

Points along individual demand functions for rice are connected by straight lines in Figure 10-7.† Points on the aggregate demand function for the two consumers are found by adding quantities at each price, a procedure that can be repeated until all individual demands are summed. A similar construction yields the demand function for wheat.

The exact properties of individual and total demand relationships depend on the properties of the consumers' preference orderings from which utility functions are derived. Herein lie many interesting problems that have been given much attention in the literature on the theory of demand. There is, for example, the seemingly paradoxical case of a Giffen good for which a lower price is associated with a smaller quantity demanded, and the closely related problem of distinguishing income and substitution effects of a price change. And, there is the case where, for certain sets of prices, utility maximizing choices are not unique, as in Figure 10-5, turning the demand function into a correspondence such that one price maps into many quantities. (Indifference curves with corners cause one quantity to map into many prices.)

---

*In particular cases, such as $(L^2, T^2) = (12, 6)$, and over particular ranges of prices, such as $p \leq a_{TR}/a_{TW}$ and $p \geq a_{LR}/a_{LW}$, only one intercept varies with prices. In other cases, both intercepts change.

†The coordinates of the other points in Figure 10-7 are: $(X_R^1, p) = (2, 3.6)$, $(2.4, 3)$, $(7, 0.6)$; and $(X_R^2, p) = (1, 3.6)$, $(1, 3)$, $(2.2, 0.6)$. Other points on the demand curves for wheat of the two consumers, not shown in Figure 10-7, are: $(X_W^1, 1/p) = (7.2, 5/18)$, $(4.8, 1/3)$, $(1.8, 5/3)$; and $(X_W^2, 1/p) = (3.6, 5/18)$, $(3, 1/3)$, $(0.18, 5/3)$. The sum of the two demand relationships, in the case of each commodity, is simply the sum of quantities at each value of p, or $1/p$.

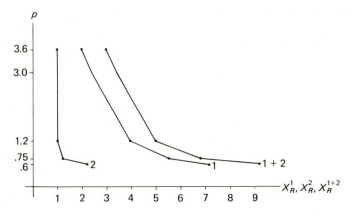

Figure 10-7. Individual and total demands for rice of two consumers, given $(L^1, T^1) = (24, 24)$ and $(L^2, T^2) = (12, 6)$:

p	w_L	w_T	X_R^1	X_R^2	X_R^{1+2}
0.6	0.0	0.25	7.0	2.2	9.2
0.75	0.0	0.25	5.6	1.2	6.8
1.2	0.1	0.2	4.0	1.0	5.0
3.0	0.5	0.0	2.4	1.0	3.4
3.6	0.6	0.0	2.0	1.0	3.0

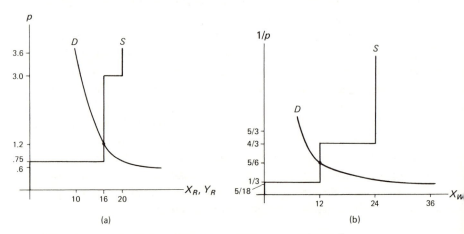

Figure 10-8. Total demand D and the supply correspondence S.

p	X_R	X_W	Y_R	Y_W	excess demand
0.6	26⅔	8	0	24	26⅔ rice
0.75	20	9	0–16	12–24	4–20 rice
1.2	16	12	16	12	zero
3.0	11	27	16–20	0–12	15–27 wheat
3.6	10	36	20	0	36 wʰ

(a) Rice   (b) Wheat

One of the authors of the present work has previously offered an elementary treatment of these matters.[7] In the arguments that concern us here, however, there are sound reasons for not developing any further the full variety of cases covered by modern demand theory since it is our purpose to present only those models which reveal the distinguishing characteristics of classical and neoclassical theories of general equilibrium. The form of the demand function is not one of these characteristics for, as will be shown in subsequent chapters on classical theory, a thoroughly orthodox (neoclassical) treatment of demand can be incorporated into a model of surplus and accumulation (but without all the entailments it has for neoclassical allocation theory). Total demand is therefore reprsented in the usual way by a function whose graph is a downward sloping curve as shown in Figure 10-8.*

A General Equilibrium of Supply and Demand

The formal structure of the neoclassical model is completed by linking production to consumption. We show first that the *value* of production is equal to the *value* of consumption for all prices and quantities that satisfy the resource constraints, price constraints, and duality conditions stated in chapters 8 and 9. This requires proof since the supply correspondence was constructed so that outputs at any given price ratio p define a maximum value given the feasible set of outputs, and it is not immediately evident that the *same* value is defined, at any given price ratio, by the quantities that satisfy the demand function. The argument, however, is straightforward.

Consider the following sum of budget equations for the set of s consumers:

$$w_L L^1 + w_T T^1 = p X_R^1 + X_W^1$$
$$w_L L^2 + w_T T^2 = p X_R^2 + X_W^2$$

$$\begin{matrix} \cdot & \cdot & \cdot & \cdot \\ \cdot & \cdot & \cdot & \cdot \\ \cdot & \cdot & \cdot & \cdot \end{matrix} \qquad (8)$$

$$w_L L^s + w_T T^s = p X_R^s + X_W^s$$

$$\overline{w_L L + w_T T = p X_R + X_W}$$

On the left-hand side of (8) is a sum equal to the total value of the economy's resource endowment, at given factor prices, while on the right-hand side is another sum measuring the value of total consumption, $x = (X_R, X_W)$, given

---

*This need not imply that *individual* demand functions are smooth curves—they may be step functions. We are assuming only that their sum has the conventional smooth shape.

$p.$* Using Walras's Law which states that the value of the resource endowment is equal to the value of goods produced:

$$w_L L + w_T T = p Y_R + Y_W \tag{9}$$

it follows that

$$p Y_R + Y_W = p X_R + X_W \tag{10}$$

The value of total production is therefore equal to the value of total consumption for any set of quantities and prices satisfying the constraints of the model.†

The graph of equation (10) is shown in Figure 10-9 for two values of p. Total demand may be an infeasible point such as $x''' = (11, 18)$, given $p = 1.2$, while having the same value as the feasible, value maximizing production point, $y = (16, 12)$. Values are also equal for certain feasible demands such as $x' = (8, 18)$ which may not be identical with a value-maximizing production point such as $y' = (12, 15)$, given $p = .75$, but which can arise when relative price is equal to opportunity cost over a range of outputs.

Values of consumption and production being equal, all that remains is to state that quantities produced and consumed must also be equal. Thus, in positions of general equilibrium:‡

$$Y_R = X_R \qquad Y_W = X_W \tag{11}$$

---

* Equation (8) follows from the assumption of nonsatiation since it is this that ensures that consumption choices will satisfy equation (4). It may be noted that there are two senses in which satiation is ruled out. On the one hand, there is no "bliss point" of *global* satiation so that we need not consider the case in which such a point belongs to the interior of the budget set for any consumer. On the other hand, the assumptions on preferences also ensure that there is no point such that all nearby points are indifferent to it. This was guaranteed by the condition that if x_2 is preferred to x_1, and there always is such a point x_2, given global nonsatiation, then all points on the straight line joining x_1 and x_2 are preferred to x_1, except x_1 itself. Thus, we need not be concerned about the problem of *local* satiation, a situation exemplified by thick indifference curves. Such bands of indifferent points must be ruled out since, otherwise, a utility maximizing point could be an interior point of a consumer's budget set, even in the absence of a bliss point. The purpose of nonsatiation assumptions is evidently to guarantee that a consumer chooses a limit point that satisfies the relevant budget constraint as an equation.

† From (10) the demand function for wheat, i.e., X_W as a function of $1/p$, can be derived from the demand function for rice since, for each value of p, the left-hand side of (10) is known from the supply correspondence, while X_R on the right-hand side is given by the demand function for rice. It follows that X_W is determined as a function of the price ratio. In the same way, given the supply correspondence, the demand function for rice can be derived from the demand function for wheat.

‡ The need to prove (10) is not made redundant by (11) since it must be established that the value of consumption choices is equal to that of production which is the source of factor payments and hence expenditure *before* it is meaningful to equate quantities. Otherwise (11) would be *ad hoc*.

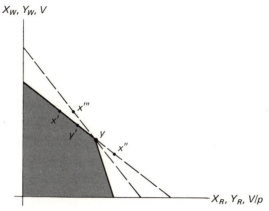

Figure 10-9. Total demand and the feasible set of outputs. Given $p = .75$, the coordinates of the indicated points are $y' = (12, 15)$, $x' = (8, 18)$, and $x'' = (20, 9)$; given $p = 1.2$, the coordinates are $y = (16, 12)$ and $x''' = (11, 18)$.

This pair of equations is satisfied only at the points of intersection of the supply correspondence and the demand function for each commodity, thereby determining an equilibrium value for the price ratio, such as $p = 1.2$ or $1/p = 5/6$ in Figure 10-8. Factor prices that minimize cost at this price ratio are such that the resulting distribution of purchasing power over commodities, given factor ownership, makes feasible a set of utility maximizing consumption choices, given preferences, that add up to the coordinates $x = (X_R, X_W)$ on the demand functions. These are equilibrium quantities since they also belong to the supply correspondence for each commodity so that the value of production is a maximum, given technology and factor supplies, at the same point $y = (Y_R, Y_W)$. At other nonequilibrium values of p there is either an excess demand for rice or an excess demand for wheat as measured in Figure 10-8 by the horizontal distance between the demand curve and the supply correspondence in the relevant diagram.

Demand functions differ with each specification of resource endowments and preferences. Various functions can, however, be associated with the same equilibrium quantities and factor allocations just so long as the point of equality between supply and demand occurs along some vertical segment of the given supply correspondence. See D_1 and D_2 in Figure 10-10 indicating a shift in demand that requires only a change in the equilibrium price ratio p with accompanying changes in factor prices. Individual consumption choices may differ since budget lines will be affected by the difference in prices, but

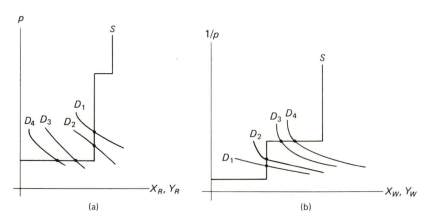

Figure 10-10. Shifts in demand alter equilibrium prices and quantities.
(a) Rice   (b) Wheat

as long as the total quantity demanded is constant, factor allocations need not change. On the other hand, differences in demand may be associated with differences in *quantities* instead of prices. This is illustrated by the shift from D_3 to D_4 in Figure 10-10 which requires a reallocation of factor services consistent with the pattern of production that satisfies the new demand. Equilibrium prices, however, are the same. Sufficiently large shifts in demand would, of course, cause *both* prices and quantities to change.*

A Summary Statement and Interpretation

The completed structure of the two-factor two-commodity allocation model may now be summarized as follows:

*Our analysis is confined to a comparison of different equilibrium configurations. In order to describe a process of *change* in factor allocations or prices, it is necessary to formulate a dynamic theory of adjustment under disequilibrium. This is because when there is excess demand there will be "profits" or "losses" in production and hence a violation of the price constraints and duality conditions of the model. See, for example, the discussion in chapter 9 of the equality between maximum value and minimum cost in the situation in which the price ratio, $p = 1.2$, exceeds the opportunity cost of rice at $y_2 = (Y_R, Y_W) = (8, 18)$. In the present context this may be interpreted as a situation in which the initial equilibrium at y_2, where $p = a_{TR}/a_{TW} = 0.75$, $w_L = 0$, $w_T = 1/a_{TW} = p/a_{TR} = 0.25$, is disturbed by an excess demand for rice associated with a shift from D_4 to D_2 in Figure 10-10. Equilibrium is now at $y_3 = (16, 12)$ with prices: $(p, w_L, w_T) = (1.2, .1, .2)$. During the "movement" from y_2 to y_3, however, there will be either profits in the rice sector if factor prices remain at their initial values, or losses in the wheat sector if factor prices move immediately to their new equilibrium values, or some combination of profits and losses. The equilibrium structure of the theory cannot account for such differences between price and cost, since there is no specification of how to allocate such profits and losses to resource owners. To avoid the problem one simply assumes that equilibrium prices and allocations are the only ones that occur, an unsatisfactory but not uncommon procedure.

Resource Constraints:

$$L \geq a_{LR} Y_R + a_{LW} Y_W \qquad \text{if a strict inequality, } w_L = 0 \qquad (12)$$

$$T \geq a_{TR} Y_R + a_{TW} Y_W \qquad \text{if a strict inequality, } w_T = 0 \qquad (13)$$

$$Y_R \geq 0 \qquad Y_W \geq 0 \qquad (14)$$

Price Constraints:

$$w_L a_{LR} + w_T a_{TR} \geq p \qquad \text{if a strict inequality, } Y_R = 0 \qquad (15)$$

$$w_L a_{LW} + w_T a_{TW} \geq 1 \qquad \text{if a strict inequality, } Y_W = 0 \qquad (16)$$

$$w_L \geq 0 \qquad w_T \geq 0 \qquad p \geq 0 \qquad (17)$$

Budget Equations:

$$w_L L^h + w_T T^h = p X_R^h + X_W^h \qquad h = 1, \ldots, s \qquad (18)$$

Supply-Demand Equations:

$$Y_R = X_R \qquad Y_W = X_W \qquad (19)$$

Walras's Law is omitted since it is implicit in the resource and price constraints, given the duality conditions. Specific reference to the role of preferences in determining the consumption choices of individuals which appear in the budget equations can be formalized in terms of:

Demand Functions:

$$\left. \begin{array}{l} X_R^h = X_R^h(p,\ w_L,\ w_T;\ L^h,\ T^h,\ \Pi^h) \\ X_W^h = X_W^h(p,\ w_L,\ w_T;\ L^h,\ T^h,\ \Pi^h) \end{array} \right\} \quad h = 1, \ldots, s \qquad \begin{array}{l}(20)\\(21)\end{array}$$

The quantity demanded of each commodity by consumer h depends on all prices, given a resource endowment and a preference ordering represented by the symbol Π^h. The chosen bundle $(X_R^h,\ X_W^h)$ is a limit point of the budget set, satisfying the relevant equation in (18), such that no alternative bundle in the budget set is preferred to the one that is chosen, thereby maximizing the value of a utility function derivable from the preference ordering.

In summarizing the structure of the neoclassical model it is helpful to recall the distinction between parameters and variables. In terms of our notation, the parameters are:

Resources: $(L,\ T)$

Technology: $(a_{LR},\ a_{TR});\ (a_{LW},\ a_{TW})$

Factor Ownership: $(L^h,\ T^h) \qquad h = 1, \ldots, s$

Preferences: $\Pi^h \qquad h = 1, \ldots, s$

The variables determined by the model are:

$$\text{Production: } (Y_R, Y_W)$$
$$\text{Consumption Choices: } (X_R^h, X_W^h) \qquad h = 1, \dots, s$$
$$\text{Factor Prices: } w_L, w_T$$
$$\text{Commodity Price Ratio: } p$$

Note that allocations of labor and land $(L_R, L_W) = (a_{LR}Y_R, a_{LW}Y_W)$ and $(T_R, T_W) = (a_{TR}Y_R, a_{TW}Y_W)$ are variables determined simultaneously with production, given the technical coefficients;* and, on the consumption side, total demand (X_R, X_W) is a variable defined by the sum of individual demands.

The neoclassical allocation model, like all scientific models, is a conscious simplification of reality. Interpretation of its structure can therefore focus on either the respects in which it fails to account for certain aspects of the problems with which it is ostensibly concerned, or on those features of reality that *are* captured and regarded as essential. Certainly the two-sector model we have analyzed is constructed on the basis of a restrictive set of assumptions, but many of these can be relaxed to meet various objections. We have already indicated certain directions in which the theory can be elaborated, allowing for arbitrary numbers of factors and commodities distinguished on the basis of physical, temporal, and spatial characteristics. It has also been noted that the representation of preferences can be made less restrictive; and, in chapter 14, we address the problem of choice of technique in greater detail. None of these complications, however, would in any important way alter or modify the basic conceptual structure of the theory which, in all its versions, explains prices and quantities in terms of the dual notions of opportunity cost and relative factor scarcity within the context of a general equilibrium of supply and demand.

We shall not therefore attempt to draw up a list of the ways in which a simple (or complicated) neoclassical model fails as a basis for description, or of the ways in which these deficiences can be rectified, but turn instead to the question: What features of competitive market economies does the theory isolate as fundamental to an understanding of their structure?

The most important aspect of neoclassical theory lies in showing the effects of differences in demand on prices and allocations. The unique view implicit in the theory is that, by taking resources and technology as given, individual consumption choices can be regarded as determining all important variables: factor allocations, prices, incomes, and commodity allocations. This explains

---

* When there is choice of technique, the coefficients must also be determined simultaneously with outputs in order to establish factor allocations. See chapter 14.

why, for the neoclassics, the theory of choice is the core of economic science, a point of view which has never been better expressed than by Lord Robbins in *An Essay on the Nature and Significance of Economic Science.*[8]

Neoclassical theory propounds the view that the important decisions in a market economy are those made by the undifferentiated resource owner *qua* consumer. This is particularly evident in the widespread use of *pure exchange* models to elucidate the principles of the theory, production being added on later as a generalization of the concept of exchange. Thus, it is the exchange of given quantities (either final commodities for each other in pure exchange, or factor services indirectly for commodities in allocation theory) that occupies center stage. Within such a framework, the prime movers in any interpretation of the analysis will necessarily be the owners of the given quantities and their preferences for final goods.

It is often claimed that households and firms occupy positions of equal importance in a neoclassical model. Such an interpretation gains little support from the theory's structure. Thus, at the very outset, three of the four categories of parametric data bear on the description of households. It is they who offer the given supply of factors to producing agents. It is they who exercise a preference for one set of goods over another. And it is they whose individual tastes are weighted in the balance of total demand according to the given distribution of ownership of the factors of production, a distribution that determines the purchasing power exercised by individual households over commodities at each set of prices. It is true that firms utilize the given technology of production, minimizing factor cost and thereby ensuring that relative price does not exceed opportunity cost (a role that takes on an added dimension when there is a choice of processes in production), but this function is essentially one of intermediation. Even the *entrepreneur* in the Walrasian sense, interpreted as one who allocates additional resources to sectors where net receipts are positive, disappears the moment the neoclassical price constraints are written down. Decisions to allocate factors in a particular way are therefore ultimately determined by consumption choices within the context of a general equilibrium in which there is no unsatisfied demand for any input or output.

The decisions of households, or more generally of consumers/resource owners, are so basic to the interpretation of neoclassical theory that the phrase "consumer's sovereignty" is used to emphasize their central role. Certain aspects of this sovereignty come out clearly in the context of the two-sector model. Suppose, on the one hand, that a shift in demand (associated with a difference either in the preference orderings of consumers, or in the pattern of ownership of the factors of production) is represented by the movement of the demand function from D_3 to D_4 in Figure 10-10. Equilibrium is altered in such a way that only production and hence factor allocations are changed; prices and income distribution are the same. The theory suggests that demand and therefore tastes determine the composition of output (given the list of commodities specified by the technology of production). On the other hand, suppose that a shift in demand is represented by the movement of the demand curve from D_1 to D_2 in Figure 10-10. A new equilibrium is defined in which only prices are different, outputs being unchanged. A difference in tastes or factor ownership, which causes the shift in demand, may therefore entail simply a reevaluation of factor services without any change in factor allocations. The only effect is to redistribute a given total output among consumers in a manner consistent with equilibrium under the new pattern of demand.*

The double influence of demand on the composition of output and the distribution of output is a hallmark of neoclassical allocation theory. The implication is clear that among the participants in exchange in a system of competitive markets, households are mutually responsible through the intermediation of firms for the resulting allocation. These households are indirectly but collectively responsible for determining what quantities of goods and services are produced and for determining who shall consume these commodities.† Differences in technology or factor supplies alter the context in which the exchange of factors for goods takes place, but in any given context it is the preferences of factor-owning households that determine how given means will be allocated among alternative uses.

A Final Caveat

Throughout our discussion of neoclassical theory we have avoided explicit reference to the structure and functioning of markets. Indirect reference was perhaps unavoidable to the extent that one takes the word price to imply a market. All prices, however, have been relative prices or ratios of exchange

---

* The two cases considered can also be illustrated in Figure 10-9. The first shift in demand from D_3 to D_4 in Figure 10-10 corresponds in Figure 10-9 to a movement of the total consumption point from $(X_R, X_W) = (12, 15)$ to $(X_R, X_W) = (8, 18)$. There is no change in equilibrium prices, only a change in equilibrium outputs (Y_R, Y_W). The second shift in demand from D_1 to D_2 in Figure 10-10 would correspond in Figure 10-9 to a counterclockwise pivot of the price line around the point $(X_R, X_W) = (16, 12)$ altering prices of factors and goods while leaving equilibrium factor allocations and total outputs unchanged at $(Y_R, Y_W) = (16, 12)$.
† The question of *how* goods are produced cannot arise in a simple model with fixed production coefficients. In chapter 14, it will be seen that the influence of demand on prices is indirectly an influence on choice of technique via the effect of factor prices on costs of production.

and do not therefore require markets in order to be defined. An exchange, however consummated, may be thought of as defining a relative price in the sense of a ratio of quantitites.

One cannot avoid all discussion of market behavior when one is considering the intended interpretation of the core of neoclassical theory which is continually used by its authors to describe economic relationships in a market economy. This is especially true for a theory that analyzes those relationships as a mechanism of exchange—if the exchange does not involve markets, how does it come about?

We have adopted the widely used method of comparative statics in our analysis of quantities and prices, thereby confining attention strictly to a comparison of equilibrium positions, leaving aside the problem of describing the process by which prices get established. Equilibrium must therefore be defined carefully as Hahn does when he writes that "prices . . . are said to be equilibrium prices . . . if, when they rule . . . no input or output is in excess demand." [9] Emphasis should be on the phrase "when they rule," for it is only after equilibrium prices have been established by some unspecified process that we can say that consuming and producing agents, in *reacting* to these prices *as if* they were parameters, determine a set of utility maximizing consumption choices and value maximizing factor allocations for which excess demand is everywhere zero. Since the definition of equilibrium takes prices as established, producing and consuming agents must be regarded as "price takers." They do not *perceive* the effect of their decisions on prices and, in that sense, are "atomistic" in the markets in which they buy and sell. Such markets are usually described as competitive. The static theory says nothing, however, about how competitive prices are formed, or how they change when the parameters of exchange are altered.

Consistent with our practice of adopting ruthless simplifications wherever a complicated analysis would not serve the objective of making clear the contrast between classical and neoclassical models of general equilibrium, we shall not now pursue the problem of constructing a theory of the *formation* of prices, i.e., a theory of markets. Our classical model, in any case, will contain no such theory so that the contrast between the models does not turn on this issue. We note, however, that there is a sizeable literature on the problem of establishing general equilibrium prices.[10] In these post-Walrasian models an "auctioneer" is invented to "call out" prices according to a particular sequence that converges to a set of equilibrium prices (given certain assumptions), but no transactions are allowed to take place until the equilibrium position is reached. Early attempts to formalize such a process succeeded only in the context of pure exchange models, and even now the general problem of dynamic adjustment out of equilibrium remains largely unsolved.

Notes

1. Frank H. Hahn, *The Share of Wages in the National Income, An Enquiry into the Theory of Distribution,* Wiedenfeld and Nicolson, London, 1972, p. 3.
2. See, for example, the concept of "resource relatedness" in Kenneth J. Arrow and Frank H. Hahn, *General Competitive Analysis,* Holden-Day, San Francisco, 1971, pp. 117 ff.
3. See, however, the many references to subsistence in Tjalling C. Koopmans, *Three Essays on the State of Economic Science,* McGraw-Hill, New York, 1957.
4. Arrow and Hahn, *General Competitive Analysis,* p. 82.
5. *Ibid.,* pp. 82–7.
6. *Ibid.,* p. 78.
7. Vivian Charles Walsh, *Introduction to Contemporary Microeconomics,* McGraw-Hill, New York, 1970.
8. Lord Robbins of Claremarket, *An Essay on the Nature and Significance of Economic Science,* Macmillan, London, 1932.
9. See note 1, above.
10. See, for example, Arrow and Hahn, *General Competitive Analysis,* pp. 263–346.

11

The Classical Theory of Surplus and the Accumulation of Capital: Quantity Relations

> It is of course in Quesnay's *Tableau Économique* that is found the original picture of the system of production and consumption as a circular process, and it stands in striking contrast to the view presented by modern theory, of a one-way avenue that leads from 'Factors of production' to 'Consumption goods.'
>
> PIERO SRAFFA [1]

The accumulation of the means of production was an essential element in the classical analysis of the emergence of capitalism. For an economy to be capable of expansion, the classical economists showed that the technology of production must yield a net output over and above the requirements for replacement of various stocks of commodities used up in the process of production. In chapter 2 this viability condition was given its simplest formulation in terms of a one-sector corn economy. In such a case there is only one input and it is a currently produced input so that viability may be expressed in terms of a single, weak inequality:

$$Y_C - a_{CC} Y_C \geq 0 \qquad \text{or simply} \qquad 1 - a_{CC} \geq 0 \qquad (1)$$

where Y_C is the gross output of corn, a_{CC} is the input of corn required per unit of output, and $a_{CC} Y_C$ is the total input of corn which must at least be replaced in order to sustain Y_C over time. A dynamic element enters into the analysis at the very outset (in marked contrast with the neoclassical theory of the allocation of given resources at a point in time).

The existence of a positive surplus, as expressed by a *strict* inequality in (1), is a characteristic of technology: the coefficient measuring the input of corn per unit of output must be less than unity. This input includes both the technical requirement of corn as seed and the subsistence requirement of corn as food during the growing season. Labor as an input is not therefore made explicit since, from the point of view of production, it is equivalent to a quantity of corn, subsistence, included in a_{CC}. (Other nonproduced inputs such as land need not be considered in the basic outline of a classical model since, as

Ricardo made clear, it is the conditions of production on marginal, *no-rent* land that determine the rents on intramarginal lands.*)

In models with more than one sector the existence of a surplus is a problem separate from the composition of the surplus in terms of particular commodities. In the two-sector model discussed in chapters 2 and 3, corn and iron are used in the production of themselves. Again, labor is hidden from view on the assumption that insofar as production is concerned it is equivalent to that quantity of corn and iron necessary for subsistence. Thus, nonproduced inputs initially have no role to play in the analysis. Subsistence and the technical requirements of corn and iron define commodity inputs per unit of output in each sector. Following our established notation, we incorporate this data in the specification of production processes:

corn sector: (a_{CC}, a_{IC}) iron sector: (a_{CI}, a_{II})

which together form a technique matrix:

$$\mathbf{A} = \begin{bmatrix} a_{CC} & a_{CI} \\ a_{IC} & a_{II} \end{bmatrix}$$

where a_{ij} measures the per-unit requirement of commodity i in the production of commodity j; $i, j = C, I$. There is one process in each sector and therefore one technique † characterized by constant returns to scale so that production coefficients do not vary with a change in the scale of output.

The viability condition for a two-sector classical model is a generalization of condition (1) for the corn model. The first inequality in (1) has as its counterpart a pair of weak inequalities:

$$a_{CC} Y_C + a_{CI} Y_I \le Y_C \tag{2}$$
$$a_{IC} Y_C + a_{II} Y_I \le Y_I \tag{3}$$

The corn input into the corn sector, $a_{CC} Y_C$, plus the corn input into the iron sector, $a_{CI} Y_I$, cannot be greater than the output of corn Y_C; and at the same time, the iron input into corn, $a_{IC} Y_C$, plus the iron input into its own production, $a_{II} Y_I$, cannot exceed the output of iron Y_I. If both of these conditions are not met the economy is using up more of at least one of the commodities

---

* See chapter 4, pp. 100–102.
† In chapter 15 on choice of technique in a classical model, it will be shown that, in equilibrium, one pair of processes dominates all other pairs, so that it is not necessarily a restrictive assumption to treat production coefficients as fixed.

than is currently produced in which case Y_C and Y_I are not sustainable outputs.*

Just as the first inequality in (1) reduces to a restriction on technology alone, so the pair of conditions, (2) and (3), may be rewritten as a single restriction on the elements of the technique matrix **A**. First, rewrite (2) and (3) as:

$$a_{CI} Y_I \leq (1 - a_{CC})Y_C \quad \text{or} \quad Y_C/Y_I \geq a_{CI}/(1 - a_{CC})$$
$$a_{IC} Y_C \leq (1 - a_{II})Y_I \quad \text{or} \quad Y_C/Y_I \leq (1 - a_{II})/a_{IC}$$

assuming $(1 - a_{CC}) > 0$.† Thus:

$$a_{CI}/(1 - a_{CC}) \leq Y_C/Y_I \leq (1 - a_{II})/a_{IC}$$

so that the viability conditions (2) and (3) may be simplified to:

$$(1 - a_{CC})(1 - a_{II}) - a_{CI}a_{IC} \geq 0 \tag{4}$$

assuming $(1 - a_{II}) > 0$.‡ Given constant returns to scale, the restriction on technology in (4) must be fulfilled if the viability conditions (2) and (3) are to be satisfied for any levels of output, Y_C and Y_I.[2] Later, after we have constructed a diagram of the set of viable outputs, the interpretation of (4) will be straightforward.

The Rate of Accumulation in One- and Two-Sector Models

In discussing the composition of surplus output we begin by considering the relationship between the creation of surplus and the possibility of accumulation. The corn model serves as an introduction and a basis for generalization.

Suppose the technical and subsistence requirements of corn input per unit of output are such that a positive surplus exists. The economy is more than just viable so that the measure of surplus and the implied restriction on technology in (1) are written as strict inequalities:

$$Y_C - a_{CC} Y_C > 0 \qquad 1 - a_{CC} > 0 \tag{1'}$$

---

* One might imagine an economy temporarily in a position which, if it continued, would eventually be self-destroying. Pollution problems, for example, can turn otherwise viable technologies into nonviable ones. We leave this matter aside, however, just as we do not attempt an analysis of how viable technologies come into existence in the first place.

† This may be interpreted to mean that if we were to extract a one-sector corn model from the two-sector model, it would be capable of producing a surplus in its own right.

‡ Again, the iron input into iron production absorbs less than the output of iron. Note that (4) can be satisfied as an equation when either of the coefficients, a_{CC} or a_{II}, is unity, but then only if one of the other coefficients, a_{CI} or a_{IC}, is zero.

Surplus may be used either for accumulating a larger stock of corn as input so that a larger crop can be planted and a larger work force maintained during the next growing season, or for sustaining a level of consumption over and above the subsistence requirement already taken into account in a_{cc}. Consumption of the surplus may support a social class not directly engaged in production: courtiers, a buraucracy or military establishment, or capitalists who own and exercise control over the means of production. If consumed by those who produce the corn, surplus output may lead to a change in the socially defined category, subsistence, and thus to a change in the corn requirement per unit of output.

As in our discussion of the physiocrats and of Adam Smith, the trade-off between accumulation and consumption of the surplus can be treated formally by introducing into the analysis a rate of accumulation g and a fraction of gross output consumed (over and above subsistence), written λ_C. Starting from (1)', subtract from Y_C a fraction of that output, λ_C, to obtain:

$$a_{cc} Y_C \leq Y_C - \lambda_C Y_C = (1 - \lambda_C) Y_C \tag{1''}$$

The strong inequality in (1)' is replaced by a weak one since λ_C may be large enough to absorb the whole surplus. In any case, there is also the possibility of growth which may be accounted for by multiplying the stock of corn $a_{cc} Y_C$ by the rate of growth g and then adding the result to the stock itself to indicate that it is being *more* than just replaced. Thus:

$$a_{cc} Y_C + (g \times a_{cc} Y_C) = Y_C - \lambda_C Y_C \tag{1'''}$$

which we write as the quantity equation for a one-sector model:

$$a_{cc} Y_C (1 + g) = (1 - \lambda_C) Y_C \tag{5}$$

or: $$a_{cc} Y_C (1 + R) = Y_C \qquad \text{where} \qquad 1 + R = (1 + g)/(1 - \lambda_C) \tag{6}$$

Note that a strict equality in (1)''' replaces the weak inequality in (1)'' since we are assuming that consumption plus accumulation absorb the entire surplus. Then from (5) it follows that g has the quite natural interpretation as a ratio of corn output, net of consumption and replacement of stock, to the stock itself:

$$g = \frac{Y_C - \lambda_C Y_C - a_{cc} Y_C}{a_{cc} Y_C} \tag{5'}$$

The interpretation of R in (6) is also as a ratio, but simply of net output to the stock of corn, leaving open the question of how the surplus is allocated:

$$R = \frac{Y_C - a_{cc} Y_C}{a_{cc} Y_C} = (1/a_{cc}) - 1 \tag{6'}$$

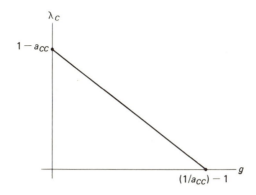

Figure 11-1. Consumption–growth trade-off in a one-commodity corn model.

Thus, R is a "rate of surplus," positive only when (1) is a strict inequality.

The accumulation-consumption trade-off may be expressed as a linear relationship in g and λ_C. Simply rewrite (5) in standard form (after dividing by Y_C) so that the equation can be graphed in a coordinate space with λ_C on the vertical axis and g on the horizontal axis:

$$\lambda_C = -a_{CC}g + (1 - a_{CC}) \tag{7}$$

Thus, $\lambda_{C_{max}} = 1 - a_{CC}$ and $g_{max} = (1/a_{CC}) - 1 = R$; the slope of the trade-off, $-a_{CC}$, is determined by technology. Figure 11-1 illustrates all possible values for λ_C and g in the corn model.

In a two-sector model the analysis of the consumption-growth trade-off also begins with the assumption that a surplus exists, i.e., that there are gross outputs, Y_C and Y_I, such that strict inequalities hold in (2) and (3):

$$a_{CC}Y_C + a_{CI}Y_I < Y_C \tag{2$'$}$$
$$a_{IC}Y_C + a_{II}Y_I < Y_I \tag{3$'$}$$

As in (1)″, fractions of gross output, λ_C and λ_I, are subtracted from the right-hand side of each inequality thereby defining output net of consumption:*

$$a_{CC}Y_C + a_{CI}Y_I \le (1 - \lambda_C)Y_C \tag{2$''$}$$
$$a_{IC}Y_C + a_{II}Y_I \le (1 - \lambda_I)Y_I \tag{3$''$}$$

Allowing for a strict equality means that the surplus in one or both sectors

---

* The symbol λ_C was used in chapter 2 to indicate direct consumption of corn as a luxury. It may come as a surprise, however, to find λ_I in the iron sector in place of the explicit sector manufacturing a luxury commodity, Y_X, described as "carriages" in chapter 2. The explanation is that we are, for the moment, burying all luxury consumption whatever its concrete form in λ_j, $j = C, I$ to make the model as simple as possible. In chapter 2 it was necessary to extract the manufactured luxury commodity in order to analyze the physiocratic model.

may be entirely consumed. But since there is also the possibility of growth, we write the quantity relations as equations by treating any remaining surplus in either sector as a percentage of the stock of corn and iron used up in the two processes of production. In general, this percentage rate of accumulation may differ for each of the four components of the stock of capital, $a_{ij} Y_j$, $i,j = C,I$. To keep the analysis simple, however, it is assumed that growth is *balanced* which is to say that when there is accumulation, every component of the commodity means of production grows at the same rate g.* On this assumption, quantity equations for a two-sector model of surplus and accumulation are written as generalizations of (5) and (6):

$$(a_{CC} Y_C + a_{CI} Y_I)(1 + g) = (1 - \lambda_C) Y_C \tag{8}$$

$$(a_{IC} Y_C + a_{II} Y_I)(1 + g) = (1 - \lambda_I) Y_I \tag{9}$$

or:

$$(a_{CC} Y_C + a_{CI} Y_I)(1 + R_C) = Y_C \tag{10}$$

$$(a_{IC} Y_C + a_{II} Y_I)(1 + R_I) = Y_I \tag{11}$$

where $R_j = (1 + g)/(1 - \lambda_j)$, $j = C,I$. As in the one-sector corn model, growth rates in (8) and (9) are ratios of output net of consumption and replacement of stock divided by the relevant component of the stock of capital: either $K_C = a_{CC} Y_C + a_{CI} Y_I$ in (8) or $K_I = a_{IC} Y_C + a_{II} Y_I$ in (9). Thus:

$$g = \frac{Y_C - \lambda_C Y_C - K_C}{K_C} \tag{8'}$$

$$g = \frac{Y_I - \lambda_I Y_I - K_I}{K_I} \tag{9'}$$

Rates of corn surplus and iron surplus in (10) and (11), on the other hand, are ratios of output net of replacement of stock divided by stock, defined independently of the allocation of the surplus:

$$R_C = \frac{Y_C - K_C}{K_C} \tag{10'}$$

$$R_I = \frac{Y_I - K_I}{K_I} \tag{11'}$$

Rates of surplus need not be equal, even in the case of balanced growth, except in the event that λ_C and λ_I are also equal. That R_C and R_I are non-negative is implied by (and implies) the viability conditions, (2) and (3), which, as we have shown, are equivalent to the restriction on technology given in (4).

---

*This was not done in chapter 3 where our model would have departed unnecessarily far from Smith if we had incorporated the assumption of balanced growth. See pp. 71–2.

Although the consumption-growth trade-off in the two-sector model is more complicated than in the corn model (since the quantity equations (8) and (9) determine a relationship in three variables, g, λ_C, and λ_I, instead of two) we may still obtain the linear function in Figure 11-1 as a special case if we assume balanced growth *and* equal fractions, $\lambda_C = \lambda = \lambda_I$, so that rates of surplus, R_C and R_I, are equal. The intercepts have the same interpretation as in the corn model. Thus, λ_{max} on the vertical axis would correspond to a zero rate of growth, and g_{max} on the horizontal axis to zero consumption out of surplus. The exact equation for this trade-off, however, requires the solution to a quadratic equation which we leave aside for the moment.

The Composition of Surplus Output

The set of viable net outputs of corn and iron consistent with a given technique matrix can be illustrated graphically as a *surplus possibilities schedule*. Since inputs and outputs are physically homogeneous, the convention is adopted of measuring inputs as negative quantities and outputs as positive quantities. Thus, in Figure 11-2, all four quadrants have meaning: negative quantities of corn being measured as inputs to the left of the origin and positive outputs to the right; while negative quantities of iron are measured as inputs below the origin and positive outputs above the origin. The unit process of production in each sector is therefore given by a point in quadrant III. As an illustration let:

$$(a_{CC}, a_{IC}) = (.4, .2) \qquad \text{and} \qquad (a_{CI}, a_{II}) = (.2, .7)$$

Giving each number a negative sign to show that it is an input, the resulting points in quadrant III are joined to the origin, thereby graphing unit process vectors for each commodity. Their slopes, a_{IC}/a_{CC} and a_{II}/a_{CI}, measure iron to corn ratios in production. Multiplying their lengths by any positive number locates a new point along either ray or its extension which measures inputs corresponding to that number of units of production of the relevant commodity.

Next, consider the gross output $(Y_C, Y_I) = (1, 0)$, to the right of the origin in Figure 11-2. To sustain this output requires using up a_{CC} units of corn and a_{IC} units of iron. Thus, *net* output is given by the point $(1 - a_{CC}, -a_{IC})$ in quadrant IV, so that in joining this point to the origin we obtain a graph of the net activity vector in the corn sector. One sees immediately that specialization in the production of corn is not viable since net output of iron is negative (as long as a_{IC} is not zero). Still, it is necessary to have this net activity vector in our construction of the surplus possibilities schedule.

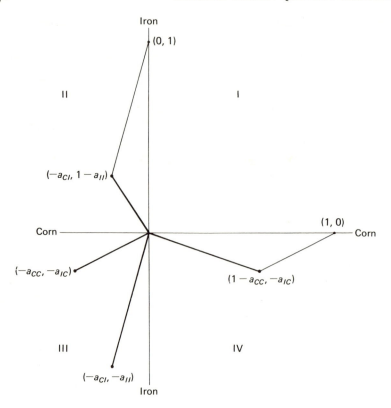

Figure 11-2. Gross and net activity vectors, given $(a_{CC},\ a_{IC}) = (.4,\ .2)$ and $(a_{CI},\ a_{II}) = (.2,\ .7)$.

A net iron activity vector is constructed in exactly the same way. Starting from the point $(Y_C,\ Y_I) = (0,\ 1)$, we observe that to sustain this output requires a_{CI} units of corn and a_{II} units of iron leaving a net output given by the point, $(-a_{CI},\ 1 - a_{II})$, in quadrant II. A line joining this point to the origin graphs the desired net activity vector, and, as in the case of $(Y_C,\ Y_I) = (1,\ 0)$, it is evident that the initial gross output consisting only of iron is not viable since it requires a negative output of corn (except in the special case where $a_{CI} = 0$). Just as the vectors in quadrant III can be lengthened or shortened to define inputs for nonunit levels of production, so the net activity vectors have lengths which when multiplied by any positive number extend or shorten them to end in a point with coordinates corresponding to that number of units of output. For example, a point ¾ of the distance from the origin along the ray in quadrant II defines net outputs corresponding to $(Y_C,\ Y_I) = (0,\ ¾)$.

An economy in which commodities are produced by means of commodities cannot, in general, be specialized in production (unless certain input–output coefficients are zero), since to sustain itself over time, the system must at least replace all the various commodity components in its capital stock. Having said this, the question remains as to which gross outputs are viable, and what these outputs imply about the resulting (non-negative) surplus output. We approach the problem by first defining, for any non-negative gross outputs (Y_C, Y_I), a pair of non-negative fractions adding up to unity:

$$\frac{Y_C}{Y_C + Y_I} + \frac{Y_I}{Y_C + Y_I} = 1 \tag{12}$$

This is a normalization* of quantities which we write more briefly as:

$$\psi + \phi = 1 \tag{12'}$$

Since any point along the line joining $(0, 1)$ and $(1, 0)$ in Figure 11-3 has coordinates (ψ, ϕ) satisfying $(12)'$, our question concerning the composition of the surplus amounts to asking which of these points corresponds to viable gross outputs (Y_C, Y_I) in (12), and what are the associated net outputs.

To find net outputs corresponding to gross outputs in any given proportions, drop perpendiculars from (ψ, ϕ) to the coordinate axes in Figure 11-3, and from these points draw lines parallel to the original (quadrant III) process vectors to intersect the net activity vectors in the two points:

$$[\psi(1 - a_{CC}), -\psi a_{IC}] \qquad [-\phi a_{CI}, \phi(1 - a_{II})] \tag{13}$$

This is simply a graphical method of marking off on the net activity vectors distances from the origin that are the same proportions of the unit distances that the initial gross outputs are of total production, namely (ψ, ϕ). Then, to discover if the initial gross output proportions are viable, we ask if this *combination* of net activities produces a non-negative surplus. The requirement is that the net output of corn, $\psi(1 - a_{CC})$, be at least sufficient to supply the corn needs of the iron sector, $-\phi a_{CI}$; and, at the same time, that the net output of iron, $\phi(1 - a_{II})$, be at least sufficient to supply the iron needs of the corn sector, $-\psi a_{IC}$. Thus, we add the respective coordinates of the two points in (13) and impose the condition:

---

* Normalizations remove indeterminant elements of scale as, for example, in the choice of wheat as *numeraire* in chapter 9's analysis of prices in a neoclassical model. Prices are sometimes normalized by setting their *sum* equal to unity. In such procedures it appears as if incommensurables are being added, as in the sum of Y_C and Y_I which have different units of measurement. This is only apparent, however, since there is always an implicit coefficient preceding, say, Y_I measuring "one unit of corn per unit of iron" so that the two quantities can, in fact, be added.

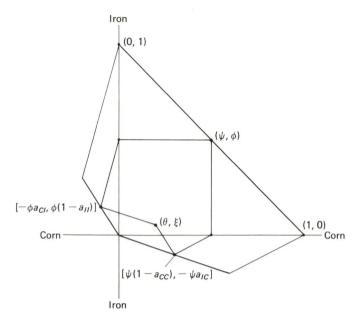

Figure 11-3. Viable gross outputs yield non-negative net outputs. The coordinates of the indicated points are $(\psi, \phi) = (.5, .5)$, $(\theta, \xi) = (.2, .05)$, $[-\phi a_{CI}, \phi(1 - a_{II})] = (-.1, .15)$, $[\psi(1 - a_{CC}), -\psi a_{IC}] = (.3, -.1)$, given the coefficients in Figure 11-2.

$$\theta = \psi(1 - a_{CC}) - \phi a_{CI} \geq 0 \qquad \xi = \phi(1 - a_{II}) - \psi a_{IC} \geq 0 \qquad (14)$$

It is easy to check that (14) is satisfied in Figure 11-3 by drawing the indicated parallelogram that has as one of its corners the point (θ, ξ). If this point lies in the non-negative quadrant, the initial gross outputs that defined the proportions (ψ, ϕ) are viable and the coordinates of (θ, ξ) measure the corresponding surplus outputs.

In constructing (θ, ξ) we began with arbitrary initial proportions, (ψ, ϕ) so that it is possible to repeat the argument for any such point. In Figure 11-4 two particular gross output proportions are chosen such that the corresponding net outputs consist of only one commodity. Where net output is entirely in the form of surplus iron at (θ'', ξ'') there must still be enough gross output of corn at (ψ'', ϕ'') to replace the stock of corn, even if no addition is made to that stock. And, if surplus is entirely in corn at (θ', ξ'), gross iron production must still be just sufficient at (ψ', ϕ') to replace the stock of iron used up. (In each case, replacement output is divided between the two sectors, although the way in which this is accomplished must await an analysis of prices.)

The various surplus outputs constructed according to the parallelogram method in Figures 11-3 and 11-4 lie along a straight line joining the end-

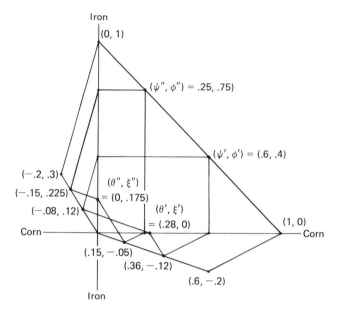

Figure 11-4. Surplus outputs consisting of only one commodity. Net output of iron is zero given $(\psi', \phi') = (.6, .4)$, $(\theta', \xi') = (.28, 0)$. Net output of corn is zero given $(\psi'', \phi'') = (.25, .75)$, $(\theta'', \xi'') = (0, .175)$.

points of the net activity vectors.* The surplus possibilities schedule is that portion of this line passing through the non-negative quadrant in Figure 11-5. Each point along this schedule maps into a unique point on the gross output schedule joining $(0, 1)$ and $(1, 0)$, subject to (14) which is written $.25 \leq \psi \leq .6$ or $.75 \geq \phi \geq .4$, using the coefficients in our example. Table 11-1 identifies the location of five surplus outputs and corresponding gross outputs, each pair of points, (ψ, ϕ) and (θ, ξ) in the table, being joined by a straight line in Figure 11-5. The slopes of these lines measure the various ratios of iron to corn in the means of production:†

$$\frac{K_I}{K_C} = \frac{a_{IC} Y_C + a_{II} Y_I}{a_{CC} Y_C + a_{CI} Y_I} = \frac{a_{IC}\psi + a_{II}\phi}{a_{CC}\psi + a_{CI}\phi} \tag{15}$$

*This line is a graph of linear combinations of the net activity vectors, each point along the line being a vector sum (θ, ξ) defined in (14).
†The slope of each line is $(\phi - \xi)/(\psi - \theta)$. On substituting the values for θ and ξ from (14), this ratio reduces to the final expression in (15), itself a ratio of the coordinates of a linear combination of the gross activity vectors in quadrant III of Figure 11-2.

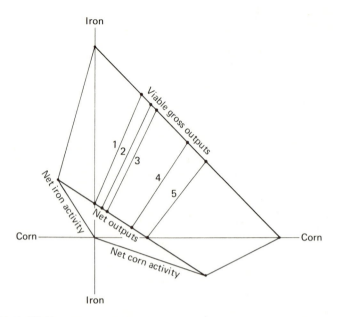

Figure 11-5. Viable gross outputs and corresponding net outputs along the surplus possibilities schedule.

TABLE 11-1. Gross and Net Outputs
Technology: $(a_{CC}, a_{IC}) = (.4, .2)$
$(a_{CI}, a_{II}) = (.2, .7)$

Label in Figure 11-5	(ψ, ϕ) on gross output schedule	Gross outputs		Total inputs		Net outputs		(θ, ξ) on net output schedule
		Y_C	Y_I	K_C	K_I	$Y_C - K_C$	$Y_I - K_I$	
1	(.25, .75)	15	45	15.0	34.5	0.0	10.5	(0, .175)
2	(.3, .7)	18	42	15.6	33.0	2.4	9.0	(.04, .15)
3	(.33, .66)	20	40	16.0	32.0	4.0	8.0	(.06, .13)
4	(.5, .5)	30	30	18.0	27.0	12.0	3.0	(.2, .05)
5	(.6, .4)	36	24	19.2	24.0	16.8	0.0	(.28, 0)

The corn-capital and iron-capital aggregates, K_C and K_I, are given in the total input columns of Table 11-1, where calculations have been made on the assumption that the number of units of corn production plus the number of units of iron production add up to 60, a convenient number given the values of the technical coefficients in our example. Gross and net output columns are therefore obtained by multiplying (ψ, ϕ) and (θ, ξ), respectively, by 60. Inputs can then be calculated, given the coefficients.

Accumulation versus Consumption of the Surplus

Differences in gross and net output in a model of surplus and accumulation entail differences in the composition of the stock of capital: the commodity inputs, K_C and K_I, entering into production in the two sectors of our model. This, of course, is in sharp contrast with the neoclassical allocation model in which all inputs are parameters. Moreover, it follows that a comparison of points along any given surplus possibilities schedule is a comparison of different economic systems, each with its own particular past investment in commodity capital. An analysis of "movement" or "change" from one point along the schedule to another is therefore even more problematical than an analysis of changing factor allocations along the boundary of the set of feasible outputs in a neoclassical model.* But, just as we learned something about the structure of the latter theory through a comparison of equilibrium positions, so in the classical model such comparisons tell us how quantities would have to be altered in order for the stock of capital to accommodate itself to the composition of output, subject to the quantity equations of the model, (8) and (9).

Suppose, for example, that accumulation is zero, i.e., the economy simply replaces its means of production during each time period. Of course, if there is no surplus, there is nothing further to discuss, but if a surplus exists its allocation must be specified. At one extreme, surplus may be entirely in the form of iron. This is expressed formally in the quantity equations by setting both the rate of accumulation and the fraction of corn output consumed as a luxury equal to zero so that (8) and (9) become:

$$a_{CC} Y_C + a_{CI} Y_I = Y_C \qquad \text{or} \qquad .4Y_C + .2Y_I = Y_C \qquad (16)$$

$$a_{IC} Y_C + a_{II} Y_I = (1 - \lambda_I)Y_I \qquad \text{or} \qquad .2Y_C + .7Y_I = (1 - \lambda_I)Y_I \qquad (17)$$

---

* In neoclassical theory disequilibrium factor allocations gave rise to positive or negative receipts in production which violated the price constraints or duality conditions of the model. In classical theory disequilibrium allocations of the surplus result in *unequal* rates of profit. Our subsequent analysis of prices, however, considers only the case of a uniform rate of profit characteristic of classical analysis from Smith onwards.

The numbers in the first row of Table 11-1, and hence the point labelled 1 in Figure 11-5, are consistent with these equations. The rate of balanced growth in zero since corn production is entirely for replacement of stock while the fraction of iron output consumed is a maximum, $\lambda_I = 7/30$. As for rates of surplus, R_C is zero while R_I is a maximum:

$$R_I = [(1+g)/(1-\lambda_I)] - 1 = \lambda_I/(1-\lambda_I) = 7/23 \tag{18}$$

since $g = 0$. The proportion of iron to corn in the stock of capital, $K_I/K_C = 34.5/15$, is weighted relatively in favor of iron since iron production is assumed to be relatively iron intensive given the sectoral commodity input ratios: $a_{II}/a_{CI} > a_{IC}/a_{CC}$.

With accumulation set equal to zero, surplus output may also exist entirely in the form of corn. This is illustrated by the fifth row in Table 11-1 and by the point labelled 5 in Figure 11-5 for which the quantity equations are written:

$$a_{CC} Y_C + a_{CI} Y_I = (1-\lambda_C)Y_C \quad \text{or} \quad .4Y_C + .2Y_I = (1-\lambda_C)Y_C \tag{19}$$

$$a_{IC} Y_C + a_{II} Y_I = Y_I \quad \text{or} \quad .2Y_C + .7Y_I = Y_I \tag{20}$$

Both g and λ_I are zero so that λ_C is a maximum, $7/15$. The rate of surplus in the iron sector is zero while in the corn sector it is a maximum:

$$R_C = [(1+g)/(1-\lambda_C)] - 1 = \lambda_C/(1-\lambda_C) = 7/8 \tag{21}$$

As expected, the composition of the stock of capital is now weighted in favor of corn as measured by the ratio, $K_I/K_C = 24/19.2$, since corn production is relatively corn intensive.

All the remaining points in Table 11-1, and therefore any point along the surplus schedule in Figure 11-5, can be interpreted as satisfying the quantity equations for the case in which $g = 0$ while λ_C and λ_I are positive. Thus, (8) and (9) would be written:

$$a_{CC} Y_C + a_{CI} Y_I = (1-\lambda_C)Y_C \quad \text{or} \quad .4Y_C + .2Y_I = (1-\lambda_C)Y_C \tag{22}$$

$$a_{IC} Y_C + a_{II} Y_I = (1-\lambda_I)Y_I \quad \text{or} \quad .2Y_C + .7Y_I = (1-\lambda_I)Y_I \tag{23}$$

However, when a surplus of both commodities exists, balanced growth is also possible, and it is to this case that we now turn.

In the extreme case, consumption out of surplus is zero and we have the situation made famous by Neumann.[3] Fractions of gross output consumed are set equal to zero in (8) and (9) so that:

$$(a_{CC} Y_C + a_{CI} Y_I)(1+g) = Y_C \quad \text{or} \quad (.4Y_C + .2Y_I)(1+g) = Y_C \quad (24)$$

$$(a_{IC} Y_C + a_{II} Y_I)(1+g) = Y_I \quad \text{or} \quad (.2Y_C + .7Y_I)(1+g) = Y_I \quad (25)$$

Quantities in the third line of Table 11-1 satisfy these equations and since each net output is 25% larger than the total input of the same commodity we may conclude that the growth rate attains its maximum value, $g_{max} = .25$. And at the point labelled 3 in Figure 11-5 we find the unique case in which the line joining gross and net outputs, if extended, would pass through the origin, indicating that the ratio of gross outputs is equal to the ratio of inputs and therefore the ratio of net outputs:

$$\frac{Y_I}{Y_C} = \frac{K_I}{K_C} = \frac{Y_I - K_I}{Y_C - K_C} \quad (26)$$

Each net output is the same maximum proportion, $g = .25$ in our example, of the corresponding input, a proportionality which does not hold for any other gross and net outputs in Figure 11-5. There is always such a point, unique except in special cases, for any given technique matrix **A**.

The situation just considered plays an important role in the next chapter's analysis of prices and it is therefore worth noting that all that it requires is that rates of physical surplus R_C and R_I be equal, the case of maximum balanced growth and zero consumption of the surplus being only one such case. This is evident when we write the condition:

$$1 + R_C = \frac{1+g}{1-\lambda_C} = 1 + R = \frac{1+g}{1-\lambda_I} = 1 + R_I \quad (27)$$

which is certainly satisfied when $\lambda_C = 0 = \lambda_I$. It is also satisfied, however, when $\lambda_C = \lambda = \lambda_I$, for $\lambda > 0$ and $g < g_{max}$. Thus, we may simply replace $(1 + g)$ by $(1 + R) = (1 + g)/(1 - \lambda)$ in (24) and (25) and not affect the equivalence of proportions between inputs and outputs. Then $R = .25$ and the allocation of surplus to accumulation and consumption is left unspecified.

Finally, there are intermediate cases where growth is balanced but not at a maximal rate since part of the surplus is consumed, and where $\lambda_C \neq \lambda_I$ so that rates of surplus are not equal. At point 2 in Figure 11-5, for example, the corresponding outputs in the second line of Table 11-1 show that growth may occur at the rate of 5%, thereby absorbing .78 units of corn surplus and 1.65 units of iron surplus leaving for consumption 1.62 units of corn and 7.35 units of iron, in which case $\lambda_C = 9\%$ and $\lambda_I = 17.5\%$, as can be verified from the table. Other allocations of the surplus in line 2 are also possible. Similarly, in line 4 of the table and at point 4 in Figure 11-5 growth may occur at the rate

$g = 5\%$, absorbing .9 units of surplus corn and 1.35 units of surplus iron leaving 11.1 units of corn surplus ($\lambda_C = 37\%$ of gross output) and 1.65 units of iron surplus ($\lambda_I = 5.5\%$ of gross output) for consumption. Thus, when the growth rate is less than its maximum value, the composition of surplus output can be weighted either in favor of corn or iron depending on the proportions, λ_C and λ_I. The extreme cases are those analyzed above in which one of these proportions is zero, the other a maximum, and the rate of accumulation zero.

To obtain a more general form of these various results, the quantity equations, (8) and (9), are rewritten after isolating the ratio of gross outputs on one side:

$$\frac{Y_I}{Y_C} = \frac{(1 - \lambda_C) - a_{CC}(1 + g)}{a_{CI}(1 + g)} \tag{28}$$

$$\frac{Y_I}{Y_C} = \frac{a_{IC}(1 + g)}{(1 - \lambda_I) - a_{II}(1 + g)} \tag{29}$$

Owing to the assumption of constant returns to scale, the ratio of gross outputs is determined by the proportions of gross output consumed, the rate of accumulation, and per-unit commodity requirements in production independently of the scale of output. We therefore obtain from (28) and (29) a function in g, λ_C, and λ_I by setting the two right-hand sides equal:

$$\frac{(1 - \lambda_C) - a_{CC}(1 + g)}{a_{CI}(1 + g)} = \frac{a_{IC}(1 + g)}{(1 - \lambda_I) - a_{II}(1 + g)} \tag{30}$$

Cross multiplying and rearranging terms:

$$(1 + g)^2 \left(\frac{a_{CC} a_{II} - a_{CI} a_{IC}}{(1 - \lambda_C)(1 - \lambda_I)} \right) - (1 + g) \left(\frac{a_{CC}}{1 - \lambda_C} + \frac{a_{II}}{1 - \lambda_I} \right) + 1 = 0 \tag{31}$$

This second-order equation in the unknowns, g, λ_C, and λ_I has, in our example, the form:

$$.24 \left(\frac{(1 + g)^2}{(1 - \lambda_C)(1 - \lambda_I)} \right) - .4 \left(\frac{1 + g}{1 - \lambda_C} \right) - .7 \left(\frac{1 + g}{1 - \lambda_I} \right) + 1 = 0 \tag{31$'$}$$

given $(a_{CC}, a_{IC}) = (.4, .2)$ and $(a_{CI}, a_{II}) = (.2, .7)$.

Various points along the surplus possibilities schedule may now be seen as satisfying (31) or its particular case (31)$'$. If the whole surplus is consumed, $g = 0$, and these equations become:

$$(1 - \lambda_C)(1 - \lambda_I) - a_{II}(1 - \lambda_C) - a_{CC}(1 - \lambda_I) + a_{CC} a_{II} - a_{CI} a_{IC} = 0 \tag{32}$$

$$(1 - \lambda_C)(1 - \lambda_I) - .7(1 - \lambda_C) - .4(1 - \lambda_I) + .24 = 0 \tag{32$'$}$$

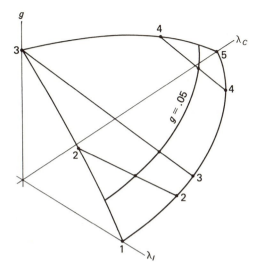

Figure 11-6. Consumption–growth trade-off in a two commodity corn and iron model. The numbered points and lines correspond to the like-numbered points in Figure 11-5 and to the numbered rows in Table 11-1.

Although only the first and last lines in Table 11-1 were used to illustrate situations in which all the surplus is consumed, any viable outputs in the quantity equations (for which surplus is non-negative) are consistent with zero growth. Various values for λ_C and λ_I satisfying $(32)'$, and the associated ratios of gross outputs Y_I/Y_C found by substituting λ_C or λ_I into (28) or (29), are:

$$(\lambda_C, \lambda_I, Y_I/Y_C) = \begin{cases} (0, 7/30, 3) \\ (2/15, 3/14, 7/3) \\ (.2, .2, 2) \\ (.4, .1, 1) \\ (7/15, 0, 2/3) \end{cases} \qquad (33)$$

Any outputs, Y_C and Y_I, forming the ratios given in (33) such as the ones in Table 11-1 can be substituted into the quantity equations (8) and (9). Figure 11-6 which is an approximate graph of the surface defined in $(31)'$ locates the five zero-growth values for λ_C and λ_I along the curve that lies in the plane where $g = 0$.

At the other extreme where consumption out of surplus is zero and growth a maximum, (31) and $(31)'$ are written:

$$(a_{cc}a_{II} - a_{CI}a_{IC})(1+g)^2 - (a_{CC} + a_{II})(1+g) + 1 = 0 \qquad (34)$$

$$.24(1+g)^2 - 1.1(1+g) + 1 = 0 \qquad (34)'$$

The growth rate calculated from the third row in Table 11-1 is now seen to be the solution to (34)′ since $1+g = 1.25$ so that $g = .25$.* As we remarked earlier, the case in which $\lambda_C = 0 = \lambda_I$ is a particular case of the more general situation in which $\lambda_C = \lambda = \lambda_I$. Physical rates of surplus are equal and (31)′ becomes:

$$.24[(1+g)/(1-\lambda)]^2 - 1.1[(1+g)/(1-\lambda)] + 1 = 0 \qquad (31)''$$

or: $.24(1+R)^2 - 1.1(1+R) + 1 = 0$ \qquad (34)''

Having simply replaced $1+g$ where $g = g_{max}$ by $1+R = (1+g)/(1-\lambda)$ where $g < g_{max}$ we immediately obtain from (34)″, which has exactly the form of (34)′, the solution:

$$1 + R = (1+g)/(1-\lambda) = 1.25$$

so that: $\lambda = -.8g + .2$ \qquad (35)

Now, this last equation has precisely the form of the consumption-growth trade-off in the one-sector corn model as shown in Figure 11-1, except that now $g_{max} = .25$ is the solution to (34)′ and $\lambda_{max} = .2$ is the solution to (32)′ given $\lambda_C = \lambda_I$.† For all values of λ and g that satisfy (35) along the straight line ending in the points marked 3 in Figure 11-6, the common rate of surplus in each sector is 25%, the solution to (34)″. The ratio of gross and net outputs and of total inputs in (26) is 2 which may be found from (28) or (29) after dividing everywhere by $1 - \lambda_C = 1 - \lambda_I$. Thus:

$$\frac{Y_I}{Y_C} = \frac{1 - a_{CC}(1+R)}{a_{CI}(1+R)} = 2 \qquad (28)'$$

$$\frac{Y_I}{Y_C} = \frac{a_{IC}(1+R)}{1 - a_{II}(1+R)} = 2 \qquad (29)'$$

The cases we have considered isolate the extremes, but there are, of course, many other particular cases of (31)′ corresponding to various points or sets of points on the surface graphed in Figure 11-6. Equation (32)′ defines the curve

---

* The   solution   to   an   equation   of   the   form $ax^2 + bx + c = 0$ is   written $x = (-b \pm \sqrt{b^2 - 4ac})/2a$. In our case, $x = 1+g$, $a = .24$, $b = -1.1$, $c = 1$. Hence $1+g = 1.25$ or $10/3$. The latter root can be ignored since it yields a negative solution for the ratio of outputs in (28) and (29). This is a general result: whenever there is more than one solution for g, take the smallest.

† Again, if there are two solutions take the smaller since the larger will result in a negative ratio of outputs.

of intersection of this surface with the $\lambda_C - \lambda_I$ plane. The other two curves of intersection with the coordinate planes are found in the usual way by setting one variable equal to zero: $\lambda_I = 0$ in (31)' produces a second-order equation in g and λ_C; $\lambda_C = 0$ produces a second-order equation in g and λ_I.* Finally, we note that the interpretation given earlier for lines 2 and 4 in Table 11-1 locates two points on the surface in Figure 11-6 which lie along the contour for which $g = .05$. They have the respective coordinates: $(g, \lambda_C, \lambda_I) = (.05, .09, .175)$ and $(.05, .37, .055)$ and also lie along the *straight* lines ending in the points marked 2 and 4. Any point along the line ending in 2 in Figure 11-6 is consistent with the quantities in the second line in Table 11-1; and any point along the line ending in 4 is consistent with the quantities in the fourth line of Table 11-1.

The Viability Condition and the Surplus Possibilities Schedule

Having analyzed the relationship between the surplus possibilities schedule and the consumption-growth trade-off, we turn to the question of how this schedule and hence the possibilities for accumulation and consumption of the surplus are affected by differences in the technical coefficients of production.

One simple but important result (which can easily be shown in a diagram) is that a reduction in any of the coefficients of production moves the surplus possibilities schedule further away from the origin along any ray. This makes possible certain net outputs not previously viable and, for that reason, always increases the maximum rate at which the economy can grow (when consumption out of surplus is zero) or the proportions of gross output that may be consumed over and above subsistence for any growth rate less than the maximum. For example, if all the coefficients in our model are reduced by 50% to $(a_{CC}, a_{IC}) = (.2, .1)$ and $(a_{CI}, a_{II}) = (.1, .35)$, the solution for the maximum rate of growth in (34)' increases from 25% to 150%; and the maximum proportion, $\lambda_C = \lambda = \lambda_I$, increases from 20% to 60%.

An increase in commodity requirements per unit of output has the effect of shrinking the viable set of net outputs so that we may ask at what point the surplus vanishes altogether. In Figure 11-7 schedules of surplus output are drawn for four different technologies. In one instance the line that joins the

---

* Using the coefficients in our example, these equations are:

$$.24g^2 + .7\lambda_C g - .62g - .3\lambda_C + .14 = 0$$
$$.24g^2 + .4\lambda_I g - .62g - .6\lambda_I + .14 = 0$$

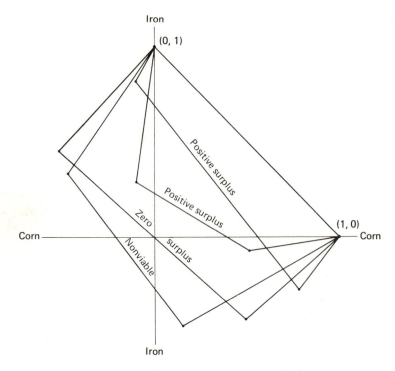

Figure 11-7. Viable and nonviable technologies.

net activity vectors coincides with these vectors, thereby passing through the origin and reducing the surplus to zero. Another case shows the line joining net activity vectors passing through the negative quadrant. It is no surprise that there is a straightforward relationship between the various cases indicated in Figure 11-7 and the viability criterion stated previously, namely:

$$(1 - a_{CC})(1 - a_{II}) - a_{CI}a_{IC} \geq 0 \tag{4}$$

Note, first of all, that the slope of the net activity vector in the iron sector is $(1 - a_{II})/(- a_{CI})$ while the slope of the corresponding vector in the corn sector is $(- a_{IC})/(1 - a_{CC})$. A look at Figure 11-7 shows that in the two cases where the surplus possibilities schedule passes through the positive quadrant, the slope of the iron sector net activity vector is steeper with respect to the horizontal axis than that of the corn sector net activity vector. Its algebraic slope is therefore smaller, meaning more negative so that:

$$(1 - a_{II})/(- a_{CI}) < (- a_{IC})/(1 - a_{CC})$$

which may be rewritten (assuming $1 - a_{CC} > 0$) as:

$$(1 - a_{CC})(1 - a_{II}) - a_{CI}a_{IC} > 0 \qquad (4)'$$

It follows that a strict inequality in the viability condition (4) is associated with a surplus possibilities schedule that passes through the positive quadrant. On the other hand, when the two net activity vectors have the same slope, the two inequalities above are replaced by equations and so we have:

$$(1 - a_{CC})(1 - a_{II}) - a_{CI}a_{IC} = 0 \qquad (4)''$$

A strict equality in the viability condition means that the surplus possibilities schedule reduces to a point, the origin, so that it is just possible to replace the commodity stock of capital during each period of production.

We conclude that the case that must be ruled out is the one in Figure 11-7 where the coefficients are such that the slope of the iron sector net activity vector is flatter (or greater in algebraic value) than the slope of the corn sector net activity vector. In that case the strict inequality in (4)' would be reversed and the technology becomes nonviable. There is then no composition of output such that the net product in each sector, after allowing for replacement of stock, is sufficient to meet the replacement needs in the other sector, much less to allow for accumulation or consumption above subsistence.*

Parameters and Variables

We have not yet commented on the dividing line between parameters and variables in a classical model, although in certain respects this may be obvious. Certainly, subsistence and the technical requirements of commodities in production are parametric to the quantity equations of a classical model, and in the formal structure they are expressed in terms of the coefficients of the technique matrix **A**. Moreover, there is a restriction on these parameters in the form of the viability condition (4) which is also a given piece of data—the theory does not explain how a viable technology came into existence.

Outputs are variables in the theory, as are inputs and net outputs, but only their ratios are determined: Y_I/Y_C and K_I/K_C and hence $(Y_I - K_I)/(Y_C - K_C)$. Given the technique matrix, only one of these is independent. Finally, there are three other symbols, g, λ_C, and λ_I, and the derivative rates of surplus R_C and R_I. At this stage in the argument, prior to any discussion of the role of demand, it is convenient to treat as parameters the proportions of gross output

---

* As we noted in our initial statement of (4), there are special cases which may be of interest in particular applications. For example, if $a_{CI} = 0$ the system is *just* viable if $1 - a_{CC} = 0$; and if $1 - a_{II} = 0$, we must have $a_{IC} = 0$. In each case surplus is zero, but note that $a_{CI}a_{IC} = 0$ does not imply a zero surplus by itself.

consumed. The growth rate is a determined variable as may be seen from equation (31).

Summing up, we take as given parameters:

(1) subsistence and technical commodity requirements per unit of output in each sector: $\mathbf{A}$;
(2) fractions of gross output consumed: λ_C, λ_I.

The quantity equations of the two-sector classical model then determine two variables:

(1) the non-negative rate of accumulation in a state of balanced growth: g;
(2) the ratio of gross outputs: Y_I/Y_C.

All the other variables follow: inputs in each sector, $a_{ij}Y_j$, i, $j = C$, I for any arbitrary outputs in the ratio Y_I/Y_C; the ratio of iron to corn in the stock of capital, K_I/K_C; the ratio of iron to corn in surplus output, $(Y_I - K_I)/(Y_C - K_C)$; and the rates of surplus in each sector, R_C and R_I.

This interpretation of the model has had a famous lineage since it is in the spirit of Neumann's analysis where consumption was treated as a fixed parameter.[4] The growth rate is then a variable to be maximized subject to the constraints of technology and the fixed proportions of output consumed. Anything that reduces consumption (by lowering λ_C or λ_I, or for that matter by lowering the customary level of subsistence) releases surplus for accumulation, and, through appropriate changes in the composition of output and of the means of production, allows for a higher rate of balanced growth. Accumulation of an ever expanding stock of produced means of production makes possible a larger future surplus—a theme which was fundamental to the conceptual scheme of the classical economists, especially those who wrote during the Industrial Revolution.

Appendix to Chapter 11

A generalization of the corn and iron model allows for n sectors of production where all inputs are simultaneously outputs. Commodity j, $j = 1, \ldots, n$ is produced by a constant-returns-to-scale process:

$$a_j = (a_{1j}, a_{2j}, \ldots, a_{nj}) \qquad j = 1, \ldots, n$$

where $a_{ij} \geq 0$ is the input of commodity i per unit of output of commodity j. Each process yields a single output. A set of processes, one for each commodity, defines a technique matrix:

$$\mathbf{A} = \begin{bmatrix} a_{11} & a_{12} & \cdots & a_{1n} \\ a_{21} & a_{22} & \cdots & a_{2n} \\ \cdot & \cdot & & \cdot \\ \cdot & \cdot & & \cdot \\ \cdot & \cdot & & \cdot \\ a_{n1} & a_{n2} & \cdots & a_{nn} \end{bmatrix}$$

The process vectors appear as the columns of $\mathbf{A}$; the rows define per-unit inputs of each commodity in the n sectors of production.

The technique matrix is viable if there exists a vector of gross outputs, $\mathbf{Y} = (Y_1, Y_2, \ldots, Y_n)$, the components of which are not less than the vector of total input requirements needed in their production. Net output in all sectors must be non-negative in order to allow for at least the replacement of the means of production. Formally:

$$a_{11} Y_1 + a_{12} Y_2 + \ldots + a_{1n} Y_n \leq Y_1$$
$$a_{21} Y_1 + a_{22} Y_2 + \ldots + a_{2n} Y_n \leq Y_2$$
$$\phantom{a_{21} Y_1 + a_{22} Y_2}\cdot \qquad \cdot \qquad \cdot \qquad \cdot \tag{A1}$$
$$a_{n1} Y_1 + a_{n2} Y_2 + \ldots + a_{nn} Y_n \leq Y_n$$
$$Y_j \geq 0 \qquad j = 1, \ldots, n$$

If the technique matrix is more than just viable, the set of relationships in (A1) can be satisfied as strict inequalities. Quantity equations are formed by subtracting from each gross output a proportion of that output, $\lambda_j Y_j$, $j = 1, \ldots, n$, measuring consumption of the net product, and adding to each sum of input requirements, $K_i = a_{i1} Y_1 + \ldots + a_{in} Y_n$, $i = 1, \ldots, n$, a sum, gK_i, $i = 1, \ldots, n$, measuring total accumulation of each commodity component of the stock of capital. Formally:

$$(a_{11} Y_1 + a_{12} Y_2 + \ldots + a_{1n} Y_n)(1 + g) = (1 - \lambda_1) Y_1$$
$$(a_{21} Y_1 + a_{22} Y_2 + \ldots + a_{2n} Y_n)(1 + g) = (1 - \lambda_2) Y_2$$
$$\phantom{(a_{21} Y_1 + a_{22} Y_2}\cdot \qquad \cdot \qquad \cdot \qquad \cdot \tag{A2}$$
$$(a_{n1} Y_1 + a_{n2} Y_2 + \ldots + a_{nn} Y_n)(1 + g) = (1 - \lambda_n) Y_n$$
$$Y_j \geq 0 \qquad j = 1, \ldots, n$$

Equations (A2) define a balanced growth path for any $g \leq g_{max}$. If $\lambda_j = \lambda$, $j = 1, \ldots, n$, rates of surplus, $R_j = (Y_j - K_i)/K_i = [(1 + g)/(1 - \lambda_j)] - 1$, $i = j = 1, \ldots, n$, have a common value, $R = [(1 + g)/(1 - \lambda)] - 1$. In that event R is equal to the maximum rate of balanced growth, g_{max}, given $\lambda = 0$. Hence:

$$1 + g_{max} = (1 + g)/(1 - \lambda)$$

or: $\lambda = \dfrac{g}{1 + g_{max}} + \dfrac{g_{max}}{1 + g_{max}}$ (A3)

This defines a linear trade-off between λ and g in an n-commodity model with equal rates of surplus in all sectors.

With unequal rates of surplus, the quantity equations may be written, after dividing each by $(1 - \lambda_j), j = 1, \ldots, n$, as:

$$(a_{11} Y_1 + a_{12} Y_2 + \ldots + a_{1n} Y_n)(1 + R_1) = Y_1$$

$$(a_{21} Y_1 + a_{22} Y_2 + \ldots + a_{2n} Y_n)(1 + R_2) = Y_2$$

$$\vdots \qquad \vdots \qquad \qquad \vdots \qquad \vdots \qquad \vdots \qquad \text{(A4)}$$

$$(a_{n1} Y_1 + a_{n2} Y_2 + \ldots + a_{nn} Y_n)(1 + R_n) = Y_n$$

In the notation of matrix algebra, this set of equations is simply:

$$\text{diag}(1 + R)\mathbf{A}\mathbf{Y} = \mathbf{Y} \qquad \text{(A4)}'$$

where $\mathbf{A}$ is the $n \times n$ technique matrix, $\mathbf{Y}$ is the column vector of gross outputs, and $\text{diag}(1 + R)$ is a diagonal matrix:

$$\begin{bmatrix} 1 + R_1 & 0 & \cdots & 0 \\ 0 & 1 + R_2 & \cdots & 0 \\ \cdot & \cdot & & \cdot \\ \cdot & \cdot & & \cdot \\ \cdot & \cdot & & \cdot \\ 0 & 0 & \cdots & 1 + R_n \end{bmatrix}$$

Rewriting (A4)' as:

$$[\mathbf{I} - \text{diag}(1 + R)\mathbf{A}]\mathbf{Y} = 0 \qquad \text{(A4)}''$$

it follows that there exists a nontrivial solution for the vector $\mathbf{Y}$, i.e., a solution such that $Y_j \neq 0$ for at least one value of j, if and only if the following determinant condition is satisfied:

$$|\mathbf{I} - \text{diag}(1 + R)\mathbf{A}| = 0 \tag{A5}$$

This imposes a restriction on the values of R_j, $j = 1, \ldots, n$ which is a generalization of (31). In the two-sector model (A5) reduces to (31) written:

$$(1 + R_1)(1 + R_2)(a_{11}a_{22} - a_{12}a_{21}) - (1 + R_1)a_{11} - (1 + R_2)a_{22} + 1 = 0 \tag{A5$'$}$$

using $1 + R_j = (1 + g)/(1 - \lambda_j)$, $j = 1,2$ instead of C, I as in the text.

In the case of equal rates of surplus (A4)″ becomes:

$$[\mathbf{I} - (1 + R)\mathbf{A}]\mathbf{Y} = 0 \tag{A4$'''$}$$

where R is a scalar, the uniform rate of surplus or maximum rate of balanced growth. To find $R = g_{max}$ it is necessary to solve:

$$|\mathbf{I} - (1 + R)\mathbf{A}| = 0 \tag{A5$'$}$$

This is a polynomial in R of, at most, order n. The relevant root is the smallest one since only then will the associated vector of net outputs be non-negative.

We have here provided only the briefest sketch of certain properties of an n-commodity classical model. The mathematical results that lie behind the theory have to do with generalizations of the Perron-Frobenius theorems for non-negative square matrices.[5]

Notes

1. Piero Sraffa, *Production of Commodities by Means of Commodities. Prelude to a Critique of Economic Theory,* Cambridge University Press, 1960, p. 93.
2. The viability condition is also referred to in the literature as the Hawkins-Simon condition. See D. Hawkins and H. A. Simon, "Note: Some Conditions of Macroeconomic Stability," *Econometrica,* Vol. 17 (1949), pp. 245–48.
3. John von Neumann, "A Model of General Economic Equilibrium," *Review of Economic Studies,* Vol. 13 (1945–46), pp. 1–9. For a full reference see chapter 1, note 2.
4. *Ibid.*
5. See Michio Morishima, *Equilibrium Stability, and Growth. A Multi-sectoral Analysis,* Oxford at the Clarendon Press, 1964, pp. 195–215.

12

The Classical Theory of Surplus
and the Accumulation of Capital:
Dual Price Relations

> The rate of profits and of interest must depend on the proportion of production to the consumption necessary to such production,—this again essentially depends upon the cheapness of provisions, which is after all, whatever intervals we may be willing to allow, the great regulator of the wages of labour.
>
> DAVID RICARDO [1]

For the classical economists the structure of society was an important element in the analysis of how a surplus arises in production and is then allocated among different uses. An analysis of the price relations of our model brings out this aspect of their theory.

In the quantity relations of the last chapter the coefficients of production were interpreted as including not only certain technical commodity requirements, but also a necessary input of commodities consumed by those directly engaged in the process of production. But we did not have to identify this group with any particular social class. They might be peasant farmers with traditional rights to the land, or "free" laborers seeking work in return for wages, or perhaps robots in some space-age economy that require some form of maintenance. And, although we specified certain fractions of gross output of corn and iron consumed, treating this consumption as part of surplus output, we did not identify the consumers of surplus as a particular social group. They may be landed gentry receiving traditionally determined rents, a ruling bureaucracy with taxing powers, or a capitalist class with control over the means of production. Consumption out of surplus may even be regarded as an addition to subsistence.

To further analyze the two-sector model of surplus and accumulation, these social relations must be made more definite. Since our primary interest lies in the analysis of capitalism, we identify those directly engaged in production as laborers without property in the means of production as opposed to capitalists who own the stock of commodity capital and make decisions regarding the composition and allocation of surplus output.* It should be noted, however, that neoclassical economists, used to thinking in terms of post-Walrasian allocation theory, might object that even under capitalism—especially twentieth century capitalism—social distinctions are of no consequence in economic analysis. Do not workers frequently own capital in the form of financial claims that yield them a share of profits through the payments of dividends and interest? And do not "capitalists" provide labor services in the form of management services and entrepreneurial talent which is, in principle, just like any other kind of labor? And, as for the idle landowners who played such an important role in classical analysis (though not in our simple models), where are they now? Even if one occasionally finds a pure rentier living off accumulated wealth, is he not being paid for a factor service in the form of finance still committed to some business enterprise, i.e., is he not being rewarded for postponing the consumption of his wealth?†

Such arguments have been advanced against the notion that social class should be given any specific analytical role in economic theory. Certainly, within neoclassical theory, there is a good reason for denying that social divisions have any explanatory role to play in determining prices, quantities, and income. Since every category of income is already determined within the structure of theory, as a payment corresponding to the marginal or scarcity value of some given factor of production, there can be no role for social class or any other parameter as a further basis for explaining these incomes. Given the parametric distribution of ownership of the factors of production in neoclassical theory, any additional structure would overdetermine the model.

The point is not, therefore, that under modern capitalism class distinctions have become blurred. Rather, it is that neoclassical allocation theory makes no *analytical* distinction between an economy in which the distribution of ownership of the means of production is, for example, egalitarian, and one in which workers have only labor services to sell to capitalists. Neoclassical models of these two economies would differ in their specification of factor ownership, but there would be no other difference in the structure of the

---

* One might include in the class of capitalists those who obtain a share of the surplus output in the form of interest income simply because they have acquired some accumulation of financial wealth, but who do not take any active part in decisions regarding production. We shall not, however, include this complication here.

† Abstinence, defined as postponement of consumption associated with the holding of physical wealth, both land and capital, has at various points in the history of economic analysis provided the basis for a "subjective" theory of interest, profit, and even rent. Maurice Dobb has written a critical survey of these theories.[2]

model or in the method of analysis. Each is viewed as a particular case of a system of exchange in which given resources are allocated among alternative uses.

This point of view about class becomes untenable as soon as one abandons the assumption that resources are given, thereby allowing for reproducible inputs and with that the concept of surplus. In a market economy it follows immediately that there must be certain categories of income that correspond to the surplus.* Rents and (later) profits were the obvious candidates to the classical economists who then developed their analysis in terms of the behavior of the social classes receiving these incomes. In this way social class and surplus were inextricably bound up in the analysis, and the consequence of this link was profit. Indeed, one might say that in any analysis of capitalism it is only by systematically removing surplus as an analytical category (as happens in neoclassical allocation theory) that one removes at one and the same time the relevance of social class and the existence of profit in the classical sense. Relative scarcity can then take over as the basis for interpreting prices; class behavior becomes irrelevant. As a result, any effort to introduce profit into neoclassical theory must, of logical necessity, interpret it as a return to a scarce factor—it cannot be analyzed as a category of income specific to a particular social system.

It is for these reasons that, in the present analysis of income distribution and relative prices in classical theory, we make quite specific assumptions about the division of society by class: capitalists own the stock of capital goods and hire laborers who own only their labor-power. Moreover, wages are for the moment considered fixed in terms of a subsistence bundle of commodities, although this assumption will be relaxed in the next chapter. Finally, competition among capitalists is taken to mean that, in equilibrium, the rate of profit is equalized among all sectors of production. This is crucial to the theory's explanation of the allocation of surplus output and of capital goods designated for replacement of used up stock.

Profits in a One-Sector Corn Model

The one-sector corn model remains a useful starting point in our analysis because, in such a model, there can be no problem of determining relative prices; the price of corn in terms of itself is unity. The only problem lies in determining the distribution of income, and although that, too, is almost triv-

---

*This is a consequence of duality between quantity and price relations in a general equilibrium model of the classical type.

ial, its solution points up an interesting and important aspect of models of surplus and accumulation; namely, the relationship between the rate of profit and the rate of growth.

We start with a viable corn economy in which surplus is non-negative:

$$a_{cc} Y_C \leq Y_C \quad \text{or} \quad 1 - a_{cc} \geq 0 \tag{1}$$

A rate of profit r on an investment in corn is then simply the rate of surplus R: the ratio of net output to the stock of corn since wages are fixed at subsistence and included in the specification of technology. Thus:

$$r = \frac{Y_C - a_{cc} Y_C}{a_{cc} Y_C} = (1/a_{cc}) - 1 = R \tag{2}$$

Here we have the simplest case of duality in classical theory: the rate of profit and the rate of surplus are not only reflections of viability—they are identical.

Condition (1) ensures that the rate of profit is non-negative in the following price equation for the one-sector model where we introduce somewhat artificially an indeterminate, nominal price of corn P_C:

$$P_C a_{cc}(1 + r) = P_C \tag{3}$$

or:
$$a_{cc}(1 + r) = 1 \tag{3'}$$

The cost of replacing the means of production, $P_C a_{cc}$ in nominal terms or a_{cc} in terms of corn, plus the rate of profit on the value of this capital investment, $r P_C a_{cc}$ in nominal terms or $r a_{cc}$ in terms of corn, is just equal to the price of corn, P_C or 1 in terms of the commodity itself. The rate of profit is a variable determined by technology (which includes the cost of labor in terms of corn), whereas P_C is an indeterminate nominal price which cancels out on both sides of (3). (It is introduced to show why it is indeterminate, and to provide a form for the price equation which is comparable to the price equations for a two-sector model discussed below.)

In a corn model the rate of profit is a ratio of physically homogeneous quantities: net corn output to the stock of corn used up during the period of production; and for this reason r depends simply on the technology of production. But subsistence consumption of workers per unit of output is included as part of the capitalists' investment in corn. It is this assumption that yields a determinate rate of profit, for as Ricardo remarked, "The rate of profits . . . must depend on the proportion of production . . . necessary to such production,"[3] where "necessary" includes both technical and social requirements per unit of output.

The relationship between the rate of profit and the allocation of the surplus is easy to see. Since $r = (1/a_{CC}) - 1$ is determined by technology alone, it follows that the rate of profit is independent of whether the surplus is used for accumulation of capital or for consumption. Recalling the consumption-growth trade-off (chapter 11, eq. (7)):

$$\lambda_C = -a_{CC}g + (1 - a_{CC})$$

it follows that only when $\lambda_C = 0$ will the rate of growth be equal to the rate of profit and the rate of surplus: $g = g_{max} = (1/a_{CC}) - 1 = r = R$. Thus, whenever $\lambda_C > 0$, the rate of profit and the rate of surplus are bound to exceed the rate of growth. The difference between r and g (or R and g) can therefore be used as a measure of the extent to which surplus is consumed, reflecting the capitalists' decision to accumulate corn at a less than maximal rate.

Price Equations in a Two-Sector Model

In generalizing our analysis of profit in the corn model it is evident that we cannot begin by defining the rate of profit as a ratio of *homogeneous* quantities—a physical ratio of surplus to the stock of capital. This is because although we assume only one output in each sector,* there is now more than one input.† The stock of capital is a heterogeneous bundle of commodities which cannot simply be added up since corn and iron have different units of measurement. If the rate of profit is to be expressed as a ratio of surplus to stock, it will therefore be necessary in forming such a ratio to know the relative prices of the various components of the stock. Only then can these components be added up to obtain a measure of the value of capital, and only then can surplus in either sector be measured in terms of the units of capital thereby determining a percentage rate of profit.

In a two-commodity model there is one rate of exchange which may be expressed in our example as the iron price of corn, P_C/P_I, or the corn price of iron, P_I/P_C. It is this ratio that we need to know in order to measure the stock of capital in each sector, either as a quantity of corn or as a quantity of iron. Nominal prices are introduced into the analysis and then one commodity is chosen as *numeraire*. We shall use iron.

In the corn sector the nominal value of commodity inputs per unit of output is $P_C a_{CC} + P_I a_{IC}$; while in the iron sector it is $P_C a_{CI} + P_I a_{II}$. To begin our

---

* Joint production is ruled out in all our models.
† Recall Malthus's letter to F. Horner in which he pointed out that the consumption of workers will generally consist of more than just corn. See above, p. 93.

analysis suppose that these unit costs measuring the required investment per unit of output are just equal to the price of the product in each sector. Thus:

$$P_C a_{CC} + P_I a_{IC} = P_C \tag{4}$$

$$P_C a_{CI} + P_I a_{II} = P_I \tag{5}$$

From these equations it is easily shown that surplus must be zero,* and so it follows that if the technology admits a surplus it cannot be the case that unit cost is equal to price in each sector. Prices must instead exceed cost giving rise to profit. This dual property of the model, that profits arise in the price relations if and only if surplus exists in the quantity relations, is developed by first of all rewriting (4) and (5) as inequalities:†

$$P_C a_{CC} + P_I a_{IC} \leq P_C \tag{6}$$

$$P_C a_{CI} + P_I a_{II} \leq P_I \tag{7}$$

We now introduce r, the ratio of profit to the value of capital, which is uniform across sectors on the assumption that capitalists are free to move from one line of production to another so that no permanent difference in profit rates can be sustained, an assumption which was a basic element in Smith's analysis of surplus and accumulation. In per-unit terms, the value of capital is that of the commodities used up in producing a unit of either corn or iron, and profit is the excess of price over this value. Price equations therefore incorporate r in the following way:

$$(P_C a_{CC} + P_I a_{IC})(1 + r) = P_C \tag{8}$$

$$(P_C a_{CI} + P_I a_{II})(1 + r) = P_I \tag{9}$$

The dual form of the quantity and price equations of the two-sector model is now apparent from a comparison of (8) and (9) with equations (10) and (11) of chapter 11. Coefficients in each of the price equations are lined up as columns in the two quantity equations; outputs are replaced by prices; and rates of surplus by the uniform rate of profit.

Although rates of surplus in the quantity equations are ratios of homoge-

* Solve each equation for the price ratio:

$$P_C/P_I = a_{IC}/(1 - a_{CC}) \text{ and } P_C/P_I = (1 - a_{II})/a_{CI}$$

so that, equating right-hand sides:

$$(1 - a_{CC})(1 - a_{II}) - a_{CI}a_{IC} = 0$$

which is the condition for a zero surplus.
† If the inequalities ran the other way, the technology would not be viable. Thus, the existence of a surplus implies (6) and (7).

neous quantities, the rate of profit in the price equations is not: it is neither the physical corn surplus divided by the requirement of corn (in one or both sectors); nor is it the physical iron surplus divided by the requirement of iron (in one or both sectors). Rather, it is a ratio of values that can only be discovered by simultaneously determining the price ratio P_C/P_I, a modern variant of a problem faced by Ricardo early in his work. There are different ways to state the problem formally. One might solve each of the price equations for the rate of profit, thereby showing how the price ratio enters into defining the ratio of profit to capital in each sector.* It is a little more straightforward, however, to solve the price equations in terms of P_C/P_I, showing how this ratio depends on r:

$$P_C/P_I = \frac{a_{IC}(1+r)}{1 - a_{CC}(1+r)} \tag{10}$$

$$P_C/P_I = \frac{1 - a_{II}(1+r)}{a_{CI}(1+r)} \tag{11}$$

Equating the right-hand sides, cross multiplying, and rearranging terms we obtain a quadratic equation in r:

$$(1+r)^2(a_{CC}a_{II} - a_{CI}a_{IC}) - (1+r)(a_{CC} + a_{II}) + 1 = 0 \tag{12}$$

As in the corn model the rate of profit depends only on the input–output coefficients, although the relationship is more complicated now that there are four coefficients instead of one. Notice again that since subsistence is included along with strictly technical requirements in the specification of these coefficients, it is, in effect, the given wage together with the technically required commodity inputs that determines the rate of profit, echoing once more Ricardo's dictum which heads this chapter.

A further similarity with the corn model exists in the relationship between the rate of profit and the rate of growth. In the simpler case consumption out of surplus implied $g < r$, and the same result holds here. If consumption out of surplus is zero, $\lambda_C = 0 = \lambda_I$ in the quantity equations and the rate of growth is found as the solution to equation (34) in chapter 11:

$$(1+g)^2(a_{CC}a_{II} - a_{CI}a_{IC}) - (1+g)(a_{CC} + a_{II}) + 1 = 0$$

---

* The price equations would be written as follows where per-unit profit and per unit value of capital in each sector appear in numerator and denominator, respectively:

$$r = \frac{P_j - (P_C a_{Cj} + P_I a_{Ij})}{(P_C a_{Cj} + P_I a_{Ij})} \qquad j = C, I$$

But this has exactly the form of (12) so that the rate of profit is equal to the *maximum* rate of growth.* We conclude that any excess of r over g is a measure of the extent to which surplus is consumed by the capitalists rather than being invested in an expanding stock of capital. In this respect the one- and two-sector models are the same.

With the rate of profit determined by technology as the solution to (12) it follows that the price ratio is simultaneously determined as the solution to (10) or (11). This is the ratio consistent with a uniform rate of profit in both sectors, and that is the sense in which prices are equilibrium prices in a classical model. This interpretation is perhaps clearest within the context of an example to which we now turn.

A Numerical Illustration of the Allocation of Surplus

The input–output coefficients used in chapter 11 provide the basis for an illustration of the relationship between the relative price of corn in terms of iron and the rate of profit. We take as given the matrix:

$$\mathbf{A} = \begin{bmatrix} a_{CC} & a_{IC} \\ a_{CI} & a_{II} \end{bmatrix} = \begin{bmatrix} .4 & .2 \\ .2 & .7 \end{bmatrix}$$

Price equations are written:

$$(.4P_C + .2P_I)(1 + r) = P_C \tag{8'}$$

$$(.2P_C + .7P_I)(1 + r) = P_I \tag{9'}$$

so that:

$$P_C/P_I = \frac{.2(1 + r)}{1 - .4(1 + r)} \tag{10'}$$

$$P_C/P_I = \frac{1 - .7(1 + r)}{.2(1 + r)} \tag{11'}$$

Equating the right-hand sides and simplifying:

$$.24(1 + r)^2 - 1.1(1 + r) + 1 = 0 \tag{12'}$$

A value of $r = .25$ satisfies this equation and, on substitution into (10)' or (11)', the relative price ratio is found to be $P_C/P_I = .5$.†

---

* Also, recall that the rate of profit is equal to the rate of surplus when the latter is uniform. See the discussion following equation (34) in chapter 11.

† The other, larger root for r in (12)' is to be ignored since on substitution into (10)' or (11)' it determines a meaningless negative price ratio.

Suppose the economy under consideration is accumulating stocks of corn and iron at the maximum rate of balanced growth which, from the solution to equation (34) of chapter 11, is $g = g_{max} = .25$. Using the relevant illustration in the third line of Table 11-1, gross output of corn is 20 units so that inputs into that sector are 8 units of corn and 4 units of iron, while in the iron sector where gross output is 40, inputs are 8 units of corn and 28 units of iron. Schematically:

$$\begin{array}{l} 8 \text{ units of corn} + 4 \text{ units of iron} \rightarrow 20 \text{ units of corn} \\ 8 \text{ units of corn} + 28 \text{ units of iron} \rightarrow 40 \text{ units of iron} \\ \hline 16 \text{ units of corn} + 32 \text{ units of iron} \end{array}$$

Each output is 25% larger than the total amount of the corresponding input, summed over both sectors. Since the total surplus is allocated to accumulation, the maximum rate of balanced growth is achieved in all components of the stock of capital.

Now, consider the following problem. At the end of a period of production each capitalist has either a stock of corn or a stock of iron. Corn producers, in order to restore their capital and, in the present case, to augment it by 25% must purchase iron from iron producers; and, of course, iron producers are in the same position vis à vis corn producers since they must purchase corn in order to reconstitute and augment their own stocks. The relative price ratio that allows the necessary exchange to take place while ensuring a uniform rate of profit is just that ratio P_C/P_I that satisfies the price equations of the model. Thus, if $P_C/P_I = .5$, the iron sector capitalists can keep 35 units of iron (25% more than the 28 units in their initial stock) and sell the remaining 5 units of iron to corn sector capitalists in exchange for 10 units of corn (also 25% more than the 8 units in their initial stock). The corn producers, having sold 10 units are left with 10 units (25% more than the 8 units of corn in their initial stock) and have acquired in the exchange 5 units of iron (which is also 25% more than the 4 units in their initial stock). This exchange allows all stocks to grow by $g = 25\%$.

As for profits, if we use the same price ratio, $P_C/P_I = .5$, to calculate the value of capital in each sector, the corn sector capitalists have an initial stock worth 8 units of iron (8 units of corn times the relative price of corn plus 4 units of iron); and since the iron value of the corn they produce is 10 (20 units of corn times the price ratio), it follows that profit in that sector is 2 which is 25% of the value of the capital stock. In the iron sector, the value of initial capital is 32 units of iron (8 units of corn times the price ratio plus 28 units of iron); and since the iron value of the output of iron is simply 40 (since this is the *numeraire* commodity) it follows that net profit is 8 which is also 25% of the value of capital. The same rate of profit is realized in both sectors after allowing for replacement of stock.

It is an important feature of the present model that the same relative price ratio and profit rate characterize all equilibrium solutions to the model regardless of the composition and allocation of surplus output. For example, in the first line of Table 11-1 where surplus exists entirely in the form of iron, flows of production appear as follows:

6 units of corn +   3 units of iron   →15 units of corn
9 units of corn + 31.5 units of iron →45 units of iron

15 units of corn + 34.5 units of iron

And the same question arises: what relative price P_C/P_I is consistent with an exchange of commodities that replenishes the stock of capital in each sector, allocates the surplus of iron, and yields an equal rate of profit on the value of capital in each sector? To illustrate the solution, corn sector capitalists sell 9 units of corn to iron sector capitalists leaving for themselves only what they need for replacement of stock, namely, 6 units of corn, since there is no accumulation of stock. At $P_C/P_I = .5$, this yields the corn sector 4.5 units of iron which is 1.5 units more than what is necessary for replacement of stock. Meanwhile the iron sector has the corn needed for the next cycle of production plus the remaining iron, 40.5 units, which is 9 more than what is necessary for replacement of stock. The allocation of surplus iron for consumption is therefore 1.5 units to the corn sector and 9 units to the iron sector. This is not the imbalance it appears to be, however, since the *value* of capital in the corn sector is 6 units of iron and in the iron sector 36 units of iron. Thus, the ratio of allocated surplus to the value of capital is 1.5/6 = 25% in the corn sector and 9/36 = 25% in the iron sector. Again, the profit rate is equalized.

At the other extreme where surplus exists entirely in corn, gross and net outputs are given by the last line in Table 11-1, and input–output flows appear as:

14.4 units of corn +   7.2 units of iron→ 36 units of corn
4.8 units of corn + 16.8 units of iron→ 24 units of iron

19.2 units of corn + 24 units of iron

Despite this difference in the composition of output, the solution to the problem of allocating surplus in such a way as to equalize the profit rate still requires a rate of exchange, $P_C/P_I = .5$ or, more conveniently in this case,

$P_I/P_C = 2$. Iron sector capitalists sell 7.2 units of iron in exchange for 14.4 units of corn leaving themselves with 16.8 units of iron and 4.8 units of corn for replacement of stock plus an extra 9.6 units of corn for consumption. As a result, corn sector capitalists have the necessary stock of 7.2 units of iron and 14.4 units of corn for the next cycle of production plus another 7.2 units of corn for consumption. This is an equilibrium allocation of surplus corn since each quantity bears a uniform proportion to the value of capital in each sector. (In the corn sector this value is 28.8 units of corn of which the allocated surplus corn is 25%; and in the iron sector capital is valued at 38.4 units of corn of which the allocated surplus is also 25%.)

These examples and others (see the remaining two lines in Table 11-1) illustrate a distinguishing property of classical models: relative prices and the rate of profit are independent of the composition of gross and net output. And, since the composition of the stock of capital goods varies with the composition of output it follows that the rate of profit is independent of the mix of corn and iron in the means of production. In particular, the rate of profit is not related to any concept of relative scarcity of factors of production since commodity inputs in a classical model are variables and not parameters of its structure.

To see the contrast between the determinants of the uniform rate of profit in classical theory and the determinants of factor prices in neoclassical theory, it is helpful to analyze one of the cases just considered in terms of neoclassical theory. This requires that we treat stocks of corn and iron as given resources, i.e., as parameters. On that interpretation the third line in Table 11.1, for example, would have to be characterized as an situation in which available factor services are $F_C = 16$ units of corn and $F_I = 32$ units of iron. Using the same technical coefficients (but interpreting them as factor requirements per unit of final output), resource and price constraints, illustrated in Figure 12-1, are written just as in chapters 8 and 9:

$$F_C \geq a_{CC} Y_C + a_{CI} Y_I \qquad \text{or} \qquad 16 \geq .4Y_C + .2Y_I \qquad (13)$$

$$F_I \geq a_{IC} Y_C + a_{II} Y_I \qquad \text{or} \qquad 32 \geq .2Y_C + .7Y_I \qquad (14)$$

$$Y_C \geq 0 \qquad Y_I \geq 0 \qquad (15)$$

$$w_C a_{CC} + w_I a_{IC} \geq p \qquad \text{or} \qquad .4w_C + .2w_I \geq p \qquad (16)$$

$$w_C a_{CI} + w_I a_{II} \geq 1 \qquad \text{or} \qquad .2w_C + .7w_I \geq 1 \qquad (17)$$

$$w_C \geq 0 \qquad w_I \geq 0 \qquad p \geq 0 \qquad (18)$$

where Y_C, Y_I, and $p = P_C/P_I$ have the same interpretation as in the classical model, but where w_C and w_I are factor prices measuring the relative scarcity of the services of corn and iron in production.

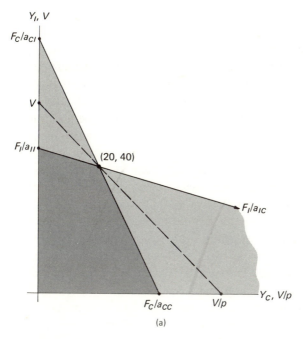

(a)

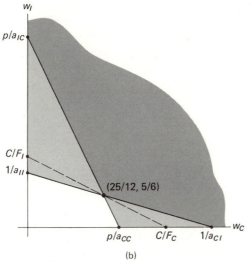

(b)

Figure 12-1. A neoclassical treatment of the classical model, given $(F_C, F_I) = (16, 32)$, $(a_{CC}, a_{IC}) = (.4, .2)$, $(a_{CI}, a_{II}) = (.2, .7)$.

(a) Feasible outputs. Total value, $V = pY_C + Y_I = 60$, is a maximum at $(Y_C, Y_I) = 20, 40)$ given $p = 1$.

(b) Feasible factor prices, given $p = 1$. Total factor cost, $C = w_C F_C + w_I F_I = 60$, is a minimum at $(w_C, w_I) = (25/12, 5/6)$.

The profit rate does not appear in the price relations (16) and (17), nor is there any surplus in the quantity relations (13) and (14). Moreover, it is no longer necessary or meaningful to make any assumption on the viability of technology since all that the neoclassical theory requires is that the coefficients be non-negative and finite, and that each process require an input of at least one factor. Commodity interest rates,* however, can be defined even in this static allocation model if it is assumed that the allocation in question is but one in a sequence of allocations. Factors are outputs of a previous equilibrium of supply and demand (although they are regarded as different commodities in neoclassical theory since they occur in a different time period†), while current outputs will either be consumed or become factors in a "future" allocation. We may then give the following interpretation to prices. When producing agents buy the factor services of, say, iron from resource owners for w_I per unit (measured in terms of iron as *numeraire*) the commodity rate of interest on iron is positive if and only if w_I exceeds unity. Thus, if $w_I = 1.25$, iron as a factor can be sold for 25% more than it costs to buy at the end of the production period.‡ Similarly, if w_C is 25% greater than P_C/P_I, resource owners can sell the factor services of corn for 25% more than its end-of-production-period price. In this particular case commodity interest rates are therefore equalized.

A relationship among factor and commodity prices in a neoclassical model that results in equal commodity rates of interest is, of course, entirely fortuitous since it requires that demand be such that the equilibrium solution to the price relations (16) and (17) is, in our example, $(P_C/P_I, w_C, w_I) = (.5, .625, 1.25)$. Suppose, therefore, since there is no reason not to, that the parameters of demand are such that only at the price $P_C/P_I = 1$ is there no excess demand for goods or factors (the neoclassical concept of equilibrium). Production occurs at the maximum value output, $(Y_C, Y_I) = (20, 40)$ in Figure 12-1(a); and factor prices are given by the minimum cost point, $(w_C, w_I) = (5/6, 25/12)$ in Figure 12-1(b). It follows that the corn rate of interest is -16.6% and the iron rate of interest is 108.3%.§ Now, there is nothing wrong with this solution to

---

*See chapter 9, pp. 234–7.

† See the remarks of Koopmans quoted above, p. 234.

‡ Since we assume that commodity inputs are used up in the process of production (depreciation is 100%), iron cannot simply be returned to resource owners by producing agents who have utilized its services in production. For this reason resource owners are to be thought of as maintaining their factor endowments through repurchase of commodities, and that is why we say the factor is bought at the end of the production period.

§ The corn rate of interest is the ratio of the factor price for corn as an input to the commodity price of corn as an output. This determines a gross rate of return to the resource owner. Then subtract one, the rate of depreciation of corn in production (100%), in order to account for the buying back of corn to replace the used-up factor. Hence, $[w_C/(P_C/P_I)] - 1 = -1/6$. The iron rate of interest is easier to calculate since w_I is already expressed in terms of iron: $w_I - 1 = 13/12$.

the neoclassical version of our classical model since there is nothing in an equilibrium of supply and demand (with given factors) to guarantee positive commodity rates of interest, much less *equal* rates of interest. Classical theory, on the other hand, builds into the structure of its models the equilibrium condition of a uniform rate of profit which, as we have remarked, may be interpreted to mean that capitalists are free to shift among various lines of production until profit rates are equalized and the stock of produced inputs is made appropriate to the composition of output. Equilibrium prices in a classical model show how the surplus is allocated through exchange among capitalists in such a way as to generate a uniform profit rate; whereas, in neoclassical theory equilibrium prices correspond to zero excess demand in a system in which factors (unlike the produced commodity inputs of a classical model) are given parameters. The derived commodity rates of interest in neoclassical theory do not correspond to the classical concept of a uniform rate of profit.

A Relationship Between Prices and Technology

In a subsistence wage model of classical theory there is an interpretation of prices which is of particular interest since it yields a graph of the relative price ratio. We begin by rewriting (10) and (11) as:

$$P_C/P_I = a'_{IC}/(1 - a'_{CC}) \tag{19}$$

$$P_C/P_I = (1 - a'_{II})/a'_{CI} \tag{20}$$

where $a'_{ij} = a_{ij}(1 + r)$, and so, in our example $(a'_{CC}, a'_{IC}) = (.5, .25)$ and $(a'_{CI}, a'_{II}) = (.25, .875)$ using $1 + r = 1.25$, the solution to $(12)'$. The coefficients, $a'_{ij}, i, j = C, I$, are larger than the original input–output requirements by just enough to cause the vectors drawn through the relevant points in quadrants II and IV of Figure 12-2 to form a straight line passing through the origin. Thus, by multiplying each coefficient by $1 + r$, the entire surplus disappears, as it were, into profits. As (19) and (20) show, the common slope of the new pair of net-of-profit activity vectors measures (apart from a negative sign) the relative price of corn in terms of iron.[4] We therefore obtain a graph of the price ratio P_C/P_I consistent with a uniform rate of profit.

The commodity price ratio may also be interpreted as the rate at which commodity inputs in each sector can be varied while leaving the rate of profit on the value of capital unchanged. To show this, draw through the end points of the activity vectors in quadrant III of Figure 12-2 a pair of lines each having a slope given by the (negative) price ratio, $-P_C/P_I = -.5$. It can then be shown that any pair of process vectors, one for corn and one for iron, ending in points belonging to these respective lines, defines a technology matrix that

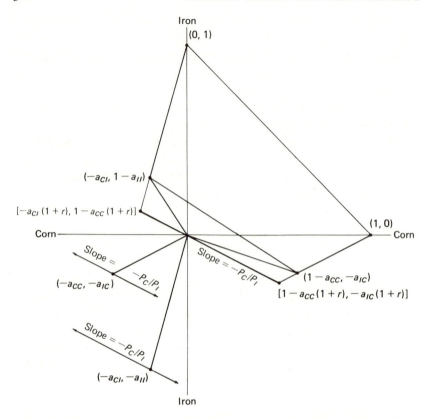

Figure 12-2. Relative price of corn in terms of iron. Given the technology in Figure 11-2, $P_C/P_I = .5$ and $r = .25$. Any pair of activity vectors ending in points along the negatively sloped lines in quadrant III will determine the same profit rate and price ratio.

yields an unchanged rate of profit, $r = .25\%$. The proof is straightforward. Substitute for (a_{CC}, a_{IC}) and (a_{CI}, a_{II}) in equations (10) and (11) new coefficients $(a_{CC} + \Delta a_{CC}, a_{IC} + \Delta a_{IC})$ and $(a_{CI} + \Delta a_{CI}, a_{II} + \Delta a_{II})$ where $\Delta a_{IC}/\Delta a_{CC} = -P_C/P_I = \Delta a_{II}/\Delta a_{CI}$. Then, after simplifying, it will be found that the solution for P_C/P_I is unchanged; and, by a similar substitution in (12), the solution for r will be shown unchanged. Alternatively, substitute the new coefficients directly in (8) and (9) on the assumption that the ratio of changes, $\Delta a_{Ij}/\Delta a_{Cj}, j = C, I$, is equal to $-P_C/P_I$ and it will be seen immediately that the price equations are unchanged and that their solution is therefore unchanged.*

* It may be noted here that other sets of coefficients not belonging to the two parallel lines in quadrant III of Figure 12-2 can still yield the same rate of profit, $r = 25\%$, if not the same price

It is this result that allows the price ratio to be interpreted as a measure of the rate at which changes in commodity requirements per unit of output can occur without altering the solution for the uniform rate of profit, and in this sense the price ratio measures a technologically determined trade-off (one which will play a role in our discussion of choice of technique in chapter 15). There are, however, two points to be made in connection with this interpretation of prices.

First, although the hypothetical changes in input–output requirements just considered leave the solution to the price equations unchanged, the solution to the quantity equations *does* change (except in special cases). Suppose, for example, that technology is given by:

$$(a_{CC}, \, a_{IC}) = (.2, \, .3) \qquad \text{and} \qquad (a_{CI}, \, a_{II}) = (.8, \, .4)$$

where, relative to our previous coefficients, $\Delta a_{Ij}/\Delta a_{Cj} = -P_C/P_I = -.5$, $j = C, I$. The rate of profit and price ratio remain what they were, but on substitution of the new technology into the quantity equations of chapter 11, it will be found that the ratio of outputs corresponding, for example, to the maximum rate of balanced growth (or simply equal rates of surplus) is $Y_I/Y_C = 3/4$ instead of 2 as in the third line of Table 11-1.*

Second, and more important, this technologically oriented interpretation of prices is valid only on the assumption that wages are given, as in the present analysis, by a fixed basket of commodities or subsistence wage included in the specification of technology. In a model with a variable wage the same result holds in terms of a link between prices and technology, but, again, only when the rate of wages (or of profits) has been given. This will be evident in the price equations of the next chapter where labor is treated as a separate input and where the wage rate is made explicit.

Parameters, Variables, and the Role of Demand

In concluding our discussion of a two-sector subsistence wage model of surplus and accumulation, we again take up the question of parameters and variables: what is given and what is determined? For this purpose it is useful to bring together the four relationships which have thus far defined the model:

ratio, $P_C/P_I = .5$. An example is $(a_{CC}, \, a_{IC}) = (56/115, \, 12/575)$ and $(a_{CI}, \, a_{II}) = (6, \, 0.4)$ for which $P_C/P_I = 1/15$.
* A table of values for gross and net output, such as the one used in the preceding chapter to describe points along the surplus possibilities schedule, may be drawn up for the present technology. For convenience of calculation, let the sum of units of gross output be 42 and let ψ take on the values, 1/2, 4/7, and 2/3. The resulting input–output flows illustrate, respectively, a surplus of iron only, equal rates of surplus, and a surplus of corn only.

$$(a_{CC} Y_C + a_{CI} Y_I)(1 + g) = (1 - \lambda_C) Y_C \qquad (21)$$

$$(a_{IC} Y_C + a_{II} Y_I)(1 + g) = (1 - \lambda_I) Y_I \qquad (22)$$

$$(P_C a_{CC} + P_I a_{IC})(1 + r) = P_C \qquad (23)$$

$$(P_C a_{CI} + P_I a_{II})(1 + r) = P_I \qquad (24)$$

At the end of chapter 11 two parameters were specified, giving enough information to determine the solution to the quantity equations (21) and (22). These data were the technical coefficients of production (including subsistence) and the fractions of gross output consumed, subject to the condition that the technology be at least viable and (implicitly) that the fractions of output consumed over and above subsistence be non-negative. The rate of accumulation was then determined along with the ratio of iron to corn in gross and net output and in the means of production.

In the price relations, technology alone (given subsistence) is sufficient for determining the rate of profit and the price ratio. Consequently, the solution to (23) and (24) is independent of the solution to (21) and (22) in the sense that the allocation of the surplus, whether to consumption or accumulation of capital, does not affect the determination of the profit rate or associated prices. But, although one may therefore conclude that in classical theory distribution and prices are independent of allocations of inputs and outputs, a reverse linkage from prices to quantities *can* be established if the proportions of gross outputs consumed by the capitalists are sensitive to the price ratio, given their preferences for corn and iron as consumption goods. In this way the choices of capitalists concerning the use to which surplus is put can affect the composition of output without there being any reciprocal effect since prices and the profit rate are the same whatever the allocation of the surplus.

The independence of prices from quantities is evident in our numerical example. Thus, we have seen that a 5% growth rate is consistent with two different allocations of the remaining surplus to consumption. (The second and fourth lines of Table 11-1 satisfy the quantity equations for $(g, \lambda_C, \lambda_I) = (.05, .09, .175)$ and $(.05, .37, .055)$, respectively.) And yet, the relative price ratio and uniform profit rate are the same in each case. Now, we are certainly free to interpret these two situations as differing only in respect of the preferences of capitalists for surplus corn and iron as consumption goods, given the relative price ratio (which is unchanged) and their individual profit incomes. Indeed, every difference in net output along the surplus possibilities schedule may be so interpreted.

Formally, capitalists' consumption, written $(X_C, X_I) = (\lambda_C Y_C, \lambda_I Y_I)$, may be regarded as the solution to maximizing utility subject to a budget constraint (as in chapter 10), the latter equating the value of commodities consumed to the profits not earmarked for accumulation. The simplest procedure is to assume that capitalists have similar tastes and can therefore be aggregated into one giant Capitalist.[5] Moreover, the preferences of the Capitalist are assumed to be such that "a proportional change in the quantities of goods [consumed] does not give rise to any change in the preference ordering."[6] As a result, consumption out of profits is split between the two commodities, corn and iron, in proportions that vary only with the relative price ratio; in particular, they are independent of the level of profits.[7] To express this in equations we need some additional notation. Recalling our use of K_i, $i = C, I$ to measure physical stocks of capital, $a_{iC} Y_C + a_{iI} Y_I$, $i = C, I$, we define the value of the stock of capital as:

$$K = P_C K_C + P_I K_I \tag{25}$$

in nominal terms, and in terms of either commodity as *numeraire:*

$$K/P_I = (P_C/P_I)K_C + K_I \tag{25}'$$
$$K/P_C = K_C + (P_I/P_C)K_C \tag{25}''$$

Total profit, in nominal terms, is simply the rate of profit times the value of capital rK; whereas the nominal value of the addition to the stock of capital is gK, since in (25) the increments to the commodity components of the stock of capital are gK_C and gK_I as can be seen from (21) and (22). Consumption out of profits, in nominal terms, is therefore $rK - gK$, and so the budget equation for the Capitalist is:*

$$P_C X_C + P_I X_I = P_C \lambda_C Y_C + P_I \lambda_I Y_I = rK - gK \tag{28}$$

Now, since the preferences of the Capitalist are such that expenditure on each commodity is a fraction of profit consumed, denoted α_i, $i = C, I$ and assumed to be dependent only on the ratio of prices, we write:

$$P_C X_C = \alpha_C(r - g)K \quad \text{or} \quad X_C = \alpha_C(r - g)(K/P_C) \tag{29}$$
$$P_I X_I = \alpha_I(r - g)K \quad \text{or} \quad X_I = \alpha_I(r - g)(K/P_I) \tag{30}$$

*Equation (28) may also be derived from (21) − (24). Multiply (21) by P_C and (24) by P_I, add the two equations, and group terms to obtain:

$$P_C Y_C + P_I Y_I - P_C a_{CC} Y_C - P_C a_{CI} Y_I - P_I a_{IC} Y_C - P_I a_{II} Y_I - P_C \lambda_C Y_C - P_I \lambda_I Y_I$$
$$= g(P_C a_{CC} Y_C + P_C a_{CI} Y_I + P_I a_{IC} Y_C + P_I a_{II} Y_I) = gK \tag{26}$$

Then multiply (23) by Y_C and (24) by Y_I, add the two equations, and group terms to obtain:

$$P_C Y_C + P_I Y_I - P_C a_{CC} Y_C - P_C a_{CI} Y_I - P_I a_{IC} Y_C - P_I a_{II} Y_I$$
$$= r(P_C a_{CC} Y_C + P_C a_{CI} Y_I + P_I a_{IC} Y_I + P_I a_{II} Y_I) = rK \tag{27}$$

Finally, subtract (26) from (27) to obtain (28).

which, when substituted into (28), yields $\alpha_C + \alpha_I = 1$, a not unexpected result since the fractions of consumed profits spent on the two commodities must clearly add up to one. Note in (29) and (30) that X_C and X_I are non-negative if and only if the rate of profit exceeds the rate of growth, reflecting the fact that λ_C and λ_I are non-negative in the quantity equations if and only if $g < r$. Finally, since $\lambda_j = X_j / Y_j$, $j = C, I$:

$$\lambda_C = \alpha_C (r - g) K / P_C Y_C \tag{31}$$

$$\lambda_I = \alpha_I (r - g) K / P_I Y_I \tag{32}$$

Then, writing out K using the definitions of K_C and K_I we obtain λ_C and λ_I as functions of r, P_C/P_I, and Y_I/Y_C, given the coefficients of production and the proportions α_C and α_I which depend only on P_C/P_I:

$$\lambda_C = \alpha_C (r - g)[a_{CC} + a_{CI}(Y_I/Y_C) + (P_I/P_C)a_{IC} + (P_I/P_C)a_{II}(Y_I/Y_C)] \tag{33}$$

$$\lambda_I = \alpha_I (r - g)[(P_C/P_I)a_{CC}(Y_C/Y_I) + (P_C/P_I)a_{CI} + a_{IC}(Y_C/Y_I) + a_{II}] \tag{34}$$

In this highly simplified treatment of demand, the rate of growth is treated as a parameter while the fractions of gross output consumed are variables determined simultaneously with the composition of output. This differs from the Neumann interpretation of the model at the end of chapter 11 in which λ_C and λ_I are the fixed parameters and g is the determined variable. And, of course, there are more complicated models in which λ_C, λ_I, and g are all treated as simultaneously determined variables. But, however complicated the structure, the importance of demand in a subsistence wage model lies only in the determination of quantities. Equilibrium prices and the uniform rate of profit are independent of demand.

For completeness we now write down a list of parameters and variables consistent with our interpretation of equations $(21) - (34)$. The given data are:

(1) A viable technique matrix, **A**.
(2) The rate of accumulation, g, such that $0 \leq g \leq g_{max}$.
(3) Fractions of profits consumed, α_j, $j = C, I$, determined by the Capitalist's preferences and assumed to vary only with the ratio of prices.

The variables determined by the model are:

(1) The rate of profit r;
(2) The relative price ratio P_C/P_I;
(3) Proportions of gross output consumed, λ_j, $j = C, I$;
(4) The ratio of gross outputs Y_I/Y_C, and thus the ratio of inputs, K_I/K_C.

The ratio of iron to corn in the means of production K_I/K_C and in surplus output, $(Y_I - K_I)/(Y_C - K_C)$, can be found using the technical coefficients and the ratio of gross outputs, absolute quantities being fixed by choosing numbers for Y_C and Y_I that form this ratio. Nominal values are determined by choosing prices in the ratio P_C/P_I; otherwise, all values are expressed in terms of the *numeraire*.

We conclude by emphasizing the main point of contrast between our interpretation of a two-sector classical model and what was previously offered as a basis for understanding the two-sector neoclassical model; namely, the question of *what* is being allocated. In neoclassical theory, it is given resources; in classical theory it is surplus output after replacement of stock. This difference has far-reaching implications for the interpretation of prices. Thus, in neoclassical theory an exchange among resource owners of factor services indirectly for final commodities via the intermediation of producing agents provides the basis for the view that relative prices are measures of opportunity cost and of relative scarcity. It is a distinguishing feature of the neoclassical system that distribution, in particular, is sensitive to shifts in demand associated with differences in either preference orderings or factor ownership, given technology and factor supplies. In classical theory, on the other hand, analysis focuses on the production of a surplus and its distribution among capitalists (in a subsistence wage model) through the formation of prices consistent with a uniform rate of profit. Exchange is now an aspect of production, reversing the neoclassical priorities. Inputs are variables since commodities are produced means of production so that given factors and their relative scarcity do not provide the basis for explaining distribution; nor does the relative price of one commodity in terms of another measure its opportunity cost in the neoclassical sense.* Equilibrium prices conform to the requirement of a uniform rate of profit and are insensitive to the pattern of demand. Demand influences the composition of inputs and of gross and net outputs, but, however sensitive it may be to relative prices and the rate of profit, demand has no reciprocal effect on these variables.

The classical model we have used for the purpose of isolating and emphasizing these various points of contrast with neoclassical theory is in the spirit of Neumann's analysis since it takes the wage as a fixed basket of com-

* It cannot since resources are not given parameters. And, even if we were to define opportunity cost in a classical model in the most obvious manner as the value of the (absolute) slope of the surplus possibilities schedule, it would be clear from our analysis that this slope is different from the relative price ratio (except in highly special cases). Thus, in our example, $P_C/P_I = .5$, whereas the absolute slope of the schedule of net outputs is $(1 - a_{II} + a_{IC})/(1 - a_{CC} + a_{CI}) = .625$. We shall make further use of this result in the next chapter.

modities included in the specification of technology. This, of course, is a very rigid formulation so that the question naturally arises as to the extent to which the contrast between classical and neoclassical theory turns on the assumption that the wage is fixed. To answer this question, we require a further chapter for the treatment of variable wages (and profits) in a classical model in which labor is made an explicit input.

Appendix to Chapter 12

The generalization of the corn and iron model outlined in the appendix to chapter 11 has a dual formulation in terms of a set of price relations for a model with n sectors of production where all inputs are simultaneously outputs. In these relations the relevant technique matrix is the transpose of $\dot{A}$:

$$\mathbf{A}^t = \begin{bmatrix} a_{11} & a_{21} & \cdots & a_{n1} \\ a_{12} & a_{22} & \cdots & a_{n2} \\ \cdot & \cdot & & \cdot \\ \cdot & \cdot & & \cdot \\ \cdot & \cdot & & \cdot \\ a_{1n} & a_{2n} & & a_{nn} \end{bmatrix}$$

The coefficients of single-output constant-returns-to-scale production processes are written as the rows of $\mathbf{A}^t$, each row corresponding to a different sector.

The following inequalities must hold if the technique matrix is viable, i.e., if the inequalities in (A1) of the appendix to chapter 11 are satisfied:

$$P_1 a_{11} + P_2 a_{21} + \ldots + P_n a_{n1} \leq P_1$$

$$P_1 a_{12} + P_2 a_{22} + \ldots + P_n a_{n2} \leq P_2$$

$$\begin{matrix} \cdot & \cdot & & \cdot & \cdot \\ \cdot & \cdot & & \cdot & \cdot \\ \cdot & \cdot & & \cdot & \cdot \end{matrix} \qquad \text{(A1)}$$

$$P_1 a_{1n} + P_2 a_{2n} + \ldots + P_n a_{nn} \leq P_n$$

$$P_j \geq 0 \qquad j = 1, \ldots, n$$

If the technique matrix is more than just viable these inequalities can be satisfied as strict inequalities. Price equations are formed by multiplying the sum of value on each left-hand side by a profit factor, $1 + r$. Formally:

$$(P_1 a_{11} + P_2 a_{21} + \ldots + P_n a_{n1})(1+r) = P_1$$

$$(P_1 a_{12} + P_2 a_{22} + \ldots + P_n a_{n2})(1+r) = P_2$$

$$\text{(A2)}$$

$$(P_1 a_{1n} + P_2 a_{2n} + \ldots + P_n a_{nn})(1+r) = P_n$$

$$P_j \geq 0 \qquad j = 1, \ldots, n$$

In the notation of matrix algebra, this set of equations is simply:

$$\mathbf{A}^t \mathbf{P}(1+r) = \mathbf{P} \tag{A2$'$}$$

where $\mathbf{P}$ is a column vector and r is a scalar, or:

$$\mathbf{P}^t \mathbf{A}(1+r) = \mathbf{P}^t \tag{A2$''$}$$

where $\mathbf{P}^t$ is a row vector of prices, namely, the transpose of $\mathbf{P}$. This latter form may be written in a manner dual to (A4) $'''$ of the appendix to chapter 11:

$$\mathbf{P}^t[\mathbf{I} - (1+r)\mathbf{A}] = \mathbf{P}^t \tag{A2$'''$}$$

There is a nontrivial solution for the price vector, i.e., a solution such that at least one price is positive, if and only if:

$$|\mathbf{I} - (1+r)\mathbf{A}| = 0 \tag{A3}$$

This polynomial in r is of order n or less and has exactly the same form as equation (A5)$'$ in the appendix to chapter 11. The relevant solution is the smallest one; otherwise the price vector will contain negative components. And, because (A3) is identical in form to (A5)$'$ of the previous chapter, it follows that $r = R = g_{max}$. Since the profit rate is equal to the maximum rate of balanced growth, consumption out of surplus implies that $r > g$ when $g < g_{max}$.

This brief sketch of the price structure of an n-commodity model of the production of commodities by means of commodities, like the sketch of the quantity relations in the appendix to the last chapter, relies on certain mathematical results concerning the properties of non-negative square matrices.[8]

Notes

1. David Ricardo, *Works and Correspondence,* ed. P. Sraffa, Cambridge University Press, 1951 *et seq.,* Vol. VI, p. 108.
2. Maurice Dobb, "The Trend of Modern Economics," in *Political Economy and*

Capitalism, Routledge and Kegan Paul, London, 1937, 1961, pp. 127–84; reprinted in E. K. Hunt and Jesse G. Schwartz, eds., *A Critique of Economic Theory,* Penguin, Harmondsworth, 1972, pp. 39–82.

3. See n. 1.

4. This construction is adapted from R. M. Goodwin, *Elementary Economics from the Higher Standpoint,* Cambridge University Press, 1970, pp. 13–19.

5. The treatment of demand which follows is adapted from M. Morishima, *Theory of Economic Growth,* Oxford University Press, 1969, pp. 89–114.

6. *Ibid.,* p. 98.

7. See *ibid.* where Morishima writes that this "is a restrictive assumption, for it means that the Engel-elasticities of all goods (i.e., the elasticities of demand with respect to income) are unity." The assumption is necessary, however, in the context of a balanced growth equilibrium. Otherwise, an increase in the level of profits as capital accumulates can lead to changes in the composition of consumption expenditure, and hence to changes in the composition of output which would throw the system out of equilibrium and require an analysis of *changing* allocations of the surplus. Throughout our analysis we confine attention to *comparisons* of equilibrium.

8. See Michio Morishima, *Equilibrium Stability, and Growth. A Multi-sectoral Analysis,* Oxford at the Clarendon Press, 1964, pp. 195–215; and, for a less formal development, Sir John Hicks, *Capital and Growth,* Oxford at the Clarendon Press, 1965, pp. 316–21. Hicks's discussion incorporates variable wages and so provides a generalization to *n* sectors of the model we develop in the next chapter. By setting the wage equal to zero, one obtains the appropriate generalization for this chapter where wages are treated as subsistence and therefore as part of the technical requirements of production.

13

Wages and Profits in Classical Theory

> We must now take into account the other aspect of wages since, besides
> the ever-present element of subsistence, they may include a share of the
> surplus product.
>
> PIERO SRAFFA [1]

In classical models of surplus and accumulation where all inputs are currently
produced commodities, the question of income distribution takes on a starkly
simple form. Workers' consumption is simply included as part of the means
of production—hidden, as it were, behind the input–output coefficients of
production. There is no symbol denoting the wage rate as such since what the
workers consume is, in the one- and two-sector models we have used, either a
given amount of corn or a particular "basket" of corn and iron.

This treatment of wages, classical in spirit, corresponds in the strictest
sense to the notion of a given subsistence (although certainly Smith, Ricardo,
and Marx recognized variations over time and place in what counts as a
minimum acceptable standard of life). All that remains of the distribution
problem is to find the residual profit which is the dual of surplus output.*
What is not so obvious is how this surplus finds expression in terms of
a uniform rate of profit on the value of the means of production in each sector
of production, thereby defining equilibrium rates of exchange among various
produced inputs. It is this problem that the formal analysis of the price relations solves. With the solution in hand, however, new questions immediately
arise.

Suppose, for example, that subsistence were redefined in terms of a basket
of commodities different from the one initially included in the specification of
technology. This would alter the values of coefficients of production, thereby
changing the solution to the price equations of the model: the profit rate and rela-

---

* Profit can arise in the price relations of a classical model only if there is surplus in the quantity
relations. Other incomes corresponding to the surplus, such as rent and interest, are not analyzed
here since there is no class of landlords in our simple models and since no attention has been
given to the underlying financial structure which would, in a more complete discussion, require
an analysis of how interest is paid on capitalist debt.

317

tive price of one commodity in terms of another. In general, a different rate of profit is associated with each definition of subsistence so that the notion of subsistence as a parameter of the model might be dropped altogether and replaced by a variable wage. As a result, a given technology defined independently of subsistence would be capable of generating a whole range of wage–profit distributions. Now, although such a generalization seems natural, it is important to note certain difficulties that arise in connection with dropping the concept of subsistence as a parameter of the argument.

First of all, if the notion of subsistence is abandoned altogether, it follows by definition that surplus may be positive in a situation in which there is insufficient net output to support even the labor force, much less to allow for growth in the stock of capital. In the corn economy, for example, if the only input taken into account in defining the means of production is seed, with no allowance made for consumption of corn by the workers during the growing season, then gross output minus the requirement for replacing the stock of seed can be positive and yet insufficient to support the working population. Surplus then loses its historical significance since a positive surplus no longer implies the basis for accumulation or for the support of the capitalist class. Of course, the classical economists never fell into this trap since they always treated wages as a necessary input into the process of production.

A related problem arises in connection with the formal statement of a model in which there is no element of subsistence in the specification of technology. On the one hand, if the wage rate is restricted simply to being non-negative there may be nothing to ensure a strictly positive wage. On the other hand, to rule out this case by imposing a limit below which the wage cannot fall is, in effect, to let in the notion of subsistence by the back door.

The issues are summed up by Sraffa as follows:

> We have up to this point regarded wages as consisting of the necessary subsistence of the workers and thus entering the system on the same footing as the fuel for the engines or the feed for the cattle. We must now take into account the other aspect of wages since, besides the ever-present element of subsistence, they may include a share of the surplus product. In view of this double character of the wage it would be appropriate, when we come to consider the division of the surplus between capitalists and workers, to separate the two component parts of the wage and regard only the 'surplus' part as variable; whereas the goods necessary for the subsistence of the workers would continue to appear, with the fuel, etc., among the means of production.[2]

Despite the appeal of this approach, Sraffa opts for the more conventional method of treating the whole wage as variable. He then notes that:

The drawback of this course is that it involves relegating the necessaries of consumption to the limbo of non-basic products [products that do not enter directly or indirectly into every sector of production]. This is due to their no longer appearing among the means of production on the left hand side of the [price and quantity] equations: so that an improvement in the methods of production of necessaries of life will no longer directly affect the rate of profits and the prices of other products. Necessaries however are essentially basic [products that *do* enter directly or indirectly into every sector] and if they are prevented from exerting their influence on prices and profits under that label, they must do so in devious ways (e.g. by setting a limit below which the wage cannot fall; a limit which would itself fall with any improvement in the methods of production of necessaries, carrying with it a rise in the rate of profits and a change in the prices of other products.)[3]

It is therefore to avoid this problem of defining a limit below which the wage cannot fall that we shall continue to interpret the input–output coefficients as defining both technical and subsistence requirements per unit of output. In our models the variable component of the wage can fall to zero without contradiction. With this in mind, we now take up the problem of giving formal expression to the trade-off between wages and profit.

Variable Wages and Profits in a One-Sector Model

In constructing a model with a variable wage rate, labor can no longer be treated as the equivalent of a certain quantity of reproducible commodities. Instead, labor enters as a separate input measured in terms of labor-hours. The structure of the corn model is hardly changed, however, since we merely add to the quantity equation:

$$a_{CC} Y_C (1 + g) = (1 - \lambda_C) Y_C \tag{1}$$

a second equation defining the relation between the level of output and the level of employment E which we normalize at unity:

$$a_{LC} Y_C = E = 1 \tag{2}$$

The coefficient a_{LC} measures the number of units of labor required per unit of production of corn under constant returns to scale so that $a_{LC} Y_C$ measures the number of units of labor needed to produce Y_C units of corn. Output will therefore determine employment which is assumed to be less than or equal to the available supply of labor. It is convenient in our analysis to set employment equal to one unit of labor but this does not alter the meaning of (2); it merely changes units. Thus, if 1000 labor-hours are utilized in producing 10 units of corn it would follow that $a_{LC} = 100$; but if we then call 1000 labor-hours a unit of labor this will change the labor coefficient to 0.1 units of labor per unit of output without altering the interpretation of equation (2).*

The addition to the corn model of equation (2) does not alter the form of the trade-off between λ_C and g which can still be derived from (1) alone:

$$\lambda_C = -a_{CC}g + (1 - a_{CC}) \tag{1}'$$

The matter of the distribution of the surplus is therefore left open; further progress can be made only by introducing prices.

We retain for the moment a nominal price for corn P_C and simply add to the left-hand side of the corn model's price equation a term measuring wage cost per unit of output:

$$P_C a_{CC}(1 + r) + W a_{LC} = P_C \tag{3}$$

where W is the nominal wage per unit of labor so that $W a_{LC}$ is the nominal wage cost per unit of output. Price is then normalized in such a way that the value of total output is unity: †

$$P_C Y_C = 1 \tag{4}$$

This means, for example, that if 1000 units of output cost $1000 we simply change the meaning of a ''dollar'' so that each unit costs $0.001.

Given the normalization of quantities and prices in equations (2) and (4), it is easy to show that the price equation (3) has exactly the same form as the consumption–growth trade-off, (1)'. Simply multiply each term in (3) by the output of corn, Y_C, to obtain:

$$P_C a_{CC} Y_C (1 + r) + W a_{LC} Y_C = P_C Y_C \tag{5}$$

Using (2) and (4) this simplifies to

$$a_{CC}(1 + r) + W = 1 \tag{6}$$

or: $$W = -a_{CC}r + (1 - a_{CC}) \tag{6}'$$

This is identical with (1)' except for a change of variables so that we may graph the two equations back-to-back in Figure 13-1. The maximum rate of

* An alternative procedure is to divide (1) and (2) by E obtaining:

   $a_{CC} y_C (1 + g) = (1 - \lambda_C) y_C$ and $a_{CC} y_C = 1$

where $y_C = Y_C / E$ is output per man. There is then no need to reinterpret a_{LC}. We choose the normalization in the text since it is needed in our discussion of the Standard Commodity below.
† The more usual procedure is to divide by P_C in (3) which would then give the wage rate in corn as a function of the profit rate; but again we choose (4) in preparation for a discussion of the Standard Commodity.

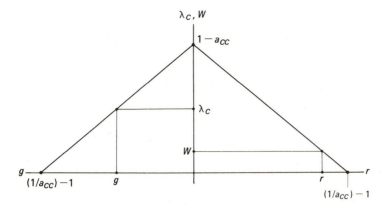

Figure 13-1. Wage–profit and consumption–growth trade-offs in a one-commodity corn model.

growth, $(1/a_{CC}) - 1$, is equal to the maximum rate of profit; and the maximum proportion of corn output consumed, $1 - a_{CC}$, is equal to the maximum real wage measured as a fraction of gross output.

Figure 13-1 shows clearly that if the growth rate is equal to the profit rate, the proportion of gross output consumed is equal to the proportion paid out as wages. Thus, if wages are entirely consumed, consumption out of profits must be zero, the whole being reinvested in the accumulation of stock. On the other hand, if part of profits are consumed in addition to the consumption of wages, it must be the case that $\lambda_C > W$ and hence $g < r$: the profit rate exceeds the growth rate. Thus, for a given rate of accumulation and a given proportion of profits consumed, it follows that the rate of profit must be such that the difference between λ_C and W measures the fraction of gross output consumed by the capitalists.* In this way the decisions of the capitalists regarding consumption and accumulation of the surplus are seen as determinants of the distribution of income between wages and profits.

Labor Coefficients in a Two-Sector Model

In generalizing the argument to two-commodity production we once again add to the quantity equations a further equation defining the relationship between outputs and employment. In the corn and iron model:

---

* Note that W, like λ_C, is a fraction of gross output since the proportion $WE/P_C Y_C$ is simply W, using (2) and (4). Assuming that wages are consumed, the fraction of gross output consumed by the capitalists is $(\lambda_C - W) Y_C$ which is $(r - g) a_{CC} Y_C$, using (1)' and (6)'. But this last term is just the difference between profits and the addition to capital, i.e., profits consumed.

$$(a_{CC} Y_C + a_{CI} Y_I)(1 + g) = (1 - \lambda_C) Y_C \tag{7}$$

$$(a_{IC} Y_C + a_{II} Y_I)(1 + g) = (1 - \lambda_I) Y_I \tag{8}$$

$$a_{LC} Y_C^S + a_{LI} Y_I^S = E = 1 \tag{9}$$

The labor coefficients a_{LC} and a_{LI} measure labor requirements per unit of output in each sector so that $a_{LC} Y_C^S$ and $a_{LI} Y_I^S$ define employment in each sector, given outputs Y_C^S and Y_I^S where the superscript S is used to signify the *Standard Commodity*. The latter is simply the particular solution to (7) and (8) corresponding to equal rates of surplus as discussed in chapter 11. Given these outputs, employment E is again normalized at one unit of labor, as in our discussion of the corn model.

Note that since (7) and (8) are identical with the quantity equations of a subsistence wage model, the trade-off between growth and consumption and the solution for the ratio of outputs are independent of labor requirements. Thus, as in chapter 11:

$$\frac{Y_I}{Y_C} = \frac{(1 - \lambda_C) - a_{CC}(1 + g)}{a_{CI}(1 + g)} \tag{10}$$

$$\frac{Y_I}{Y_C} = \frac{a_{IC}(1 + g)}{(1 - \lambda_I) - a_{II}(1 + g)} \tag{11}$$

from which we obtain the consumption–growth trade-off as a function in g, λ_C, and λ_I, given the technology of production:

$$(1 + g)^2 \left[\frac{a_{CC} a_{II} - a_{CI} a_{IC}}{(1 - \lambda_C)(1 - \lambda_I)} \right] - (1 + g) \left[\frac{a_{CC}}{(1 - \lambda_C)} + \frac{a_{II}}{(1 - \lambda_I)} \right] + 1 = 0 \tag{12}$$

This relationship was analyzed in chapter 11 under various assumptions concerning the allocation of the surplus to accumulation and consumption. The outputs in (9) correspond to the solution for (10) and (11) in which rates of surplus R_C and R_I are equal. This requires $\lambda_C = \lambda_I$ in (12) since, by definition:

$$1 + R_C = \frac{1 + g}{1 - \lambda_C} = \frac{1 + g}{1 - \lambda_I} = 1 + R_I \tag{13}$$

Using the coefficients in our example $(a_{CC}, a_{IC}) = (.4, .2)$ and $(a_{CI}, a_{II}) = (.2, .7)$, equations (10) and (11) are written:

$$\frac{Y_I^S}{Y_C^S} = \frac{1 - a_{CC}(1 + R)}{a_{CI}(1 + R)} = \frac{1 - .4(1.25)}{.2(1.25)} = 2 \tag{10$'$}$$

$$\frac{Y_I^S}{Y_C^S} = \frac{a_{IC}(1 + R)}{1 - a_{II}(1 + R)} = \frac{.2(1.25)}{1 - .7(1.25)} = 2 \tag{11$'$}$$

where $R = R_C = R_I$ in (13) is the smaller root for R in: *

$$(1 + R)^2(a_{CC}a_{II} - a_{CI}a_{IC}) - (1 + R)(a_{CC} + a_{II}) + 1$$
$$= .24(1 + R)^2 - 1.1(1 + R) + 1 \qquad (12)'$$

The ratio of outputs Y_I^S/Y_C^S corresponding to equal rates of surplus in the quantity equations defines the relative proportions of iron to corn in what Sraffa calls the Standard Commodity.[4] It will be seen presently that when the Standard Commodity is chosen as *numeraire* in the price relations a very simple relationship is obtained between profit rate and wage rate, a relationship which is otherwise complicated even in the simplified context of a two-commodity model. As for the normalization of employment in (9), this may now be stated explicitly in terms of our example. Taking the sum of units of corn and iron production to be 60, it follows from (10)' or (11)' that (Y_C^S, Y_I^S) = (20, 40), an example we discussed previously as line three of Table 11-1. Equation (9) therefore becomes:

$$20a_{LC} + 40a_{LI} = 1 \qquad (9)'$$

Note that for other outputs in *non*-Standard proportions the level of employment will not generally be 1, although such outputs can always be appropriately scaled (up or down) in order to fix E at unity.

Turning to the price equations of chapter 12 we add a new term to each left-hand side, which measures variable wage cost per unit of output:

$$(P_C a_{CC} + P_I a_{IC})(1 + r) + Wa_{LC} = P_C \qquad (14)$$
$$(P_C a_{CI} + P_I a_{II})(1 + r) + Wa_{LI} = P_I \qquad (15)$$

As in the one-sector model, W is the nominal wage per unit of labor so that Wa_{LC} and Wa_{LI} measure nominal wage cost per unit of output in each sector. We then remove the indeterminate element of scale in nominal prices by setting equal to unity the nominal value of the Standard Commodity which therefore becomes the *numeraire:*

$$P_C Y_C^S + P_I Y_I^S = 1 \qquad (16)$$

The allocation of the surplus may entail a composition of output entirely different from the Standard Commodity, but for the purpose of normalizing prices including the wage rate, Y_C^S and Y_I^S are chosen as weights in (16). Thus, in our example:

$$20P_C + 40P_I = 1 \qquad (16)'$$

---

* It is always the smaller root since the larger root results in a negative ratio of gross outputs in (11)'.

Real wages are therefore measured, not in terms of one commodity, but in terms of units of a given basket of commodities (Y_C^S, Y_I^S). In light of this, we replace W by W^S to remind us that the wage rate as well as total wages (since $E = 1$) is measured in units of the Standard Commodity.

To illustrate the usefulness of the Standard Commodity in the analysis of prices, we begin with the special case in which the actual composition of output is the Standard Commodity: $(Y_C, Y_I) = (Y_C^S, Y_I^S) = (20, 40)$. The maximum wage is $W^S = .2$ since in that case wages absorb 20% of the Standard Commodity, namely, 4 units of corn and 8 units of iron, and, since this is the whole surplus, profit (and the rate of profit) must be zero. At the other extreme, W^S is zero, a case we have already considered in chapter 12 where it was shown that the rate of profit, which we now write r_{max}, is 25%. The interesting thing to note is that when the Standard Commodity is the actual composition of output, the rate of profit can be calculated without knowing relative prices because each component of the surplus is the same proportion of the corresponding component of the stock of capital goods: 4 units is 25% of the stock of 16 units of corn, and 8 units of iron is 25% of the stock of 32 units of iron (see Table 11-1). The maximum rate of profit is therefore 25% as a proportion of the stock of capital which accounts for 100% of the surplus; if only 20% of the surplus accrued in the form of profits, the rate of profit would likewise be 20% of its maximum value which is 5%.

The reason for choosing to measure the wage in terms of the Standard Commodity is now becoming clear for, as Sraffa remarks, when the actual composition of output is the Standard Commodity, the "residue left over for profits will itself be a quantity of [the] Standard commodity and therefore similar in composition to the means of production."[5] This means that "the rate of profits, being the ratio of two homogeneous [bundles of corn and iron] can be *seen* to rise in direct proportion to any reduction in the wage."[6] For example, if W^S falls by 25% from .2 to .15, then 75% of the surplus or 3 units of corn and 6 units of iron are paid out as wages leaving 1 unit of corn and 2 units of iron as profit. This is 6.25% of the means of production so that $r = .0625$ which is 25% of the maximum rate of profit. A further fall in the wage to .1 distributes the surplus evenly: 2 units of corn and 4 units of iron to wages (50% of the surplus) and the same amounts to profits, the *rate* of profit having risen to 12.5% of the means of production so that $r = .125$ which is 50% of its maximum value. In general, any reduction in the wage W^S raises the profit rate r by a constant proportion which in our example is 1.25 times the change in W^S. Equivalently, any change in r alters W^S by the reciprocal proportion, $1/1.25 = .8$ times the change in r.

We must now ask if these results are only a special case, invalid when quantities other than the Standard Commodity are produced. This is important because we know that in general the means of production will not be similar in composition to gross and net output and that therefore the rate of profit cannot in general be measured as a ratio of homogeneous bundles of commodities. As Sraffa puts the matter:

> There would therefore appear to be no reason to expect that in the actual system, when the equivalent of the same quantity of Standard commodity has been paid for wages, the *value* of what is left over for profits should stand in the same ratio to the *value* of the means of production as the corresponding *quantities* do in the Standard system.[7]

Nevertheless, that relationship between wages and profits in which a change in the wage is accompanied by an invervse *proportional* change in the rate of profit, does hold true in all cases, just as long as the wage is measured in terms of units of the Standard Commodity (irrespective of the composition of expenditure out of wages). We prove this result and then illustrate it with an example.

First, multiply (14) and (15) by Y_C^S and Y_I^S, respectively, to obtain:

$$(P_C a_{CC} Y_C^S + P_I a_{IC} Y_C^S)(1+r) + W a_{LC} Y_C^S = P_C Y_C^S \tag{17}$$

$$(P_C a_{CI} Y_I^S + P_I a_{II} Y_I^S)(1+r) + W a_{LI} Y_I^S = P_I Y_I^S \tag{18}$$

Then add (17) and (18) and group terms as follows:

$$(P_C a_{CC} Y_C^S + P_C a_{CI} Y_I^S + P_I a_{IC} Y_C^S + P_I a_{II} Y_I^S)(1+r)$$
$$+ (a_{LC} Y_C^S + a_{LI} Y_I^S)W = P_C Y_C^S + P_I Y_I^S \tag{19}$$

The first four terms in parentheses in (19) can be shown to equal $1/(1 + g_{max})$ which is equal to $1/(1 + r_{max})$ since the maximum rate of growth and the maximum rate of profit are equal.* Then using (9) and (16) so that W^S replaces W in (19), we obtain:

---

* Let $\lambda_C = 0 = \lambda_I$ in (7) and (8). Then $g = g_{max}$ and gross outputs have the values Y_C^S and Y_I^S since this is a particular case of (10)' and (11)' in which $\lambda = 0$. Then multiply (7) and (8) by P_C and P_I:

$$(P_C a_{CC} Y_C^S + P_C a_{CI} Y_I^S)(1 + g_{max}) = P_C Y_C^S$$
$$(P_I a_{IC} Y_C^S + P_I a_{II} Y_I^S)(1 + g_{max}) = P_I Y_I^S$$

Adding terms and dividing by $(1 + g_{max})$ yields:

$$(P_C a_{CC} Y_C^S + P_C a_{CI} Y_I^S + P_I a_{IC} Y_C^S + P_I a_{II} Y_I^S) = (P_C Y_C^S + P_I Y_I^S)/(1 + g_{max}) = 1/(1 + g_{max})$$

using (16). Finally, recall from chapters 11 and 12 that $g_{max} = r$ in the quantity and price equations which are identical to the quantity and price equations of this chapter on the assumption that $W = 0$. Thus, in the present model, $g_{max} = r_{max}$ which establishes the result used in deriving (20) from (17) and (18).

$$\frac{1+r}{1+r_{max}} + W^S = 1 \tag{20}$$

or:

$$W^S = -\frac{r}{1+r_{max}} + \frac{r_{max}}{1+r_{max}} = -.8r + .2 \tag{20}'$$

where $r_{max} = .25$ is the solution for r in (14) and (15) given $W = 0$. Thus, the choice of *numeraire* in (16) yields a linear relationship between the real wage measured as a proportion of the Standard Commodity, and the rate of profit. Now, it is true that in deriving (20) we have used the particular quantities (Y_C^S, Y_I^S) to weight the price relations of the model, but this does not imply that these are the actual quantities produced. The relationship therefore holds regardless of the composition of output just so long as employment and prices are normalized according to (9) and (16). Note that (20)' establishes the result stated earlier that a change in the rate of profit is associated with a proportional and opposite change in the Standard Commodity wage where the factor of proportionality is $1/(1+r_{max}) = .8$.

The *form* of the relationship between W^S and r is exactly the same as that of the relationship between λ and g, given equal rates of surplus, for in that event:

$$1 + R = (1+g)/(1-\lambda) = 1 + g_{max} = 1.25 \tag{21}$$

so that:

$$\lambda = -\frac{g}{1+g_{max}} + \frac{g_{max}}{1+g_{max}} = -.8g + .2 \tag{21}'$$

The division of the Standard Commodity between consumption and growth is therefore dual to the division of income between wages and profits as indicated in Figure 13-2 which shows virtually the same dual trade-offs as in the corn model. See Figure 13-1. Since the two relationships in the diagram, equations (20)' and (21)', are derived independently, however, it follows that the wage–profit trade-off holds for all outputs and not just for those defined by the Standard Commodity. This independence of prices from quantities is a property of classical theory already noted in connection with the subsistence wage model of chapters 11 and 12. We wish to develop this point further by showing that even with a variable wage the link between quantities and prices is, in an important respect, one-way. A given profit rate, wage rate, and relative price ratio may be associated with very different outputs and corre-

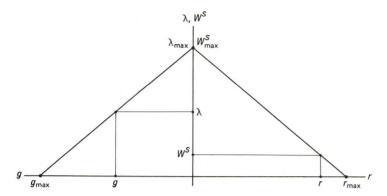

Figure 13-2. Wage–profit and consumption–growth trade-offs in a two-commodity corn and iron model, given equal rates of surplus and a wage measured in terms of the Standard Commodity.

sponding allocations of the surplus. Thus, different patterns of demand in a classical (unlike a neoclassical) model will not entail any differences in prices or the distribution of income.

A Numerical Example

Values for the labor coefficients in the quantity and price equations are chosen to satisfy (9) so that whenever the Standard Commodity (Y_C^S, Y_I^S) = (20, 40) is produced, given our assumption that the sum of units of production is 60, the level of employment will be unity. We therefore let a_{LC} = .03 and a_{LI} = .01. and write (14) and (15) as:

$$(.4P_C + .2P_I)(1 + r) + .03W = P_C \qquad (14)'$$

$$(.2P_C + .7P_I)(1 + r) + .01W = P_I \qquad (15)'$$

In this system there are four unknowns: r, W, P_C, and P_I. One solution is already known from chapter 12 since if $W = 0$, (14)' and (15)' reduce to equations (8)' and (9)' of chapter 12, for which $r = .25$ and $P_C/P_1 = .5$, absolute prices remaining indeterminate. Rates of profit less than $r_{max} = .25$ are associated with positive wage rates. In particular, we may solve the price equations for W/P_C, the real wage in terms of corn, and W/P_I, the real wage in terms of iron, thereby obtaining the price ratio as $(W/P_I)/(W/P_C) = P_C/P_I$. Each of these variables is a function of the rate of profit, given the technology of production:

$$W/P_C = \frac{(a_{CC}a_{II} - a_{CI}a_{IC})(1+r)^2 - (a_{CC} + a_{II})(1+r) + 1}{(a_{LI}a_{IC} - a_{LC}a_{II})(1+r) + a_{LC}}$$

$$= \frac{.24(1+r)^2 - 1.1(1+r) + 1}{-0.019(1+r) + .03} \tag{22}$$

$$W/P_I = \frac{(a_{CC}a_{II} - a_{CI}a_{IC})(1+r)^2 - (a_{CC} + a_{II})(1+r) + 1}{(a_{LC}a_{CI} - a_{LI}a_{CC})(1+r) + a_{LI}}$$

$$= \frac{.24(1+r)^2 - 1.1(1+r) + 1}{.002(1+r) + .01} \tag{23}$$

$$P_C/P_I = \frac{(a_{LI}a_{IC} - a_{LC}a_{II})(1+r) + a_{LC}}{(a_{LC}a_{CI} - a_{LI}a_{CC})(1+r) + a_{LI}}$$

$$= \frac{-.019(1+r) + .03}{.002(1+r) + .01} \tag{24}$$

Wage rates in terms of corn and iron are second-order functions of the rate of profit as can be seen from (22) and (23), whereas W^S in terms of the Standard Commodity is a much simpler linear function as shown in (20)'. All, however, vary inversely with the profit rate.* The price ratio P_C/P_I, on the other hand, can either increase or decrease with r,† although in our example, it too is an inverse function of r.

Various solutions to the price equations, written as (22)–(24), together with the corresponding Standard Commodity wage, are given in Table 13-1 for rates of profit ranging from 4% to 24%. We shall use nominal prices that satisfy the ratios in Table 13-1 to value the gross and net outputs in Table 13-2 (which is a modified version of Table 11-1).

We now illustrate a property of the classical model by showing that the first two columns in Table 13-1 measuring r and the associated Standard Commodity wage W^S correctly describe the distribution of income between profits and wages in situations for which the composition of output is *not* in Standard Commodity proportions, as in all but the third line of Table 13-2. Suppose then that the profit rate is 4% and the Standard Commodity wage is .168 with nominal prices satisfying the first row in Table 13-1: $W = \$1,444.80$, $P_C = \$128$, and $P_I = \$151$. Suppose also that the composition of output is given by the first line in Table 13-2, consumption out of wages and profits after replacement of stock being restricted to expenditure on iron. Equilibrium

---

* This may be shown by taking the first derivative of (20)', (22) and (23) with respect to the rate of profit. In the case of (20)' this is simply the constant slope, $-1/(1 + r_{max})$; whereas in (22) and (23) the slope of the function varies although it is always negative.

† Note that equation (24) is that of a rectangular hyperbola with asymptotes parallel to the coordinate axes. The slope of the hyperbola has the sign of $a_{LI}(a_{LI}a_{IC} - a_{LC}a_{II}) - a_{LC}(a_{LC}a_{CI} - a_{LI}a_{CC})$, so that in our example where this number is $-.00025$, P_C/P_I varies inversely with r.

TABLE 13-1. Solutions to the Price Equations
Technology: $(a_{CC}, a_{IC}, a_{LC}) = (.4, .2, .03)$
$(a_{CI}, a_{II}, a_{LI}) = (.2, .7, .01)$

r	W^s	W/P_C	W/P_I	P_C/P_I
.04	.168	11.2875	9.5682	.8477
.08	.136	9.6979	7.5605	.7796
.12	.104	7.9193	5.6418	.7124
.16	.072	5.8975	3.8104	.6461
.20	.040	3.5556	2.0645	.5806
.24	.004	0.7801	0.4026	.5160

net output consists of a surplus of 10.5 units of iron valued at $1,585.50. Given what is clearly a non-Standard output, is the wage, in units of the Standard Commodity, still .168? To find out we must subtract from the value of the actual net output the equivalent of .168 units of the Standard Commodity and then show that what remains of the surplus is 4% of the value of the means of production.

Since total labor employed in the first line of Table 13-2 is .9 instead of 1, the Standard Commodity corresponding to the actual output is 90% of the quantities in the third line of Table 13-2; namely, 18 units of corn and 36 units of iron. At nominal prices corresponding to the given distribution of income, the value of this Standard Commodity is $7,740.00: 18 units of corn at $128 per unit plus 36 units of iron at $151 per unit. Thus, the equivalent of $W^s = .168$ units of the Standard Commodity is $(.168)(\$7,740.00) = \$1,300.32$. Subtracting this from the value of the actual output, $1,585.50,

TABLE 13-2. Gross and Surplus Outputs and Employment
Technology as in Table 13-1.

Gross outputs		Total inputs		Surplus outputs		Employment
Y_C	Y_I	K_C	K_I	$Y_C - K_C$	$Y_I - K_I$	E
15	45	15.0	34.5	0.0	10.5	0.90
18	42	15.6	33.0	2.4	9.0	0.96
20	40	16.0	32.0	4.0	8.0	1.00
30	30	18.0	27.0	12.0	3.0	1.20
36	24	19.2	24.0	16.8	0.0	1.32

leaves $285.18. Is this 4% of the value of the stock of capital? Since 15 units of corn at $128 per unit plus 34.5 units of iron at $151 per unit comes to $7,129.50 the answer is yes since 4% of this value is $285.18.

This example illustrates the fact that $(r, W^S) = (.04, .168)$ which satisfies (20)′ independently of any calculation of prices correctly describes the distribution of income between wages and profits in a situation which does not correspond to production of the Standard Commodity. Thus, Sraffa remarks:

. . . when the equivalent of the same quantity of Standard commodity has been paid for wages, the *value* of what is left over for profits should stand in the same ratio to the *value* of the means of production as the corresponding *quantities* do in the Standard system.[8]

Hence, the simplicity of the Standard system in which the rate of profit is a ratio of physically heterogeneous bundles of commodities bearing the same relative proportions to one another carries over to non-Standard systems just so long as the wage is measured in terms of units of the Standard Commodity. Expenditure of wages and profits on consumer goods may, however, be restricted entirely to one commodity as in the above example.

Other illustrations of this general result may be constructed for any composition of output satisfying the quantity equations of the model. Table 13-3 summarizes the various calculations needed to show that, when the profit rate is 4%, the wage is always equivalent to .168 times the value of the Standard

TABLE 13-3. Nominal values corresponding to quantities in Table 13-2, and prices satisfying the ratios in the first line of Table 13-1: $W = \$1444.8$, $P_C = \$128$, $P_I = \$151$, given a profit rate of 4% and a Standard Commodity wage, $W^S = .168$.

1	2	3	4	5	6	7
Value of actual net product	Equivalent standard commodity, (EY_C^S, EY_I^S)	Value of standard commodity, $P_C EY_C^S + P_I EY_I^S$	Equivalent of wages, WE, or W^S times column 3	Profit: column 1 minus column 4	Value of actual means of production	Profit: 4% of column 6
$1,585.5	(18, 36)	$7,740	$1,300.32	$285.18	$7,129.5	$285.18
$1,666.2	(19.2, 38.4)	$8,256	$1,387.008	$279.192	$6,979.8	$279.192
$1,720.0	(20, 40)	$8,600	$1,444.80	$275.20	$6,880.0	$275.20
$1,989.0	(24, 48)	$10,320	$1,733.76	$255.24	$6,381.0	$255.24
$2,150.4	(26.4, 52.8)	$11,352	$1,907.136	$243.246	$6,081.6	$243.246

TABLE 13-4. Nominal values corresponding to quantities in Table 13-2, and prices satisfying the ratios in the fifth line of Table 13-1: $W = \$64$, $P_C = \$18$, $P_I = \$31$, given a profit rate of 20% and a Standard Commodity wage, $W^S = .04$.

1	2	3	4	5	6	7
Value of actual net product	Equivalent standard commodity, (EY_C^S, EY_I^S)	Value of standard commodity $P_C EY_C^S + P_I EY_I^S$	Equivalent of wages, WE, or W^S times column 3	Profit: column 1 minus column 4	Value of actual means of production	Profit: 20% of column 6
$325.5	(18, 36)	$1,440	$57.60	$267.90	$1,339.5	$267.90
$322.2	(19.2, 38.4)	$1,536	$61.44	$260.76	$1,303.8	$260.76
$320.0	(20, 40)	$1,600	$64.00	$256.00	$1,280.0	$256.00
$309.0	(24, 48)	$1,920	$76.80	$232.20	$1,161.0	$232.20
$302.4	(26.4, 52.8)	$2,112	$84.48	$217.92	$1,089.6	$217.92

Commodity which corresponds to each line in Table 13-2, irrespective of the way in which wages and profits are actually spent on the consumption of corn and iron. The point is simply that if one subtracts this equivalent wage (column 4 in the table) from the value of the actual net product, the profit residual (column 5) is always equal to $r = 4\%$ of the value of the means of production (column 7).

Table 13-3 also illustrates a distinguishing characteristic of classical theory which we have remarked upon previously; namely, that the composition of output and the allocation of the surplus are free to vary without affecting the equilibrium distribution of income corresponding to a uniform rate of profit. For this reason distribution and the theory of relative prices can be formulated independently of a theory of demand, an aspect of the analysis which differentiates it sharply from neoclassical theory where, in general, prices and distribution are sensitive to the structure of demand. Conversely, various income distributions are consistent with given outputs. This is shown in Table 13-4 where the physical flows in Table 13-2 are valued at nominal prices, $W = \$64$, $P_C = \$18$, and $P_I = \$31$, that satisfy the price constraints, given a 20% rate of profit. (See the fourth line of Table 13-1.) Once again, the point $(r, W^S) = (.2, .04)$ satisfying (20) correctly describes the distribution of income prior to the calculation of prices and values. And, comparing Tables 13-3 and 13-4, it is evident that a given composition of output in Table 13-2 is consistent with widely separated distributions of income in Table 13-1.

Parameters, Variables, and the Role of Demand

At the end of the last chapter it was remarked that various points along the surplus possibilities schedule may be associated with differences in the pattern of demand. The point of the argument was to show that, regardless of the way in which demand is introduced into the model, it has importance only insofar as quantities are concerned. In this regard classical theory differs from neo-classical theory in which incomes reflect the relative scarcity of given factors, and in general relative scarcity varies with the pattern of demand. Since this contrast is so important to our discussion of the differences between classical and neoclassical theories of general equilibrium, it is essential at this point to reexamine our earlier conclusions in light of the foregoing analysis of *variable* wages and profits.

For ease of reference, the formal structure of the present model is repeated but without the normalizations in (9) and (16) since they have now served their purpose:

$$(a_{CC}Y_C + a_{CI}Y_I)(1 + g) = (1 - \lambda_C)Y_C \tag{25}$$

$$(a_{IC}Y_C + a_{II}Y_I)(1 + g) = (1 - \lambda_I)Y_I \tag{26}$$

$$a_{LC}Y_C + a_{LI}Y_I = E \tag{27}$$

$$(P_C a_{CC} + P_I a_{IC})(1 + r) + Wa_{LC} = P_C \tag{28}$$

$$(P_C a_{CI} + P_I a_{II})(1 + r) + Wa_{LI} = P_I \tag{29}$$

Given technology (including subsistence), the quantity equations contain six unknowns: λ_C, λ_I, g, Y_C, Y_I, and E; and the price equations a further four unknowns: r, W, P_C, P_I.

In chapter 12 the price equations were equivalent to (28) and (29) only for the special case in which $W = 0$. This assumption yielded a solution for r and the price ratio P_C/P_I, absolute prices remaining indeterminate. Proportions of gross output consumed, λ_C and λ_I, were treated as variables dependent on the preferences of the Capitalist for corn and iron as consumption goods, given the rate of accumulation g as a parameter. Equations (25) and (26) then gave a solution for Y_I/Y_C which was indirectly a function of prices since the proportions of output consumed depended on prices. Absolute quantities were left indeterminate, or fixed arbitrarily given the *ratio* of outputs. Employment was not an explicit variable since labor coefficients were unnecessary in the analysis of a subsistence wage model.

In the present model surplus is divided not only between consumption and growth, but also between wages and profits. The proportions of gross output consumed cannot be regarded simply as functions of the preferences of capitalists for corn and iron in consumption, since they depend also on the division of income between wages and profits. The decisions of laborers concerning what part of their incomes they will spend and what part they will save (subsistence consumption having already been accounted for) must also be considered. Given these complications, the argument proceeds on the basis of a simplifying assumption often referred to as the classical savings hypothesis; namely, that workers spend all of their income on consumption while capitalists consume only a fraction of total profits, the remainder being invested in accumulating a larger stock of capital. Then, if the rate of growth and the fraction of profits invested are specified as parameters, equilibrium requires that the rate of profit be such that total profits invested be just equal to the value of the addition to the stock of capital. For example, if g is 5% and the fraction of profits saved and invested is 25%, it follows that the *rate* of profit must be 20%. This is because a 5% addition to the value of the stock of capital requires profits to be equal to 20% of that value if 25% of profits are earmarked for investment. If 50% of profits are saved and invested the rate of profit need only be 10% to sustain growth at 5%. And, in the event that all profits are invested, the profit rate need only just equal the growth rate. This relationship may be written:

$$g = s_c r \qquad \text{or} \qquad r = g/s_c \tag{30}$$

where s_c is the fraction of profits saved, i.e., not consumed. It is this saving that finances accumulation at the rate g (although we give no account of the financial mechanism involved since we have nowhere attempted to integrate monetary variables into our analysis).

The rate of profit that satisfies (30) for given values of g and s_c can be substituted into the price equations thereby determining the real wage in terms of corn W/P_C, or iron W/P_I, or the Standard Commodity W^S; and the relative price ratio P_C/P_I. Consumption expenditure by workers and capitalists fixes the exact composition of output, the proportions λ_C and λ_I being determined simultaneously with the ratio of outputs Y_I/Y_C. The ratio of iron to corn in the stock of capital, the composition and allocation of the surplus, and the ratio of employment to output can then be calculated.

The role of demand in determining the composition of output may be stated formally by writing out equations that show how consumption depends on prices, income distribution, and the preferences of both capitalists and workers for corn and iron. As in chapter 12, it is assumed that the capitalists' choices can be aggregated, on the basis of similar tastes, into the choice of one giant Capitalist; and that the preferences of workers, too, can be treated simply as the preferences of the Worker.[9] In a crude way this expresses a social distinction in patterns of consumption that mirrors the social relations of production. Again, we assume that the fractions of consumed profits spent on corn and iron, α_C and α_I, respectively, depend *only* on the price ratio and are thus independent of the level of profits. The Worker's preferences also have this property, where the fractions of total wages spent on corn and iron are denoted β_C and β_I, respectively, and are assumed to be independent of the level of wages. Denoting consumption by the Capitalist as (X_C^C, X_I^C) and by the Worker as (X_C^W, X_I^W) we then have:

$$P_C X_C^C = \alpha_C (r-g)K \quad \text{or} \quad X_C^C = \alpha_C (r-g)K/P_C \tag{31}$$

$$P_I X_I^C = \alpha_I (r-g)K \quad \text{or} \quad X_I^C = \alpha_I (r-g)K/P_I \tag{32}$$

$$P_C X_C^W = \beta_C WE \quad \text{or} \quad X_C^W = \beta_C (W/P_C)E \tag{33}$$

$$P_I X_I^W = \beta_I WE \quad \text{or} \quad X_I^W = \beta_I (W/P_I)E \tag{34}$$

where $(r-g)K$ has exactly the same meaning as in chapter 12, namely, the difference between profits and the value of the addition to the stock of capital, or simply consumed profit which, from (30), is $(1-s_c)rK$. In (33) and (34), on the other hand, WE measures total wages which is expressed in terms of corn or iron after dividing by P_C or P_I.

The budget equations for Capitalist and Worker are, respectively:

$$P_C X_C^C + P_I X_I^C = (r-g)K \tag{35}$$

$$P_C X_C^W + P_I X_I^W = WE \tag{36}$$

which, together with:

$$X_C^C + X_C^W = \lambda_C Y_C \tag{37}$$

$$X_I^C + X_I^W = \lambda_I Y_I \tag{38}$$

imply an aggregate budget constraint:

$$P_C \lambda_C Y_C + P_I \lambda_I Y_I = (r-g)K + WE \tag{39}$$

which can also be derived directly from the quantity and price equations.*

Finally, the proportions, λ_j, $j = C,I$, can be written as the sum of Capitalist's and Worker's consumption per unit of output in each sector after substituting (31)–(34) into (37) and (38). We also substitute for K, the value of the

---

*To do so requires multiplying quantity equations by prices and price equations by quantities, adding the resulting equations, and then rearranging terms in a manner exactly parallel to the calculation in the note on page 311.

means of production,* in order to show a relationship between the proportions of output consumed and the ratio of outputs Y_I/Y_C. Thus:

$$\lambda_C = X_C^C/Y_C + X_C^W/Y_C$$
$$= \alpha_C(r-g)[a_{CC} + a_{CI}(Y_I/Y_C) + (P_I/P_C)a_{IC} + (P_I/P_C)a_{II}(Y_I/Y_C)] \qquad (40)$$
$$+ \beta_C(W/P_C)(E/Y_C)$$

$$\lambda_I = X_I^C/Y_I + X_I^W/Y_I$$
$$= \alpha_I(r-g)[(P_C/P_I)a_{CC}(Y_C/Y_I) + (P_C/P_I)a_{CI} + a_{IC}(Y_C/Y_I) + a_{II}] \qquad (41)$$
$$+ \beta_I(W/P_I)(E/Y_I)$$

The ratios E/Y_C and E/Y_I in (40) and (41), are found be dividing (27) first by Y_C and then by Y_I substituting for Y_I/Y_C or Y_C/Y_I using (28) and (29) from chapter 11:

$$E/Y_C = \frac{a_{LI}(1-\lambda_C) - (a_{LI}a_{CC} - a_{LC}a_{CI})(1+g)}{a_{CI}(1+g)}$$

$$= \frac{a_{LC}(1-\lambda_I) - (a_{LC}a_{II} - a_{LI}a_{IC})(1+g)}{(1-\lambda_I) - a_{II}(1+g)} \qquad (42)$$

$$E/Y_I = \frac{a_{LI}(1-\lambda_C) - (a_{LI}a_{CC} - a_{LC}a_{CI})(1+g)}{(1-\lambda_C) - a_{CC}(1+g)}$$

$$= \frac{a_{LC}(1-\lambda_I) - (a_{LC}a_{II} - a_{LI}a_{IC})(1+g)}{a_{IC}(1+g)} \qquad (43)$$

We are now in a position to summarize the model's structure. There are four groups of parameters:

(1) A viable technology: (a_{CC}, a_{IC}, a_{LC}); (a_{CI}, a_{II}, a_{LI});†
(2) The rate of accumulation g; and the fraction of profits saved and invested s_c,
(3) Fractions of consumed profits spent on each commodity, α_C and α_I, determined by the Capitalist's preferences and assumed to vary only with the commodity price ratio;
(4) Fractions of total wages spent on each commodity, β_C and β_I, determined by the Worker's preferences and assumed to vary only with the commodity price ratio.

---

*Recall from chapter 12 that K is the value sum $P_C K_C + P_I K_I$ where $K_j = a_{jC} Y_C + a_{jI} Y_I$, $j = C, I$. Dividing by a price expresses K in terms of one of the commodities.
†The viability condition of chapter 11, inequality (4), is unchanged when labor coefficients are introduced since the slopes of the net activity vectors are independent of these coefficients, and it is these slopes that determine whether or not the surplus possibilities schedule passes through the non-negative quadrant (as it must if the technology is to be viable).

The equations of the model, (25)–(38), determine four groups of variables:

(1) The rate of profit r and the wage in terms of the Standard Commodity W^S;

(2) Relative prices W/P_C, W/P_I, P_C/P_I;

(3) Proportions of gross output consumed λ_C and λ_I;

(4) Quantity ratios: Y_I/Y_C, X_C^C/Y_C, X_C^W/Y_C, X_I^C/Y_I, X_I^W/Y_I, E/Y_C, E/Y_I, K_I/K_C.

In one respect the model divides into two parts since the first two groups of parameters are sufficient to determine the first two groups of variables. The model thus shows that a theory of distribution and hence prices can be formulated in a classical model prior to a treatment of the composition of output and of the allocation of surplus.* Quantities, on the other hand, are not independent of distribution and prices as is clear from (40) and (41) where each ratio of consumption to output, X_j^k/Y_j^k, $j = C, I$, $k = C, W$, depends on either the real wage or profit rate as well as the ratio of prices which determines each of the fractions, α_j and β_j, $j = C, I$. Moreover, all ratios of quantities must be found simultaneously since the ratios of consumption to output as much determine as they are determined by the ratio of gross outputs and the ratio of employment to output. And, as chapter 11 shows, the ratio of gross outputs also determines the ratio of iron to corn in the stock of capital K_I/K_C and in the surplus output $(Y_I - K_I)/(Y_C - K_C)$. Any absolute quantities and nominal prices that form the ratios determined by the model can then be substituted into its equations.

Summing up, we have found that in a classical model relative prices or rates of exchange are independent of consumers' preferences. On the other hand, the decisions of capitalists regarding growth and the reinvestment of profits determine the rate of profit as in equation (30). This fixes the division of income between wages and profits and determines relative prices. Preferences for consumption goods come into the argument only insofar as they affect the composition of output and the allocation of surplus. Thus, the independence of prices from quantities that characterizes a subsistence model continues to hold, although in a modified way, when wages are variable.

---

* This partial decomposibility of the model has been used to provide modern reinforcement for the Ricardian view that a theory of income distribution, i.e., a theory of the rate of profit, has a certain priority, the intended contrast being with the theory of demand which may be said to have prior importance in the structure of neoclassical theory.

Appendix 13A: Basic and Nonbasic Commodities

An aspect of the classical model which we have not yet developed, and which has particular relevance to the wage–profit trade-off, concerns Sraffa's distinction between basic and nonbasic commodities.[10] A *basic* commodity is one that enters directly or indirectly as an input into every sector of production; a *nonbasic* does not.

In the two-sector model in which every coefficient, a_{ij}, $i, j = C, I$, is positive, both corn and iron are clearly basics. However, one can easily turn, say, iron into a nonbasic by setting $a_{IC} = 0$. Corn remains basic since it enters as an input into both sectors but iron is now an input only in its own production.* The quantity and price equations of the model may then be simplified as follows:

$$(a_{CC} Y_C + a_{CI} Y_I)(1 + g) = (1 - \lambda_C) Y_C \tag{A1}$$

$$(a_{II} Y_I)(1 + g) = (1 - \lambda_I) Y_I \tag{A2}$$

$$a_{LC} Y_C + a_{LI} Y_I = E \tag{A3}$$

$$(P_C a_{CC})(1 + r) + W a_{LC} = P_C \tag{A4}$$

$$(P_C a_{CI} + P_I a_{II})(1 + r) + W a_{LI} = P_I \tag{A5}$$

When only corn is basic it is the price equation for the corn sector that determines the real wage in corn as a function of the rate of profit independently of the price equation for the iron sector:

$$W/P_C = [1 - a_{CC}(1 + r)]/a_{LC} \tag{A4$'$}$$

The relative price of iron follows after substituting (A4)$'$ into (A5):

$$P_I/P_C = \frac{a_{LI} - (a_{LI} a_{CC} - a_{LC} a_{II})(1 + r)}{a_{LC} - a_{LC} a_{CC}(1 + r)} \tag{A5$'$}$$

On the other hand, in the quantity equations, λ_I is fixed if g is a given parameter since from (A2):

$$\lambda_I = 1 - a_{II}(1 + g) \tag{A2$'$}$$

while λ_C and Y_I/Y_C are free to vary subject to (A1) which may be written:

$$Y_I/Y_C = \frac{1 - \lambda_C - a_{CC}(1 + g)}{a_{CI}(1 + g)} \tag{A1$'$}$$

---

* If we had set only a_{II} equal to zero, iron would have remained basic since iron is an input into corn which is an input into iron. Thus, iron enters indirectly into its own production.

The effects of distinguishing basics from nonbasics may also be seen in models more complicated than the corn and iron economy. A particular case was sketched much earlier in our discussion of the physiocrats where part of the surplus was devoted to the production of a luxury good, "carriages." This is clearly a nonbasic commodity since it enters nowhere as an input in production. Formally, the equations of such a model are written:

$$(a_{CC} Y_C + a_{CI} Y_I + a_{CX} Y_X)(1+g) = (1-\lambda_C) Y_C \tag{A6}$$

$$(a_{IC} Y_C + a_{II} Y_I + a_{IX} Y_X)(1+g) = (1-\lambda_I) Y_I \tag{A7}$$

$$a_{LC} Y_C + a_{LI} Y_I + a_{LX} Y_X = E \tag{A8}$$

$$(P_C a_{CC} + P_I a_{IC})(1+r) + W a_{LC} = P_C \tag{A9}$$

$$(P_C a_{CI} + P_I a_{II})(1+r) + W a_{LI} = P_I \tag{A10}$$

$$(P_C a_{CX} + P_I a_{IX})(1+r) + W a_{LX} = P_X \tag{A11}$$

Recall that X denotes carriages, C having been used for corn. The fraction λ_I may be set equal to zero if all the surplus iron consumed is in the form of carriages, but this is not required. What is important is that the coefficients of production in the nonbasic sector do not affect the wage–profit trade-off. This is obvious from (A9) and (A10) which are identical to the price equations of the corn and iron model. The relative price of carriages does not appear in these equations so that W/P_C, W/P_I, and P_C/P_I may be written as functions of the rate of profit prior to the calculation of P_X/P_C or P_X/P_I which is then determined by the solution to the price equations of the basic sectors (given the technology of the nonbasic sector).

In more general situations with many commodities it is difficult to distinguish the basic from the nonbasic sectors by simply inspecting the input–output coefficients. Even in a three-commodity model there is a need for some definite criterion. Consider, for example, the case in which all commodities are simultaneously inputs and outputs and are therefore potentially basic. In the following matrix two coefficients are zero, the remaining ones being strictly positive:

$$\begin{bmatrix} a_{11} & a_{12} & 0 \\ a_{21} & a_{22} & a_{23} \\ a_{31} & 0 & a_{33} \end{bmatrix}$$

Commodity 2 is basic since it enters directly into the production of all three commodities. Commodity 1 is also basic since it enters into sectors 1 and 2 directly and into sector 3 indirectly as an input into commodity 2 which is required directly in sector 3. Similarly, commodity 3 is basic since it enters into sectors 1 and 3 directly and into sector 2 indirectly as an input into commodity 1 which is required directly in sector 2. An extreme case where all three commodities are basic even though there are many zeros follows. Here, again, all the a_{ij}'s not zero are assumed to be strictly positive:

$$\begin{bmatrix} 0 & a_{12} & 0 \\ 0 & 0 & a_{23} \\ a_{31} & 0 & 0 \end{bmatrix}$$

Commodity 1 is required directly in sector 2 and therefore indirectly in sector 3 which requires commodity 2 directly, and since commodity 3 is required directly in sector 1 it follows that commodity 1 is required indirectly in the production of itself. A similar argument applies in the case of the other two commodities.

It is not the *number* of zeroes but rather their position in the technique matrix that determines how many commodities are basic. This is shown in two further examples: in the first, only commodity 2 is basic, and, in the second, only commodity 3 is basic:

$$\begin{bmatrix} a_{11} & 0 & 0 \\ a_{21} & a_{22} & a_{23} \\ a_{31} & 0 & a_{33} \end{bmatrix} \qquad \begin{bmatrix} a_{11} & a_{12} & 0 \\ a_{21} & a_{22} & 0 \\ a_{31} & 0 & a_{33} \end{bmatrix}$$

In the first matrix, commodity 1 is required only in the production of itself, and commodity 3, though required in sector 1 and in its own production, is not required in sector 2. In the second matrix, commodities 1 and 2 are not required directly or indirectly in sector 3, whereas commodity 3 enters directly into sectors 1 and 3 and indirectly into sector 2 since commodity 1 is directly required in sector 2. The need for a rule to identify the basic sectors is clear—and we have only considered 4 out of 343 possible combinations of zeros and positive numbers in the three-commodity technique matrix.*

A simple concept will suffice to distinguish basic commodities. It may be asked of any square matrix of the type we are considering whether or not it is

---

* There are $2^n - 1$ ways of choosing positive or zero numbers in *each* column, the $- 1$ occurring since not all entries can be zero (each commodity requires some commodity as an input). Then, since there are n columns, there are $(2^n - 1)^n$ possible matrices, which comes to 343 in our example where $n = 3$.

possible to renumber the commodities by switching like-numbered rows and columns (i.e., if two rows are switched then the like-numbered columns must also be switched) in such a way as to place blocks of coefficients along the diagonal with only zeros below and to the left of these blocks. If so, then the first such block defines a set of basic commodities. In the last two examples such a rearrangement would result in new matrices:

$$
\begin{bmatrix}
a_{22} & a_{23} & a_{21} \\
0 & a_{33} & a_{31} \\
0 & 0 & a_{11}
\end{bmatrix}
\qquad
\begin{bmatrix}
a_{33} & a_{31} & 0 \\
0 & a_{11} & a_{12} \\
0 & a_{21} & a_{22}
\end{bmatrix}
$$

In the first matrix the blocks along the diagonal are single coefficients, the first such block defining the basic sector, 2. In the second case, the first block is again one coefficient while the second is two by two. Still there is one basic sector, 3. In the previous cases, on the other hand, where all three commodities were basic, it will be found that there is no rearrangement of like-numbered rows and columns of the technique matrix that makes it block triangular. A matrix having this property is said to be indecomposable.

Finally, having discovered the basic commodities by rearranging the technique matrix in block-triangular form, it will always be found that the wage–profit trade-off (where the real wage is measured in terms of a basic commodity or some mixture of basic commodities such as the Standard Commodity) has a form determined solely by the coefficients of production of the basic commodities. Given the solution for relative prices and the rate of profit in the basic sectors, the relative prices of all nonbasics are then determined.

Appendix 13B: The Pasinetti Theorem

The relationship $g = s_c r$ or $r = g/s_c$, used in determining the rate of profit, given g and s_c as parameters, would be of limited interest if it held only on the assumption that all wages are consumed. Without that assumption, increases in the value of the stock of capital goods gK could be financed with savings out of both wages and profits. Equation (30) would then read:

$$
gK = s_c rK + s_w WE \qquad \text{or} \qquad g = s_c r + s_w (WE/K) \tag{B1}
$$

where s_w is the fraction of wages not spent on consumption goods. Since the term WE/K depends on technology, the rate of profit, and the composition of output,* which in turn depend on the rate of accumulation and the proportions of output consumed (and therefore on preferences, incomes, and prices), it would appear that all variables must be simultaneously determined.

There is, however, an argument that establishes the relationship $r = g/s_c$ *independently* of laborers saving part of their wages and thus acquiring through the purchase of financial assets a claim to some part of total profits. Known as the Pasinetti Theorem, this important result has been the subject of much controversy.[11] It is presented briefly as follows. In a model of surplus and accumulation, equilibrium persists through time only if shares of ownership in the means of production remain unchanged. As Morishima remarks:

Since the total profits are distributed among individuals in proportion to their ownership of capital and the distribution remains unchanged over time in the state of growth equilibrium, the rate of growth of the amount of capital that each individual owns (i.e., the amount of one's savings divided by the amount of one's capital) must be the same if there is long-run balanced growth.[12]

Formally, the ratios K^W/K and K^C/K defining workers' and capitalists' shares of ownership in the value of the stock of capital must remain constant. This requires that additions to wealth remain constant proportions of wealth for each class, a proportion equal to the overall rate of accumulation. Thus, if S^W is total saving by the workers and S^C is total saving by the capitalists:

$$S^W/K^W = S^C/K^C = g \qquad (B2)$$

Moreover, since profits are paid at a uniform rate on the value of capital, the ratio of profits to capital for each class must be equal to the rate of profit. Denoting workers' profits by P^W and capitalists' profits by P^C:

$$P^W/K^W = P^C/K^C = r \qquad (B3)$$

Then, dividing (B2) by (B3) yields:

$$S^W/P^W = S^C/P^C = g/r \qquad (B4)$$

Since workers' saving out of wages and profits is:

---

*Recalling the definition of K:

$$WE/K = \frac{W/P_I}{(K/P_I)/E}$$

$$= \frac{W/P_I}{(P_C/P_I)a_{CC}(Y_C/E) + (P_C/P_I)a_{CI}(Y_I/E) + a_{IC}(Y_C/E) + a_{II}(Y_I/E)}$$

where relative prices depend on the profit rate, and ratios of output per unit of employment depend on the growth rate and proportions of output consumed.

$$S^W = s_w(WE + P^W) = s_w(WE + rK^W) \tag{B5}$$

while capitalists' saving is:

$$S^C = s_c P^C = s_c rK^C \tag{B6}$$

equation (B4) becomes:

$$\frac{s_w(WE + rK^W)}{rK^W} = s_c = g/r \tag{B7}$$

This last equation summarizes the Pasinetti Theorem. It shows that the relationship $r = g/s_c$ does not, after all, depend on the assumption that workers do not save. Thus, in the general case in which there is saving out of both types of income, the rate of profit remains independent of both the technology of production and the composition of the stock of capital goods, since neither the input–output coefficients nor the value of capital enters into the second equation in (B7). Moreover, it follows from the first equation in (B7) that:

$$s_c(WE + rK^W) = s_c rK^W \tag{B8}$$

This yields an interpretation of the Pasinetti Theorem to the effect that total savings by workers out of wages plus the share of profits that accrues to them is just equal to what the capitalists would have saved out of the workers' profit income alone *if* that profit had accrued to the capitalists instead. It is *as if* the workers saved nothing at all and profit accrued entirely to the capitalists. In this sense workers' saving is irrelevant to the determination of the rate of profit, although their propensity to save will affect equilibrium profit shares.*

To quote Pasinetti on the significance of these results:

> These conclusions, as the reader may clearly realise, now suddenly shed new light on the old Classical idea, hinted at already at the beginning, of a relation between the savings of that group of individuals who are in the position to carry on the process of production and the process of capital accumulation. This idea has always persisted in economic literature. . . . It is valid whatever the saving behavior of the workers may be.[13]

---

*To show this, let total income be written $Y = WE + rK^W + rK^C$ and let $v = K/Y$ measure the ratio of capital to income. The proportionality relation $S^W/K^W = S^C/K^C$ may then be written:

$$s_c rK^C/K^C = s_w(Y - rK^C)/K^W \qquad \text{or} \qquad s_c r(K^W/K) = s_w[(Y/K) - r + r(K^W/K)]$$

using $K = K^W + K^C$. It follows that:

$$\frac{K^W}{K} = \frac{s_w(1 - rv)}{(s_c - s_w)rv} = \frac{P^W}{P} \qquad \text{and} \qquad \frac{K^C}{K} = \frac{s_c rv - s_w}{(s_c - s_w)rv} = \frac{P^C}{P}$$

where $P = P^W + P^C$. Both savings propensities, s_w and s_c, together with the rate of profit and the share of profits in total income, $rv = rK/Y$, determine the two shares P^W/P and P^C/P.

And, on the implications of his analysis for the interpretation of the rate of profit, Pasinetti adds:

. . . the rate of profit is determined by the . . . rate of growth divided by the capital-ists' propensity to save, independently of any 'productivity' of capital (no matter how it may be defined) and indeed independently of anything else. The most surprising out-come of all is that the long-run rate of profit is even independent of 'capital'! In the long run, capital itself becomes a variable; and it is capital that has to be adapted to an exogenously determined rate of profit, not the other way round.[14]

Here we find a further expression of the essential contrast between classical and neoclassical theories of general equilibrium. The capital stock of pro-duced commodities is adjusted, in equilibrium, to the composition of output which is determined by the distribution of income, the share of profits saved, and the pattern of consumption. In a neoclassical model, on the other hand, distribution is a reflection of the relative scarcity of given factors as they con-tribute to the value of production at prices for which there is no excess demand. In one theory, capital is a variable sum of value on which profit is received at a uniform rate; in the other, capital goods (if they are so iden-tified) are simply a subset of the components of a given list of factors; and factor prices are such that, in equilibrium, profits are zero.

Notes

1. Piero Sraffa, *Production of Commodities by Means of Commodities, Prelude to a Critique of Economic Theory*, Cambridge University Press, 1960, p. 9.
2. *Ibid.*, pp. 9–10.
3. *Ibid.*, p. 10.
4. *Ibid.*, pp. 18–25.
5. *Ibid.*, p. 22.
6. *Ibid.*, pp. 22–3.
7. *Ibid.*, p. 23. Sraffa's italics.
8. *Ibid.* Sraffa's italics.
9. The argument that follows is adapted from M. Morishima, *Theory of Economic Growth*, Oxford at the Clarendon Press, 1969, pp. 89–114.
10. Sraffa, *Production of Commodities*, pp. 7–8.
11. See Luigi Pasinetti, *Growth and Income Distribution, Essays in Economic Theory*, Cambridge University Press, 1974, pp. 103–46. Pasinetti lists 28 refer-ences to the main contributions in the debate that developed following his original paper, "Rate of Profit and Income Distribution in relation to the Rate of Eco-nomic Growth," *Review of Economic Studies*, Vol. 29 (1962), pp. 267–79.
12. Morishima, *Theory of Growth*, p. 106.
13. Pasinetti, *Growth and Distribution*, pp. 112–3.
14. *Ibid.*, p. 144.

14

Choice of Technique in a Neoclassical Model

Throughout our analysis of classical and neoclassical theory all matters relating to choice of technique have been set aside by assuming that each commodity is produced by a single process exhibiting constant returns to scale. Each process is a set of coefficients measuring factor services per unit of final output in the neoclassical model, and labor and commodity inputs per unit of commodity output in the classical model. A *technique* of production is a *set* of processes, one for each commodity, so that in all our models technology has been restricted to a single technique. In this chapter we consider the implications of allowing for choice of technique in a two-sector neoclassical model and, in the following chapter, a similar analysis is undertaken for the two-sector classical model.

It is well known that standard treatments of neoclassical theory begin with a representation of technology in which variation in the methods of production plays a highly visible role in the analysis.[1] But there are good reasons for initially presenting the theory within the sparse context of a fixed-coefficients single-technique model.

To begin with, one purpose of our analysis has been to lay bare the historical roots of two great themes in economic theory: the allocation of given resources among alternative uses, and the generation and accumulation of a social surplus. Since Walras is universally recognized as the founder of modern neoclassical allocation theory, it is appropriate to present a version of post-Walrasian theory that comes as close as possible to Walras's original model in which the coefficients of production were fixed. As far as the basic theoretical structure is concerned, the only necessary change in Walras's formal model involves writing resource constraints and price constraints as weak inequalities instead of equations, thereby allowing for outputs that do not use up all of every factor service and for prices that do not allow for production of all commodities.

Secondly, a linear model of neoclassical allocation theory, although it may initially appear to limit the application of the theory to the simplest technologies, is, as Hicks remarks, "mainly interesting because it can be generalized." [2] The possible generalizations include allowing for technologies with any number of processes, as well as for systems with any number of factor inputs and final outputs (as was shown in chapters 8 and 9). But the *method* of analysis of these more complicated cases remains essentially the same as in the two-sector fixed-coefficients model. Moreover, had we begun with a representation of technology in which factor proportions (ratios of inputs in each sector) were allowed to vary continuously, the appropriate mathematics (the differential calculus) would not have allowed a straightforward analysis of cases in which factor proportions do not vary continuously, for, as Koopmans remarks, the calculus does "not permit recognition of restraints on choice that require expression by inequalities rather than by equations." [3] In presenting a linear model of neoclassical allocation theory, we have thus provided an introduction to modern methods of analysis.

Finally, it is helpful in developing the contrast with classical theory to present the basic theorems of neoclassical theory in such a way as to exclude that aspect of "marginal productivity" which goes hand in hand with continuously variable factor proportions.* What we wish to establish is that the neoclassical theory of factor prices does not require such variation in proportions, despite recent criticisms (inspired by the results of modern classical analysis) which imply that this variation is essential. [4] The discussion of relative scarcity in chapter 9 shows that the interpretation of factor prices as marginal valuations does not require any variation in factor proportions (which, in the model, were constant ratios a_{LR}/a_{TR} and a_{LW}/a_{TW}).

Having established certain essential characteristics of neoclassical allocation theory within the context of a very sparse model, we now take up the

---

* The marginal physical product of a factor of production is defined as the ratio of the change in output of a particular commodity to the change in the allocation of the factor service that makes this change in output possible, holding constant all other inputs. In our model the marginal physical product of labor in wheat is either zero, if the land services allocated to the wheat sector are fully utilized, or it is equal to the average product of labor, $1/a_{LW}$, if the land services are not fully utilized. The same is true of the other marginal physical products; they are either zero or equal to the corresponding average products. Note that marginal value products are obtained by multiplying the changes in a marginal physical product by appropriate prices. Finally, our concept of relative factor scarcity is an aggregate marginal product with a value change in the numerator and a physical change in the denominator. Since it is such a hybrid we have not chosen to call it a marginal product to avoid confusion with the more familiar definitions.

question of how a choice of processes affects the analysis. This question is narrowly formulated, however, since all we will be analyzing is the problem of choice of technique in a static sense, i.e., choice from a *given* array of production processes already "blueprinted." Questions concerning the process of technical *change* are not discussed, since the framework of analysis is static.

Variable Factor Proportions

Choice of technique in a neoclassical model is defined by variation in the proportions of a given list of factors used in the production of a particular commodity. Any given ratio or proportion of factors can be represented by a ray passing from the origin through a point of unit factor requirements in a coordinate space where factor services are measured along the axes. The wheat-sector process $(a_{LW}, a_{TW}) = (3, 4)$ is illustrated by the ray in Figure 14-1 where the factor services allocated to wheat are designated L_W and T_W. Constant returns to scale imply that equidistant points marked off along the process ray correspond to equal increments in output. On the other hand, if equidistant points were labelled 1, 2, 4, 8, 16, . . . units of output, increasing returns to scale would be implied; while a sequence, 1, 1.5, 1.75, 1.875, 1.9375, . . . for equidistant points would indicate diminishing returns to

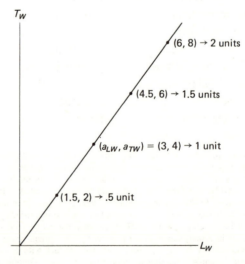

Figure 14-1. Fixed coefficients and constant returns to scale in the wheat sector.

scale. In a more complicated case there might be increasing, constant, and decreasing returns to scale over various ranges of production as in the sequence, 1, 4, 8, 9, 10, 10.5, 10.75, etc.

Let there now be a second constant-returns-to-scale process in the wheat sector, the two sets of coefficients being distinguished by superscripts, α and β:

$$(a_{LW}^\alpha, a_{TW}^\alpha) = (3, 4) \qquad (a_{LW}^\beta, a_{TW}^\beta) = (4, 3) \tag{1}$$

If both coefficients are smaller for one process, the other is technically inefficient since it requires more of both inputs at every level of production. Such processes are dominated and may be ignored in the representation of technology.

The two wheat-sector processes in (1) are represented by the rays in Figure 14-2. Hybrid "processes" can then be defined as linear combinations of the given pure processes. Thus, if one unit of wheat can be produced using either 3 units of labor and 4 units of land or 4 units of labor and 3 units of land, it is also possible (given constant returns to scale) to employ a fraction ψ of process α requirements and a fraction $1 - \psi$ of process β requirements to obtain the same unit output. Setting $\psi = .4$, the total input is given by the point:

$$\begin{aligned}
(a_{LW}', a_{TW}') &= [\psi a_{LW}^\alpha + (1 - \psi)a_{LW}^\beta, \ \psi a_{TW}^\alpha + (1 - \psi)a_{TW}^\beta] \\
&= (1.2 + 2.4, \ 1.6 + 1.8) = (3.6, 3.4)
\end{aligned} \tag{2}$$

This and all other such points for which $0 \le \psi \le 1$ lie along a straight line in Figure 14-2 joining the unit factor requirements for the pure processes in (1). A line drawn horizontally to the right of $(a_{LW}^\beta, a_{TW}^\beta)$ and another drawn vertically above $(a_{LW}^\alpha, a_{TW}^\alpha)$ indicate other points that also yield a unit of wheat on the assumption that the excess labor or excess land need not be used. All three line segments joined together define the unit isoquant in the wheat sector, a set of points measuring various combinations of the two factors that yield exactly one unit of wheat. Other isoquants are constructed in the same manner but starting from a different pair of points such as those indicated along the process rays in Figure 14-2 where $Y_W = 1.75$, namely, (5.25, 7) along the α ray, and (7, 5.25) along the β ray. The respective three line segments of each isoquant are parallel. (This is implied by constant returns to scale, but the converse need not be true since isoquants can be parallel without exhibiting constant returns to scale as, for example, when output increases by a constant percentage for equidistant points along every ray.)

Other process rays may be added, taking into account any amount of variation in factor proportions. Four processes are indicated in Figure 14-3 in order

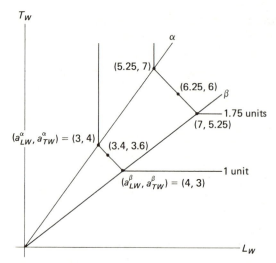

Figure 14-2. Factor proportions vary along wheat-sector isoquants, given two pure processes, α and β, and their linear combinations.

to show a case of dominance not involving pure processes alone. Thus, process γ is technically inefficient, not because it is dominated by any other pure process, but rather because a linear combination of β and δ dominates γ. Finally, it should be noted that in the limiting case, as the number of un-

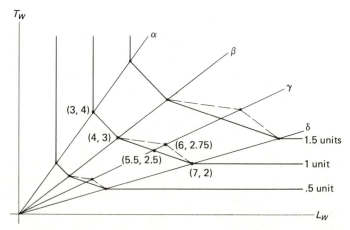

Figure 14-3. A dominated process in the wheat sector. Process γ is dominated by linear combinations of processes β and δ, given $\psi = .5$ since the resulting per-unit requirements, $(a'_{LW}, a'_{TW}) = (5.5, 2.5)$, are both less than the per-unit requirements of process γ.

dominated processes becomes infinitely large and "dense," the corners along the isoquant tend to vanish, leaving as smooth curves the unit isoquant and all other isoquants. It is this familiar limiting case that exhibits continuously variable factor proportions along the isoquant, whereas in the present illustrations proportions change discretely at points where the isoquant meets a pure process ray.

A similar analysis of the technology of rice production would generate a map of isoquants in that sector.

Resource Allocations and Variable Factor Proportions

Having allowed for variation in the ratio of labor to land, we must now determine which processes or combinations of processes are efficient, i.e. place production at a limit point of the feasible set of outputs. The simplest way to identify these efficient techniques is to combine in one diagram the process rays for each sector, together with information on factor supplies. We begin with the case of fixed coefficients in both sectors and then show the effects of allowing for variable proportions. The case considered in detail is the simplest one: there will be two processes in one sector and one in the other.

In Figure 14-4, single process rays are drawn for the rice and wheat sectors together with vertical and horizontal lines in each diagram indicating total factor supplies. We assume: $(a_{LR}, a_{TR}) = (6, 1)$; $(a_{LW}, a_{TW}) = (3, 4)$; $(L, T) = (120, 48)$. The maximum output of rice is indicated at the point where the rice sector process ray runs into a constraint, in this case the labor constraint, at $Y_R = L/a_{LR} = 20$. And, in the same way, maximum wheat output $Y_W = T/a_{TW} = 12$ occurs at the point where the wheat-sector process ray runs into the land constraint.

. Next, consider the composite diagram in Figure 14-5 constructed by placing the rice-sector origin O_R of Figure 14(a) at the point $(L_W, T_W) = (120, 48)$ in Figure 14(b) and by reversing the direction of the axes measuring L_R and T_R. Positive quantities of labor allocated to the production of rice increase to the left of O_R, while positive quantities of land allocated to rice increase below O_R. The resulting box diagram has the property that any point inside the box (including its boundaries) defines an allocation of the total supply of factors to the two sectors of production. Not all allocations are efficient, however, and among the efficient ones not all will fully utilize both factor supplies. For example, the point $(L_W, T_W) = (72, 16)$ measured relative to the wheat-sector origin O_W allocates 72 units of labor and 16 units of land to the production of wheat, the remaining 48 units of labor and 32 units of land

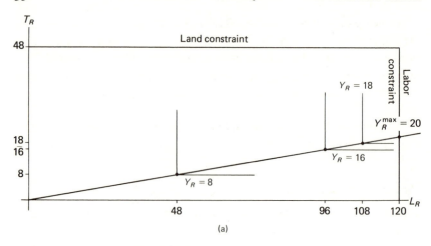

(a)

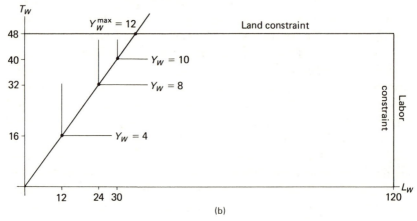

(b)

Figure 14-4. Process rays and resource constraints, given $(L, T) = (120, 48)$, $(a_{LR}, a_{TR}) = (6, 1)$, $(a_{LW}^\alpha, a_{TW}^\alpha) = (3, 4)$.
(a) Rice sector   (b) Wheat sector

being allocated to rice production. The given point therefore has a second set of coordinates, $(L - L_W, T - T_W) = (L_R, T_R) = (48, 32)$, measured from O_R, since by definition $L = L_R + L_W$ and $T = T_R + T_W$. This particular allocation is inefficient since neither factor is fully utilized. In the wheat sector where the labor–land ratio is .75 it is impossible to use more than 12 of the 72 units of allocated labor; and in the rice sector where the labor–land ratio is 6 it is impossible to use more than 8 of the 32 units of allocated land.

Efficient outputs, i.e., limit points of the feasible set of outputs in Figure

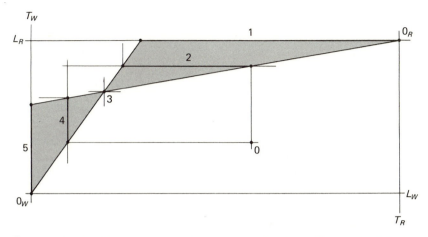

Figure 14-5. Box diagram of factor allocations given the data in Figure 14-4. Efficient allocations belong to the shaded triangles including their boundaries.

14-6, correspond to points in the box diagram through which the isoquants for each product do not cross but only just touch. Consider a line that contains at least one point belonging to a given isoquant for a particular commodity and is such that all factor allocations corresponding to larger outputs lie on one side of the line. Such a line is said to be supporting to the given isoquant. A factor allocation is efficient if and only if there exists a line that supports both isoquants corresponding to the maximum outputs of rice and wheat made possible by that allocation. This criterion is satisfied only in the shaded areas of Figure 14-5 (including their boundaries on all sides).

The relationship between efficient factor allocations and limit points of the feasible set of outputs is not one-to-one. Thus, any point along the line segment labelled 1 in the shaded area of the box diagram defines a factor allocation such that $(Y_R, Y_W) = (0, 12)$ at y_1 of the feasible set. The length of the line segment marked 1 measures 84 units of unemployed labor. Similarly, line segment 2 in the shaded area of Figure 14-5 defines a set of factor allocations all of which support production at y_2 in Figure 14-6 where $(Y_R, Y_W) = (8, 10)$, but now the line segment is shorter, indicating 42 units of unemployed labor. Vertical line segments labelled 4 and 5 in the shaded area of the box diagram map into y_4 and y_5 of the feasible set, where, respectively, 14 and 28 units of land are unutilized. At point 3 in the box diagram, on the other hand, the allocations $(L_R, T_R) = (96, 16)$ and $(L_W, T_W) = (24, 32)$ are such that the relevant isoquants have *only* this point in common, unlike the other cases just

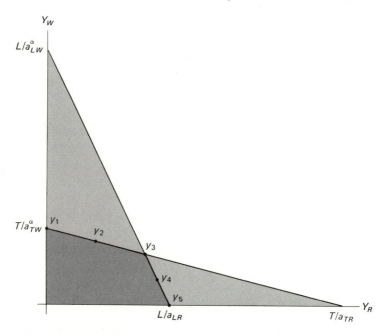

Figure 14-6. Feasible set of outputs, given the data in Figure 14-4. The coordinates (Y_R, Y_W) of the indicated points are: $y_1 = (0, 12)$, $y_2 = (8, 10)$, $y_3 = (16, 8)$, $y_4 = (18, 4)$, $y_5 = (20, 0)$.

considered where the isoquants corresponding to maximum outputs are congruent over a range of allocations. For this reason, there is full employment of both factor services at point 3 and the corresponding outputs $(Y_R, Y_W) = (16, 8)$ satisfy both resource constraints as equations at y_3 of the feasible set.

Elsewhere in the box diagram at the point marked 0, for example, rice and wheat isoquants intersect so that there is no line of mutual support to the isoquants passing through this point. In such a case there is a set of possible reallocations of factor services yielding more of at least one commodity and no less of the other. These are given by the points belonging to a smaller box bounded by the two right-angled isoquants that pass through the given point (excluding the point at the opposite corner where outputs are unchanged). Such a box may be constructed for any point outside the shaded areas in Figure 14-5, i.e., for any inefficient allocation such that the associated outputs belong to the interior of the feasible set in Figure 14-6.

A minimally complicated technology that allows for choice of technique is one that includes two processes in one sector and one process in the other. We let the choice of processes occur in the production of the *numeraire* commodity, wheat. (This makes the analysis of feasible factor prices somewhat simpler.) As an illustration, the wheat-sector processes in Figure 14-2 are combined with the rice-sector process in Figure 14-4(a), resulting in a new box diagram in Figure 14-7. (The axes of Figure 14-2 are rescaled to conform with those of Figure 14-4(a).) The important change that has occurred is that the shaded area near the rice-sector origin is now much smaller than in the case of rigidly fixed coefficients, indicating that there are now *fewer* efficient factor allocations for which labor services are less than fully employed. Putting this another way, the single point of full employment in Figure 14-5 appears in Figure 14-7 to have been "stretched out" to form the line segment joining the point marked 3 where $(L_R, T_R) = (96, 16)$ and $(L_W, T_W) = (24, 32)$, and the point marked 3' where $(L_R, T_R) = (72, 12)$ and $(L_W, T_W) = (48, 36)$.

The addition of a wheat-sector process that is more labor intensive than the initial process $(a_{LW}^\beta / a_{TW}^\beta = 4/3 > 3/4 = a_{LW}^\alpha / a_{TW}^\alpha)$ means that as the composition of output shifts away from labor-intensive rice production toward land-intensive wheat production, it is possible over some range of outputs to combine the two wheat-sector processes in such a way as to absorb all the land and labor being released from the rice sector. This range of efficient allocations is given by the set of points along the line segment joining the two points 3 and 3' in Figure 14-7. Outside that range but in the shaded areas, allocations

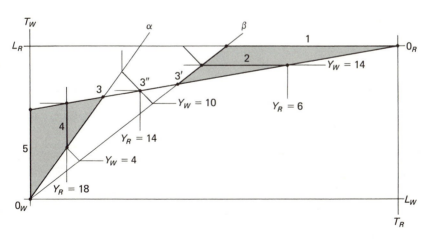

Figure 14-7. Box diagram with choice of technique, given $(L, T) = (120, 48)$, $(a_{LR}, a_{TR}) = (6, 1)$, $(a_{LW}^\alpha, a_{TW}^\alpha) = (3, 4)$, $(a_{LW}^\beta, a_{TW}^\beta) = (4, 3)$.

are efficient even though one factor service is less than fully utilized. Where land is in excess supply only, the land-intensive process α is utilized; and where labor is in excess supply process β is utilized. But between allocation 3 where $(Y_R, Y_W) = (16, 8)$ using process α and allocation 3′ where $(Y_R, Y_W) = (12, 12)$ using process β (the rice-sector process being the same), efficient allocations are associated with linear combinations of α and β. At 3″ in the box diagram $(L_R, T_R) = (84, 14)$ and $(L_W, T_W) = (36, 34)$ so that rice production is $Y_R = 14$ given $(a_{LR}, a_{TR}) = (6, 1)$. If only process α were used in the wheat sector, output would be determined by the available land, $Y_W = T_W / a_{TW}^{\alpha} = 34/4 = 8.5$, leaving unemployed labor equal to $L_W - a_{LW}^{\alpha} Y_W \doteq 36 - 25.5 = 10.5$. On the other hand, if only process β were used, output would be determined by the available labor, $Y_W = L_W / a_{LW}^{\beta} = 9$, with land unused in the amount $T_W - a_{TW}^{\beta} Y_W = 34 - 27 = 7$. Since one process leaves labor unemployed and the other leaves land uncultivated, it follows that a linear combination of the two will absorb the total allocation $(L_W, T_W) = (36, 34)$ and produce a larger output. This defines an efficient combination of pure processes utilizing factor services in the given ratio $T_W / L_W = 34/36$.

Formally, the combination of processes associated with 3″ in Figure 14-7 is found by solving the following equation for ψ:

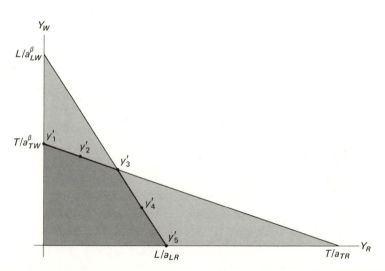

Figure 14-8. Feasible set of outputs, given $(L, T) = (120, 48)$, $(a_{LR}, a_{TR}) = (6, 1)$, $(a_{LW}^{\beta}, a_{TW}^{\beta}) = (4, 3)$. The coordinates (Y_R, Y_W) of the indicated points are: $y_1' = (0, 16)$, $y_2' = (6, 14)$, $y_3' = (12, 12)$, $y_4' = (16, 6)$, $y_5' = (20, 0)$.

$$T_W/L_W = 34/36 = a'_{TW}/a'_{LW} = \frac{\psi a^\alpha_{TW} + (1 - \psi)a^\beta_{TW}}{\psi a^\alpha_{LW} + (1 - \psi)a^\beta_{LW}} \tag{3}$$

On substituting the coefficients from (1), this determines $\psi = .4$ and $(a'_{LW}, a'_{TW}) = (3.6, 3.4)$, the case initially considered in our discussion of the unit isoquant in Figure 14-2. It follows that outputs corresponding to the point $3''$ in the box diagram are $(Y_R, Y_W) = (14, 10)$. This is a limit point of the feasible set of outputs because it is not possible to reallocate factor services in such a way as to increase the output of one commodity without at the same time reducing the output of the other commodity. Notice that the line that supports the two isoquants at $3''$ in the box diagram is congruent with that segment of the wheat-sector isoquant defining the set of linear combinations of processes.

We now construct the diagram of the feasible set of outputs corresponding to the set of factor allocations in Figure 14-7. Figure 14-6 has already been constructed for technique α (process α in the wheat sector and the given process in the rice sector). Figure 14-8 repeats the construction for technique β (process β in the wheat sector plus the rice sector process). In Figure 14-9 these two diagrams are superimposed and a line is drawn connecting y_3 and y'_3. This line passes through y''_3 where outputs correspond to the factor allocation at $3''$ in the box diagram. Now, as long as the composition of output satisfies the two inequalities, $0 \le Y_R \le 12$ and $12 \le Y_W \le 16$, it is efficient to use only process β in wheat production, as can be shown using the box diagram; while, for outputs satisfying $16 \le Y_R \le 20$ and $0 \le Y_W \le 8$, it is efficient to use only process α. However, when $12 \le Y_R \le 16$ and $8 \le Y_W \le 12$, the box diagram shows that techniques utilizing linear combinations of the two wheat-sector processes are efficient and utilize the total supply of both factors. As

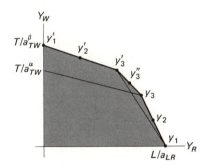

Figure 14-9. Feasible set of outputs, given the data in Figure 14-7. The coordinates of the indicated points are the same as in Figures 14-6 and 14-8. At y''_3, $(Y_R, Y_W) = (14, 10)$.

will be shown presently, the straight line joining y_3 and y_3' in Figure 14-9 is the locus of all full employment outputs, namely, the points of intersection of labor and land constraints (as equations) corresponding to the set of techniques utilizing linear combinations of the two wheat-sector processes. The feasible set of outputs therefore includes the outputs corresponding to the use of pure processes in Figures 14-6 and 14-8 plus those additional outputs made possible by the use of linear combinations of processes in the wheat sector.

There are two ways of stating resource constraints for this two-technique model. The first corresponds to the diagram in Figure 14-9 and is written:

$$L \geq a_{LR} Y_R + a_{LW}' Y_W \tag{4}$$

$$T \geq a_{TR} Y_R + a_{TW}' Y_W \tag{5}$$

$$Y_R \geq 0 \qquad Y_W \geq 0 \tag{6}$$

$$a_{iW}' = a_{iW}^\alpha + (1 - \psi) a_{iW}^\beta \qquad i = L, T \qquad 0 \leq \psi \leq 1 \tag{7}$$

The equation of the line joining y_3 and y_3' in Figure 14-9 is then obtained by writing (4) and (5) as equations, substituting (7), and eliminating ψ. Thus:

$$
\begin{aligned}
Y_W &= -\frac{a_{LR}(a_{TW}^\alpha - a_{TW}^\beta) - a_{TR}(a_{LW}^\alpha - a_{LW}^\beta)}{a_{TW}^\alpha a_{LW}^\beta - a_{TW}^\beta a_{LW}^\alpha} Y_R \\
&\quad + \frac{L(a_{TW}^\alpha - a_{TW}^\beta) - T(a_{LW}^\alpha - a_{LW}^\beta)}{a_{TW}^\alpha a_{LW}^\beta - a_{TW}^\beta a_{LW}^\alpha} \\
&= -Y_R + 24
\end{aligned}
\tag{8}
$$

Note that the coordinates of y_3, y_3', and y_3'', namely, (16, 8), (12, 12), and (14, 10), all satisfy this equation.

Alternatively, and from a mathematical point of view more simply, the two-technique model may be considered as a particular case of a two-factor three-commodity model where two "types" of wheat are distinguished: one produced according to process α and the other produced according to process β, Y_W^α and Y_W^β. Together with rice Y_R there are three outputs or, more correctly, three *activities* to which the given factors are allocated. The feasible set of outputs is then defined by two constraints in three dimensions:

$$L \geq a_{LR} Y_R + a_{LW}^\alpha Y_W^\alpha + a_{LW}^\beta Y_W^\beta \tag{9}$$

$$T \geq a_{TR} Y_R + a_{TW}^\alpha Y_W^\alpha + a_{TW}^\beta Y_W^\beta \tag{10}$$

$$Y_R \geq 0 \qquad Y_W^k \geq 0 \qquad k = \alpha, \beta \tag{11}$$

If all outputs are positive this means that a linear combination of processes is being used in the wheat sector, but if only Y_R and Y_W^α are positive, only process α is used (and similarly for β). Finally, it may be noted that this second way of defining the feasible set of outputs is very easily generalized to allow for more than two wheat-sector proceses as well as for a choice of processes in the rice sector. Thus, a neoclassical model with a finite number of processes in each sector can be represented mathematically as a model with n activities for arbitrarily large finite n.

Prices, Opportunity Cost, and Relative Scarcity

A change in the feasible set of outputs must alter the relationship between the commodity price ratio $p = P_R / P_W$ and the outputs of rice and wheat that satisfy the equilibrium condition: relative price cannot exceed opportunity cost. Figure 14-9 shows that for all limit points of the feasible set of outputs from y_1 to y'_3 (but excluding the latter) the opportunity cost of rice is $a_{TR}/a_{TW}^\beta = 1/3$, the absolute value of the slope of the land constraint in Figure 14-8. At points along the full employment line segment joining y'_3 and y_3 (but excluding the latter) the opportunity cost of rice has a higher value, the absolute value of the coefficient of Y_R in equation (8) which in our example is unity. And, over the range of outputs along the line segment joining y_3 to y_5 (but excluding the latter), the opportunity cost of rice is given by the absolute slope of the labor constraint in Figure 14-6, $a_{LR}/a_{LW}^\alpha = 2$. At y_5 the opportunity cost of rice becomes infinite. The reciprocal (absolute) values of the slopes of the line segments just considered measure the opportunity cost of wheat.

In Figure 14-10 step functions are drawn showing this relationship between output and opportunity cost in each sector. (For the moment ignore the dotted lines.) These are the supply correspondences since for each value of p and its reciprocal $1/p$, the step functions define the output or outputs for which relative price does not exceed opportunity cost. Vertical segments in each graph define a set of prices all of which are less than or equal to opportunity cost at the corresponding outputs in Figure 14-9. The horizontal segments correspond to limit points of the feasible set where a given price ratio is equal to opportunity cost over a range of outputs.

The effect of allowing for variable factor proportions in the wheat sector is to decrease the output of rice over some range of prices p while increasing the output of wheat over the corresponding range of reciprocal prices $1/p$. This is illustrated by the shifts in the supply correspondence where the dotted lines in Figure 14-10 show the position of the graph *before* the introduction of process β. Thus, a larger feasible set, associated with variable factor proportions in one sector, does not imply a larger output of both commodities at every rel-

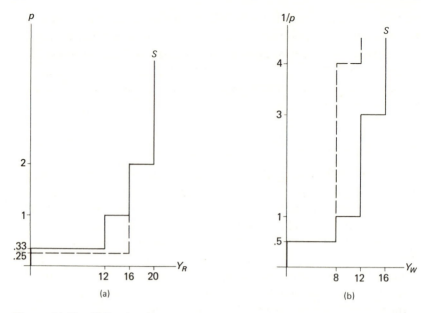

Figure 14-10. Shifts in the supply correspondence associated with choice of technique.
(a) Rice   (b) Wheat

ative price ratio since a reduction in the opportunity cost of one commodity necessarily implies an increase in the opportunity cost of the other.

A further implication of choice of technique may also be seen using the diagram of the feasible set and a graph of the price ratio p. Recall from chapter 9 that the relative scarcity of a given factor service is measured by the increase in the value of output that would be possible if an extra or marginal unit of that factor service were to become available, other things equal (i.e., technology and prices). Here we apply the same argument in the situation in which there is choice of technique. Consider an increase in the supply of land services from $T^1 = 48$ to $T^2 = 69$ (a convenient number, given the technical coefficients in our example). This has the effect of shifting the land constraints in Figures 14-6 and 14-8 away from the origin (without changing their slopes), thereby moving the points of full employment of both factors up and to the left along the given labor constraint (since the labor constraint is in each case steeper relative to the rice axis than the land constraint). Thus, y_3 in Figure 14-6 would be (13, 14) instead of (16, 8) and y_3' in Figure 14-8 would be (6, 21) instead of (12, 12). The new feasible set of outputs is then redrawn in

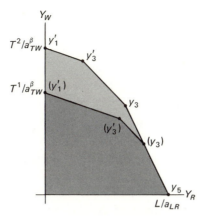

Figure 14-11. The effect of an increase in the supply of land services from $T^1 = 48$ to $T^2 = 69$, given the other data used in constructing Figures 14-7 and 14-9. The coordinates (Y_R, Y_W) of the indicated points are $y_1' = (0, 23)$, $y_3' = (6, 21)$, $y_3 = (13, 14)$. These replace the points with the same labels in Figure 14-9, indicated here in parentheses.

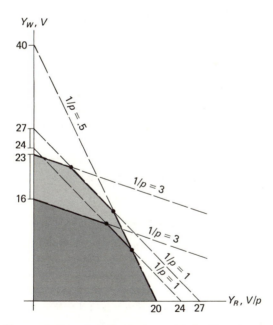

Figure 14-12. Changes in the value of output associated with an increase in the supply of land services are measured by changes in the intercepts of the maximum value price line. These changes are larger the higher the price of the land-intensive product, wheat, in terms of the labor-intensive product, rice. The value changes, measured in wheat, are: 0 given $1/p = .5$, 3 given $1/p = 1$, and 7 given $1/p = 3$.

Figure 14-11 which replaces Figure 14-9, the lines inside the feasible set indicating the initial position of the constraints.

Depending on the price ratio, the change in the value of production associated with the increased supply of land can range from zero, when the price ratio $1/p$ is less than or equal to $a_{LW}^{\alpha}/a_{LR} = .5$, to a maximum of 7 units of wheat when $1/p$ is greater than or equal to $a_{TW}^{\beta}/a_{TR} = 3$. These extremes are illustrated in Figure 14-12 by the indicated price lines. An intermediate case is also shown where $1/p = 1$ so that the increase in the maximum value of production associated with the given increase in land is neither zero nor a maximum. It follows that, as in the simpler case without choice of technique, an increase in the relative price of the land-intensive product is associated with an increase in the relative scarcity of land (which is shown below to measure the rental rate for land services). A similar analysis shows that the relative scarcity of labor services is greater the higher the price of the labor-intensive product.*

Factor Prices and Choice of Technique

Already implicit in our discussion is a relationship between factor prices and choice of technique. This characteristic feature of neoclassical theory establishes a link between the distribution of income and the technology of production and thus provides the basis for a generalization of the proposition that factor prices measure relative factor scarcity. As we have remarked, such an interpretation of factor prices is a hallmark of neoclassical theory.

The connection between factor prices and factor proportions is established by showing how costs of production are minimized at each set of factor prices and for each level of output. Cost in each sector measured in terms of wheat as *numeraire* is given by the pair of equations:

$$C_R = w_L L_R + w_T T_R = w_L a_{LR} Y_R + w_T a_{TR} Y_R \tag{12}$$

$$C_W = w_L L_W + w_T T_W = w_L a_{LW} Y_W + w_T a_{TW} Y_W \tag{13}$$

The first of these linear relationships is graphed in Figure 14-13 as a set of parallel *cost lines* drawn for the rice sector on the assumption that the factor price ratio is constant. The slope of the cost lines is a constant, $-w_L/w_T$, while the level of cost in terms of either input, C_R/w_L or C_R/w_T, varies. For the unit level of production indicated by the given isoquant, there is a unique

---

*Given the coefficients in our example, a convenient way of illustrating this is to let L increase from 120 to 138.

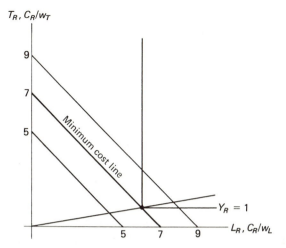

Figure 14-13. Cost minimization in the rice sector, given $(a_{LR}, a_{TR}) = (6, 1)$ and $(w_L, w_T) = (1/7, 1/7)$ so that $w_L/w_T = 1$. Minimum cost for $Y_R = 1$ is $C_R = w_L L_R + w_T T_R = w_L a_{LR} + w_T a_{TR} = 1$ measured in terms of wheat as *numeraire*. In terms of labor, minimum cost is $C_R/w_L = 7$, and in terms of land, $C_R/w_T = 7$.

minimum value for C_R (given w_L and w_T) such that any lower cost outlay would not purchase sufficient factor services to sustain a unit level of output. Alternatively, every cost line may be considered as a set of limit points of a feasible set of factor allocations, given C_R, w_L, and w_T. Output is then maximized, in the present case at a point along the given process ray where it cuts the cost line.

In the rice sector there is no problem of choosing one process over another except in the sense of not using more of any factor service than is necessary when both factor prices are positive.* Thus, a change in the absolute slope of the cost line w_L/w_T simply swings the line around the point of unit factor requirements, altering minimum cost in terms of each input, but not changing the fixed ratio of inputs. In the wheat sector, on the other hand, the process that minimizes unit cost varies with the slope of the cost line and is therefore sensitive to the ratio of factor prices. As Figure 14-14 shows, the relatively land-intensive process α is associated with relatively high values for labor in

* If $w_L = 0$ the cost line $C_R = w_T a_{TR}$ has a zero slope in the diagram so that in minimizing cost all points along the horizontal segment of the isoquant qualify as minimum cost points; in other words, excess labor allocated to the rice sector does not raise cost. On the other hand, if $w_T = 0$ the cost line $C_R = w_L a_{LR}$ is vertical and any point along that segment of the isoquant is cost minimizing since an excess land allocation does not raise cost.

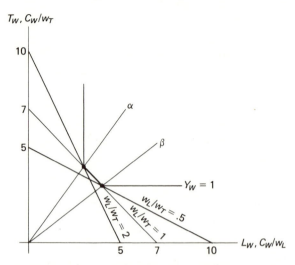

Figure 14-14. Cost minimization in the wheat sector, given $(a_{LW}^{\alpha}, a_{TW}^{\alpha}) = (3, 4)$ and $(a_{LW}^{\beta}, a_{TW}^{\beta}) = (4, 3)$. For each factor price ratio, minimum cost in terms of labor is given by the intercept of the cost line with the horizontal axis; and in terms of land, by the intercept with the vertical axis.

terms of land, specifically, $w_L/w_T > -(a_{TW}^{\alpha} - a_{TW}^{\beta})/(a_{LW}^{\alpha} - a_{LW}^{\beta}) = 1$, while for price ratios less than this value the relatively labor-intensive process β is cost minimizing. At the cross-over point where w_L/w_T is just equal to the ratio of unit factor differences (comparing the two processes) any linear combination of processes is cost minimizing. Note, that as w_L/w_T falls from a high value to a low value, the cross-over points never cause a process which was cost minimizing at one factor price ratio to come back as the cost-minimizing process at some lower ratio. Thus, for each factor ratio there is a single interval of factor price ratios (which may reduce to a point) such that the corresponding process is cost minimizing; and, conversely, for each ratio of prices there is a single interval of factor ratios (which may reduce to one ratio) for which cost is, again, a minimum. In the limiting case of smoothly curved isoquants, there is a *unique* cost minimizing (pure) process of production associated with each factor price ratio.

Factor Prices and Commodity Prices

The various elements in our analysis can now be drawn together. On the one hand, the supply correspondence in Figure 14-10 establishes a relationship between outputs and the commodity price ratio. Using the box diagram, we also have a relationship between efficient processes and limit points of the feasible set of outputs, and thus a relationship between efficient processes and the commodity price ratio. Cost minimization further implies that for any factor price ratio, the corresponding cost line is supporting to the relevant isoquant (since the cost line contains at least one point that belongs to the isoquant such that all factor allocations corresponding to larger outputs lie on one side of the line). It follows that efficient allocations define minimum cost methods of production. To complete the discussion it is only necessary to make explicit the relationship between commodity prices and factor prices, and (in the next section) to link this up with relative factor scarcity.

The price constraints of the model formalize the relationship between prices of inputs and outputs. Following the argument in chapter 9:

$$w_L a_{LR} + w_T a_{TR} \geq p \tag{14}$$

$$w_L a'_{LW} + w_T a'_{TW} \geq 1 \tag{15}$$

$$w_i \geq 0 \qquad i = L, T \qquad p \geq 0 \tag{16}$$

where: $\quad a'_{iW} = \psi a^{\alpha}_{iW} + (1 - \psi) a^{\beta}_{iW} \qquad i = L, T \qquad 0 \leq \psi \leq 1 \tag{17}$

Alternatively, treating wheat as two commodities distinguished by process of production, but having the *same* price (which is unity since wheat is *numeraire*):

$$w_L a_{LR} + w_T a_{TR} \geq p \tag{18}$$

$$w_L a^{\alpha}_{LW} + w_T a^{\alpha}_{TW} \geq 1 \tag{19}$$

$$w_L a^{\beta}_{LW} + w_T a^{\beta}_{TW} \geq 1 \tag{20}$$

$$w_i \geq 0 \qquad i = L, T \qquad p \geq 0 \tag{21}$$

As in our earlier discussion, the interpretation of the neoclassical price constraints is that, for an equilibrium allocation of factors to exist, price cannot exceed unit cost in any sector. Otherwise, "profits" would arise and the existing allocation would not be sustained owing to an excess demand for factor services in the relevant sector.

It is now a simple matter to construct a graph of the feasible set of factor prices. We first draw a pair of factor price frontiers in Figure 14-15. The rice-sector frontier is the set of non-negative prices (w_L, w_T) that satisfy (18) as an equation for a given value of p. The wheat-sector frontier is the set of factor prices that satisfy (19) and (20), where at least one is an equation. This is shown in Figure 14-15(b). Only points along the solid sections of each line

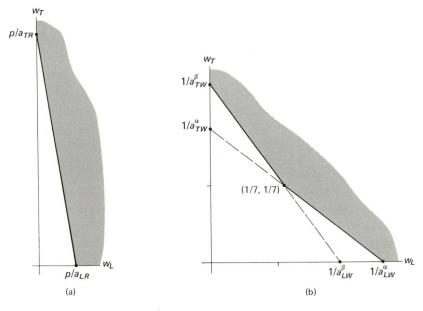

Figure 14-15. Factor price frontiers.
(a) Rice sector, given $(a_{LR}, a_{TR}) = (6, 1)$ and $p = 3/7$.
(b) Wheat sector, given $(a_{LW}^{\alpha}, a_{TW}^{\alpha}) = (3, 4)$ and $(a_{LW}^{\beta}, a_{TW}^{\beta}) = (4, 3)$.

belong to the frontier since factor prices along the dashed lines, though satisfying one constraint as an equation, violate the other and so give rise to "profits" when that process is used. In the event that $0 < \psi < 1$, (15), (19), and (20) are all satisfied at the point of intersection in Figure 14-15(b) where $(w_L, w_T) = (1/7, 1/7)$ in our example. At any other point satisfying (15) as an equation, given $0 < \psi < 1$, either (19) or (20) will be violated so that *only* this point is feasible when a linear combination of processes is used in the wheat sector.

The two factor-price frontiers are superimposed in Figure 14-16 for various values of the commodity price ratio which alter the position of the rice-sector frontier, and thus alter the set of factor prices that are feasible. In each situation total factor cost, given $(L, T) = (120, 48)$, is shown as a minimum by drawing the graph of the cost line:

$$C = w_L L + w_T T = 120 w_L + 48 w_T \tag{22}$$

as close to the origin as possible while still containing at least one point belonging to the feasible set of prices. This is illustrated in Figure 14-16 by

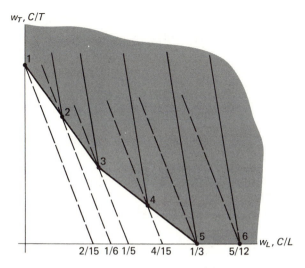

Figure 14-16. Feasible set of factor prices for various values of p, given the coefficients in Figure 14-15. The dashed minimum total cost lines each has the same absolute slope, $L/T = 120/48 = 2.5$. Labelled points correspond to the following prices and costs:

	p	w_L	w_T	C
1	1/3	0	1/3	16
2	2/3	1/14	5/21	20
3	1	1/7	1/7	24
4	3/2	5/21	1/14	32
5	2	1/3	0	40
6	5/2	5/12	0	50

the dashed lines whose intercepts with the axes measure minimum ratios, C/L and C/T, converted to cost in terms of the numeraire simply by being multiplied by L and T, respectively. The corresponding minimum-cost prices have non-negative coordinates that satisfy at least two of the constraints, (18)–(20), as equations given a commodity price ratio in the full employment interval, $a_{TR}/a_{TW}^\beta < p < a_{LR}/a_{LW}^\alpha$. Over this range of prices both outputs are positive, although wheat may be produced by a combination of processes or by a single process.

Within the context of our example, a more explicit statement of the relationship between factor prices and commodity prices can be given. Thus, over the range of prices, $a_{TR}/a_{TW}^\beta = 1/3 \le p < 1$ where the last number is the absolute slope of the line in Figure 14-9 joining y_3 and y_3', we know that both outputs can be positive and that only technique β is used so that (18) and (20) may be solved as equations just as in the model of chapter 9. This yields:

$$w_L = (3/14)p - (1/14) \tag{23}$$

$$w_T = (3/7) - (2/7)p \tag{24}$$

On the other hand, over the range of prices, $1 < p \leq 2 = a_{LR}/a_{LW}^{\alpha}$, we know that both outputs can be positive and that only technique α is used so that (18) and (19) may be solved as equations. This yields:

$$w_L = (4/21)p - (1/21) \tag{25}$$

$$w_T = (2/7) - (1/7)p \tag{26}$$

And, at the cross-over point where $p = 1$ (the absolute value of the coefficient of Y_R in equation (8) w_L is $1/7$ in both (23) and (25), and w_T is $1/7$ in both (24) and (26). This is exactly the pair of factor prices that are cost minimizing in Figure 14-16 (given $p = 1$) and for which any combination of processes is cost minimizing in the wheat sector, as shown in Figure 14-14. Finally, for values of p outside the two intervals just considered, Figure 14-16 shows that $(w_L, w_T) = (0, 1/a_{TW}^{\beta}) = (0, 1/3)$ for $p \leq a_{TR}/a_{TW}^{\beta} = 1/3$; and $(w_L/p, w_T/p) = (1/a_{LR}, 0) = (1/6, 0)$ for $p \geq a_{LR}/a_{LW}^{\alpha} = 2$. The first of these values satisfy (23) and (24) given $p = 1/3$; the second satisfy (25) and (26) given $p = 2$.*

Factor Prices and Relative Factor Scarcity

It is a feature of the present model just as it was of the simpler one-technique model that the relative scarcity of each factor—the change in the value of production made possible by a unit increase in the supply of the factor—is equal to the corresponding factor price. Here we consider the case in which the supply of land increases without any change in the supply of labor since we have already constructed the relevant diagrams in Figure 14-12. (The other case, an increase only in the supply of labor services, is symmetrical.)

The argument showing equality of factor prices and relative factor scarcity in chapter 9 was based on a simple manipulation of Walras's Law, and, in the present context that demonstration is also valid. But, rather than repeat it, we

---

* Given these various results it is possible to construct graphs of the relationships implicit in Figure 14-16 between w_L and p, and between w_T and p. Each is a series of connected line segments so that the functions are continuous, but have corners: w_L as a function of p is nondecreasing, and w_T as a function of p is nonincreasing. Prices that satisfy the relationships are: $(p, w_L, w_T) = (1/3, 0, 1/3), (2/3, 1/14, 5/21), (1, 1/7, 1/7), (3/2, 5/21, 1/14)$, and $(2, 1/3, 0)$, as indicated in Figure 14-16 by the points of intersection of the factor-price frontiers.

offer a slightly different analysis intended to bring out a further aspect of the problem. To begin with, we have the indentities:

$$\Delta L_R + \Delta L_W = 0 \tag{27}$$

$$\Delta T_R + \Delta T_W = \Delta T > 0 \tag{28}$$

which we write:

$$a_{LR}\Delta Y_R + a'_{LW}\Delta Y_W = 0 \tag{29}$$

$$a_{TR}\Delta Y_T + a'_{TW}\Delta Y_W = \Delta T \tag{30}$$

on the assumption that the coefficients of production are constant, i.e., ψ does not change in the definition of the coefficients a'_{iW}, $i = L, T$. Solving (29) and (30) for changes in output:

$$\Delta Y_R = \frac{-a'_{LW}}{a_{LR}a'_{TW} - a_{LW}a'_{TR}}\Delta T < 0 \tag{31}$$

$$\Delta Y_W = \frac{a_{LR}}{a_{LR}a'_{TW} - a_{LW}a'_{TR}}\Delta T > 0 \tag{32}$$

Rice output decreases and wheat output increases since the factor that is now in greater supply is the one that is used relatively intensively in the production of wheat. Thus, the only way to absorb the additional factor service (given that the coefficients of production are unchanged) is to alter the composition of output.[5]

We now multiply (31) by the price ratio p which is assumed to be constant in the calculation of relative factor scarcity and form the ratio:

$$\frac{p\Delta Y_R + \Delta Y_W}{\Delta T} = \frac{a_{LR} - pa'_{LW}}{a_{LR}a'_{TW} - a_{LW}a'_{TR}} \tag{33}$$

But the right-hand side of (33) is just the solution for w_T in (14) and (15) written as equations. The relative scarcity of land, defined on the left-hand side of (33) is therefore equal to the rental rate w_T whenever both outputs can be positive, i.e., whenever the price ratio falls in the interval, $a_{TR}/a_{TW}^\beta \leq p \leq a_{LR}/a_{LW}^\alpha$. Outside this interval the price ratio is such that only one output is positive. An increase in the supply of land will have no effect on the value of production if $p > a_{LR}/a_{LW}^\alpha$, and this is just the case in which the rental rate is zero at the point of minimum factor cost. However, for $p < a_{TR}/a_{TW}^\beta$, the change in the value of production in terms of wheat (the only commodity produced) is $\Delta T/a_{TW}$ so the relative scarcity of land is $1/a_{TW}$ which, again, is

the minimum cost solution for the rental rate consistent with the price constraints of the model. The rental rate thus measures the relative scarcity of
land services in all cases that satisfy the equilibrium conditions of the model.
And, by a parallel analysis, it can be shown that the wage rate measures the
relative scarcity of labor.

The main conclusion to be drawn from the foregoing analysis is that variation in factor proportions complicates the neoclassical allocation model but
does not alter its basic structure in any essential way. It is true that the set of
feasible outputs is altered when input–output coefficients are allowed to vary,
but the basic conceptual framework in which output is limited by resource
constraints that embody parametric data on technology and factor supplies
remains unchanged. It is also true that choice of technique allows, in general,
an expansion of the set of feasible outputs for which all factors (or perhaps a
subset of factors in a model with more than two inputs) are fully utilized.
Over this range the equilibrium commodity price ratio implies positive prices
for both factors. Whatever the associated complications, however, the result
obtained in the very simplest case—that relative factor scarcity is measured by
price—continues to hold.

The remaining structure of the model can now be sketched in to show how
the present analysis relates to the interpretation of neoclassical theory offered
in chapter 10. The relationship between factor and commodity prices implicit
in the price constraints of the model establishes that, for each set of prices,
there is a particular distribution of purchasing power over commodities corresponding to the given distribution of ownership of the factors of production.
The preferences of consumers determine individual demands (at limit points
of consumers' budget sets) and these may be summed to yield total demands
for rice and wheat. If the total demand is feasible, the initial prices are equilibrium prices. It will then be possible to produce these outputs, which are
maximum-value outputs given Walras's Law, without violating the resource
constraints or the condition that relative price cannot exceed opportunity cost.
If total demand is not feasible, the chosen prices are disequilibrium prices and
therefore not a solution to the model.

If we restrict our attention as always to equilibrium positions, it may be
said that, in general, a difference in the parameters of the model will be associated with differences in prices and quantities. Thus, since the technique of
production is now variable, a difference in consumers' preferences may be associated with a change in factor proportions. This aspect of ''consumers' sov-

ereignty'' was mentioned briefly in chapter 10 where it was remarked that, given the other parameters of the model, consumers' tastes may be said to determine not only what quantities of goods are produced and how these are distributed among resource owners in the final allocation, but also what processes are used in transforming factor services into final commodities. The relationship between tastes and technique is indirect since it is the cost-minimizing behavior of producing agents that results in one particular method of production being chosen over another. However, since it is prices that determine which technique is cost minimizing, it may still be held that consumers' preferences ultimately determine the technique in use.

Finally, the analysis in this chapter establishes, at least for the two-sector model, an important inverse relationship between relative factor scarcity and the relative factor intensity of production, as measured by relative factor proportions (where these are variable). Thus, income distribution, which reflects the relative scarcity of factors, is functionally related to the technology of production. This is a striking result for it establishes a definite link between the composition of output, the technique of production, and the distribution of output. Neither the particular mix of goods produced nor the technology in use can therefore be viewed, according to neoclassical allocation theory, as an economic problem independent of distribution; and, conversely, distribution cannot be analyzed independently of the determination of outputs and techniques. All are tied together in an interdependent system of constraints on inputs, outputs, and prices. For this reason, one may go so far as to say that there is a ''natural'' distribution of output implicit in the interaction between supply (factors and technology) and demand (preferences and factor ownership). This distribution is an aspect of the exchange of factors among households who desire final goods through the intermediation of cost-minimizing producers. Any other distribution would be inconsistent with equilibrium exchange.

Notes

1. See, for example, Harry G. Johnson, *The Two-Sector Model of General Equilibrium,* George Allen and Unwin, London, 1971.
2. Sir John Hicks, "Linear Theory," in *Surveys of Economic Theory,* Vol. III, St. Martin's, New York, 1967, p. 81.
3. Tjalling C. Koopmans, *Three Essays on The State of Economic Science,* McGraw-Hill, New York, 1967, p. 81.
4. This may be unfair to the critics of marginal productivity theory since one of their purposes has been to expose the precise implications of particular models of neo-

classical theory in which variable factor proportions do play an important role. See, for example, P. Garegnani, "Heterogeneous Capital, the Production Function and the Theory of Distribution," *Review of Economic Studies,* Vol. 37 (1970), pp. 407–36. However, this type of criticism can leave the impression that it has no relevance for neoclassical models that do not exhibit the particular characteristics of marginal productivity being discussed. See, for example, the brief remarks by Franklin M. Fisher, "Reply," *Econometrica,* Vol. 39 (1971), p. 405; and Robert M. Solow, "Brief Comments," *Quarterly Journal of Economics,* Vol. 89 (1975), pp. 48–52. Many of the elements in the critique of the marginal productivity theory of distribution do not depend on the "smoothness" of technology, however, and we have therefore chosen to present the theory on the assumption that coefficients are fixed.

5. In the theory of international trade, which relies on general equilibrium models to a large extent, this result has been referred to as the "magnification effect." See Ronald W. Jones, "The Structure of Simple General Equilibrium Models," *Journal of Political Economy,* Vol. 73 (1965), p. 561.

15

Choice of Technique in a Classical Model

In this chapter our purpose is to show how the structure of classical theory leads to conclusions concerning the implications of choice of technique that are at variance with those obtained for the neoclassical allocation model—except in certain special and therefore illuminating cases. The analysis starts within the context of a subsistence wage model where choice of technique is introduced in terms of variation in commodity input proportions along isoquants of exactly the kind analyzed in the previous chapter. In general, only one technique (or a pair of indifferent techniques, from the point of view of the capitalists) will characterize an equilibrium solution to the model regardless of the composition of surplus output. The relationship between the profit rate and the technique of production is then analyzed in a model with a variable wage and hence a variable rate of profit. One of our primary concerns is to show that the technique that sustains the highest rate of profit in both types of classical model is not necessarily the one that generates the largest physical surplus, and in that sense an equilibrium solution may have nonoptimal properties.

Choice of Technique in a Subsistence Wage Model

Variable input proportions are easily introduced into a corn and iron model with a subsistence wage of the type considered in chapters 11 and 12. In Figure 15-1 a unit isoquant is constructed in quadrant III of each diagram, one for the corn sector and one for the iron sector. The line segments joining the points of unit commodity requirements define per-unit commodity requirements for various linear combinations of processes as described in the preceding chapter.

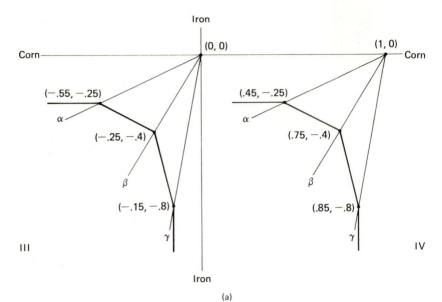

(a)

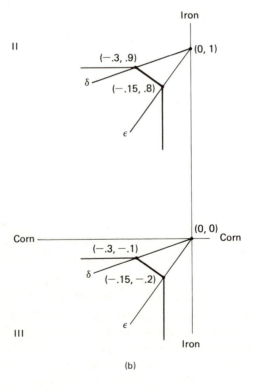

(b)

The set of unit net activities in each sector is obtained by shifting the isoquants of quadrant III into quadrants II and IV, i.e., displacing the unit iron-sector isoquant one unit vertically, and the unit corn isoquant one unit horizontally. Net activities per unit of output in each sector are indicated by vectors from the origin ending in points along these displaced isoquants. Such points measure a positive net output of one commodity plus the (negative) input of the other commodity associated with each unit of production. A given gross output (Y_C, Y_I) is then viable if its corresponding net outputs are non-negative. This results in the construction of surplus possibilities schedules defined by linear combinations of *each pair* of processes, as indicated in Figure 15-2. From the diagram (which shows only two of six possible schedules) it appears that one pair of processes, β and ϵ, wins out over all other pairs since the corresponding surplus possibilities schedule joining the β process in the corn sector and the ϵ process in the iron sector lies further from the origin along any ray than the schedule for any other technique. But this conclusion must be examined closely.

Consider the following numerical example of two techniques, $\mathbf{T}^\alpha$ and $\mathbf{T}^\beta$, that share a common iron-sector process (to simplify the analysis) while using different corn-sector processes:*

$$\mathbf{T}^\alpha = \begin{bmatrix} a_{CC}^\alpha & a_{IC}^\alpha \\ a_{CI} & a_{II} \end{bmatrix} = \begin{bmatrix} .38 & .48 \\ .08 & .18 \end{bmatrix}; \mathbf{T}^\beta = \begin{bmatrix} a_{CC}^\beta & a_{IC}^\beta \\ a_{CI} & a_{II} \end{bmatrix} = \begin{bmatrix} .48 & .08 \\ .08 & .18 \end{bmatrix}$$

*The set of all processes is written in matrix form as:

$$\mathbf{A} = \begin{bmatrix} a_{CC}^\alpha & a_{IC}^\alpha \\ a_{CC}^\beta & a_{IC}^\beta \\ a_{CI} & a_{II} \end{bmatrix}$$

A particular technique matrix $\mathbf{T}^i$, $i = \alpha, \beta$ is then extracted from $\mathbf{A}$ by choosing one process for each sector. In the present case, either corn process can be combined with the single iron process.

Figure 15-1. Unit isoquants in a two-commodity corn and iron model are defined in quadrant III by commodity requirements for pure processes together with their linear combinations. Net outputs are found by shifting the unit corn isoquant one unit to the right along the corn axis, and the unit iron isoquant one unit up along the iron axis.

(a) Corn sector. Unit commodity requirements are given by the coordinates $(-a_{CC}^k, -a_{IC}^k)$ defining activity vectors in quadrant III, $k = \alpha, \beta, \gamma$. Net outputs are given by the coordinates $(1 - a_{CC}^k, -a_{IC}^k)$ in quadrant IV.

(b) Iron sector. Unit commodity requirements are given by the coordinates $(-a_{CI}^k, -a_{II}^k)$ defining activity vectors in quadrant III, $k = \delta, \epsilon$. Net outputs are given by the coordinates $(-a_{CI}^k, 1 - a_{II}^k)$ in quadrant II.

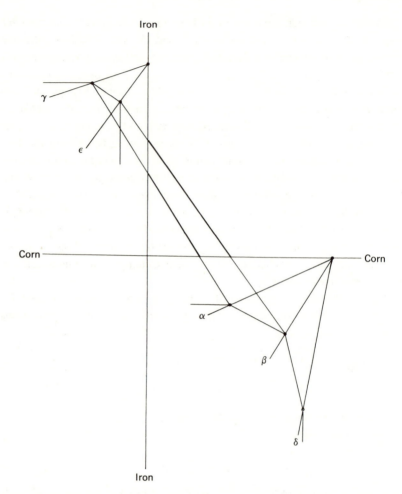

Figure 15-2. Surplus possibilities schedules. The technique defined by processes β and ϵ in Figure 15-1 yields a schedule furthest from the origin along any ray. The schedule for the technique defined by processes α and δ lies closest to the origin of all the schedules constructed from the pure process vectors in Figure 15-1.

It is easily verified using the results of chapters 11 and 12 that both techniques sustain the same rate of profit and the same maximum rate of balanced growth, namely, 100% (a large value being convenient for the purpose of constructing diagrams); while the price ratio P_C/P_I is, in each case, 4 units of iron per unit of corn.* The output ratio corresponding to equal rates of surplus in each sector, and hence the maximum rate of balanced growth, is $Y_I/Y_C = 3/2$ for technique α and $Y_I/Y_C = 1/4$ for technique β.

Surplus possibilities schedules for $\mathbf{T}^\alpha$ and $\mathbf{T}^\beta$ are drawn in Figure 15-3 using the method described in chapter 11. A line with a slope measuring the price ratio P_C/P_I is constructed by joining the end points of the gross activity vectors after lengthening each by a factor, $1 + r$, which is 2 in our example. It is the requirement that such a line pass through the origin that determines r. In quadrant I, output ratios for which the rate of growth is a maximum are constructed as follows. First, a dashed line is drawn parallel to the gross output schedule such that its intercepts with the axes are both $g_{max}/(1 + g_{max}) = .5$ in our example. This line and the parallel gross output schedule cut any ray through the origin into two segments, the first from the origin to the dashed line having a length equal to g_{max} times the remaining distance to the gross output schedule.[1] Two such rays are drawn through points where the dashed line intersects each of the surplus possibilities schedules in Figure 15-3. It is their slopes that define the ratios of iron to corn along the maximal growth path for each technique, or, more generally, the path along which rates of surplus in each sector are equal. These slopes also define the proportion of iron to corn in the Standard Commodity for each technique.

The two diagrams in Figure 15-3 are drawn together, omitting unnecessary lines, in Figure 15-4 in order to show that the surplus possibilities schedule for technique β lies entirely outside the schedule for technique α, i.e., further away from the origin along any ray in quadrant I. This is the case despite the fact that each technique sustains the same rate of profit, and the same rate of maximum growth. Thus, if the profit rate were used as the criterion for choice of technique, it would follow that techniques α and β are equivalent, even though technique β generates an unambiguously larger surplus.

A third technique $\mathbf{T}^\gamma$ which dominates both $\mathbf{T}^\alpha$ and $\mathbf{T}^\beta$ in terms of its rate of profit is now introduced to show first of all how the diagram of the surplus possibilities schedule illustrates such dominance. To keep the construction as

---

* In the example, $P_C/P_I = -(a_{IC}^\alpha - a_{IC}^\beta)/(a_{CC}^\alpha - a_{CC}^\beta) = -\Delta a_{IC}/\Delta a_{CC}$. We have made use of a result from chapter 12 showing that for a given technique the equilibrium price ratio measures the rate at which the coefficients can change in each sector without affecting the rate of profit or the maximum rate of balanced growth.

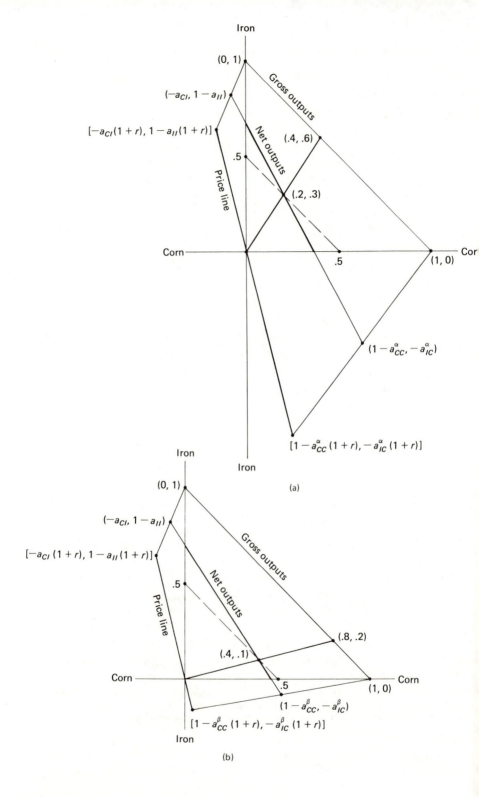

(a)

(b)

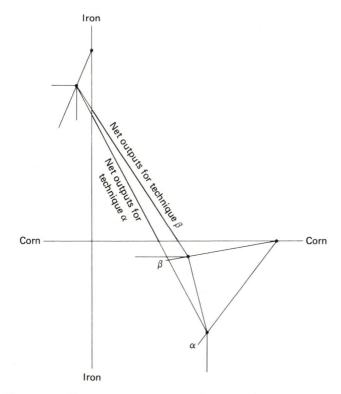

Figure 15-4. Technique β generates a larger surplus than technique α.

simple as possible, technique γ is defined simply in terms of a third process in the corn sector without any change in the iron-sector coefficients. Thus:

$$
\mathbf{T}^\gamma = \begin{bmatrix} a_{CC}^\gamma & a_{IC}^\gamma \\ a_{CI} & a_{II} \end{bmatrix} = \begin{bmatrix} .40 & .28 \\ .08 & .18 \end{bmatrix}
$$

Surplus possibilities schedules for all three techniques are shown in Figure 15-5. In the diagram the rate of profit is held constant at 100% so that each

---

Figure 15-3. Net outputs, price line, and maximum growth input–output ray for which rates of surplus are equal.

(a) Given $\mathbf{T}^\alpha$, $g_{\max} = r = 100\%$, $P_C/P_I = 4$, and $Y_I/Y_C = 1.5$ when rates of surplus are equal.

(b) Given $\mathbf{T}^\beta$, $g_{\max} = r = 100\%$, $P_C/P_I = 4$, and $Y_I/Y_C = .25$ when rates of surplus are equal.

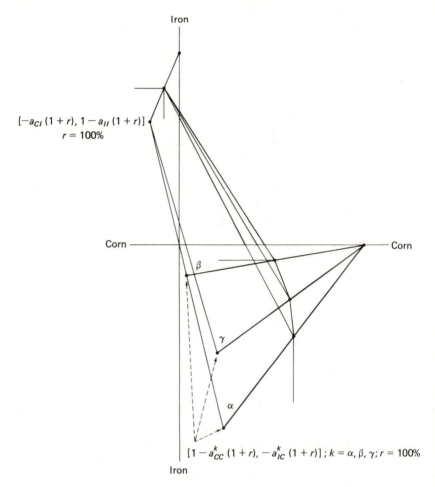

Figure 15-5. Technique γ leaves an unappropriated surplus when the profit rate is 100%, the rate for which the whole surplus is absorbed under techniques α and β.

activity vector is lengthened by a factor, $1 + r = 2$. The lines joining the extended activity vectors for $\mathbf{T}^\alpha$ and $\mathbf{T}^\beta$ pass through the origin as before, but the line joining the extended vectors for $\mathbf{T}^\gamma$ passes through the positive quadrant. A higher profit rate is therefore needed to "absorb" the entire surplus generated by this technique; it may be found by solving equation (12) in chapter 12 for r, taking the smaller root. On substituting the relevant coefficients, the solution to:

$$(1+r)^2(a_{CC}^\gamma a_{II} - a_{CI}a_{IC}^\gamma) - (1+r)(a_{CC}^\gamma + a_{II}) + 1$$
$$= (.0496)(1+r)^2 - (.58)(1+r) + 1 = 0 \tag{1}$$

determines a rate of profit of approximately 110%. A profit factor, $1+r \approx 2.1$, will then lengthen the activity vectors of technique γ to the extent required to force a line joining their end points through the origin. The absolute value of the slope of this line measures $P_C/P_I \approx 3.7$, given $\mathbf{T}^\gamma$ and $1+r \approx 2.1$, as may be verified using the price equations of chapter 12. Note that if this profit factor were used to extend the activity vectors of techniques α and β, the line joining their end points would pass through the negative quadrant in Figure 15-5. In other words, a rate of profit of 110% requires a larger surplus than either of these techniques can sustain.

Technique α and β generate the same rate of profit, 100%, while technique γ dominates both α and β by sustaining a higher profit rate, approximately 110%. It follows immediately from Figure 15-5 that the surplus possibilities schedule furthest from the origin along any ray does not necessarily coincide with the profit-maximizing technique. Moreover, in the present example, since technique γ yields the highest rate of profit, it is also the technique that sustains the highest rate of balanced growth, or the largest value of $\lambda = \lambda_C = \lambda_I$ for $g < g_{max}$.* On the other hand, it should be noted that for $\lambda_C \neq \lambda_I$, given $g < g_{max}$, technique γ may not be superior to α and β. To take an extreme case, let $\lambda_I = 0 = g$. Using equation (31) of chapter 11:

$$\lambda_{C_{max}} = \frac{(1 - a_{CC})(1 - a_{II}) - a_{CI}a_{IC}}{(1 - a_{II})} \tag{2}$$

Then, substituting the coefficients of $\mathbf{T}^\alpha$, $\mathbf{T}^\beta$, and $\mathbf{T}^\gamma$ yields:

$$\lambda_{C_{max}}^\alpha > \lambda_{C_{max}}^\gamma > \lambda_{C_{max}}^\beta \tag{3}$$

so that technique α offers the largest fraction of gross corn output as a surplus when surplus exists entirely in the form of corn. Alternatively, let $\lambda_C = 0 = g$. Again, using equation (31) of chapter 11:

$$\lambda_{I_{max}} = \frac{(1 - a_{CC})(1 - a_{II}) - a_{CI}a_{IC}}{(1 - a_{CC})} \tag{4}$$

in which case:

$$\lambda_{I_{max}}^\beta > \lambda_{I_{max}}^\gamma > \lambda_{I_{max}}^\alpha \tag{5}$$

---

* Recall from chapter 11 that $\lambda = 1 - (1 + g)/(1 + g_{max})$. Thus, if $g = 100\%$, $\lambda = 0$ using $\mathbf{T}^\alpha$ or $\mathbf{T}^\beta$; whereas $\lambda \approx .05$ when $g = 100\%$ using $\mathbf{T}^\gamma$.

Technique β now offers the largest fraction of gross iron output as a surplus when the surplus exists entirely in the form of iron.

Summing up, given the *composition* of the surplus, the technique that maximizes the rate of profit does not necessarily coincide with the technique that generates the largest physical surplus. It may therefore happen that the technique that maximizes the capitalists' rate of profit is, in fact, dominated by some other technique that yields an unambiguously larger output. This matter of "inefficiency" in choice of technique will be discussed further at the end of the chapter.

Choice of Technique with a Variable Wage

The analysis of choice of technique in a subsistence wage model is extended in a fairly straightforward manner to cover the case in which the wage includes not only subsistence but also a variable component consisting of part of the surplus. This component can vary from zero, given $r = r_{\max}$ (the case just considered), to a maximum value for which profits are zero. Formally, such a trade-off is expressed in terms of a function showing how the real wage (measured in corn, or iron, or a mixture of the two) changes with the rate of profit in such a way as to satisfy the price equations of chapter 13. Here we repeat the wage–profit curves previously given as equations (13-22) and (13-23):

$$W/P_C = \frac{(a_{CC}a_{II} - a_{CI}a_{IC})(1+r)^2 - (a_{CC} + a_{II})(1+r) + 1}{(a_{LI}a_{IC} - a_{LC}a_{II})(1+r) + a_{LC}} \tag{6}$$

$$W/P_I = \frac{(a_{CC}a_{II} - a_{CI}a_{IC})(1+r)^2 - (a_{CC} + a_{II})(1+r) + 1}{(a_{LC}a_{CI} - a_{LI}a_{CC})(1+r) + a_{LI}} \tag{7}$$

The relative price P_C/P_I is the ratio of the iron wage to the corn wage:

$$P_C/P_I = \frac{(a_{LI}a_{IC} - a_{LC}a_{II})(1+r) + a_{LC}}{(a_{LC}a_{CI} - a_{LI}a_{CC})(1+r) + a_{LI}} \tag{8}$$

In our analysis of the wage–profit curves, (6) and (7), it is convenient to study first their relationship to the surplus possibilities schedule. In the present context this schedule must be somewhat altered to take account of the labor coefficients. Thus, we change the normalization of quantities used in chapter 11 to the following:

$$a_{LC}y_C + a_{LI}y_I = 1 \tag{9}$$

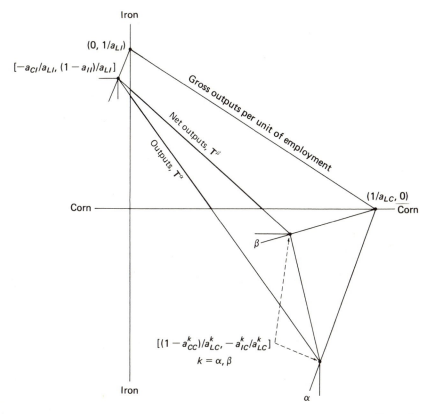

Figure 15-6. Gross and net outputs per unit of employment, given $(a_{CC}^\alpha, a_{IC}^\alpha, a_{LC}^\alpha) = (.38, .48, .5)$, $(a_{CC}^\beta, a_{IC}^\beta, a_{LC}^\beta) = (.48, .08, .5)$, $(a_{CI}, a_{II}, a_{LI}) = (.08, .18, 1)$.

where $y_j = Y_j/E$, $j = C, I$ measure output per worker employed, taking E as total employment. This changes the gross output schedule from a line joining $(0, 1)$ and $(1, 0)$ to one joining $(0, 1/a_{LC})$ and $(1/a_{LI}, 0)$ in Figure 15-6 where, for convenience, we assume $a_{LC} < 1$ and $a_{LI} = 1$, although this does not affect the analysis. The construction of the surplus possibilities schedule of net outputs per unit of labor is accomplished in the same manner as in the subsistence wage model. Simply draw the net activity vectors for $1/a_{LC}$ units of corn per unit of labor and $1/a_{LI}$ units of iron per unit of labor by dividing the former net activities, $(1 - a_{CC}, -a_{IC})$ and $(-a_{CI}, 1 - a_{II})$ by a_{LC} and a_{LI}, respectively. This will lengthen or shorten the vectors in our earlier diagrams, depending on whether the relevant labor coefficient is less than or greater than unity. Having completed this step as shown in Figure 15-6, join the end points of the net activity vectors to form the surplus possibilities schedule defining net outputs per unit of employment.

If the surplus possibilities schedule passes through the positive quadrant in the subsistence wage model, i.e., if the technology in that model is viable, then it must also pass through the positive quadrant in the present model (the converse also being true). This follows from the fact that our modification of the net activity vectors has not altered their slopes; it has only lengthened or shortened them. Moreover, the equilibrium profit factor, $1 + r$, previously associated in the subsistence wage model with a widening of the angle formed by the net activity vectors to $180°$ (to form a price line through the origin) turns out to accomplish exactly the same thing in the present model. Formally, if r is the solution to the equation formed by equating the slopes of the net activity vectors in the subsistence model, after increasing each coefficient by the factor $1 + r$:

$$\frac{-a_{IC}(1+r)}{1-a_{CC}(1+r)} = \frac{1-a_{II}(1+r)}{-a_{CI}(1+r)} \tag{10}$$

then it is also the solution to a similar equation for the present model where the coefficients of the net activity vectors are defined per unit of employment, namely:

$$\frac{-(a_{IC}/a_{LC})(1+r)}{(1/a_{LC})-(a_{CC}/a_{LC})(1+r)} = \frac{(1/a_{LI})-(a_{II}/a_{LI})(1+r)}{-(a_{CI}/a_{LI})(1+r)} \tag{11}$$

Since the labor coefficients on each side cancel out, it follows that the solution for r in (10) is also the solution for r in (11). Thus, the maximum rate of profit is not altered by the inclusion of labor coefficients in the specification of technology. The variable component of the wage is zero given $r = r_{max}$ and the relative price of corn in terms of iron is the same as in the subsistence model.

The opposite case—in which the rate of profit is zero so that the entire surplus is absorbed by the variable component of the wage—provides an interesting illustration of how a classical model can take on some of the characteristics of a neoclassical allocation model. It also provides a particular solution to the wage–profit curves which we shall use in our analysis of the problem of choice of technique. Thus, we set $r = 0$ in (6) and (7) to obtain:

$$W/P_C = \frac{(a_{CC}a_{II}-a_{CI}a_{IC})-(a_{CC}+a_{II})+1}{(a_{LI}a_{IC}-a_{LC}a_{II})+a_{LC}} \tag{12}$$

$$W/P_I = \frac{(a_{CC}a_{II} - a_{CI}a_{IC}) - (a_{CC} + a_{II}) + 1}{(a_{LC}a_{CI} - a_{LI}a_{CC}) + a_{LI}} \qquad (13)$$

in which case the price ratio is given by:

$$P_C/P_I = \frac{(a_{LI}a_{IC} - a_{LC}a_{II}) + a_{LC}}{(a_{LC}a_{CI} - a_{LI}a_{CC}) + a_{LI}} \qquad (14)$$

It can then be shown that in the particular case of zero profits the intercepts of the surplus possibilities schedule with the horizontal and vertical axes measure the real wage in terms of each commodity as given in (12) and (13), and that the slope of the schedule is measured by the price ratio in (14). For this purpose it is necessary to have an equation of the line of the surplus possibilities schedule joining the end points of the net activity vectors. In standard form it is written:*

$$y_I = -\frac{(a_{LI}a_{IC} - a_{LC}a_{II}) + a_{LC}}{(a_{LC}a_{CI} - a_{LI}a_{CC}) + a_{LI}} y_C + \frac{(a_{CC}a_{II} - a_{CI}a_{IC}) - (a_{CC} + a_{II}) + 1}{(a_{LC}a_{CI} - a_{LI}a_{CC}) + a_{LI}} \qquad (15)$$

Setting $y_C = 0$ in (15) shows that the intercept of the surplus schedule with the iron axis measures W/P_I, given $r = 0$, since the second term in (15) is the right-hand side of (13). Similarly, setting $y_I = 0$ and solving for y_C shows that the intercept of the surplus schedule with the corn axis measures W/P_C, given $r = 0$, since the solution for y_C is the right-hand side of (12). Finally, the ratio that multiplies y_C in (15) measures the slope of the schedule of surplus outputs whose absolute value is the price ratio in (14).

Given a zero rate of profit the classical model is now seen to have certain "neoclassical" features. Using neoclassical terminology, the slope of the boundary of the feasible set of outputs (net outputs) measures the relative price of one commodity in terms of the other. This is exactly the interpretation of the slope of the boundary of a single binding constraint in a neoclassical model with one scarce factor and two sectors of production (assuming both outputs positive). Also, where profits are zero, real wage rates in a classical model can be shown to measure total (direct and indirect) labor requirements per unit of output in the production of the two commodities. Thus, proportionality of prices to labor values holds in a model in which the rate of profit is zero and labor is the only nonproduced input.

---

* The equation of a straight line passing through arbitrary points, (x_1, y_1) and (x_2, y_2), is written $(y - y_1)/(x - x_1) = (y_2 - y_1)/(x_2 - x_1)$. Here we identify (x, y) with (y_C, y_I); (x_1, y_1) with $[(1 - a_{CC})/a_{LC}, -a_{IC}/a_{LC}]$; and (x_2, y_2) with $[-a_{CI}/a_{LI}, (1 - a_{II})/a_{LI}]$. Then rearrange terms to obtain (15).

In formulating a model where prices are proportional to labor values, the quantity equations of a classical model are first written as:[2]

$$a_{CC} Y_C + a_{CI} Y_I = (1 - \lambda_C) Y_C = Y_C - X_C \tag{16}$$

$$a_{IC} Y_C + a_{II} Y_I = (1 - \lambda_I) Y_I = Y_I - X_I \tag{17}$$

where, assuming zero growth, $X_j = \lambda_j Y_j$, $j = C,I$, are "final demands" for corn and iron resulting from expenditure of wage income, profits being zero. Rewriting (16) and (17) as:

$$(1 - a_{CC}) Y_C - a_{CI} Y_I = X_C \tag{16$'$}$$

$$- a_{IC} Y_C + (1 - a_{II}) Y_I = X_I \tag{17$'$}$$

one may solve for gross outputs (Y_C, Y_I) in terms of net outputs (X_C, X_I), using, for example, Cramer's Rule:

$$Y_C = \frac{(1 - a_{II})}{(1 - a_{CC})(1 - a_{II}) - a_{CI} a_{IC}} X_C + \frac{a_{CI}}{(1 - a_{CC})(1 - a_{II}) - a_{CI} a_{IC}} X_I \tag{18}$$
$$= A_{CC} X_C + A_{CI} X_I$$

$$Y_I = \frac{a_{IC}}{(1 - a_{CC})(1 - a_{II}) - a_{CI} a_{IC}} X_C + \frac{(1 - a_{CC})}{(1 - a_{CC})(1 - a_{II}) - a_{CI} a_{IC}} X_I \tag{19}$$
$$= A_{IC} X_C + A_{II} X_I$$

The interpretation of the coefficients, A_{ij}, $i,j = C,I$, is "the total direct and indirect gross output of Commodity i needed to support 1 unit of final consumption of Commodity j."[3] Thus, $A_{CC} X_C$ is the amount of gross corn needed to support X_C; $A_{CI} X_I$ is the amount of gross corn needed to support X_I; and $A_{IC} X_C$ and $A_{II} X_I$ are the amounts of gross iron needed to support the same net outputs, X_C and X_I. Given these direct and indirect commodity requirements, gross outputs (Y_C, Y_I) can be calculated for any final net outputs (X_C, X_I).

To show that at a zero profit rate, real wage rates W/P_C and W/P_I measure output per unit of labor in terms of corn and iron, we first write the reciprocal wage rates in terms of labor coefficients and the direct and indirect commodity requirements per unit of output. Using (12), (13), (18), and (19):

$$P_C/W = \frac{a_{LC} + (a_{LI} a_{IC} - a_{LC} a_{II})}{(1 - a_{CC})(1 - a_{II}) - a_{CI} a_{IC}} = a_{LC} A_{CC} + a_{LI} A_{IC} = A_{LC} \tag{20}$$

$$P_I/W = \frac{a_{LI} + (a_{LC} a_{CI} - a_{LI} a_{CC})}{(1 - a_{CC})(1 - a_{II}) - a_{CI} a_{IC}} = a_{LC} A_{CI} + a_{LI} A_{II} = A_{LI} \tag{21}$$

The coefficients A_{Lj}, $j = C,I$ measure direct and indirect labor requirements per unit of net output since A_{Cj} and A_{Ij}, $j = C,I$ measure direct and indirect commodity requirements and these are multiplied by direct labor coefficients, a_{Lj}, $j = C,I$. We conclude that since the intercepts of the surplus possibilities schedule are already shown in equation (15) to be identical with the right-hand sides of (12) and (13), it follows that when profits are zero wage rates W/P_C and W/P_I are equal to $1/A_{LC}$ and $1/A_{LI}$, respectively. The wage in corn therefore measures corn per unit of direct and indirect labor in the production of corn; and, similarly, the wage in iron measures iron per unit of direct and indirect labor in the production of iron. This is a modern classical model where prices are proportional to labor values.

The link between classical theory under zero profits and neoclassical theory is completed by showing that in an allocation model where only a labor constraint is binding and outputs of two commodities are positive, real wage rates are also measured by reciprocal labor coefficients. Such a model would have the following structure where, for the moment, we return to rice and wheat as our commodities:

$$L \geq a_{LR} Y_R + a_{LW} Y_W \tag{22}$$

$$W_L a_{LR} \geq P_R \tag{23}$$

$$W_L a_{LW} \geq P_W \tag{24}$$

Assuming both commodities produced and the labor constraint binding, it follows that $W_L/P_R = 1/a_{LR}$ and $W_L/P_W = 1/a_{LW}$. This result exactly parallels what was just obtained for the classical model under zero profits except, of course, that there is no indirect production of commodities and therefore no indirect labor requirements to account for in (22)–(24).

We have now shown that when profits are zero, the technique of production that sustains the highest real wage in terms of either commodity is the one for which the surplus possibilities schedule is furthest from the origin along any ray. This is because the intercepts of the schedule measure $1/A_{LC}$ and $1/A_{LI}$ and these also measure the wage in corn and iron when $r = 0$. In Figure 15-7 technique β therefore sustains higher maximum wage rates than technique α. But we have already seen that in the opposite case of zero wages and maximum profits, the profit-maximizing technique cannot be chosen simply by inspection of the surplus possibilities schedules. In Figure 15-7, for example, r_{max} is greater for technique α than for technique β, as will be shown presently.

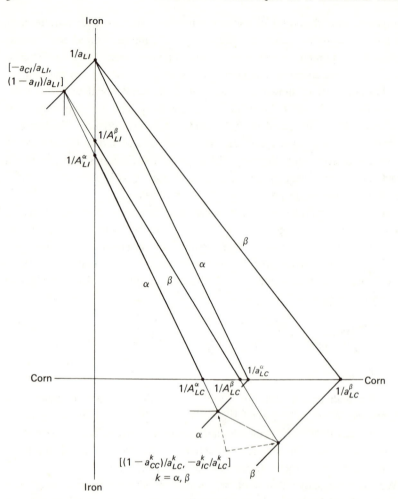

Figure 15-7. The maximum-wage technique has a surplus possibilities schedule furthest from the origin along any ray since its intercepts with the coordinate axes are $(W/P_j)^k_{max} = 1/A^k_{Lj}$, $j = C, I$, $k = \alpha, \beta$. The technical coefficients are: $(a^\alpha_{CC}, a^\alpha_{IC}, a^\alpha_{LC}) = (.2, .2, .8)$, $(a^\beta_{CC}, a^\beta_{IC}, a^\beta_{LC}) = (.25, .25, .5)$, $(a_{CI}, a_{II}, a_{LI}) = (.1, .1, .4)$.

When the profit rate is neither zero nor a maximum, it is necessary to analyze the form of the wage–profit curves (6) and (7) over the range of profit rates, $0 \le r \le r_{max}$. The simplest procedure is to visualize the problem in a diagram. Thus, for each value of the profit rate we define a pair of modified net activity vectors obtained by multiplying all commodity requirements by the profit factor $1 + r$:

$$[(1/a_{LC}) - (a_{CC}/a_{LC})(1 + r), - (a_{IC}/a_{LC})(1 + r)] \qquad (25)$$

$$[- (a_{CI}/a_{LI})(1 + r), (1/a_{LI}) - (a_{II}/a_{LI})(1 + r)] \qquad (26)$$

The line joining these points defines a net-of-profit surplus possibilities schedule which may be thought of as that part of the original surplus schedule left over for variable wages after the payment of profit at the given rate, r. If $r = r_{max}$ the net-of-profit schedule is simply the price line of the subsistence wage model. If $r = 0$ the original schedule is unchanged and so the whole surplus accrues in the form of wages. For intermediate values of r the net-of-profit schedule passes through the positive quadrant but is closer to the origin along any ray than the original schedule, as shown in Figure 15-8. It is the intercepts of the net-of-profit schedule that measure real wage rates in terms of each commodity so that as the profit rate rises and the net-of-profit schedule moves toward the origin, these wage rates fall. This may be shown by writing an equation for the line that joins the two points given in (25) and (26), namely:

$$y_I = - \frac{(a_{LI}a_{IC} - a_{LC}a_{II})(1 + r) + a_{LC}}{(a_{LC}a_{CI} - a_{LI}a_{CC})(1 + r) + a_{LI}} y_C$$
$$\frac{(a_{CC}a_{II} - a_{CI}a_{IC})(1 + r)^2 - (a_{CC} + a_{II})(1 + r) + 1}{(a_{LC}a_{CI} - a_{LI}a_{CC})(1 + r) + a_{LI}} \qquad (27)$$

If $y_C = 0$, $y_I = W/P_I$ in (7); if $y_I = 0$, $y_C = W/P_C$ in (6). Thus, the intercepts of the net-of-profit schedule measure real wage rates; and its slope, given by the coefficient of y_C, measures the price ratio in (8).

In comparing the wage–profit trade-offs for two techniques, it is convenient to remove the squared term in (6), (7), and (27) since this only complicates the discussion unnecessarily. We therefore assume that $a_{CC}a_{II} - a_{CI}a_{IC} = 0$ which has the effect of making parallel all gross activity vectors in Figures 15-7 and 15-8. Equations (6) and (7) simplify:

$$W/P_C = \frac{- (a_{CC} + a_{II})(1 + r) + 1}{(a_{LI}a_{IC} - a_{LC}a_{II})(1 + r) + a_{LC}} \qquad (28)$$

$$W/P_I = \frac{- (a_{CC} + a_{II})(1 + r) + 1}{(a_{LC}a_{CI} - a_{LI}a_{CC})(1 + r) + a_{LI}} \qquad (29)$$

The price ratio in (8), however, is unchanged.

The two techniques used in constructing Figure 15-7 are:

$$\mathbf{T}^\alpha = \begin{bmatrix} a_{CC}^\alpha & a_{IC}^\alpha & a_{LC}^\alpha \\ a_{CI} & a_{II} & a_{LI} \end{bmatrix} = \begin{bmatrix} .2 & .2 & .8 \\ .1 & .1 & .4 \end{bmatrix}$$

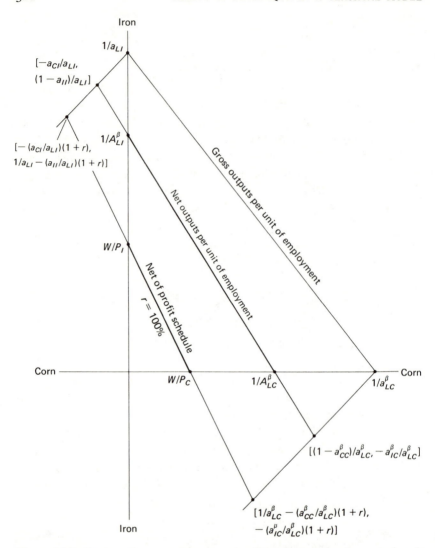

Figure 15-8. Gross and net outputs per unit of employment, and a net-of-profit schedule for technique β using the coefficients in Figure 15-7 given $r = 100\%$.

$$\mathbf{T}^\beta = \begin{bmatrix} a_{CC}^\beta & a_{IC}^\beta & a_{LC}^\beta \\ a_{CI} & a_{II} & a_{LI} \end{bmatrix} = \begin{bmatrix} .25 & .25 & .5 \\ .1 & .1 & .4 \end{bmatrix}$$

Both matrices satisfy the condition $a_{CC}\,a_{II} - a_{CI}\,a_{IC} = 0$. The first also satisfies $a_{LI}\,a_{IC} - a_{LC}\,a_{II} = 0$ and hence $a_{LC}\,a_{CI} - a_{LI}\,a_{CC} = 0$ which is to say that the co-

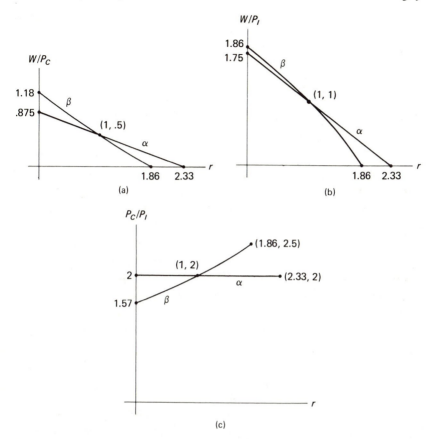

Figure 15-9. A switch point occurs at $r = 100\%$ where wage–profit trade-offs and price functions intersect, given the coefficients for techniques α and β in Figure 15-7.
(a) Corn wage W/P_C as a function of r.
(b) Iron wage W/P_I as a function of r.
(c) Relative price P_C/P_I as a function of r.

efficients in one row are a common multiple of those in the other. As a result the wage–profit curves are straight lines and the price ratio is constant. The lines in Figure 15-9 are graphs of functions obtained by substituting $\mathbf{T}^\alpha$ and $\mathbf{T}^\beta$ into (28), (29), and (8):

$$(W/P_C)^\alpha = \frac{1 - .3(1 + r)}{.8} \tag{30}$$

$$(W/P_I)^\alpha = \frac{1 - .3(1 + r)}{.4} \tag{31}$$

$$(P_C/P_I)^\alpha = 2 \tag{32}$$

$$(W/P_C)^\beta = \frac{1 - .35(1 + r)}{.5 + .05(1 + r)} \tag{33}$$

$$(W/P_I)^\beta = \frac{1 - .35(1 + r)}{.4 - .05(1 + r)} \tag{34}$$

$$(P_C/P_I)^\beta = \frac{.5 + .05(1 + r)}{.4 - .05(1 + r)} \tag{35}$$

Figure 15-9 shows that real wage rates are inverse functions of the rate of profit, a result which is only implicit in Figure 15-8.* The *rate* at which W/P_C and W/P_I fall, however, depends on how the price ratio P_C/P_I varies with r, and this in turn depends on the structure of the technique matrix. In general, if the surplus possibilities schedule has a slope that is steeper (greater in absolute value) than the slope of the gross output schedule, then P_C/P_I increases with r: the slope of the net-of-profit schedule becomes steeper as the activity vectors emanating from $(1/a_{LC}, 0)$ and $(0, 1/a_{LI})$ are progressively lengthened by an increasing factor $1 + r$. Since the slope of the gross output schedule is $-a_{LC}/a_{LI}$ and the slope of the net output schedule is $-A_{LC}/A_{LI}$ from (15), it follows that P_C/P_I increases with r if and only if:

$$A_{LC}/A_{LI} > a_{LC}/a_{LI} \tag{36}$$

On the assumption that $a_{CC}a_{II} - a_{CI}a_{IC} = 0$ it can be shown that (36) implies an unambiguously labor-intensive iron sector, i.e., the ratios of labor to corn and of labor to iron in that sector exceed the corresponding ratios in the corn sector.† This means that a higher rate of profit increases the costs of commod-

---

* The wage–profit curves in Figure 15-9 must not be confused with the factor–price frontiers of neoclassical theory. The latter define factor prices for which the price relation in a given *sector* is satisfied as an equation. A wage–profit curve is defined by a *set* of price equations corresponding to a technique of production which is a set of processes, one for each basic commodity. (On basic commodities, see Appendix 11A.)

† Since both numerator and denominator on the left-hand side of (36) are positive, given $1 - a_{CC} > 0$ and $1 - a_{II} > 0$, we may cross multiply and drop the term $a_{LC}a_{LI}$ from each side leaving:

$$a_{LI}(a_{LI}a_{IC} - a_{LC}a_{II}) > a_{LC}(a_{LC}a_{CI} - a_{LI}a_{CC})$$

Since $(a_{LC}a_{CI} - a_{LI}a_{CC}) = -(a_{CC}/a_{IC})(a_{LI}a_{IC} - a_{LC}a_{II})$, given $a_{CC}a_{II} = a_{CI}a_{IC}$, it follows that:

$$a_{LI}(a_{LI}a_{IC} - a_{LC}a_{II}) > -(a_{LC}a_{CC}/a_{IC})(a_{LI}a_{IC} - a_{LC}a_{II})$$

or:

$$(a_{LI}a_{IC} + a_{LC}a_{CC})(a_{LI}a_{IC} - a_{LC}a_{II}) > 0$$

so that $(a_{LI}a_{IC} - a_{LC}a_{II}) > 0$, in which case $(a_{LC}a_{CI} - a_{LI}a_{CC}) < 0$, given $(a_{CC}a_{II} - a_{CI}a_{IC}) = 0$. Thus, $a_{LI}/a_{II} > a_{LC}/a_{IC}$, and $a_{LI}/a_{CI} > a_{LC}/a_{CC}$. The ratios of labor to each commodity are greater in the production of iron than in the production of corn.

ity inputs *more* in the corn sector than in the labor-intensive iron sector so that, to allow both industries to pay the same wage after a rise in the (uniform) profit rate, the price of corn must rise relatively to the price of iron. This is shown for technique β in Figure 15-9(c). Alternatively, since a higher rate of profit is associated with a higher value of commodity inputs measured in terms of iron as *numeraire,* equal increments in the rate of profit will be associated with *increasing* increments in the iron value of profits. The wage in terms of iron must therefore fall at an increasing rate for each given increase in the profit rate. This is shown for technique β in Figure 15-9(b). By a similar argument, the wage in corn falls at a decreasing rate for each given increase in the profit rate as shown for technique β in Figure 15-9(a).

The *linear* wage–profit trade-offs for technique α in Figure 15-9 illustrate the special case of "constant organic composition of capital": the ratios of direct labor to indirect labor are the same in both sectors, so that a difference in wages or profits does not result in any change in relative costs.* The equilibrium price ratio P_C/P_I is therefore constant and equal to the ratio of direct and indirect labor requirements A_{LC}/A_{LI} which is equal to a_{LC}/a_{LI}. Prices are proportional to labor inputs for all rates of profit.

Our illustration of wage–profit curves for two techniques is constructed to show that one technique can sustain a higher maximum profit rate and the other a higher maximum wage rate. At an intermediate switch point the two techniques sustain equal profit rates and real wage rates. In Figure 15-9 this occurs at $r = 100\%$ where the corn wage is .5 and the iron wage is 1 for both techniques. For lower rates of profit, technique β sustains a higher real wage (in terms of either commodity); for higher rates of profit it is technique α that can support a higher real wage. The technique of production can therefore be considered as a function of the rate of profit if we assume that competition results in a choice of technique for which the real wage is a maximum given the profit rate.

Re-switching of Techniques

A problem which has received considerable attention in the literature[4] concerns the invertibility of the relationship between profit rates and techniques

---

*In the case of $\mathbf{T}^\alpha$ all input proportions are equal so that $A_{LC}/A_{LI} = a_{LC}/a_{LI}$: the ratio of direct and indirect labor requirements is equal to the ratio of direct requirements. The same situation can arise, however, without assuming $a_{CC}a_{II} - a_{CI}a_{IC} = 0$, $a_{LC}a_{CI} - a_{LI}a_{CC} = 0$, and $a_{LI}a_{IC} - a_{LC}a_{II} = 0$, where one of these conditions is implied by the other two. For example, the price ratio is a constant for all profit rates, and real wage rates are linear functions of r given $(a_{CC}, a_{IC}, a_{LC}) = (.4, .2, .01)$ and $(a_{CI}, a_{II}, a_{LI}) = (.2, .7, .02)$. On substituting these coefficients in $(6) - (8)$: $W/P_C = -80(1 + r) + 100$; $W/P_I = -40(1 + r) + 50$; and $P_C/P_I = .5 = A_{LC}/A_{LI} = a_{LC}/a_{LI}$.

of production. It is one thing to say that at a given profit rate there is one technique or a pair of techniques (at a switch point) that maximizes the real wage. It is another to say that, given the technique, the profit rate (or wage rate) is fixed at a given value or restricted to a single interval of values. In general, the latter statement is false, as we now show in terms of an example.

We assume that corn is the only commodity consumed so that techniques are to be compared, at a given rate of profit, only in terms of the corn value of the wage. Iron is a commodity that enters only into production and it is assumed to have a specific form appropriate to each technique. Thus, iron is no longer homogeneous across techniques so that, in effect, we have a three-commodity model, but only two commodities are produced with any given technique of production. It follows that we cannot combine the *processes* belonging to different techniques since each matrix has its own particular units of measurement for the input of iron: *

$$\mathbf{T}^{\alpha} = \begin{bmatrix} a_{CC}^{\alpha} & a_{IC}^{\alpha} & a_{LC}^{\alpha} \\ a_{CI}^{\alpha} & a_{II}^{\alpha} & a_{LI}^{\alpha} \end{bmatrix} = \begin{bmatrix} 20/164 & 100/164 & 25/164 \\ 12/164 & 60/164 & 220/164 \end{bmatrix}$$

$$\mathbf{T}^{\beta} = \begin{bmatrix} a_{CC}^{\beta} & a_{IC}^{\beta} & a_{LC}^{\beta} \\ a_{CI}^{\beta} & a_{II}^{\beta} & a_{LI}^{\beta} \end{bmatrix} = \begin{bmatrix} 55/667 & 100/667 & 1250/667 \\ 165/667 & 300/667 & 415/667 \end{bmatrix}$$

Substituting these coefficients into equations (28) and (29), we then graph the resulting curves in Figure 15-10. Evidently, if it were known that technique α was in use, it could not be said whether the profit rate was high or low. This is because there are two switch points: technique α maximizes the real wage when r is greater than 80% and also maximizes the real wage when r is less than 24%. Technique β, on the other hand, is chosen under competitive conditions when the profit rate lies in the interval between these values.

This result, first regarded as a curiosity,[5] is interesting mainly because it cannot arise in a neoclassical allocation model of the type we have consid-

---

*Formally, the matrix **A** from which $\mathbf{T}^{\alpha}$ and $\mathbf{T}^{\beta}$ are extracted would be written:

$$\mathbf{A} = \begin{bmatrix} a_{CC}^{\alpha} & a_{IC}^{\alpha} & 0 & a_{LC}^{\alpha} \\ a_{CC}^{\beta} & 0 & a_{IC}^{\beta} & a_{LC}^{\beta} \\ a_{CI}^{\alpha} & a_{II}^{\alpha} & 0 & a_{LI}^{\alpha} \\ a_{CI}^{\beta} & 0 & a_{II}^{\beta} & a_{LI}^{\beta} \end{bmatrix}$$

where each row defines a process of production (the first two for corn, the third for iron of type α, and the fourth for iron of type β), the columns corresponding to inputs of corn, iron of type α, iron of type β, and labor.

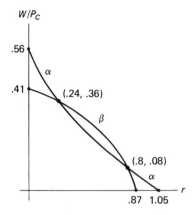

Figure 15-10. Reswitching of techniques.

ered. This is clear from the construction of the isoquant in chapter 14 where each process is cost minimizing for a *single interval* of factor prices, and where each combination of processes is cost minimizing at exactly one set of factor prices. Thus, for any given technique of production in a neoclassical model, the distribution of income is determined, if not uniquely, then at least within only *one* interval of values. In a classical model, on the other hand, a given technique may be associated with widely *separated* distributions, other techniques corresponding to intermediate distributions.

"Efficient" Techniques in a Classical Model

It was shown in the subsistence wage model that the technique associated with the highest rate of profit may not be the one that generates the largest physical surplus. In the present context where the wage includes a variable component over and above subsistence, a similar phenomenon arises.

In comparing techniques α and β in Figure 15-7, it is apparent that if the whole net output is consumed, technique β is superior to technique α since the surplus possibilities schedule for T^β lies further from the origin along any ray. There is no ambiguity in identifying technique β as superior since for any composition of final demand, given zero growth, a larger surplus is obtained under T^β than under T^α.[6] This result can be generalized for the case in which the rate of growth is positive. Thus, for any g, a net-of-accumulation schedule may be constructed defining all possible net outputs available for consumption. This is accomplished by multiplying the commodity coefficients of production by a growth factor $1 + g$. The resulting net-of-accumulation schedule lies inside the surplus possibilities schedule, and is formally identical to the net-of-profit schedule constructed for a profit rate equal to the given value of g. Figure 15-11 illustrates two such schedules for $g = 60\%$, using the coefficients of $\mathbf{T}^\alpha$ and $\mathbf{T}^\beta$ from Figure 15-7. Technique β yields the larger surplus for consumption, making this the *optimal* technique for this rate of growth; and, whatever the number of techniques, there will always be such an optimal technique. In the diagram, net-of-profit schedules are also con-structed assuming $r = 120\%$. A higher real wage (measured in either corn or iron) is sustained by $\mathbf{T}^\alpha$ than by $\mathbf{T}^\beta$, so that the former is the *equilibrium* tech-nique at $r = 120\%$. There is no incentive to switch to the optimal technique since the real wage is already a maximum for the given profit rate. Such a nonoptimal position would correspond, for example, to zero savings out of wages and a propensity to save out of profits of .5. (See equation (30) of chapter 13 where $g = 60\%$ implies $r = 120\%$, given $s_c = .5$.)

In the case of smooth isoquants in quadrants II and IV of our diagrams, an optimal technique would be associated with a line drawn tangent to the isoquants after extending each process ray, emanating from $(1/a_{LC}, 0)$ and $(0, 1/a_{LI})$, by a factor $(1 + g)$ where g is given. The optimal processes are the ones that meet the isoquants at the points of tangency. If the rate of profit is equal to the rate of growth, the technique generating the largest surplus for consumption also generates the highest real wage. However, since in general the rate of profit will exceed the rate of growth, the maximum wage technique will not, in general, be the optimal technique. Thus, a larger surplus for con-sumption could be obtained by switching to the optimal technique, but there is no incentive on the part of either capitalists or workers to bring about this change since the wage is already a maximum, given the profit rate.

The nonoptimality of choice of technique in a classical model is, of course, at sharp variance with the results obtained by neoclassical theory where vari-able factor proportions only expand the set of feasible outputs corresponding to efficient allocations of resources. From the point of view of neoclassical theory, the classical results are therefore "surprising and disturbing." [7] At the same time, the classical analysis also shows how to avoid a nonoptimal choice of technique simply by ensuring that the growth rate and the profit rate are equal.

This result, that optimality with steady growth requires profit rate equal to growth rate and profits equal to saving and investment has come to be called the Golden Rule because it makes consumption as great as possible subject to the growth rate. It is a direct consequence of von Neumann's analysis with the difference that, whereas he took

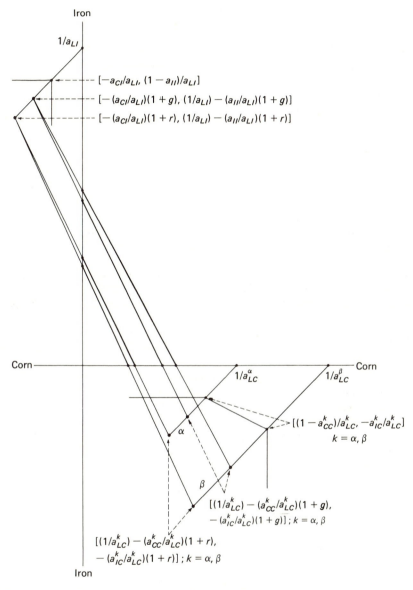

Figure 15-11. Net-of-accumulation and net-of-profit schedules for techniques α and β in Figure 15-7, given $g = 60\%$ and $r = 120\%$. Technique β generates a larger surplus for consumption while technique α sustains a higher real wage.

consumption as given and maximized growth rate, here the growth is given and consumption is maximized.[8]

Thus, we are alerted to the fact that in classical theory, the distribution of income between wages and profits influences not only the allocation of the surplus, but also the *size* of the surplus through its effect on choice of technique. In neoclassical theory, on the other hand, the distribution of the product is simply a corollary to an explanation of the allocation of given resources among alternative uses.

Notes

1. This construction is from R. M. Goodwin, *Elementary Economics from the Higher Standpoint,* Cambridge University Press, 1970, pp. 33–7.
2. See Robert Dorfman, Paul A. Samuelson, and Robert M. Solow, *Linear Programming and Economic Analysis,* McGraw-Hill, New York, 1958, pp. 215–24.
3. *Ibid.,* p. 218.
4. See "Paradoxes in Capital Theory: A Symposium," *Quarterly Journal of Economics,* Vol. 80 (1966), pp. 503–83.
5. Joan Robinson, *The Accumulation of Capital,* Macmillan, London, 1956, pp. 109–10.
6. Thus, despite the ability to substitute labor for commodities in production, one technique is best whatever the composition of output. This result, when first discovered, was named the nonsubstitution theorem since it was at variance with the results on substitution usually obtained in neoclassical allocation models. See T. C. Koopmans, ed., *Activity Analysis of Production and Allocation,* Wiley, New York, 1949, chapters 7–10 by P. Samuelson, T. C. Koopmans, K. J. Arrow, and N. Georgescu-Roegen, respectively, pp. 142–73. See also P. Samuelson, "A New Theorem on Nonsubstitution," in Hugo Hegeland, ed., *Money, Growth and Methodology and Other Essays in Economics,* Lund, Sweden, CWK Gleerup, 1961.
7. Goodwin, *Elementary Economics,* p. 56.
8. *Ibid.,* p. 80.

16

A Concluding Assessment of the Two Theories

Classical Theory

Classical theory developed concurrently with the transition from feudalism to the capitalist mode of production. For its inventors it was a theory consciously concerned with the emerging capitalist phase of history, and for that reason its methods or form of abstraction took account not only of the structure of society, but also of the expanding character of the process of production typical of capitalism.

The reproduction of commodities by means of commodities is central to all modern treatments of classical theory: an economy exists through time only if it continually replaces the material basis for production. This is the starting point for classical theory and the associated condition of viability, its initial concept.

Mathematical methods of analysis deal systematically with the implications of viability. In our formal argument, we began with a statement of quantity relations for certain linear models of production. Here, the most important and historically significant insight is the distinction between systems that are just viable and those that yield a surplus over the inputs needed to maintain the flow of production. Viability is a condition relevant not to particular sectors but to the system of reproduction as a whole. It is not, however, simply a matter of technology in an engineering sense, since part of the material basis for production includes subsistence commodities sufficient for the reproduction of the labor force. This latter process, though left unspecified in our model, is an essential aspect of the social relations of production. Thus, to ignore subsistence requirements would be to render the viability concept meaningless: a capitalist economy could not maintain its capacity to produce if the labor force were not maintained. What counts as subsistence, however, is historically determined, in part by the very process of reproduction and expansion of capital.

In an economy that is more than just viable there is a trade-off between accumulation and consumption of the surplus. The existence of a surplus, though necessary for the expansion of capital, is not therefore sufficient: part of the surplus must be diverted to expansion of the means of production. Capitalist economies are distinguished by the unique social conditions under which the surplus or net product is extracted.

For the classical economists the key to an analysis of accumulation under capitalism lay in the division of society into landlords, capitalists, and workers, and the consequent division of income into rents, profits, and wages. The observations that landlords consumed their rents in "riotous living," capitalists reinvested a part of their profits, and workers lived on subsistence wages provided the basis for an analysis of accumulation in terms of the distribution of income and the behavior of the capitalist class. For our purposes, a two-class division sufficed: propertyless workers receive only wages, with a minimum defined by subsistence, while capitalists receive profits in proportion to the value of the stock of capital they own. In the simplest model, workers consume the whole of their wages while capitalists consume part of the profit, reinvesting the remainder and thus accumulating a still larger stock of capital. This link between distribution and accumulation is fundamental to classical theory, hence the famous remark: "To determine the laws which regulate this distribution, is the principal problem of Political Economy. . . ."[1]

Real wages were typically regarded as a parameter in classical models of the long run. A fast enough rate of accumulation might, however, cause a temporary shortage of labor and higher wages in the short run. This was looked upon with approval by Ricardo since it might lead to a rise in customary standards of subsistence and thus to an increase in the long-run level of wages. In any case, Ricardo treated the long-run supply of labor as perfectly elastic at the customary level of subsistence, thus explaining the long-run price of labor in terms of a Malthusian theory of the growth of population. Marx used instead a theory of the reserve army of the unemployed, always available at a given subsistence wage. In either case, profits are dependent on the technical conditions of production, given the level of wages. Accumulation is then greater to the extent that profits are reinvested, and less to the extent that they are consumed.

In analyzing modern capitalist economies, classical views concerning the growth of population seriously misrepresent the complex process of the repro-

duction of the labor force. The Marxian theory of the reserve army of the unemployed provides a starting point for the analysis of the link between labor
supply and changes in technology inherent in the process of capitalist accumulation, but this link has not yet been adequately formulated. Meanwhile,
the basic structure and conceptual foundation of classical theory remains intact and has been given a new interpretation by treating wages rather than
profits as the residual category of income. This requires a theory of the rate of
profit to replace the classical or Marxian determinants of the real wage.

In its most incisive form the new theory can be stated in terms of three variables: the rate of growth of the stock of capital, the rate of profit, and the
proportion of profits reinvested in the accumulation of a larger stock of capital. The relationship among these variables, all defined in terms of the system
of reproduction as a whole, states that the growth rate is equal to the proportion of profits saved multiplied by the rate of profit. Capitalists therefore determine the rate of profit since both the rate of accumulation and the proportion of profits saved and reinvested are under their control: for any given rate
of growth the smaller the fraction of profits reinvested the greater the rate of
profit and the lower the real wage.

Classical theory, both ancient and modern, is concerned at the outset with
an analysis of long-run tendencies under capitalism and thus with the on-going nature of capitalist reproduction. The theory of the profit rate just outlined
is formulated within the context of long-run balanced growth since the notion
of a single rate of growth implies proportional expansion of all components of
the physical stock of capital and thus a proportional expansion of capacity in
all sectors of production. The replacement and accumulation of commodities
used up in production require an exchange of commodities among capitalists
at prices that allow each to pay the same wage per unit of labor and to recover
profit at the same rate on the value of the stock of capital in every line of
production. Otherwise, in a competitive system, labor and commodities will
be reallocated between sectors as long as there remain any differences in wage
rates or profit rates. The physical form of the stock of capital embodies the
technique of production that sustains the highest wage rate consistent with the
overall rate of profit. The physical form of the surplus makes possible a net
accumulation of capital at the given rate plus consumption corresponding to
the pattern of expenditure of the households of workers and capitalists. Total
savings out of wages and profits, after allowing for replacement of commodities used up in production are then equal in every period to the value of the
addition to the stock of capital.

Such a path of development moves through what Joan Robinson has called "logical" as opposed to "historical" time since the expectations of capitalists concerning future sales and profits are being continually realized.[2] Thus:

> We may speak of an economy in a state of *tranquillity* when it develops in a smooth regular manner without internal contradictions or external shocks, so that expectations based upon past experience are very confidently held, and are in fact constantly fulfilled and therefore renewed as time goes by. In a state of perfect tranquillity the prices ruling to-day, in every market, are those which were expected to rule to-day when any relevant decisions were taken in the past; the quantities of goods being sold, costs, profits and all relevant characteristics of the situation are turning out according to expectations; and the expectations being held to-day about the future are those that were expected in the past to be held to-day.[3]

These conditions, when combined with the further requirement of full employment, i.e., that the pace of accumulation be just sufficient to offer additional employment to a labor force growing at a given proportional rate, have been called "a golden age (thus indicating that it represents a mythical state of affairs not likely to obtain in any actual economy)."[4]

The equilibrium conditions of a classical model should therefore be regarded as a mutually consistent set of relationships which serve "as a reference point against which various patterns of imbalance can be studied and their causes investigated."[5] This point of view is fundamental to an understanding of modern classical analysis. Thus, in presenting Marx's schemes of reproduction (which were formulated in chapter 4 using equilibrium quantity equations), Donald Harris remarks:

> In identifying the specific conditions that are required for continued reproduction, the scheme has an analytic content which is of a *dual* character. On the one hand, the scheme indicates precisely how it is possible for reproduction to take place, or, in other words, what the necessary conditions are for reproduction. It is evident that these are conditions that the system *as a whole* must satisfy. . . . On the other hand, and at the same time, the scheme locates in these conditions specific points at which inconsistency may arise in the course of reproduction in the capitalist economy.[6]

Harris notes that this use of an equilibrium framework to identify sources of disequilibrium is clearly recognized by Marx who, having considered the "normal course of reproduction [adds that] balance is itself an accident,"[7] his ultimate purpose being to analyze the cycles and crises characteristic of capitalist economies. The work of Joan Robinson[8] and Sir Roy Harrod[9] may also be seen in this light, i.e., as consisting of models whose purpose is to highlight sources of imbalance through a statement of the conditions necessary for balance.

One source of imbalance or disequilibrium arises when the pattern of demand is inappropriate to the composition of output. What the equilibrium structure of the model shows is only that it is *possible* for the commodity structure of the stock of capital, given the technique of production, to be appropriate to a given pattern of expenditure out of wages and profits, net of accumulation. But, for this, it is necessary to assume that an increase in income at constant relative prices, associated with balanced growth and a uniform rate of profit, does not result in any change in the proportions of commodities consumed, for only then can a steady expansion of output be matched by a steady expansion of expenditure in all sectors. Otherwise, production and demand diverge, an excess of output in one sector corresponding to a deficit in some other sector. If prices respond by falling where there is excess supply and rising where there is excess demand, sectoral profit rates will also diverge (since the solution for prices at a uniform rate of profit is unique). Outputs and sectoral rates of accumulation will therefore change as labor and commodities are reallocated to the more profitable sector(s). The resulting disturbances need not converge to an equilibrium path, although the underlying solution for prices (given the profit rate and the technique of production) may in some sense provide a "center of gravity" around which various oscillations occur.[10]

Disequilibrium may also occur because of an imbalance between savings and investment. Again, what the equilibrium model shows is only that, for any given rate of growth (between zero and the maximum rate the technology can sustain), it is possible to find a distribution of income between wages and profits for which total savings is equal to total investment.* In the simplest case of zero saving out of wages it follows that expenditure by the capitalist class, either in the form of accumulation or consumption of the surplus, enables them to obtain as profits on the sale of the net product a share of that product. Having said this, however, it is natural to take the argument a step further, recognizing, as Robinson remarks, "that profits are desired for the sake of growth rather than growth for the sake of profits. . . ."[11] Suppose, for example, that the rate of growth is an increasing function of the expected rate of profit which, in the simplest case, is equal to the realized rate. Equality between savings and investment will then be maintained only if the equilibrium rate of profit is such as to induce the exact rate of growth which is a parameter in determining that rate of profit. If the induced rate of growth

---

*This is a generalization of the Keynesian equality between saving and investment with the difference that, whereas in the Keynesian model the equilibrating variable is the level of production and income, in a classical equilibrium saving and investment are brought into line through changes in the distribution of income between wages and profits, given different propensities to save on the part of workers and capitalists.

exceeds the given rate, the equilibrium profit rate will be higher; if the induced rate of growth falls short of the given rate, the equilibrium profit rate will be lower.[12] How such a disequilibrium works itself out requires an analysis of the relationship between expected profits, realized profits, and the rate of accumulation within the context of various "short period limits to investment."[13] Finally, there is a further source of difficulty in establishing an equality between saving and investment if the equilibrium profit rate is not free to vary. In a subsistence wage model, for example, it attains a maximum value which may induce a rate of growth that exceeds the maximum possible rate after allowing for consumption out of profits. This "crisis . . . may be manifested, for instance, in the form of an inflationary spiral."[14] Alternatively, the maximum rate of profit in such a model may induce a rate of growth that falls short of what is needed to absorb the surplus net of consumption out of profits. Total spending is insufficient to absorb production because savings exceeds investment.

These two sources of imbalance, one caused by an allocation of labor and commodities inappropriate to the pattern of demand and the other by an overall inequality between savings and investment, have been studied by Harris within a Marxian framework of analysis. The first gives rise to a *disproportionality crisis* and the second to a *realization crisis* (which may degenerate into a *stagnation crisis*).[15] And, of course, both may occur together, the case of imbalance between supply and demand in particular sectors giving rise to a situation of general overproduction.[16] Additionally, there is the problem of the supply of labor, or more generally of the reproduction process of labor, which we have left entirely to one side.* Harris incorporates this process by treating the supply of labor as, in part, determined by the rate of accumulation where the latter causes "changes in the techniques of production involving increased mechanization, through increase in the number of hours worked per worker, or through absorption of an existing reserve army of labor. . . ."[17] This, combined with the demand for labor, which also depends on the rate of accumulation of capital, determines a particular rate of growth which is compatible with an unchanging wage rate. But the associated rate of profit in a model with a variable wage (such as the one developed in chapter 13) may not induce the rate of growth consistent with a constant wage. Thus, where the growth rate depends on the profit rate and the wage

---

* In chapter 13 employment was measured by the symbol E for any given levels of output of corn and iron. This left open the question as to whether there is an excess demand for labor or an excess supply, and thus upward or downward pressure on the wage.

rate depends on the growth rate, one finds a further source of disequilibrium or "crisis."

Harris concludes his analysis of "crises" by remarking that:

All of the foregoing discussion is not to be taken to deny that expanded reproduction is possible and does occur in fact in capitalist economies. Rather, it means that recognition must be given here to Marx's argument that the process of reproduction under capitalist conditions is a *contradictory* process.[18]

He then quotes Marx's position that:

The crises are always but momentary and forcible solutions of the existing contradictions. They are violent eruptions which for a time restore the disturbed equilibrium.[19]

Our concluding assessment of the equilibrium structure of classical theory is that it provides an initial framework of analysis containing concepts and categories relevant to a study of the on-going process of accumulation under capitalism. The structure itself is mainly interesting, however, because of what it implies concerning imbalance within that process. Thus, no claim is made that an equilibrium model of balanced growth contains sufficient structure for an analysis of such disturbances—it is only a first step in providing such an analysis.

Neoclassical Theory

We have remarked at various points in our discussion that neoclassical theory reverses the priorities of classical analysis, beginning not with production but with exchange, and then "adding on" production to make possible the indirect exchange of factor services for final commodities. For this reason much can be learned about the structure of neoclassical theory by looking first at a model in which the goods to be traded already exist and the only problem is to allocate them among consumers. This would be inconceivable in classical theory where the social conditions of production determine the context in which exchange takes place.

A model for the pure theory of exchange was discussed informally in chapter 7 where we took as an illustration Radford's famous account of a prisoner-of-war camp. The given data of the model are the quantities of goods to be exchanged, the tastes or preferences of consumers, and the initial allocation of goods among consumers. As in other neoclassical models, the concept of feasibility is central; in the exchange model it finds expression in the set of alternative final allocations that do not require more than the total supply of commodities. An equilibrium allocation defines a set of prices corresponding to rates of exchange among consumers (all consumers facing the same set of prices) such that the sum of individual consumption choices does not exceed the given supply of any commodity. Not every set of prices will have this property; hence, the problem of finding equilibrium prices.

In the pure-exchange model prices have nothing to do with production. Also, the mere fact that a commodity may be useful in some sense does not mean that it has value—that its price is positive. Certain goods and services may be in such plentiful supply relative to the demand for them that no unit commands a positive price. For commodities that have value, equilibrium prices measure a balance between supply and demand, where demand itself depends on prices and the given endowments and preferences of consumers. The balance of supply and demand for all commodities is therefore interdependent and thus requires the simultaneous solution of a whole set of relationships between quantities and prices.

A further property of an equilibirum exchange is that no consumer is willing to give up a unit of one commodity in exchange for another at a rate that exceeds the ratio of their prices. In this sense all consumers are in a position where their individual utility indexes (which can be derived from their preferences) are maximized. This characteristic of the solution to the model, however, cannot bear a normative interpretation since the initial endowments of factors are given arbitrarily.

Neoclassical allocation models depict an indirect exchange of given factors for final outputs and so generalize the model of pure exchange. In such a scheme there is no place for the classical notion of a system of reproduction. Viability is not a concept of the theory since its resources are parametric. In this way the theory incorporates production simply by changing the given quantities of goods and services of the pure-exchange model into variables and then adding sufficient structure to determine these variables from other data: given factors and their distribution among resource owners *qua* consumers, and the technology that specifies how inputs are transformed into outputs. Feasibility is again central to the analysis, the starting point being the production possibilities set defined by the intersection of resource constraints.

Feasibility is a static concept in neoclassical theory. In the pure-exchange model the existence of the given commodities is not explained by any process internal to the model, so that it cannot be known if the exchanges that occur are repeatable. In a model of the allocation of given resources the situation is the same: there is no presumption that the use of factor services is accompanied by any activity that reconstitutes their productive powers so that it cannot be known that the allocations which now yield an output of commodities will, in the future, be repeatable. Feasibility in neoclassical theory therefore lacks the dynamic character of viability in classical theory.

As in the pure-exchange model, prices in a static allocation model are to be interpreted within the context of a balance of forces affecting supply and demand. Again, there is an interdependence among prices since, on the one hand, the purchasing power commanded by any given resource endowment, and hence the consumption choices available to resource owners, depend on factor prices and commodity prices; while, on the other hand, these same prices must satisfy both the price constraints of the model and the condition that the sum of individual consumption choices nowhere exceed the total supply of a commodity.

The most important aspect of this analysis of production as an exchange of given factors concerns the interpretation of factor prices as measures of the relative "intensity" with which the various resources restrict production. The interdependent balance of supply and demand therefore entails the result that consumers, who own the resources and make the choices that determine their allocation, are ultimately responsible for relative values, and thus for the distribution of output. This follows from the equilibrium relationship between factor prices and the composition of output; namely, that there is, in general, a different measure of relative factor scarcity, and hence a different set of factor prices and a different distribution of purchasing power, associated with each efficient output.* In an indirect way, what consumers demand, given their preferences and the "weight" attached to these preferences through the initial endowments of factors, determines not only the quantities of goods produced, but also the distribution of this output among consumers.

An equilibrium relationship between opportunity cost and marginal rates of substitution in consumption adds a further dimension to the role of resource owners *qua* consumers, the "households" of neoclassical theory. On the one hand, the relative price of one commodity in terms of another cannot exceed the opportunity cost of the first in terms of the second for, if it did, the total value of production could be increased through a reallocation of factors. On

---

* In linear models for neoclassical theory such as the ones considered in this book, the relationship between allocations, prices, and distribution is not one-to-one. There may be many prices and distributions consistent with a given allocation of factors at a feasible output where at least two resource constraints are binding. The range of prices that corresponds to each such allocation diminishes, however, as the number of processes of production of each commodity increases. In the limiting case, the possibilities for substitution between factors is such that every limit point of the feasible set of outputs is associated with a unique distribution of income.

the other hand, the marginal rate of substitution of one commodity in terms of another in consumption cannot exceed the ratio of their prices (as in the pure-exchange model). It follows that opportunity cost ratios are never less than marginal rates of substitution so that the rate at which one commodity can be "transformed" into another through a reallocation of resources is never less than the rate at which any consumer is willing to give up one commodity in order to have another. In this sense production is in accordance with the wishes of consumers, although, again, this aspect of equilibrium cannot be interpreted normatively since the initial endowments of factors are arbitrary.

An important contrast now emerges between the determinants of value in classical and neoclassical theory. In the latter, social class is subsumed in the given pattern of ownership of factors, a pattern which may be egalitarian or extremely uneven. This treats class division solely in terms of demand; the preferences of certain consumers happen to have more weight in the balance that determines the allocation of resources and the distribution of output. Production, on the other hand, is analyzed independently of the distribution of these endowments, and thus of social class. There is no counterpart in neoclassical theory to the classical idea that private ownership of produced means of production as such has an important bearing on the analysis of production in a capitalist economy. At the same time, the irrelevance of class relations in production is entirely consistent with the neoclassical view of the economic problem as that of exchange of the productive powers of given resources. Differences in factor ownership may alter the terms of this exchange, it is argued, but not the structure of the theory.* This is most readily apparent in the form of the price relations of a neoclassical model where prices are dual to the concepts of opportunity cost and relative factor scarcity implicit in the quantity relations. In classical theory, on the other hand, the dual of surplus is reflected as profit in the price relations only for the case of capitalism. Other social structures would require a different manifestation of surplus in the price relations: as taxes on net wages, for example, in a planned economy.

The absence of excess demand, as the essential characteristic of a neoclassical equilibrium, has been regarded as the basis for an analysis of capitalism in terms of a simultaneous equilibrium of a set of interdependent markets. We have not presented the theory within the setting of a market economy (at least not explicitly) since to do so would beg the question of how prices are

---

*Recall, however, the discussion in chapter 10 where it was pointed out that to ensure the existence of a solution to the model, some restriction must be placed on the distribution of ownership of the factors of production.

formed, that is to say, of how the system "gets into equilibrium." At one level of analysis, post-Walrasian theory finesses the problem by appealing to the concept of an "auctioneer" whose function is to "cry out" prices, to register excess demands at these prices, and then to adjust prices in such a way as to remove the excess demand. No transactions take place, however, until equilibrium prices have been found. Even granting this last assumption, it is a difficult problem to know how equilibrium prices are to be found when, for example, to raise the price of a product that is in excess demand is to raise the incomes of certain factor owners who may then increase their demand for the given product all the more. But, suppose that assumptions can be made to ensure that a sequence of notional price changes (unaccompanied by any transactions) "converges" to an equilibrium solution (at which transactions do occur).[20] The real difficulty comes in finding appropriate contexts for such a "tâtonnement" process, as it is usually called. Hicks remarks that it is relevant only in "very sophisticated markets, requiring a lot of organisation; for who is to pay the official who is to 'cry' the prices . . . ? There must be a prior agreement among the parties to play the game according to these rules: but how is such an agreement to come about?"[21] The closest approximation we have are commodity and stock exchanges, but like the Paris Bourse, Walras's own prototype, these are markets where only pure exchange occurs. It is a much more difficult task to conceive of a set of rules concerning price formation that would bring a whole set of markets into simultaneous equilibrium within a system in which production is going on, even granting the neoclassical assumption that resources are parameters of the problem.

It must be insisted, however, that the problem of the formation of prices is of central importance in neoclassical theory insofar as it provides insight into the workings of a market economy. But to give up the fiction of the auctioneer, or some equivalent set of "rules," is to raise the issue of uncertainty for, as Hicks points out, in any complicated system of markets there arises "an opportunity for the development of specialised merchanting—a merchant being defined as one who buys not for his own use but in order to sell again."[22] The holding of stocks of commodities, however, depends on decisions taken in the past with a view to an uncertain future. When the future becomes present, stocks will be appropriate if expectations have been realized, inappropriate and therefore out of equilibrium if they have not. Thus, a difficult analytical problem arises. Either the concept of a static equilibrium of supply and demand must be abandoned and the theory reformulated in terms of disequilibrium relations among prices and quantities; or the problem must be reformulated so as to be amenable to an equilibrium analysis that preserves the essentially static properties of the neoclassical framework. Only the latter course has appeared tractable.

Thus, there begins with the work of Frank Ramsey in 1928[23] a branch of theory that generalizes the neoclassical framework of analysis to a finite (or infinite) number of timeless allocations, the total allocation problem being defined over this set of individual allocations regarded, not individually, but as a whole. Within each momentary allocation the variables and parameters of the model are the same as in our simple neoclassical model. To connect the allocations requires linking the variables of one to the parameters of the next since, in multiple allocations, outputs not consumed in allocation t may become factors of production in allocation $t + 1$.* The resulting sequence of allocations can be looked at together, as if they constituted a consistent plan worked out at the beginning of the first "period." It is in this sense that the static properties of the theory are preserved since a "multiperiod" allocation problem is defined as a sequence of timeless allocations. What are called "momentary" positions of equilibrium are linked forward and backward in such a manner that data concerning "future" states (factor supplies, technology, tastes, and endowments) can influence "present" allocations and prices just as much as data about "present" states can influence "future" allocations and prices.

> The plan is mutually determined; there is no movement from past to future, except in the sense that there is also a movement from future to past. There is no room for the unexpected.[24]

The only sense in which these models are temporal consists in isolating those sequences of allocations which are optimal from the point of view of the intertemporal preferences of consumers with given initial factor endowments. Thus, as Harris remarks:

> When it comes to the problem of accumulation, this is treated in neoclassical theory essentially as a matter of the exchange of commodities through time, or the exchange of "time-dated" commodities. As such, the problem of accumulation has no special significance in this theory apart from the problem of exchange per se. . . . The basic object of the economy is consumption; accumulation is an incidental feature of individuals' consumption decisions. . . .[25]

---

* See the generalizations of the neoclassical model in chapters 8 and 9 where it was remarked that in "multiperiod" neoclassical allocations models, commodity interest rates can be defined. But they are not uniquely determined nor are they equal among commodities or equal across time periods. They do not correspond to the uniform rate of profit of classical theory, and bear no relationship to the concept of surplus which is not defined in the quantity relations of the model.

Within this context the most significant feature of the theory of intertemporally efficient resource allocation is that the methods used to solve the problem typically involve perfect foresight at every point in time.[26] This is not, however, the foresight implicit in the conditions of "tranquillity" that characterize a classical equilibrium of balanced growth since the theory will generally involve the correct anticipation of a complicated pattern of future prices and quantities. But, as the basis for an analysis of intertemporal exchange among autonomous "households," correct foresight about the future raises fundamental epistemological questions which led Oskar Morgenstern to argue that, "Unlimited foresight and economic equilibrium are . . . irreconcilable with one another."[27]

Our concluding assessment of neoclassical theory is that when generalized to the context of a "multiperiod" framework of analysis, it treats time in such a way as to restrict the application of the theory to situations in which there must be a significant element of control over future events, thus making the implicit assumption of foresight meaningful. But within that context, models for the theory, though unavoidably complex, have properties essentially similar to those of the one-period allocation model. As for the relevance of the theory to an analysis of capitalism, Robert Solow has remarked:

By asking planning questions, allocation questions, we can . . . dodge many embarrassing questions of definition and their ideological overtones. The fundamental difficulty of uncertainty cannot really be dodged; and since it cannot be faced, it must simply be ignored. If I am right in thinking that much empty controversy arises because the questions asked are pointless, then the planning point of view may be a useful one. A planning question, after all, is likely to have an answer.[28]

Harris points out, however, that, "Against [this] claim it could be argued, as Solow recognizes . . . that 'a capital theory erected on planning grounds has no relevance to the actual behavior of any real capitalist economy.' This argument has never been effectively rebutted."[29]

Our position may now be summed up. Classical theory is a theory of reproduction in which the dynamic concept of viability is central and where the fundamental problem is to show how the social relations of production under capitalism determine the nature of the process of extraction, accumulation, and consumption of the surplus product. It is a theory containing concepts and categories appropriate to an analysis of on-going production in an economy of capitalist firms, where conditions of crisis and imbalance periodically arise. In classical theory the role of equilibrium relationships is to shed light on the causes of imbalance and on the various ways in which these imbalances may be resolved. Neoclassical theory is a theory of exchange in which the static concept of feasibility is central and where the fundamental problem is to show how a system of prices can sustain an efficient allocation of resources. Its equilibrium structure defines relationships among prices, opportunity cost, and relative factor scarcity in the context of an indirect exchange of factors for commodities. Thus, its concepts and categories, though ostensibly concerned with a ubiquitous feature of capitalism, the interdependence of markets, lead inevitably to a static perspective appropriate only to problems of economic planning.

Despite the classical revival, neoclassical general-equilibrium theory continues to be thought relevant to an analysis of capitalism—possibly because the latter theory analyzes prices and hence income distribution in a way that effectively succeeds in distracting attention from the problem of class relations in production. The concept of relative factor scarcity, in particular, has the appearance of objectivity, even granting the arbitrariness (in the theory) of factor endowments. Thus, as Solow remarks in the passage quoted above, economists may avoid embarrassing questions of definition and their ideological overtones simply through the expedient of confining attention to problems of the allocation of given means among alternative uses. To give up the preoccupation with marginal valuation and efficiency and to face instead the classical questions concerning the production, extraction, and accumulation of surplus requires a conceptual framework in which social class is an important variable. In adopting such a framework, however, the seeming objectivity of neoclassical theory would necessarily give way to an analysis reformulated in light of the historically determined character of the capitalist system.

Notes

1. David Ricardo, *On the Principles of Political Economy and Taxation,* ed. P. Sraffa, *The Works and Correspondence of David Ricardo,* Vol. I, Cambridge University Press, 1951, p. 5.
2. Joan Robinson, *Essays in the Theory of Economic Growth,* St. Martin's, New York, 1968, pp. 23–4.
3. Joan Robinson, *The Accumulation of Capital,* 3rd ed., St. Martin's, New York, 1969, p. 59. Robinson's italics.
4. *Ibid.,* p. 99.
5. Donald J. Harris, *Capital Accumulation and Income Distribution,* Stanford University Press, 1978, p. 41.
6. *Ibid.,* p. 250. Harris's italics.

7. *Ibid.* The citation is to K. Marx, *Capital,* Volume II, International Publishers, New York, 1967, p. 495.

8. See especially *The Accumulation of Capital* and *Essays in the Theory of Economic Growth* cited above.

9. Sir Roy Harrod, "An Essay in Dynamic Theory," *Economic Journal,* Vol. 49 (March 1939), pp. 14–33; and *Towards a Dynamic Economics,* Macmillan, London, 1948.

10. See, for example, R. M. Goodwin, *Elementary Economics from the Higher Standpoint,* Cambridge University Press, 1970, pp. 19–23.

11. Robinson, *Essays,* p. 45.

12. *Ibid.,* pp. 46–51; also, Harris, *Accumulation and Distribution,* pp. 186–92.

13. Robinson, *Accumulation,* pp. 48–53, cited by Harris, *Accumulation and Distribution,* p. 190.

14. Harris, *Accumulation and Distribution,* p. 272.

15. *Ibid.,* pp. 269–73.

16. Harris remarks that this "was an explicit element in Marx's attack on Say's Law. . . ." *Ibid.,* p. 277. He cites B. Shoul, "Karl Marx and Say's Law," *Quarterly Journal of Economics,* Vol. 71 (November 1971), pp. 611–29.

17. Harris, *Accumulation and Distribution,* p. 269.

18. *Ibid.,* p. 284. Harris's italics.

19. K. Marx, *Capital,* Volume III, International Publishers, New York, 1967, p. 249. Cited by Harris, *Capital and Distribution,* p. 284.

20. See, for example, Kenneth J. Arrow and Frank H. Hahn, *General Competitive Analysis,* Holden-Day, San Francisco, 1971, pp. 282–323.

21. Sir John Hicks, "Some Questions of Time in Economics," in Anthony M. Tang, Fred M. Westfield, and James S. Worley, eds., *Evolution, Welfare, and Time in Economics, Essays in Honor of Nicholas Georgescu-Roegen,* D. C. Heath, Lexington, Mass., 1976, p. 147.

22. Hicks, "Questions of Time," p. 147.

23. Frank P. Ramsey, "A Mathematical Theory of Saving," *Economic Journal,* Vol. 38 (1928), pp. 543–59.

24. Hicks, "Questions of Time," p. 144.

25. Harris, *Accumulation and Distribution,* p. 20.

26. The methods used are those of optimal control theory. For an explicit recognition of the perfect foresight assumption, see Michael Bruno, "Optimal Accumulation in Discrete Capital Models," in Karl Shell, ed., *Essays on the Theory of Optimal Economic Growth,* M.I.T. Press, Cambridge, Mass., 1967, p. 184.

27. Oskar Morgenstern, "Perfect Foresight and Economic Equilibrium," trans. Frank H. Knight, unpublished. This article appears in German in *Zeitschrift für Nationalökonomie,* Vol. VI, Part 3, 1935. Despite Morgenstern's compelling arguments, nonsteady-state models *with* perfect foresight, i.e., models where Robinson's conditions of "tranquillity" cannot hold, continue to proliferate. Thus, in a survey article, Avinash Dixit remarks, "No account is taken of any imperfections of information, and the possibility of acquiring new information and revising plans in course of time. This is tantamount to assuming perfect foresight or perfect futures markets. . . . any further discussion of the patent unrealism of such an

equilibrium over time is surely unnecessary. However, for all its shortcomings, it does highlight important questions of intertemporal resource allocation, and it is the framework used in most of capital theory." See "The Accumulation of Capital Theory," *Oxford Economic Papers,* (New Series), Vol. 29 (March 1977), p. 14.

28. Robert M. Solow, *Capital Theory and the Rate of Return,* Rand McNally, Chicago, 1965, pp. 15–16.

29. Harris, *Accumulation and Distribution,* p. 44. Harris quotes Solow, *Capital Theory,* p. 16.

Author Index

Arrow, Kenneth J., 175n.12; with Frank H. Hahn, 148–49, 215n.3, 247n.2, 250; with David Starrett, 4n.11, 123–24

Barone, Enrico, 162
Baudeau, Abbé, 24n.42
Black, R. D. Collison, 62, 131; with Rosamond Könekamp, 124, 126–27
Blaug, Mark, 131
Böhm-Bawerk, Eugen von, 132
Bortkiewicz, Ladislaus von, 122

Cannan, Edwin, 53, 56–58, 66, 71
Cantillon, Richard, 3, 7, 9, 18–23, 23–24, 26–28, 35, 39–44, 59, 63, 85, 96, 122, 148, 168

Debreu, Gerard, 197, 234, 234 *
Dimitriev, V. K., 122
Dixit, Avinash, 236, 409n.27
Dobb, Maurice, 131, 173, 295†

Eatwell, John, 90, 108n.126
Eltis, W. A., 65, 67
Engels, Friedrich, 105, 125, 133

Garegnani, Pierangelo, 4, 345n.4

Hahn, Frank H., 236, 245, 267; with Kenneth J. Arrow, 148–49, 215n.3, 247n.2, 250
Harris, D. J., 400, 402, 403, 408, 409
Harrod, Sir Roy, 400
Hartwell, R. M., 66
Hicks, Sir John, 121, 179, 184, 241, 345, 407; with W. Weber, 4
Higgs, Henry, 18
Hollander, Samuel, 9, 42–43, 61–63, 65, 73, 87, 90
Hume, David, 51–53, 60–61
Hutchison, T. W., 125, 130–31, 143–44

Jaffé, William, 142, 144, 147, 159†, 160, 162

Subject Index